非文学文体解析与翻译
——以功能文体学为理论视角

主　编　张国敬
副主编　高莉娟　吕　元
编　者　王文平　王　阳　戴宗琳

南开大学出版社

天　津

图书在版编目(CIP)数据

非文学文体解析与翻译：以功能文体学为理论视角 / 张国敬主编. —天津：南开大学出版社，2017.9
（天外"求索"文库）
ISBN 978-7-310-05472-5

Ⅰ.①非… Ⅱ.①张… Ⅲ.①文体论－研究 Ⅳ.①H052

中国版本图书馆 CIP 数据核字(2017)第 235023 号

版权所有 侵权必究

南开大学出版社出版发行
出版人：刘立松
地址：天津市南开区卫津路 94 号　邮政编码：300071
营销部电话：(022)23508339　23500755
营销部传真：(022)23508542　邮购部电话：(022)23502200

*

天津泰宇印务有限公司印刷
全国各地新华书店经销

*

2017 年 9 月第 1 版　2017 年 9 月第 1 次印刷
230×155 毫米　16 开本　23.5 印张　2 插页　323 千字
定价：69.00 元

如遇图书印装质量问题,请与本社营销部联系调换,电话：(022)23507125

天外"求索"文库

天外"求索"文库编委会

主　任：修　刚
副主任：王铭玉
编　委：余　江　刘宏伟

前　言

本书旨在以韩礼德（M. A. K. Halliday）的功能文体学为理论视角，对英语非文学文体即实用文体的构成、界定进行分析探讨，对翻译策略和方法的选择进行比较研究，从客观上澄清形式和内容的关系及相互作用，寻求更合适的翻译手段与措施，规范国内外非文学翻译的活动与效果。

国外相关的研究有吉恩•保罗•维奈（Jean-Paul Vinay）的《法英比较文体翻译》（*Comparative Stylistics of French and English*）、费德里科•费德里希（Federico Federici）的《文体的发展与翻译》（*Translation as Stylistic Evolution*）、路易斯•M. 海伍德（Louis M. Haywood）的《西班牙英语翻译》（*Spanish Translation on English*）、桑德•赫维（Sandor Hervey）的《德语翻译之思考》（*Thinking German Translation*）等。这些研究大都对问题做泛泛概述，分析探讨多为诗学翻译，且都是法语、德语、西班牙语等和英语互译研究，但所设计分析方法和翻译策略的选择对本课题有参考价值。我国对于此类研究正处在初期阶段，到目前为止，比较系统全面介绍非文学文体翻译的著作主要有：方梦之的《英汉—汉英应用翻译教程》，伍锋、何庆机的《实用文体翻译：理论与实践》，顾维勇的《实用文体翻译》以及李长栓的《非文学翻译理论与实践》。方梦之就应用文体翻译理论体系的定位、应用翻译理论原则、分类及文本类型意义应用翻译理论的组成等问题进行了深入探讨，该书可谓实用，涵盖面广，但例证分析较少，也未涉及文化与语言的关系。伍锋与何庆机主要从功能派翻译理论角度，探讨实用文体侧重交际，其翻译注重的是译文的语用功能。同时，这些作品在题材选择上也有所侧重，大都倾向于商务、旅游或公示语。

我国历史上的翻译活动开始较早。根据马祖毅的《中国翻译简史》介绍，早在周王朝，就有专门的翻译官员负责接待各民族和国家的使节及宾客；魏晋南北朝和隋朝也设置了配备译员的官方机构掌管与四方民族和外国交往的事务；从东汉末年到宋代则进行了大量的佛经翻译；而在唐朝时从日本来到中国的大量遣唐使，则引用中国的思想文化和典章制度等促进了日本封建制度的建立及巩固；辽、金、元朝等也有通事和译史，从事口笔译；为了适应外事翻译的需要，明朝设置了四夷馆；时至清初，来华的大量传教士与中国的士大夫一起翻译编写了三百多种书籍，除了经院哲学、神学和其他宗教文献之外，还包括其他一百多种科学类书籍，内容广泛，涉及天文学、数学、物理学和机械工程学、采矿冶金、军事技术、生理学、医学和语言学等，当时的清朝科举考试，还特设翻译科，并且设立了多种翻译机构。鸦片战争之后，西学翻译的规模和范围更是达到了前所未有的程度。翻译活动对国外先进思想和技术的译介促进了我国自身的进步，另一方面也将中国的思想文化等传达到了其他国家。总的来说，非文学翻译贯穿我国翻译活动的历史，历朝历代所设置的翻译机构，或出于行政目的（如掌管四方民族和外国交往），或出于典籍翻译的目的其大部分的内容还是以实用性的即非文学性文本为主。

目前，我国国内存在大量的翻译公司，除了这些商业性的翻译机构外，"国际机构、政府和非政府组织、企业、研究机构等对翻译的需求巨大，不少设有专门的翻译部门"[①]。大型的国际机构如联合国和欧盟，每天都有大量的专业文件产生，政府机构为了对外宣传也有大量政府文件需要翻译，跨国企业如 IBM 等也设有专门的语言辅助部门，并遵从特定的语言译写规范，非政府组织和各种研究机构也离不开翻译，而这些翻译活动中绝大部分都是非文学翻译。可想而知，在全球一体化的环境下，非文学翻译与这个世界的日常

---

① 李长栓：《非文学翻译理论与实践》（第二版），北京：中国对外翻译出版公司，2012年，第17页。

运转息息相关。

强调非文学翻译所占翻译活动的比例之高及其现实价值并不是要诋毁和贬低文学翻译的价值，而是希望引起翻译界内外对非文学翻译的重视。目前对非文学翻译的研究成果比起文学翻译来实在是少之又少，且不说研究成果，大部分翻译研究者对非文学翻译的研究意识也是很薄弱的。在中国学术期刊网络出版总库中输入关键词"非文学翻译"，搜索结果只有几十条，这其中真正提到"非文学翻译"的只有寥寥几篇，不少研究文章是在探讨各种实用类文本的翻译，如旅游文本翻译、科技翻译、商务翻译、法律翻译等，也就是说尽管已经有人意识到此类翻译与文学翻译的翻译理念和操作模式有所不同，但还没有建立起属于非文学翻译的完整研究框架，只有分散的各种实用型文本的翻译研究。

对非文学翻译的研究意识薄弱，一方面体现在学术论文以及研究专著的缺乏，另一方面则体现在用文学翻译的操作模式和标准来衡量和指导一切翻译活动，比如强调对原文的忠实，"信、达、雅""化境""神似"等文学翻译标准仍然应用在非文学翻译中，而如"直译/意译""归化/异化"等翻译方法也在非文学翻译中有所讨论，但正如林本椿先生所说："虽然在文学翻译研究方面的成果有许多已经运用到实用翻译的实践中，但实用翻译还是有其特殊性。"[①] 尽管冠以"非文学翻译"的研究专著为数不多，但目前出版的实用翻译类教材还是相对较多的。然而纵观这一类实用翻译教材，则出现了目前对非文学翻译研究的另一个问题，即这些专著中所探讨的一些技巧和策略等并没有突现出非文学翻译自身的特点，"大量篇幅用于讨论某特定文本（如旅游、商贸、法律等）的翻译策略（直译、意译、归化、异化、读者反应等）、翻译技巧（词性转换、肯定否定转换、主动被动转换、词序倒装、增译、减译、加注、长短句交换等），甚至一些基本的语言转换问题（一般语法分析、流水句、并列结构、核心句、美国英语和英国英语之差异等）。然而，

[①] 林本椿：《漫谈汉英实用翻译》，《福建外语》，1997年第1期，第58页。

这些策略和技巧的研究早已成熟,适用于几乎所有普通翻译文本类型。而适应于非文学翻译的应用型理论研究尚显苍白。非文学翻译研究应突出自身的学术特点,其理论研究的定位和导向性须进一步明确"①。

本书以文化与语言的关系为指导,结合韩礼德的功能文体学理论,以非文学文体的翻译为研究对象,主要在文化的层面揭示论证英汉两种语言在词汇选择、词汇含义、句法结构以及语篇结构等方面的异同,进而分析说明非文学文体翻译的特点、选择的策略、使用的翻译技巧与方法,特别是对文化因素在翻译策略的选择方面的影响进行深入的探讨,并运用大量的鲜活实例,旨在理论与实践相结合,在形式对内容所产生的作用上取得突破性进展。

张国敬
2016 年 10 月 21 日

---

① 林本椿:《漫谈汉英实用翻译》,《福建外语》,1997 年第 1 期,第 58 页。

目 录

第一章 非文学文体与翻译 ·· 1
  1.1 非文学文体的语言特征 ·· 1
  1.2 非文学文体翻译的定位与分类 ···································· 3
  1.3 非文学文体翻译的功能特征 ······································ 5
  1.4 非文学文体翻译的理念、原则和标准 ···························· 8
  1.5 非文学文体翻译的策略与方法 ··································· 10
  1.6 非文学文体翻译的研究意义 ····································· 12

第二章 功能文体学与非文学翻译 ·· 16
  2.1 功能翻译理论 ·· 16
  2.2 系统功能文体学理论 ··· 17
  2.3 功能文体学在中国的发展 ·· 21
  2.4 功能文体学视角下的非文学文体翻译 ·························· 23
  2.5 本书的研究内容 ··· 29

第三章 法律文书 ··· 34
  3.1 法律文书的文体功能 ··· 34
  3.2 英文法律文书的语言特征 ·· 35
  3.3 法律文书翻译的原则与解析 ····································· 56
  3.4 法律文书翻译实例 ·· 65

第四章 新闻报道 ··· 109
  4.1 新闻报道文体概述 ·· 109
  4.2 英文新闻报道的语言特征 ·· 110
  4.3 新闻报道翻译策略 ·· 123

第五章 商贸文本 ··· 137
  5.1 商贸文本的文体类型及功能 ····································· 137

  5.2 英文商贸文本的文体特征 ·················· 138
  5.3 商贸文本翻译的原则与解析 ················ 151
  5.4 商贸文本翻译实例 ······················ 158

第六章 影视字幕 ····························· 179
  6.1 影视字幕的特点 ······················· 180
  6.2 影视字幕翻译策略 ····················· 182
  6.3 电影《功夫熊猫》的翻译策略赏析 ············· 190
  6.4 影视片名翻译 ························ 192

第七章 广告语 ······························ 197
  7.1 广告语的文体功能 ····················· 197
  7.2 英文广告语的语言特征 ·················· 198
  7.3 汉英广告语差异 ······················ 218
  7.4 广告语翻译策略 ······················ 219

第八章 旅游宣传 ···························· 226
  8.1 旅游宣传的文体功能 ··················· 226
  8.2 旅游宣传的文体特征及风格 ··············· 227
  8.3 旅游宣传翻译的过程与原则 ··············· 233
  8.4 旅游宣传翻译技巧 ···················· 238

第九章 公示语 ····························· 245
  9.1 公示语的文体功能 ···················· 245
  9.2 英文公示语的语言特征 ················· 248
  9.3 城市公示语翻译现状的调查与研究 ·········· 252
  9.4 公示语翻译策略 ····················· 258
  9.5 公示语翻译规范解析 ·················· 262

第十章 哲学文献 ···························· 271
  10.1 哲学文献的文体功能 ·················· 271
  10.2 英文哲学文献的语言特征 ··············· 271
  10.3 哲学文献翻译的原则与解析 ············· 278
  10.4 英文哲学术语选译 ··················· 286
  10.5 哲学文献翻译实例 ··················· 290

第十一章 企业规章制度·····315
  11.1 企业规章制度的文体功能·····315
  11.2 英文企业规章制度的语言特征·····316
  11.3 企业规章制度的翻译·····326
第十二章 商务信函·····335
  12.1 商务信函的文体功能·····335
  12.2 商务信函的分类·····336
  12.3 商务信函的篇章结构·····338
  12.4 商务信函的词汇特点及翻译·····342
  12.5 商务信函的句法特点及翻译·····349
参考文献·····357
后　记·····362

第一章 非文学文体与翻译

非文学文体是相对于文学文体而言的，也称为实用文本或应用文本（applied style，practical style 或 pragmatic style）。翻译活动分为两个不同的领域：非文学翻译和文学翻译。非文学翻译强调的是事实，文学翻译强调的是价值；非文学翻译强调信息的清晰性，文学翻译强调风格。非文学翻译文本类型的特征有其共性，且共性是绝对的，所遵循的是普遍规律。这就为非文学翻译方法论研究建立了共识，提供了依据。近年来，随着经济全球化、一体化的迅速发展，国际交往日趋频繁，翻译活动日益增多，非文学文体翻译研究的重要性也日益凸显。功能文体学理论的不断发展，为非文学文体翻译研究提供了新的视角，本书力求从功能文体学的视角，探究非文学文体翻译的翻译理念、翻译策略、翻译原则，更好地指导翻译教学和实践，进一步提高非文学文体翻译的有效性和针对性。

1.1 非文学文体的语言特征

根据德国学者赖斯（Katharina Reiss）的文本类型学理论和英国学者纽马克（Peter Newmark）的观点，文本功能主要有三种类型：表达功能、信息功能和呼唤功能。文学文体属于表达功能文本，而非文学文体则属于其他两种功能性文本。由此可见，非文学文体的应用范围和种类都是非常广泛的。较文学文体而言，非文学文体的语言较少使用词语的内涵意义，主要使用词语的本意，也就是词语的指称意义。非文学文体具有很强的目的性和实用性，旨在传达信息，或者呼唤读者引起反应。不同于文学文体重形式的特点，非文学文体其形式相对于内容是次要的，以传达信息为目的，同时考虑信息的传递效果。区别于传达有较强情感意义和美学意义的文学文体，非文学文体是对现实世界的客观陈述，为社会和人类生活而服务的一种实用性文体。非文学文体重视读者，因此它注重信息的清晰、准确和简洁。而且，非文学文体注重逻辑思维，讲究逻辑严密客观、语言平铺直叙，旨在阐述事实或得出结论。另外，非文学文体有其特定的目标读者群，此类读者的主要目的是获取相关的信息。

非文学文本的范畴很广，几乎囊括了文学文体之外的所有文体，种类繁多，涉及政治、法律、经济、科技、文化等社会生活的各个领域。非文学文体的基本特点是内容具体明确、书写格式比较固定、语言简明扼要。各种文体又拥有各自的一些词汇、语法、语篇和修辞手段等风格特征。从语言层面来看，陈述性和说明性语言是这类文本的语言规范。同时，非文学文体在日益强调语言规范的基础上还追求语言的审美性。语言的审美即文采，是指经过修饰、润色、加工过的富于美感的书面语言。非文学文体的语言审美主要体现在以下四个方面。

第一，朴实。语言的朴实体现在选用质朴无华的语言，不加雕琢地表现出文本固有的原貌。非文学文体的实用性，决定了它的语言必须具有真理般的自然质朴、浑然天成、平淡本色，不饰华丽的辞藻，没有浓郁的抒情，用实实在在的语言去表述。

第二，简洁。简洁，就是用最简短的文字，表达丰富、确切的内容，言简意赅。非文学文体以高效、迅速地传递信息为己任，以反映特定的活动为内容，以取得社会效益和经济效益为目的，具有很强的时效性和实用性，因此语言的高度简洁、准确和精美就显得尤为重要。

第三，流畅。非文学文体的流畅美，主要是指文气的畅达、意脉的贯通，体现在上下文气势贯通，逻辑顺序贯通，语言整齐而不呆板，错落而不杂乱，音韵和谐，给人美感。

第四，生动。非文学文体语言的平实、直白和流畅、生动并不矛盾。虽然非文学文体不能像文学文体那样生动含蓄，文采飞扬，言有尽而意无穷，但并不排斥一定程度上的生动性。规范而生动的语言不仅深化了文章的内涵，还增添了文章的感染力。非文学文体语言的生动性主要体现在：一是精心提炼富有表现力的群众语言；二是恰当地使用专业术语；三是恰当运用比喻、拟人、借代等修辞方法，使用具有弹性的语言，达到表意上的高度精确。

1.2 非文学文体翻译的定位与分类

非文学文体翻译亦称应用文体翻译，根据美国学者约瑟夫·卡萨格兰德（Joseph B. Casagrande）的定义，实用类翻译的主要目的是"尽可能准确有效地翻译信息"，侧重"信息内容而非美学形式、语法形式或文化氛围"。[①] 实用翻译是一种目的性很强的翻译活动，要求译文在最大程度上达到并满足预期的功能，目的和功能是实用翻译文本翻译的依据和依归。关于非文学文体翻译的定义，国内学者也是众说纷纭，既有共识，也有分歧。

2003年全国应用翻译研讨会的召开，标志着我国应用翻译研究进入深入研究阶段，对应用翻译的定位、应用翻译的特点及其理论研究和创新等问题做了探讨。方梦之首次提出了"非文学文体翻译以传达信息为目的（同时考虑信息的传递效果），它有别于传达有较强情感意义和美学意义的文学翻译"[②]。贾文波认为"应用翻译是一种以传递信息为主要目的、又注重信息传递效果的实用型翻译，它的最大特点除了实用性强之外就是应用面广，其范围几乎涵盖当今政治、经济、社会、文化生活的各个领域，大大不同于强调艺术审美和文学翻译，就内容来看，它几乎囊括了除文学翻译以外的所有作品"[③]。关于实用翻译定位的依据，当前学界有三种不同的观点。林本椿等一批学者认为，实用翻译以文学翻译为参照，非文学

[①] Joseph B. Casagrande & Kenneth L. Hale. *The Translator as Communicator*. London: Routledge, 1997, p.16.

[②] 方梦之、毛忠明：《英汉—汉英应用翻译综合教程》，上海：上海外语教育出版社，2008年，第Ⅲ页。

[③] 贾文波：《功能翻译理论对应用翻译的启示》，《上海翻译》，2007年第2期，第9页。

翻译即实用翻译。有的学者把文本实用性的强弱作为定位实用翻译的依据，有的学者则把翻译的目的作为实用翻译定位的依据。李长栓、林克难、韩子满对实用翻译的定义作了较独到的阐释，其中韩子满的观点认同度比较高，他提出"应用翻译……应包括除文学翻译之外所有以信息传达为主的文本翻译。科技、法律、经贸等实用文本的翻译，以及各种应用文的翻译，以及各种应用文的翻译都应属于应用翻译"[1]。韩礼德从功能文体学的研究角度提出，对应用翻译的定位其实是对翻译客体——文本的定位，并将构成语域的情景因素分为三个变项，即语场、语旨、语式。非文学文体翻译的定位从传统的"非文学翻译""目的、功能翻译"扩大到了功能文体学视角下的非文学文体翻译，与王佐良先生在"新时期的翻译观"中提到的"根据文体定译法"[2]的观点极为呼应。

为了更加准确地进行非文学文体翻译，必须先了解非文学文体的分类。关于非文学文体的分类，学者们存在不同的见解。有人认为文艺作品以外的文字都是非文学文体，是人们交流思想、处理事务、解决问题、互通情况的一种重要工具，其特点是内容具体明确、书写格式固定、语言简明扼要、处理事务实践性强。大体上，文学文体包括小说、诗歌以及戏剧。非文学翻译的对象涵盖诸多领域，划分的基础是将具有类似学科或行业特点、翻译文本研究属性趋于一致的文本归属一类。非文学文体的主要功能在于传递信息，因此其包括政府文件、告示、科技论文、新闻报道、法律文书、商贸信函、产品说明书、使用手册、广告、技术文本、科普读物、旅游指南等各类文本。

非文学文体门类众多，涉及广泛的专业领域。在本书中，我们将非文学文体分为法律文书、商贸文本、新闻报道、影视字幕、广告语、旅游宣传、公示语、哲学文献、企业规章制度、商务信函等，并且分章进行具体论述，探讨各类文本在词汇选择、句法结构、语

---

[1] 韩子满：《应用翻译：实践与理论研究》，《中国科技翻译》，2005年第4期，第49页。

[2] 王佐良：《翻译：思考与试笔》，北京：外语教学研究与出版社，1997年，第2页。

篇结构及文体等方面的特征,并分析英汉两种语言在这些层面的异同,从而探讨适用于各类文本的翻译策略。

1.3 非文学文体翻译的功能特征

方梦之提出了非文学文体翻译的"信息性""劝导性""匿名性"三大特点[①]。几乎所有的学者都把信息性当作实用翻译文本的最主要特点。文本的应用性,实际上也就是文本的信息性。信息性、劝导性、匿名性是实用语篇的共性。贾文波则表述为"信息性、诱导性和匿名性",这种观点刚好与纽马克的文本类型说的观点不谋而合。文本按其功能主要分为"信息型""呼唤型"和"表达型"文本。有的学者以文体功能作为实用翻译定位的依据,实际上与文本的应用性为依据本质上是相同的。其实,除去非文学文体翻译的目的性、应用性,非文学文体翻译的适应性也是非文学文体翻译不容忽视的一大特点,即译文"文随其体,语随其人"。刘宓庆在《文体与翻译》中较早提出了"翻译三论",即"论严谨、论修辞、论风格"。其中"论风格"从译文对原文的适应性角度,提出"译文应适应原文文体的需要",翻译必须密切适应文体特点,译文中遣词造句务须符合文体的需要,即翻译应恪守译文的适应性原则,力求在文本体裁、语体风格上高度适应。和文学翻译相比,非文学文体翻译面广量大,文本类型各异,要求多样,非常需要有针对性的理论作指导,发挥理论的对策功能。非文学文体翻译从文本功能和翻译目的区别于一般翻译,它除了具有一般翻译的共性之外,还有其特殊之处。

虽然非文学文体具有区别于文学文体的共同特征,但是在非文学文体内部也存在一定差异,尤其是不同题材的文本以及同一题材但交际目的和对象、交际环境不同的文本,因此必须了解各类文本

[①] 方梦之、毛忠明:《英汉—汉英应用翻译综合教程》,上海:上海外语教育出版社,2008年,第16-17页。

的功能特征，并对其进行分析。

根据文本的主要功能，赖斯将文本分为四类，特点如下：（1）信息型文本以内容为主，这类文本的主要功能是交流信息、知识和意见。传递信息的语言手段是逻辑指称意义。（2）表达型文本的作者利用语言的美学意义进行创造性写作的文本。信息发出者和信息的形式均被放在突出的位置。（3）呼唤型文本的重点是呼吁、说服、劝阻、欺骗文本读者或接受者采取某种行为。（4）视听文本以图像、音乐等补充以上三种功能，如影视和口头广告。

非文学文体多具有很强的实用性和目的性，旨在传达信息，或者召唤读者引起反应。非文学类文本其形式相对于内容都是次要的，它以传达信息为目的，同时考虑信息的传递效果，是对现实世界的客观陈述，是为社会和人们生活而服务的一种实用性文体。根据上述文本特点，下面简要分析主要非文学文体（以本书所选用的为主）的功能。

1. 法律文书用词庄严、规范、严谨，多用书面语，频繁使用外来词和古体词，叠用近义词或同义词，以彰显内容准确严密、语气客观规范。法律文书以向读者传递信息为主，读者根据法律文书约束自己的行为、承担义务或履行职责，因此法律文书具有权威性和约束力，是呼唤型文本，同时兼具强制性的指令功能。

2. 新闻报道总体来说是信息性文本，以传播资讯为目的。但不同题材、文类、传播载体的新闻文本有各自的特点，需要区别对待。政治类文本为评价信息型文本，政府报告、领导言论等为表达型文本，政治宣传文本为非强制指令功能呼唤文本。

3. 商贸文本涉及金融、商业、保险、法律等诸多领域，用词简洁、准确，语气正式，非常注重礼貌原则，多使用缩略语、古体词、专业术语及近义词和同义词的叠用。商贸文本以向贸易双方传递信息为主，目的在于说服对方，促进贸易的达成。因此，商贸文本是以劝诱为主要功能的呼唤型文本。

4. 影视字幕是以视听为主要功能的信息型文本。影视剧的语言多数为对话形式，大都源于生活，词汇量较小。因此，其语言口语化、生活化，并且十分形象；句子简单且通俗易懂，还会包含十分贴近生活的很多流行语和表达方式。

5. 广告常常运用文学语言中的修辞，以加强对读者的吸引力，实现其商业目的。在选词方面，广告语通常选用大众化的词汇，口语化气息较浓，有时也会创造新词，增强吸引力。广告语是典型的以劝诱为主要功能的呼唤型文本，其目的是使人认识、理解某种商品或服务，以说服消费者产生购买的欲望和购买的行为。

6. 公示语的用语简洁明了、引人注目，常使用大写字母以显示正式庄重，有时还会图文并用，增强视觉效果。公示语具有规范、调节、制约、提示等信息功能，属于非强制性指令功能的呼唤型文本。

7. 中英文旅游宣传文本在语言使用上各有特点。中文旅游文本通常注重音韵和谐、形式对称，常常大量使用修饰语形容词、华丽之词，具有强烈的主观色彩。而英语用词朴实明快，简洁明了，句式结构严谨，表达直观通俗，注重信息的准确性和语言的实用性。旅游宣传属于呼唤功能文本，并兼具劝诱的功能。因为该类文本看似是传播旅游资讯，但目的旨在劝诱人们到所宣传的旅游地游览观光。中文旅游宣传文本多采用具有需求功能的词语来渲染气氛，而英文则是依托信息达到类似的功能。

8. 哲学是理论化、系统化的世界观，是人们对自然知识、社会知识、思维知识的概括和总结。哲学文献的语言具有高度概括性、抽象性和思辨性，常用古体词和外来词，是典型的信息型文本。

9. 企业规章制度的语言特点是简洁、精准、正式，具有刚性，鲜用形容词、副词甚至介词，祈使句比比皆是。企业规章制度用文字的形式规定企业管理的内容、程序和方法，是管理企业人员的行为规范和准则，总体来说是以强制为主要功能的呼唤型文本。

10. 商务信函主要用于向商务伙伴提供有关公司、产品规格、性能、价格、付款、装运、保险等方面的信息。在提供有关信息的同时，商务信函主要促成对方采取行动，如购买产品、装运产品、支付货款等。如今，商务信函可以通过电子邮件的方式快捷传递，为塑造友好、亲切、和谐的氛围，文字也更加简洁和口语化。

由此可见，虽然不同文体的非文学文体在功能和目的上有所区别，但总体来看都是人们传递信息、处理事务的工具。即便某种著作的主旨为传达特定具体知识，如哲学文献尽管具有文学价值，却不属于文学的范畴。

1.4 非文学文体翻译的理念、原则和标准

在国外译论中，苏联翻译理论家费道罗夫（Andrei Fedorov）的等值论是最早被引进的。该理论认为，等值翻译就是复制原文形式的特点（如果语言条件许可的话），或创作在作用上与原文特点相符合的东西，来表达原文所特有的内容与形式间的相互关系。由此可见，该理论把原文形式特点（其中包括文体特点）的再现提到了等值的高度。等值翻译要求译作必须与原作有相同的信息、相同的思想、相同的意境以及相同的文体风格。在非文学文体翻译中，体中有体，类中有类，有的体例、程式、专业术语、用词已经相对固定或者国际化，译文不得任意逾越。

美国翻译理论家尤金·奈达（Eugene A. Nida）提倡翻译的动态对等。他认为"对等"其实就是"最切近源语信息的自然对等"[①]，具体地说，就是词汇、语法、语义和文体等不同层次上，通过改变原文形式，保存原文内容，用译语最切近而又最自然的对等语把原文内容表达出来，以求功能对等。所以动态对等实际上有两种关系的对等：一边是原文对原文的接受者，另一边是译文对译文的接受者。同一信息，用两套不同的语言，受众不同，却要求有相同的效果。很显然，相应的文体是获得相应功能的条件之一。翻译对等原则既有语言结构、语言发生时态上的动态对等，也有体裁形式、语域风格上的静态对等。非文学文体的文体风格既有程式化的一面，

---

① 参见：Eugene Nida, Charles, Taber R. *The Theory and Practice of Translation*. Shanghai: Shanghai Foreign Language Education Press, 2004, p.12.

也有相对性的一面。当前，我国翻译理论界过多地推崇西方译论，认为德国学者汉斯·费米尔（Hans Vermeer）的"目的论"翻译理论、赖斯的文本类型翻译理论以及纽马克的交际翻译法事实上更适用于各类应用型翻译。

传统的翻译理论比较推崇"对等"，即译文和原文的语义对等，翻译的机理以语言学和结构学为基础。非文学翻译在实践中的的标准要求是：译文正确反映客观事实，实现原文服务社会的功能，语言规范，不用新奇的表达方法，符合一般的语法规范；因原文具有单一性，译文也要意思明确，没有歧义。非文学翻译的首要标准是准确，在翻译中，需要译者注重翻译理念，洞悉源语与目的语间的文化差异及语言特点，在深入了解专业领域知识的基础上，恰当地用直译和意译使译文行文流畅、表意清晰，忠实地再现原文的信息。

我国传统的翻译理论和翻译标准，基本上都是针对文学翻译而言的。而对广泛应用于社会生活的内容繁杂、形式多样、目的不一的非文学文体翻译很少论及，致使应用翻译理论研究一直处于一种被冷落的境地。同时，传统的翻译教材也是重视文学文体翻译，非文学文体翻译教材占比例很小，结果导致翻译课堂教学严重脱离实际，造成学习者不能很好地完成各类非文学文体的翻译任务，难以"学以致用"。黄龙在《翻译艺术教程》中阐释了翻译的 13 观 4 性 1 法，包括译学的功能、性质、原理、标准、方法、神韵、美学、风格、教学、翻译家以及语言心理学、人工智能等相关学科的研究。金隄在《等效翻译探索》中论述了他对译论的思考，分基础理论、本体理论、专项研究和技巧研究四个门类，其中，本体理论包括形式与内容、灵活与准确、语义与语境、异国情调与翻译腔、标准与其上下限等五个关系问题。刘宓庆在《西方翻译理论概评》中通过评述西方译论，构建了由内部和外部两个结构系统组成的翻译学的理论体系。内部系统由翻译理论（基本理论、方法论、程序论、美学、教学法研究）、翻译史（翻译发展史、译论史）和翻译信息工程三部分构成。外部系统包括哲学、社会文化和语言符号三部分，为译学的基础理论参照系统。李长栓在《非文学翻译理论与实践》中专门探讨了非文学翻译的特点，提出了非文学翻译要做到"方法得当、意思明确、语言朴实"的翻译策略。冯庆华的《实用翻译教程》一书，语言的功能思想贯穿始终，在翻译理念上，突破了传统翻译理论的束缚，积极倡导非文学文体翻译标准多元化。他认为，就非文学文体翻译而言，由于文体的变化与迥异，翻译标准应该是多元化的，就是说，我们应根据不同的文体来确定相应的标准。黄忠廉、信娜提出了创建应用翻译学的理论构想，认为将应用翻译作为一门独立学科开展研究，不仅可行，而且能够更好地指导实用翻译的教学和实践，有助于整个翻译学的完善。

长期以来，文学文体翻译比较恪守"信、达、雅"的翻译标准，并以此指导着翻译教学和翻译实践。但是，越来越多的研究表明，沿用此类标准并不一定适合应用文本翻译。有的学者提出"信、达、雅"并不一定是适合应用翻译的最佳标准。陈新认为"信、达、雅"的翻译标准对于文学翻译是毋庸置疑的，但是，对于实用英语翻译，它的指导意义还有待商榷。林克难结合多年的翻译实践教学，认为"信、达、雅"并不完全适合实用英语的翻译。

1.5 非文学文体翻译的策略与方法

前面我们曾提到，非文学文体是相对于文学文体而言的，由此可见非文学文体体裁的多样性。虽然非文学文体体裁多种多样，但是由于特定体裁的非文学文体具有单一性，译文需要直截了当地表达出原文文本的信息，而不是追求语言的新奇。因此，译者需要了解非文学文体的翻译策略与方法，才能更好地完成翻译工作。恰当和适合的翻译方法可以帮助译者更好地完成译文，而正确的翻译策略可以为翻译方法做指导。

本书将从以下三个方面探讨如何制定翻译策略。

第一，了解原文文本。译者在翻译前应当掌握原文文本，首先了解原文文本的类型，按照文本的功能来划分。不同文体的功能和特点都不一样，了解原文文本的类型是译者首先需要做的。然后根据原文文本的类型及其功能，了解原文文本的翻译目的，明确翻译目的。

第二，找出翻译难点。在翻译的过程中，译者会频繁地遇到自己不知道或者不了解的内容。因此，在翻译之前，译者应当找出原文文本中自己不知道或者不了解的知识，即翻译难点。译者可以借助电子工具，查找平行文本，解决原文文本中的翻译难点。只有这样，译者才能正确地把握和了解原文文本所表达的含义，也只有当译者完全理解原文文本的含义之后，才能在翻译时正确地传达原文文本信息。

第三，灵活对待原文文本。非文学文体的种类很多，每种文体对翻译的诉求也不一样，例如法律翻译、商务翻译、公示语翻译、广告翻译等。译者在翻译时不可死板地对原文文本进行翻译，应当结合原文文本的类型，在传达准确的信息基础上，灵活地进行翻译工作。

恰当的翻译方法可以帮助译者提供更好、更快捷有效的服务，帮助译者准确、完善地进行翻译。例如，我们熟知的关于非文学文体翻译的方法主要有：借助在线电子工具、查找平行文本、交叉检验法、定性与定量分析方法。

第一，借助在线电子工具。在线电子工具内容包罗万象，译者可以借助在线电子工具查找在翻译中不知道或者不了解的单词、短语或者术语。与此同时，在线电子工具检索方便，打破了普通出版物和工具书的界限，实现了全文搜索，提高了译者的翻译质量和速度。更重要的是，在线电子工具的电子资源是不断更新和增加的，这对译者来说十分重要。

第二，查找平行文本。平行文本与原文文本不仅文本类型相同，而且涉及的主题相同，内容相似。因此，译者可以通过查找平行文本来获取或弥补相关的专业知识和术语，学习相关专业领域的语言表达方式和语言风格。平行文本不仅可以提高译者的语言能力，还可以使译文变得更专业，确保翻译质量。

第三，交叉检验法。译者需要将一个汉语词语译为英文，这个汉语词语所对应的英文单词或词组有可能会有好几个，但不一定每个都能正确地反映出原文文本所要表达的含义。交叉检验法是通过英英词典提供的英语释义、例句和词源信息等，并通过查阅不同的词典和资料相互验证，从而使译者掌握英文单词或词组的准确含义及用法，选择合适的英文，更准确地传达原文含义。

第四，定性与定量分析法。定性分析是指确定某一概念在英语或汉语中可能有哪些表达方法。定量分析则是用来确定这些不同的表达方法在英语或汉语中使用的频率，以便使译者选择更准确、最常用、最符合英语或汉语习惯的表达方法。

1.6 非文学文体翻译的研究意义

1.6.1 非文学文体翻译研究的理论意义

根据奈达的统计，文学文体翻译在全部翻译活动中所占比例不超过5%（literature occupies not more than 5%）[1]。然而，国内每年正式和非正式出版的关于文学翻译研究的著作，所占比例却很高。究其原因，"文学文体翻译优于非文学文体翻译"的观点，在国内外翻译界盛行已久，导致非文学文体翻译的地位与其对翻译实践和翻译理论的贡献极不相称。如果我们查阅国内外翻译史就会发现，"非文学文体翻译"似乎被排除在翻译学研究圣殿之外。两部国外权威译学辞书（分别为 Mona Baker 和 Mark Shuttleworth 编著[2]）均未收录"非文学文体翻译"（non-literary translation）词条，而《中国翻译词典》，虽然有"法律翻译""旅游翻译""科技翻译"等词条，但

---

[1] 参见：Eugene A. Nida. *Language, Culture Contexts in Translation*. Shanghai: Shanghai Foreign Language Education Press, 2001, p. 86-95.

[2] 这两部辞书为：Mona Baker. *In Others Words: A Coursebook on Translation*. Beijing: Beijing Foreign Language Teaching and Research Press, 2000. 和 Shuttleworth Mark, Maria Cowie. *Dictionary of Translation Studies*. Shanghai: Shanghai Foreign Language Education Press, 2004.

未收录"非文学文体翻译"。

纽马克要我们重视非文学文体翻译的研究,"I close by bringing to your attention two underplayed aspects of translation theory: the approach to non-literary translation and the impact of corpora from computer database on translation."[①] 奈达也呼吁大家不要把注意力浪费在过时的翻译理论上,而应该把注意力放在翻译研究的新领域。翻译研究应该为经济建设服务,加强对非文学文体翻译的研究,提高非文学文体翻译队伍的水平,有助于增强我国在全球化经济中的竞争力。

诚然,我们无意诋毁文学翻译家所做出的杰出贡献。然而,提升非文学文体翻译的地位,需要翻译界共同努力,关心非文学文体翻译的发展以及相关的理论导向研究。虽然在文学翻译研究方面的成果有许多已经运用到非文学文体翻译的实践中,但非文学文体翻译还是有其特殊性,非文学文体翻译工作者不仅要考虑原文和译文读者,还要考虑翻译的委托人或有关领导,甚至要考虑印刷排版等问题。由于我们在汉英非文学文体翻译方面的理论研究跟不上形势的发展,一支高水平的非文学文体翻译队伍尚未形成,以致这几年在涉外出版物、对外宣传材料、商品广告等汉译英时存在许多问题和失误。这些问题已引起有关部门及学者专家的高度重视。

非文学问题涵盖面极广,在政治、经济、社会及文化等各个层面都有着密切的关联,如何界定分类是个至关重要且亟待解决的问题。对于非文学文体翻译的关注度不应仅仅停留在语言差异层面,应重视文化对翻译策略选择的影响。更应从文化层面,结合文体学理论对实用文体翻译的特点、使用的技巧和方法进行深入细致的分析,论证文化对语言的影响、对翻译策略选择的影响,超越以往非文学文体翻译过于侧重文体的语言特点以及英汉两种语言之间差异的狭隘,促进今后文化与翻译的跨学科研究,为"翻译学"更快、

---

① Peter Newmark. "Why Translation Theory What Translation Theory". *Journal of Translation Studies*, Dec. 1997: 100.

更好地发展奠定更坚实的理论基础。

1.6.2 非文学文体翻译研究的现实意义

韩礼德的功能主义语言观认为，语言的使用与其使用的情景语境之间有着十分密切的关系。语场（field of discourse）、语式（mode of discourse）和语旨（tenor of discourse）是情景语境的三个变量，它们促成不同的情景类型的形成，从而产生不同的语篇类型，即语域[①]。形成于20世纪60年代的ESP（English for Specific Purposes，专门用途英语）教学理念，正是源于韩礼德的功能语言学中的语域理论，作为一门发展迅速的学科，在英语教学领域正受到越来越多的关注。

随着经济全球化的推进和深入以及社会的发展对高素质人才的需求，中国的教育目标和课程设置都发生了深刻的变化，特别是英语课程在整个教育体系中的职能与以往相比大有不同，其目标已不仅仅是满足一般性文化教育的需要，而是更注重它的社会性和复合性。实际上，非文学文体的主要内容可以说就是专门用途英语。因此，非文学文体翻译的研究，响应了教育目标和课程设置的要求，顺应了经济全球化的发展趋势，满足了社会对翻译人才的需要，并且在很大程度上丰富了文体学的研究，具有极其重要的研究价值。

本书运用大量的实例，说明理论、文化在非文学翻译中的作用，剖析了文化、文体对语言的影响，以在文体分析和界定方面产生突破，从而在客观上厘清内容与形式的关系，指出二者之间的相互作用。同时也指出英语学习者，特别是翻译实践者在翻译活动中容易犯的错误：忽略文化与语言的关系；缺乏实践与理论相结合的意识；没有深入、系统分析发掘的方法与习惯。本书从功能文体学翻译理论角度和文化角度对非文学文体的翻译标准、策略、技巧与方法进行阐释，并辅以大量的翻译实例加以说明，有理有据，从而为进一步规范非文学文体翻译、为翻译教学及翻译实践提供有用的借鉴，提高翻译教学的效果，为培养出更加优秀的翻译人才做出贡献，并

---

① M. A. K. Halliday. *Language as Social Semiotic*. London: Edward Arnold, 1978, p.31.

为促进我国与世界的交际和交流、学习国外的先进科技与管理经验做出贡献。

第二章 功能文体学与非文学翻译

2.1 功能翻译理论

功能主义翻译理论于20世纪70年代出现在德国。它既继承了传统译论的合理的成分，又突破了其束缚，具有很强的可操作性和实践意义，为整个翻译界提供了一条新的研究发展思路，对于电影字幕的翻译具有宏观的指导和启示作用。功能翻译理论（functionalist translation theory）创始人赖斯于1971年提出了"把翻译行为所要达到的特殊目的"[①]作为翻译批评的新模式。后来赖斯的学生费米尔提出翻译目的论（Skopostheorie），从而奠定了功能派理论基础。该理论提出：（1）翻译各方面的交互作用为翻译目的所决定；（2）目的随接受对象的不同而变化。按照这两项原则，译者可以为了达到目的而采用任何他认为适当的翻译策略。

20世纪90年代初，诺德（Christina Nord）进一步拓展了功能翻译理论。她指出，原文与译文联系的质量与数量由译文的预期功能确定。这就是说，根据译文语境，原文中的哪些内容可以保留，哪些需进行调整或改写，该由译文的预期功能确定。在认同费米尔的目的原则（skopos rule）基础之上，她提出了连贯原则（coherence rule）和忠实原则（fidelity rule）。当忠实性原则与功能主义标准发生冲突时，忠实性原则服从于连贯性原则，它们二者均服从目的性原则，这样进一步完善了功能翻译理论。

---

① Katharina Reiss. *Translation Criticism: The Potentials & Limitations.* Shanghai: Shanghai Foreign Language Education Press, 2004, p.168.

功能翻译理论认为，翻译是一种复杂的交际行为，翻译目的常常是在委托人与译者之间磋商而确定的。发挥作用的是发起人或其代理，他们对翻译的时间、地点、场合、媒介、目的以及译文的读者和功能做出解释；译者根据具体的翻译要求，着眼于原作者的交际意图与译文的预期功能，结合译文读者的社会背景知识、交际需要、译文期待来决定处于特定译语文化环境中文本的具体翻译策略，而不必拘泥于原文对等而影响译文在译语文化环境中的交际功能。功能翻译理论的贡献主要是：第一，从译入者的新视角来诠释翻译活动，赋予译者更大的选择权——译者可根据译文的预期功能或目的调整翻译策略，灵活选择诸如删减、调整等翻译方法，对原文进行处理；第二，为翻译批评提出了多元化的标准，对翻译实践具有更现实的指导意义。

2.2 系统功能文体学理论

本书的主要理论依据是韩礼德的功能语言学，该理论是具有社会学倾向的功能语言学处理方法，是 20 世纪最有影响的语言学理论之一，同时也影响到和语言相关的不同领域，如语言教学、社会语言学、话语分析、文体学和机器翻译等。功能文体学是系统功能语言学的重要组成部分，本书主要关注的是功能文体学理论。功能语法的目标是要说明语言是社会交往的手段，其基础是语言系统及其组成成分，同时又不可避免地由它们所提供的作用和功能所决定。

20 世纪 70 年代初，韩礼德在论文《语言功能与文学文体》（"Linguistic Functions and Literary Style"）[①]中论述了系统功能文体学理论。之后，功能文体学在世界上产生巨大影响。"功能文体学"为"系统功能文体学"的简称，它特指以系统功能语言学为基础的

---

① 参见：M. A. K. Halliday: "Linguistic Functions and Literary Style". *Explorations in the Functions of Language*. London: Edward Arnold, 1973, p.103.

文体派别。作为功能文体学的开创人之一，韩礼德在该文中提出"语言的功能理论"是进行文体研究的较好工具，并区分了语言的三大纯理功能：表达讲话者经验的"概念功能"，表达讲话者态度、评价以及交际角色间关系的"人际功能"和组织语篇的"语篇功能"。

功能文体学的核心概念是"功能""情景语境""前景化"，这三大概念互相交融在一起，成为一个系统整体发挥效应。功能文体学理论的核心是"功能"思想。"功能"在语言学研究中主要有两层相互联系而又相互独立的意义：第一，语法功能，如主语、谓语、主位等；第二，语言的总体功能。功能文体学中的功能主要指第二种功能。韩礼德从无数具体的功能类别中归纳出三个纯理功能：概念功能、人际功能和语篇功能[①]。概念功能是讲话者作为观察者的功能，表达人们的社会经历和内心的心理经验，同时也表达事物之间的各种逻辑关系，如并列、从属等。人际功能是讲话者作为闯入者（intruder）的功能，表达他的意见、态度、评价和他与听话者的相对角色关系，包括社会角色关系和交流角色关系。语篇功能是讲话者作为组织者的功能，它把概念功能和人际功能根据情景语境在语篇中组织成一个整体，共同在语境中起作用。所有三种功能都同时存在于讲话者的语篇组织计划内。这三种意义相对来说是相互独立的。所以，三种功能组成三种意义资源。讲话者在讲话过程中要根据情景语境从这三种资源的系统网络中做出选择。从所有这三种意义中做出的选择都可对语篇的文体有意义。因此，韩礼德不同意把文体只作为一种表达，而与概念意义或者认知意义对立起来，把文体视为没有意义的特征。他认为这一方面与我们的许多文学文体是以经验意义为基础的感受不一致，另一方面，也把所谓的"非认知的"文体特征置于与那些最贴切地表现我们对文学作品的认识的语言选择相对立的地位。[②]

[①] 参见：M. A. K. Halliday. *An Introduction to Functional Grammar*. Beijing: Foreign Language Teaching and Research Press, 2000, p.114.

[②] 张德禄：《韩礼德功能文体学理论述评》，《外语教学与研究》，1999 年第 1 期，第 45 页。

"前景化"是功能文体学的一个重要概念。韩礼德把文体视为"前景化"(Style is foregrounding)①。他明确指出"前景化是有动因的突出"(motivated prominence)。韩礼德认为,"突出"是一个概括性术语,指语言显耀现象,语篇中的某些语言特征以某种方式凸露出来。那么哪些文体特征才是有动因的突出呢?韩礼德指出,单纯的语言突出不能作为有无文体价值的标准,只有当突出在表达讲话者的全部意义有一定"功能"时,才具有文体价值,才能是前景化的语言特征。"前景化,据我理解,是有动因的突出……但是,除非这种突出对作者的整体意义有贡献,否则就似乎缺乏动因;一个突出的特征只有与文本的整体意义相关时,才能真正地前景化。这种关系是一种功能关系:如果某个语言特征由于自身的突出而对整个作品的整体意义做出贡献,它凭借的是它在语言系统中的价值——凭借的是产生其意义的语言功能。当这种语言功能与我们阐释作品相关时,这种语言结构的突出看起来就是有目的的。"②

"情景语境"是功能文体学的另一个核心概念。韩礼德将语域定义为"依用法而变的变量"③。区别任何一种语域的变量(情景语境变量)有三个维度:正在谈论的事情(语场);语言是如何在互动交流中发挥作用的(语式);交流中所涉及的人及其关系和交际意图(语旨)。语旨可以进一步分为个人语旨、功能语旨和修辞语旨。个人语旨牵涉交际的参与者及其社会关系,它也决定着交际的正式程度、熟悉程度及专业程度。功能语旨是用来描述在某一情景下使用的是何种语言的一种范畴。修辞语旨涉及语言的各种修辞功能。语言可以是寒暄性的、说明性的、说服性的或者说教性的。许多学者认为语言还有其他功能。情景语境的三个变量构成不同的情景语境,因此通过不同的音、词汇及语法形式产生出不同文体类型的语

---

① 参见:M. A. K. Halliday. *An Introduction to Functional Grammar*. Beijing: Foreign Language Teaching and Research Press, 2000, p.120.

② M. A. K. Halliday. *An Introduction to Functional Grammar*. Beijing: Foreign Language Teaching and Research Press, 2000, p.126.

③ 参见:M. A. K. Halliday. "Linguistic Functions and Literary Style". *Explorations in the Functions of Language*. London: Edward Arnold, 1973, p.112.

篇（即语域）。

前景化的文体观在进行文体分析时采取的是一种相关性标准，即看语言的突出形式是否在情景语境中起到了突出的作用。由此可见，情景语境对理解语篇的整体意义、对识别某些语言特征是否被前景化以及对整个文体分析都起到了十分重要的作用。功能文体学中语境是个多层次的概念，它包括文本本身的整体意义和一切文本外的社会文化要素。对情景语境的重视使功能文体学对翻译实践和研究的各方面都具有重要的指导意义。

韩礼德认为语境变量可以分为"语场"（field of discourse）、"语式"（mode of discourse）和"语旨"（tenor of discourse）三种[①]。"语境是话语在其中行使功能的整个事件，以及说话人或写作者的目的。因此，它包括话语主题。方式是事件中话语的功能，因此，它包括语言采用的渠道（临时的或有准备的说或写），以及语言的风格或者修辞手段（叙述、说教、劝号、应酬等等）。基调指交际中的角色类型，即话语的参与者之间的一套永久性的或暂时性的相应的社会关系。范围、方式和基调一起组成了一段话语的语言情景。"[②] 这些变量分别决定他提出的概念功能（ideational function）、语篇功能（textual function）和人际功能（interpersonal function）这三大纯理功能（metafunction）。而这三大纯理功能又分别支配语义系统中的及物性系统、主位/信息系统和语气、情态系统。

概念功能又可再分为经验功能（empirical function）和逻辑功能（logical function）。经验功能与说话的内容发生关系，它是说话人对外部环境的反映的再现，是说话人关于各种现象的外部世界和自我意识的内部世界的经验。逻辑功能则仅仅是间接地从经验中取得的抽象的逻辑关系的表达。

语篇功能使说话人所说的话在语言环境中起作用，它反映语言

[①] 参见：M. A. K. Halliday. *An Introduction to Functional Grammar*. Beijing: Foreign Language Teaching and Research Press, 2000, p.130.

[②] M. A. K. Halliday. *An Introduction to Functional Grammar*. Beijing: Foreign Language Teaching and Research Press, 2000, p. 142.

使用中前后连贯的需要。例如，如何造一个句子使其与前面的句子发生关系，如何选择话题来讲话，如何区别话语中的新信息和听话人已经知道的信息，等等。它是一种给予效力的功能。没有它，概念功能和人际功能都不可能付诸实现。

人际功能是一种角色关系，它既涉及说话人在语境中所充当的角色，也涉及说话人给其他参与者所分派的角色。例如，在提问时，说话人自己充当了提问者，即要求信息的人的角色；同时，他也就分派听话人充当了答话者，即提供信息的人的角色。不同的说话人，因与听话人的关系不同，在对同一听话人说话时，会采取不同的口气；而同一说话人对不同的听话人说话时，也会采用不同的口气。

韩礼德认为，概念功能、语篇功能和人际功能是三位一体的，不存在主次问题。当语言情景的特征反映到语言结构中时，话语范围趋向于决定概念意义的选择，话语方式趋向于决定话语意义的选择，话语基调则趋向于决定交际意义的选择。功能文体学把语言现象和语篇产生的文化背景和语篇的意义较好地结合起来，通过分析在情境语境中突出的语言现象，阐释语篇的文体。因此，韩礼德的功能文体学理论为我们提供了一个比较完整、全面的文体学分析框架。

2.3 功能文体学在中国的发展

功能文体学是系统功能文体学的简称，既是文体学的一个流派，也是系统功能语言学研究的一部分。随着系统功能语言学在中国的发展，功能文体学理论自 20 世纪 70 年代诞生后，也受到不少中国学者的关注。功能文体学把语言现象和语篇产生的文化背景以及语篇意义较好地结合起来，通过分析在情景语境中突出的语言现象来阐释语篇的文体。由于韩礼德的功能文体学理论为我们提供了一个比较完整、全面的文体学分析框架，该理论自诞生以来对中国的文体学研究产生了深远的影响。功能文体学研究在中国的发展过程大致分为两个阶段：第一阶段为初步研究阶段，一些文体学家对新兴的功能文体学理论进行了简略介绍和初步研究；第二阶段是迅速发展阶段，许多文体学家和英语学习研究人员对功能文体学理论进行了深入研究和探索之后，把该理论广泛应用于对文学文体的阐释、语篇分析和英语教学实践。

根据胡壮麟、陈冬梅（1990）的综述，我国的功能文体学研究开始于20世纪80年代，一直到2000年，这十几年是功能文体学理论在中国发展的初步研究阶段。侯维瑞（1983）讨论了语域在文学作品中的应用；胡文仲（1984）以文体学的"英国学派"为名介绍了韩礼德的基本观点并加以评述；张德禄（1988）比较全面地介绍了韩礼德的观点，并且总结出了一个"前景化"的模式。1989年和1991年，在北京大学和苏州大学分别召开了第一届和第二届"全国系统功能语法研讨会"，而1993年在浙江大学召开的"第三届全国系统功能语法研讨会"上，刘世生的论文《系统功能文体学在现代文体学中的位置》拉开了中国学者探讨功能文体学理论的序幕。通过对文体学研究历史的回顾与总结，刘世生突出强调了系统功能文体学承前启后的重要位置。他认为，迄今为止文体学已形成了四个主要的发展方向：形式文体学、功能文体学、语篇文体学、社会历史文化文体学。刘世生分析了各派的特点及系统功能文体学与其他各派的关系，证明了系统功能文体学继往开来的特点。在第三届研讨会上，崔云红的论文《英诗中的词汇衔接分析》利用韩礼德提出的语言三大功能之一的语篇功能理论分析英语诗歌，把文学欣赏与语言学联系起来，是功能文体学理论早期的探索实践之一。

张德禄教授的专著《功能文体学》于1998年出版，它严格按系统功能语言学的理论来建构自己的理论体系，在理论上既有继承又有发展，较好地体现了当时中国普通文体学的研究水平。在功能文体学登上世界文体学界的舞台20年后，中国的学者才开始逐步关注这一新兴的文体学理论。屈指可数的论文和论著揭示了功能文体学在中国的发展还处于初级阶段，对该理论的简单介绍和浅略尝试远远无法揭示系统功能文体学的博大精深。

进入21世纪，中国功能文体学研究步入了迅猛发展阶段。经过了前期的积累，中国文体学界对功能文体学理论的研究成果在这期间可谓达到了"井喷"状态，无论是理论探索还是研究实践都更加深入和全面。截至本书定稿之日，在"中国知网"以"功能文体学"为关键词进行检索可以检索到582篇文章，其中期刊论文408篇、硕士论文165篇、博士论文9篇。论文大致可以分为四类：（1）分析文学作品的文体特征，探寻作者如何通过不同的语言选择来表现作品的主题意义；（2）研究非文学体裁的文体特征，如新闻、广告、科技、贸易、法律等，分析各种体裁的不同语域特征；（3）探讨如何在翻译实践中更好地实现原文篇章语言特征的翻译技巧和方式；（4）研究功能文体学在大学英语语篇和写作教学中的指导作用，并提出具体的研究方法和步骤。

迄今，功能文体学已经有了半个世纪的发展历史，在我国也有了近30年的研究积累，经历了初步阶段和迅速发展阶段，从学者对理论的简略介绍和浅略尝试到对该理论的深入研究和全面应用，现在功能文体学理论在中国已经具有巨大的影响力。我们也坚信，功能文体学在中国有着光明的发展前景，在众多文体学家、翻译研究者和英语教学研究人士的共同努力下，功能文体学一定会得到更深入的研究和更广泛的发展。

2.4　功能文体学视角下的非文学文体翻译

文体学最早发轫于古希腊的传统修辞学，是一门既古老又年轻的学科，直到20世纪才被学者们关注和认知，并开始尝试运用现代语言学的理论和分析方法去探讨研究文体的问题。文体学有传统文体学和现代文体学之分。传统文体学指运用传统的分析方法分析作家的文学风格，研究代表作者作品风格特点的语言本体，研究方向仅限于文学文体的本体研究，侧重文体风格；现代文体学则用现代语言学的原理与分析方法研究包括文学文体在内的各种文体，研究内容更加宽泛，从狭义的文学文体扩大到非文学文体，研究方法也已从单纯的文体分析法衍生为语言结构分析的层面上。随着文体学的发展和完善，翻译文体学研究日趋成为研究翻译理论和翻译标准的重要理念。文体既有内容题材也有语言风格，不同的内容决定了不同的文本本体，不同的文本决定不同的语言形式，即语体风格。

非文学文体翻译都具有实用性目的，译文不仅要保证语义信息的对等，更要求最大限度地达到并满足文体信息和文化信息的对等，最终实现文本的功能。目的和功能的实现是非文学文体翻译的基础和依据。功能文体学用现代语言学原理与分析方法研究各类文体，注重对不同的语言结构所产生的不同文体效应的描述，如语言各层面的突出形式与前景化分析、语境与语篇分析等。因此，作者通过源语文本提供的信息不仅停留在语义层面，也包含文体和语境即文化信息，而译者需首先识别出源语语言及文本特征，并考虑译入语读者对源语中文化信息的接受程度，之后将源语的语言、文体和文化信息在译文中重现，以实现文本的功能。在实用文体中，语篇是在情景语境中产生的。某个突出的语言形式特征只有在情景语境中起突出作用才是被激活的，才能产生文体效应。由此，实用文体的突出形式必须到情景语境中去寻找动因。功能文体学指导非文学翻译的理论核心在于文化对于翻译策略的选择至关重要，超越了以往非文学文体翻译过于侧重非文学文体的语言特点以及英汉两种语言之间差异的狭隘。用该理论来指导非文学文体翻译实践，能更好地解决在非文学文体翻译中遇到的诸多问题。功能文体学理论的功能观和语境理论有助于译者理解源语文本内语言现象以及文本外文化和情境因素。该理论将语言形式、内容和语言功能结合起来考虑，加深了对非文学文体实质的理解，克服了传统文体分析的缺点和不足。与其他文体理论相比较，功能文体学为非文学文体分析和翻译提供了一种更全面、更深刻、更系统的研究方法。

文体是每一个语篇必不可少的一部分，所以译者的任务之一就是要尽可能地传递原文文体特征。文本通过使用的语言呈现出一定的文体特征。探索语言使用的得体性是文体研究的一个主要目的，翻译也强调译文的得体性。翻译的文体研究一般考察译文的语言使用是否得体,是否符合原文的文体特征。脱离对原文文体的理解和再现,不可能进行成功的翻译。实际上,译文得体与否正是衡量译品高下的尺度之一。功能文体学理论以系统功能语言学为理论基础,为我们提供了一个分析和展示语体的文体特征的有效途径。功能文体学认为:所有语言都由三大元功能组成,文体则被视为"前景化",即"有动因的突出"。而概念功能、人际功能和语篇功能是文体的三个方面。如果三个元功能完整地从原文传译到译文中,那么译文就可被视为理想的翻译。然而,由于中英文之间语言和文化差异,有时要完全同时传译三个元功能就存在困难。在这种情况下,译者应根据最突出的元功能灵活地转移自己的翻译焦点,同时还应做一些调整,以便使译文符合译入语的语言和文化习惯。从原文传译到译文中的元功能越多,译文就越成功。

　　文体在翻译中起着极其重要的作用。众所周知,大多数探讨翻译理论和技巧的学者都认为翻译不仅要忠实于原文的内容、表达其意义,而且还要尽可能地忠实于原文的文体。不论是从语言描写的结构特点,还是从读者的反映的角度来看,文体特点是翻译过程中必须考虑的因素。翻译的过程就是译者将原文语义信息、文体信息和文化信息转移到译入语的过程,译文所承载的信息是经过转移后的语义信息、文体信息和文化信息的总和,缺一不可。另一方面,语义信息对等和文体信息对等必须服从于文化信息对等。换言之,在语义信息对等和文体信息对等与文化信息对等出现矛盾时,必须以文化信息对等为大局,再现原文的功能。

　　基于非文学文体的语言和功能特征,对非文学翻译的特点进行总结如下:(1)强调信息的准确性、行文的严谨性以及信息传递的有效性。(2)有明确的目的和读者,非文学翻译的主要目的是为了行之有效的交流,译者可以根据文本类型、项目特色判断翻译目的;在具体的翻译项目中,也可以与委托人交流以进一步明确目的和读者。(3)信息量大、交付时间短,有必要采用工作坊式的集体工作;有些项目具有历史性,不同时期的翻译要注意其连贯性和统一性。(4)对象文本可能不是能够达成翻译目的的"完美"文本,存在着书写质量较差、内容有误或有歧义、逻辑矛盾、行文不规范、思维不严谨等问题,因此译者不可盲目地遵从原文,要批判性地处理源语文本。非文学翻译强调客观真实性,不存在任何虚构和想象的表达,所以,翻译时即使根据需要对原文增删,改变原文的措辞,也要保证原文信息传递的准确性,否则可能引起严重后果或法律后果,如法律文书、商贸合同等文本的翻译。(5)根据具体的翻译文本和翻译目的,选择行之有效的翻译策略,必要的时候可以对原文进行变通或优化以实现翻译目的。

作为跨文化交际行为,非文学翻译功能突出,目的明确,文本的文体规范性强且一般较为统一,同类题材具有突出的共性,作者个性并不鲜明,有时文本的题材类型可以显示或制约文本的功能、文体及语言特点等。同时,虽然非文学文体具有区别于文学文体的共同特点,但在非文学文体内部,不同题材的文本以及同一题材但交际目的、对象、交际环境不同的文本,都有一定的差异。因此,我们必须了解并学会分析各类文本的功能特征,培养对文本功能和文体特点的敏感性,进而在翻译过程中实现功能转换。

由于文学文体特征突出,风格迥异,令译者十分为难,学者们普遍都很重视对文学文体及其翻译的研究;但是对于非文学文体翻译,有些学者认为其大多属于实用文体,翻译起来相对容易一些,因而不需要再花时间在文体特征的分析上了,从而往往忽略了对非文学文体及其翻译的研究。

2.4.1 功能文体学与翻译学的关系

翻译与文体学有着密切的关系,正确传神达意且连贯得体的翻译离不开文体。第一,从翻译的过程与本质来看,翻译的过程就是译者将源语的语义信息、文体信息和文化信息转移到译语的过程。译文所承载的信息是经过转移后的语义信息、风格信息和文化信息的总和,缺一不可。文体是每一个语篇必不可少的一部分,所以译者的任务之一就是要能够保留并尽可能地传递原文的文体特点。第二,从翻译的考察标准来看,翻译的文体研究一般考察译文的语言使用是否得体，是否符合原文的语言风格。众所周知，大多数探讨翻译理论和技巧的人都认为翻译不仅要忠实于原作的内容，而且还要尽可能地忠实于包括语言时代、专业、领域风格在内的原作风格。第三，从翻译的社会功能来看，文体不应该阻碍交流。虽然与作品的内容或意义相比较，形式处于次要的地位，但如果文体的形式处理不得当，就会阻碍文化的交流、意义的表达。

从翻译角度来研究文体理论可称为翻译文体论。在文体学尚未成为独立的学科时，无论国内国外，对文体的研究仅限于修辞学的认知分析。传统的翻译文体学理论一般侧重于文学翻译，主要是针对文学作家个人语言风格流派以及不同体裁的研究，而少有非文学文体翻译的理论研究，即使有，也是包含于修辞的真诚和文辞的达意之中，鲜有系统归纳之说。文体语言特征源于其社会功能，文学文体"一文独大"已成过去，各种非文学文体的社会功能日见重要。文体在应用翻译过程中起着极其重要的作用。翻译不可能脱离文体，实际上，翻译是否得体也是译品高下的重要尺度之一。因此，翻译不仅要忠实于原作的内容、表达其意义，而且还要尽可能地忠实于原作的文体。

2.4.2 功能文体学理论对非文学文体翻译的指导作用

在国外的译论研究中，功能目的论（skopos theory）对应用翻译有一定的指导意义,非文学文体翻译都有现实的甚至功利的目的，要求译文达到预期的功能。目的和功能是非文学文体翻译的依据和依归。翻译的功能目的论认为，原文和译文是两种独立的具有不同价值的文体，各有不同的目的和功能，作者通过源语文本提供信息，译者则将源语的语言和文化信息有条件地传递给目的语的接受者。至于译者对源语文本信息的选择、翻译策略的运用以及译文的表现形式，则决定于翻译委托人和译本接受者的需要和愿望。功能目的论的核心在于翻译的目的和译文的功能。

功能翻译理论注重翻译的目的和译文的预期功能，而非文学文体偏重实用性和交际目的，起着指导、警示、宣传、劝导、鼓动等实用功能。译文预期的目的在于准确、有效地传达信息，因此非文学文体翻译过程中必须充分考虑翻译的目的、读者的接受和译文的预设功能等因素。泰特勒（Alexander Fraser Tytler）指出，翻译的本质是"在接受语中重新创造源语言信息最贴近、最自然的对应项，首先是意义，其次是文体。功能文体学、翻译文体学强调翻译规范、与译文文本相适应等。翻译文体学研究是通过语言对比这一纽带将文体学与翻译研究结合起来，改变了传统翻译研究仅仅关注语言转换或文化研究的单一模式局面，而是在双语语料库基础上将语言对比、文体学研究与翻译研究对象的范围扩大到翻译文本，即以翻译文本为基础，从文体学的视角探究翻译文本所表现出的各类特征的根源"①。

文体学理论的研究和发展，为翻译理论的建设和开拓提供了理论基础，特别是为非文学文体的翻译提供了新的研究视角，能更好地体现翻译的实质。尽管国内外对非文学文体翻译理论的观点各有千秋，但是将翻译目的论与功能文体学结合起来，更加注重文本（或语言）功能在翻译中的作用，已达成共识。陈小慰认为，"功能目的论对指导整个翻译实践，包括文学翻译和实用翻译，都提供了较为客观、可行的原则和标准，相比较而言，它对实用类语篇翻译的指导作用表现得更为明显"②。刘世生提出文体学研究不只为文学研究提供理论研究方法，其实还可以应用于普通文体研究。普通文本表意的客观性有别于文学文体的客观性。对于普通文本，尤其是应用文本，如新闻、合同等问题在表述过程中的意思必须是明确的，其相对突出的时效性、客观性决定了这些文体必须寻找最恰当的文体、语体适应读者导向，来达意传神，以确保读者可以更快地接受。由此可见，功能翻译理论对指导整个翻译实践，尤其是实用类翻译，从文本分析、翻译目的、译文功能到具体的翻译策略都提出了较为

---

① Alexander Tytler. *Essay on the Principles of Translation*. Beijing: Foreign LanguageTeaching and Research Press, 2007, p.9.

② 陈小慰:《对德国翻译功能目的论的修辞反思》,《外语研究》, 2012 年第 1 期, 第 91 页。

客观、可行的原则和标准。可以说，功能翻译理论在实用翻译中有着重要且直接的指导作用。

随着经济全球化、一体化的发展，非文学文体翻译的需求日渐扩大，逐渐成为翻译研究和翻译实践的主流。郭建中认为，"翻译不同类型的文章，应该运用不同的翻译原则和方法，这是当代翻译理论的核心"[①]。由此可见，在非文学文体翻译研究过程中，不仅要注重方法、原则、策略和技巧，更要注重理论层面即方法论的研究。

2.5 本书的研究内容

语域理论是系统功能语言学的一个重要理论，以韩礼德为代表的系统功能学派特别强调语境的作用，即语言发生的环境，他们将语境分为两类：文化语境和情景语境。所谓文化语境指的是语言使用者生活在其中的社会文化或者文化背景，而情景语境指的是语言正在使用时的场合，即语言使用的实际环境。文化语境的差异导致语言产生了基于语言使用者的变体，即由于方言、社会地位、性别等语言使用者的因素所产生的语言变体。而另一种情景语境的差异则使得语言产生了基于语言运用的变体。所谓语域就是语言使用的功能变体，即因情景语境的变化而产生的语言形式的变化。[②]

语域分析是文本分类和分析的有效工具。确定文本的语域特点被认为是成功翻译的必备条件之一。在翻译前，译者必须对文本的语场、语式和语旨等语境变量进行系统分析，进而才有可能在目的语中选择相应的语域根据目的语文化背景进行调整。翻译质量的评估不仅是语义匹配的问题，也是语域匹配程度的问题。

翻译作为一种跨文化交际行为，其过程中语域匹配问题并不简单。某一话语是否达到其交际意图与一定的文化语境相关，因此在

---

① 郭建中：《实用性文章的翻译（上）》，《上海科技翻译》，2001年第3期，第14页。
② 张德禄：《语域理论简介》，《现代外语》，1987年第4期，第23页。

跨语言、跨文化的语境中，语域往往要做必要的调整，出现相应的语域转换，即有时译者需要在目的语语言文化背景下再创造一个与原文同等的交际事件，以便在译文文本中实现原本在其语言文化架构中的功能。在语言和语域层面，译者在必要的时候要做一定的调整，进而使原文和译文在这两个层面可能出现比较大的差异。因此，语域在翻译中的作用，是要根据翻译目的、源语与目的语的语言文化差异等因素来做出判断。

非文学文本交际意图与目的、话题（题材）比较明确，语域易于进行典型化的概括，属于比较容易预测语言使用的限制性语域（restricted registers）。在翻译过程中，语域是要移植到目的文本中，以求语域对等，还是应进行调整，则要看翻译的目的、翻译类型、文化背景差异等。例如新闻报道，译文的语域肯定不同于原文的语域，专业性程度和正式程度肯定要有所降低，可接受程度有所提高。一般来说，在同功能翻译中，信息型非文学文本由于交际情景的文化差异不大，语域转化（transfer of register）问题不会给译者带来太多的麻烦。而广告、旅游等文本中，由于源语和目的语交际环境中对实现同一交际意图的语域要求有所差异，译者需要以实现交际意图和文本功能为目的，对语域做相应的调整。

根据语域理论分析，不同语域有不同的语篇特征，各文体篇章都有自己的一些词汇、语法、修辞手段和文本格式，翻译时应根据不同的文体形式采用相应的翻译方法。笔者以为，在非文学文体翻译中，最重要的就是要体现其专门用途性质的篇章特征，讲究译文的正确性和得体性。而且，非文学文体翻译的优劣与否，很大程度上不仅取决于文字与格式的得体与否，更取决于译者是否对语域做出了适当的调整。

本书在理论上主要以上述功能文体学（functional stylistics）理论为指导。作者花费大量精力分析非文学文体的语域特点，即不同文化背景下具体交际场合中的语场、语式、语旨的特点，概括文本的语言特点，进而根据文本类型与功能、翻译目的与类型、目的与交际情景和文化背景因素，找出合适的翻译策略，对翻译文本做语言层面的操作。依据功能文体学理论,结合非文学文体的语言和功能特征,以下简要分析本书中所涉及的非文学文体的翻译策略。

法律文书:法律文书文体功能的特殊性主要体现其语用上,包括用词、用句、篇章结构等表达规范的逻辑性以及整体布局的周密性。中英文法律文本都有一些不尽相同的文类规范和套语,翻译的时候要遵守译入语文类规范加以套用,而不是倾向于源语采用字面翻译的方法。

新闻报道:新闻语言与具有劝说功能的广告语言不同,又与讲求生动、追求各种艺术效果和意蕴内涵的文学语言有所区别,具有自身鲜明的文体特点。新闻语言鲜明的文体特色增加了其翻译的难度。基于此,本书从功能文体学理论的角度来探讨新闻报道的翻译,并提出相应的翻译方法和策略。

商贸文本:商贸文本翻译要求译者在两种语言的同一语境中寻求功能上的对等。同时,商贸文本作为专门用途英语还要求译者遵循其专门用途要求的特定原则,根据英汉商贸文本的文体差异做出调整。各类不同题材的英汉商贸文本都有各自的文类规范、对应的专业术语,只能遵守规范要求,采用固定的专业术语。而对于固定格式的套语,也有固定的译法,不能简单照搬直译。

影视字幕:由于受时间限制,图像和语言要同步配合,其次还有空间限制,字幕每次出现一般不超过两行。因此,字幕翻译策略应是选用常用词、小词和短词;句式宜简明,力戒繁复冗长,少用过长的插入成分、分词结构和从句。翻译是一个过程,达到过程的目的则是最为重要的。在特定的翻译过程中,根据特定的目的选择相适应的翻译技巧。同翻译的原则相比,翻译技巧则更有实用导向性。一方面,翻译技巧有赖于大量实践,另一方面,它们又超脱于实践并企图更好地引领实践。因此,整理梳理影视字幕翻译策略,对于得到更好的字幕翻译效果而言是非常必要且基础性的工作。

广告语:广告翻译需要译者发挥极大的创造力,为了达到在译语文化中的宣传作用,可能需要对源语文本做出调整,甚至有时候需要抛开原文,才能创造出在译入语文化中起作用的广告。因此,译者应根据不同国家的特点考虑广告的角度和风格,用广告受众能接受、理解,能产生兴趣的方式去做新的创意构思,同时改变广告语言的战略,以达到"本土化"的效果。

旅游宣传:旅游宣传是一种典型的呼唤型文体。"从整体上来说,旅游文体具有以下特点:短小精悍,生动活泼,通俗易懂,信息量大,又不失文学性、艺术性、宣传性和广告性。"①其语言表达必须准确通俗、简洁明了,并富有吸引力,利于不同层面的读者或游客理解和接受。中英文旅游宣传文本语言差异明显。旅游文本翻译虽然总体策略上也是采用交际翻译法,但需要在侧重译语读者的原则下,对源语文本做适当的调整,以符合译入语的表达习惯和文化惯用法。

公示语:公示语的应用范围非常广泛,公共场所旅游外出者所到之处,所见的指示牌、路牌、标志、告示等具有持久性、固定性的信息都可称为公示语。在实际运用中,公示语具有指示性、提示性、限制性和强制性四种突出的应用示意功能。中英文公示语均有相应的文本规范,应该参照目标语的文本规范和相应的规定进行翻译,并注意英汉语言表达和文化思维习惯上的差异,切忌盲目直译,以免译文贻笑大方。

哲学文献:哲学文献翻译不具备开放性的特点,译者只能在有限的空间,甚至是唯一的答案里做选择。哲学文献的特点十分鲜明,据理论证涉及的范围广泛,对各个学科、不同题材文体内容信手拈来,这要求译者具有广泛的知识积累和深入的理解能力。在翻译策略上,译者需要充分体现哲学内容与语言的特点,使译语读者拥有与源语读者相同的感受,通常采用贴近源语的直译策略。

企业规章制度:企业规章制度侧重实用功能,因此对译文有一些特殊要求,不应过分注重文采,不应过于口语化,同时要向员工

---

① 伍峰等:《应用文体翻译:理论与实践》,杭州:浙江大学出版社,2008年,第319页。

传递公司核心价值观并对员工起到约束作用，这是对译者翻译水平的考验。要求译者在翻译时应更加注重翻译的逻辑性和准确性。笔者希望通过对该类文本翻译的研究，得出适用于翻译该类文本的翻译技巧，为今后该类文体的翻译提供实践经验。

商务信函： 商务信函涉及双方的权利、义务和利害关系，是达成贸易活动目的不可或缺的环节。英汉商务信函特点鲜明，涉及特有的格式、套话及惯用语，译者应都提起注意，同时译者更应认识到商务信函翻译也是一种跨文化交际行为，其主要目的在于实现英汉两种语言的功能对等。对商务信函翻译而言，应准确把握语篇，体现信函层次分明、语言简洁的语篇特色。

第三章 法律文书

法律语言是一种语言变体，属于专门用途语言（Language for Special Purposes，简称 LSP）范畴。它完全不同于日常生活中所使用的语言，也不同于文学和商务等语言，既具有自身的个性化特点和规律，又带有一定的法律功能和意义。法律文书属于庄重文体，是各种文体中正式程度最高的一种，它的翻译是一种涉及法学、语言学和翻译学的跨学科行为。法律文书不同于其他文体，在翻译时不需要进行阐释和艺术创造。有时甚至为了保持法律文书原文意思的原汁原味，翻译时要牺牲语言的流畅。做专业的法律文书翻译还需要译者精通法律知识并且具有过硬的语言功底，但在翻译时几乎不能自由发挥。因此，探讨法律文书的文体功能、研究其语言特征，都对法律文书的翻译有着极其重要的价值。

3.1 法律文书的文体功能

通常来说，法律是指由社会认可、国家确认、立法机关制定规范的行为规则，并由国家强制力保证实施，以规定当事人权利和义务为内容的，对全体社会成员具有普遍约束力的一种特殊的行为规范或社会规范。广义上的法律文书指的是一切涉及法律内容的文书，从约束力上来区分主要包括两方面：(1) 具有普遍约束力的规范性法律文件，具体指各种法律法规及规章等；(2) 不具有普遍约束力的非规范性法律文件，即狭义上的法律文书，指国家司法机关、律师及律师事务所、仲裁机关、公证机关和案件当事人依法制作的处理诉讼案件以及非诉讼案件的具有法律效力或法律意义的非规范性文件的总称。本章所指的法律文书是指广义上与法律相关的各类文本。

任何交际都有其特殊的意图或目的，法律文书是一种特殊用途语言文本，它的主要功能是规范功能（regulatory function），即以约束性来规定、规范、指导人的行为和社会活动，这种功能具有强制性，也是其区别于其他文体功能的主要原因。同时，法律文书还具有提供信息的功能（informative function），带有描写性的意义，这种功能主要体现在所有介绍法律知识的著作、论文以及普法宣传材料等文本中。因此，法律文书文体功能的特殊性主要体现在其语用上，包括用词、用句、篇章结构等表达规范的逻辑性以及整体布局的周密性。

3.2 英文法律文书的语言特征

美国语言学家马丁·裘斯（Martin Joos）在《五只钟》（*Five Clocks*）一书中按照正式程度将文体分成五种变体：冷冻体（frozen style）、正式体（formal style）、商议体（consultative style）、随意体（casual style）和亲密体（intimate style）。法律文书就属于冷冻体的范畴，它经过起草人的反复推敲，字斟句酌，并经过使用者实践的反复检验，再被进行修订之后已经形成了一种含义清晰且无歧义的文本。因此，法律文书的形成过程其实就是冷冻过程，对其文本进行领悟、解读的过程就类似于解冻过程。语言学界把法律文书归为庄重（solemn）或刻板（rigid）的文体，这种文体需要读者进行反复解读、深度理解才能挖掘蕴藏在其中的多层含义。"法律英语语句正规，有一定的程式，专用于严肃客观地表述所涉事项。也有人认为这种文体是'神秘的'（mystical），甚至是'矫揉造作的'（assiduously stilted），理由是法律英语文词艰涩难懂，语句冗长复杂。"[①] 英文法律文书的语言特征从总体上来讲主要表现在选词保守性、用词专业性、表达精确性、布局严密性、谋篇庄重性以及高

---

① 孙万彪：《英汉法律翻译教程》，上海：上海外语教育出版社，2003年，第9页。

度权威性。本章从词汇特征、语法特征和审美特征来对此进行挖掘。

3.2.1 词汇特征

A. 经常沿用古旧体词

当代英语的词汇与 1000 多年前甚至几百年以前的词汇已经发生巨大变化，不仅含义大不相同，用法也大不一样。而英文法律文书却一直频繁沿用古代英语和中世纪英语中的词汇，包括它们的意义和用法，因为这类词语可以充分地展现法律语言的正式、严谨以及庄重的文体风格。这类古旧体词中最典型的是由 here, there 和 there 加上介词构成复合副词，在法律英语中应用十分普遍，例如：

hereafter	此后
hereat	因此
herebefore	此前
hereby	兹，借此，特此
herein	此处，本文中
hereinabove	在上文中
hereinafter	以下，在下面中
hereof	于此
hereon	于是，关于这个
hereto	至此
heretofore	在此以前
hereunder	根据本文
herewith	同此
thereafter	据此
therefore	因此，因而
therefrom	由此
therein	在此文中
thereof	关于，由是
thereto	又，及
thereon	就此

whereas	鉴于，然而，尽管
whereby	由此
wherefore	为此，因此
whereof	关于那个
wherein	在那方面
wheresoever	无论何处

常见的古旧体词还有：

aforesaid	前述的
anent	关于，涉及
foregoing	前述的，前面的
forthwith	即刻
henthforth	从此以后
howbeit	尽管如此
let	障碍
nay	不，否
notwithstanding	尽管
said	上述的
thence	从那里，之后，因此

以上这些古旧体词遗留在当代法律英语中虽然会给人们的理解带来一定的障碍，但是对于规范、古板的法律语言而言，它们的使用会使法律文书的句子更加简洁紧凑，语意表达更加精练严密，体现出法律文书独特的文体特征。

B. 频繁借用外来语词汇

从词源学的角度来讲，法律英语从法语和拉丁语借用了相当多的词汇，这也是英文法律文书区别于其他文体的另一个主要特征。这些借词被英语接纳之后一直沿用至今而没有发生根本性的形式变化，成为英语法律语言的一大特色。1066年，征服者威廉把法语带到了英格兰，并对英语产生了影响，法语开始成为英国的统治语言。现代英语法律文书中大量使用的法语词很大部分便是从当时的法语法律语言中直接借用过来的。这类词的特点是在法律意义上具有相对固定且单一的词意，没有一定词源学知识的人们是无法辨认这种词的来源的。法律英语中常见的法语借词有：

action	诉讼
alien	转让
amerce	罚款
bar	禁止
complaint	起诉
culpaple	有罪，重大过失
demise	亡夫遗产
demurer	抗诉
easement	地役权
estoppel	禁止翻供
fee simple	无条件继承的不动产
feme covert	已婚妇女
feme sole	未婚女子
hue and cry	大声抗议
indictment	控告
jury	陪审团，陪审员
laches	对行使权力的懈怠
lien	抵押权，留置权
parol	口头的
plaintiff	原告
quash	废除，取消
remise	让与
residue	剩余财产
save	除……之外
specialty	盖印的契约（合同）

英语是从与拉丁语同源的盎格鲁—撒克逊语中派生出来的。盎格鲁—撒克逊语早先从拉丁语中借用过一些词汇。公元 7 世纪时，又有更多的拉丁词被吸收进来，这主要是由于基督教开始传入英国。

到了 13、14 世纪，中古英语慢慢发展出来。除了含有拉丁词根的法语词被吸收进来，还有一些词是直接从拉丁语借过来的。到了 16、17 世纪，文艺复兴重新唤起了人们对于古典作品的兴趣，从而使这一过程得到加强。从那以后，拉丁语一直是许多新词特别是科学词汇的来源。法律英语中的拉丁语词汇以其简短精辟、准确清晰的特点得到公认并一直延续使用至今，体现了法律文书的权威性和严肃性。法律英语中常见的拉丁语借词有：

ab initio	从开始起，自始
ad hoc	专门的，特别的
alibi	不在犯罪现场
alieni juris	他人权利
amicus curiae	法官顾问
bona fide	善意的，真诚的
caveat	当心
de facto	事实上，根据事实
de novo	重新
ejusdem generic	同类性质的
ex parte	片面的
flagrante delicto	犯罪时刻
in personam	对人诉讼
in re	关于，案由
in rem	反对某物
in statu quo	现状
lex loci	地方法律
pari passu	不分先后，公平地
per capita	人均
per se	自身，本身
pro rata	按比例
quasi	类似，准
res judicata	定案

seriatim	逐条，依次
sua sponte	自愿的
tulela	监护人

C. 大量选用法律术语或行话

法律英语中的许多词汇都是从英语的演变过程中分离出来的，承载着特征明显的法律含义，而法律文书的文体功能决定了大量已经约定俗成的专业术语的使用。这些术语语义精练、表意准确、严谨规范，用法相对稳定，可以非常精确地表达复杂的法律问题。它们是法律语言的重要组成部分，能够体现出法律文书庄重、正式的文体特征。常见的英文法律术语如下：

action	诉讼
alien	转让
appeal	上诉
bench	法官席
brief	辩护状
clean hands	清白
color	表面法律权利
counterpart	有同等效力的副本
depose	宣誓作证
distress	扣押
execution	签订，签署
first instance	一审
force majeure	不可抗力
variance	诉状与供词不一致
instrument	法律文件
issue	子女
jeopardy	受刑的可能性
liability	责任
limitation	时效
majority	法定年龄

negligence	过失
party	诉讼当事人
prescription	时效
principal	本人，当事人
restitution	归还，补偿，赔偿
satisfaction	清偿，补偿
serve	送达
surety	担保人
holding	裁定
verdict	裁决

英文法律文书中还通常使用大量的行话，它们与专业术语的不同之处往往体现在规范程度上。行话往往是同行之间在状辞、法庭辩论辞中使用的语言，是"专业性俚语"，非法律行内人士通常是不习惯于使用的。而法律专业术语更适用于书面文件，几乎不限制使用人士，规范程度更强一些。常见的英文法律行话如下：

accessory	从犯，帮凶
accomplice	同谋
alleged	被指控的
case at bar	正在审讯的案件
damages	赔偿金
due care	应有的谨慎
hung jury	意见分歧的陪审团
inferior court	下级法院
issue of fact	事实上的争论点
legal fiction	法律上的假定
misdemeanor	行为失检，轻罪
on all fours	完全一致的
plea bargin	认罪求情协议
process	传票
record	诉讼记录

retainer	律师聘请费	
sidebar	兼职律师	
surplusage	多余的辩解	
superior court	上级法院	
winding up	结案	

除了专业术语和行话之外，法律文书中还经常使用正式程度较高且形态上较复杂的词汇替代普通词汇来展现其严肃、郑重的风格。例如：

普通英语词汇	法律英语词汇	汉语词义
according to	in accordance with	依照，根据
after	subsequent to	在……之后
because of	by virtue of	因为，由于
before	prior to	在……之前
if	provided that	如果
the dead	the deceased	死去的人
think	hold, deem	认为

D. 故意使用叠词

在英文法律文书中，原本只需要一个词就能表达出来的意思却故意使用双叠词（doublet）或三叠词（triplet），主要表现为两个或三个同义词或近义词的叠用或并用，目的是为了刻意追求用词精确和语意确凿，同时又能增强所传达的语气。这是法律英语的一大特色，也被认为是一种相当得体的行文手法。一些近义词并用是为了用它们彼此的相同含义使原文的意思不被曲解，这属于"求同型"；另一些则是为了体现彼此之间的微弱差别以使原文的意思更加完整，这属于"存异型"。然而要识别这两种情况，非要有一些语言功力和实践经验不可。法律英语中常见的叠词如下：

求同型

acknowledge and confess	承认
act and deed	行为
charge, fees and expenses	费用

custom duties and tariffs	关税
deem and consider	认为
goods and chattels	个人财产
have and hold	持有
heirs and successors	继承人
let or hindrance	妨碍，阻碍
null and void	无效
release and discharge	解除
transfer and convey	转让
secret and confidential	机密
terms or provisions	条款
will and testament	遗嘱

存异型

alter and modify	修改和变更
executor and administrator	遗嘱执行人和遗嘱管理人
expiration and termination	期满和终止
gain, advantage and benefit	收益、优势和利益
interpretation and construction	理解和解释
loss, disadvantage and detriment	损失、劣势和损害
obligation and liability	义务和责任
solicit or accept	招引与接受

E. 惯用模糊性词语和精确性词语

法律英语中的模糊性和精确性是互为补充的矛盾体和统一体。一般来讲，法律文书的撰写起草要避免使用含糊其辞或模棱两可的表达，但为了发挥法律的调节功能，为客观存在或可能发生的事情提供一定的法律依据和处理空间，法律英语会故意采用一些具有概括性和灵活性特点的含义模糊的词语来表达准确的法律事实或概念。这一点完全不同于歧义性词语，因为后者在任何法律语言中都是绝对禁止使用的，而前者通常用来描述一些处在过渡或难以划清界限而不能确指语意的模糊现象。最常用的如 more than, not more than, less than, not less than 等，其他常见模糊性词语如下：

adequate	适当的
apparently	显然地
approximately	极尽于地，大概地
consequent	随之而来的
due	应有的，正当的
excessive	过度的，极端的
habitual	通常的，惯常的
incidental	附带的，非主要的
malice	恶意，蓄意
obviously	明显地
reasonable	应有的，合理的，理性的
serious	严重的
somewhat	有点，稍微
sufficient	足够的
unsound	不健全的，不令人满意的
virtually	实际上，事实上

精确是法律语言的生命，最重要的表现就是使用带有精确性含义的词汇做清晰表达，并防止歧义和误解现象的发生。哪怕一点点失误都会造成差之毫厘、谬以千里的后果。正是这种精确性保证了法律和其所规范内容的权威性，才能够使法律效力得以正常发挥。法律英语中词语的精确性通常表现在表达绝对概念、表达限定概念以及表达扩展概念的词汇或短语的选用上。例如：all, impossible, never, none, perpetuity, unbroken, and no more, and no other purpose, shall not be deemed a consent, as well as, including but not limit to, shall not be deemed to limit 以及 without prejudice 等。

【例 1】用人单位有下列情形之一的，由劳动行政部门责令限期支付劳动报酬、加班费或者经济补偿。劳动报酬低于当地最低工资标准的，应当支付其差额部分；逾期不支付的，责令用人单位按应付金额百分之五十以上百分之一百以下的标准向劳动者加付赔偿金。

【译文】Where an employing entity is under <u>any</u> of the following circumstances, the labor administrative department shall order it to pay the remunerations, overtime remunerations or economic compensations <u>within a time limit</u>. If the remuneration is lower than the local minimum wage, the employer shall pay the shortfall. If payment is <u>not</u> made <u>within the time limit</u>, the employer shall be ordered to pay an extra compensation to the employee at a rate of <u>not less than</u> 50 percent and <u>not more than</u> 100 percent of the payable amount.

在这个法律条文中,"any""within a time limit"和"not…within the time limit"都是精确性词语,而"not less than"和"not more than"则属于模糊性词语。"any"是一种对精确的强调,不管下列所述哪种情况发生都必须采取措施处罚,而如果换成"one"则体现不出这种强硬,只能表示一种选择。"within a time limit"和"not…within the time limit"两个短语,尤其是后者巧妙地使用了否定词"not",只有一个冠词之差却非常准确地区分了"限期"和"逾期"的不同含义,既体现出时间的限定性和不可逾越性,又把时间段的截点展示得非常清晰,做到了无懈可击。"not less than"和"not more than"用模糊的表达给出了裁决的范围,将判定处罚的权力留给司法人员,使法律更加贴近实际情况。

3.2.2 语法特征

A. 限定选用代词

在英文法律文书尤其是合同或契约中,为了避免代词的指代不明确而引起理解或解释上的麻烦,通常是不用代词或者少用代词的。在这种情况下,指代人或物的名词往往会重复出现或者使用间接代词以表示对各方一视同仁。例如:Party A(甲方)、Party B(乙方)、a third Party(第三方)、each Party(每一方)、the purchaser(买方)、the supplier(卖方)、the licensor(出让方)、the licensee(受让方)、the recipient(受方)、the transferor(转让方)、the transferee(受让方)等。在合同中很少出现人称代词,而且即使出现了人称代词通常都是泛指。合同的起草人经常用 the said 或 the same 加上一个名词来指代前文中提到的名词。

【例2】The seller shall not be held responsible for any delay in delivery or nondelivery of the goods due to Force Majeure. However, the seller shall advise the buyer immediately of such occurrence and within fourteen days thereafter, shall send by airmail to the buyer a certificate issued by the competent government authorities of the place where the accident has occurred as evidence thereof. Under such circumstances the seller, however, is still under the obligation to take all necessary measures to hasten the delivery of the goods. In case the accident lasts for more than 10 weeks, the buyer shall have the right to cancel this contract .

这是一个典型的重复使用所指名词的例子。该合同条款中没有使用一个指示代词或不定代词,使得所指代的事物明确而清楚。

B. 特定使用情态动词

法律英语中有两个情态动词有着与普通英语中不同的特定用法,即 shall 和 may,尤其以 shall 最为突出。shall 是使英文法律文书具有独特文体特征的一个非常重要的词汇。当其放在第三人称后面作为情态动词使用时,往往表示责任、义务、权利、命令和许诺等含义,带有指令性或强制性,体现出法律文书的权威性和严谨性。这种情况下,shall 一般译为"应""须""应当",甚至完全忽略不译。其否定式 shall not 表示"禁止""不得"。may 在法律文书中不如 shall 用得广泛,通过 may 提出的要求一般不具有约束力和强制性,只说明一种权利,相当于 be entitled to。may not 则表示"不得",语气较弱。

【例3】The trial of all crimes, except in cases of impeachment, shall be by jury; and such trial shall be held in the state where the said crimes shall have been committed; but when not committed within any state, the trial shall be at such place or places as the Congress may by law have directed.

【译文】除弹劾案外，一切犯罪由陪审团审判；此种审判<u>应</u>在犯罪发生的州内举行；但如犯罪不发生在任何一州之内，审判<u>应</u>在国会以法律规定的一个或几个地点举行。

【例 4】订立劳动合同，<u>应当</u>遵循合法、公平、平等自愿、协商一致、诚实信用的原则。

【译文】The principle of lawfulness, fairness, equality, free will, negotiation for agreement and good faith <u>shall</u> be observed in the formation of a labor contract.

【例 5】The price in a contract of sale <u>may</u> be fixed by the contract, or <u>may</u> be left to be fixed in a manner agreed by the contract, or <u>may</u> be determined by the course of dealing between the parties.

【译文】买卖合同中的价格<u>可</u>由合同确定，也<u>可</u>留给合同所确认的其他方式确定，或者还<u>可</u>以由双方当事人在交易过程中来确定。

C. 多用名词化结构

英文法律文书中的句子通常理解起来很困难，需要仔细分析句子成分，造成这种情况的原因之一就是名词化结构的使用。法律语言主要以陈述事实和加强限制为主，使用名词化结构可以将人称主语带来的主观性减小到最低，从而使法律文体的语言表达更加客观公正、不带主观色彩，这也与法律英语中被动结构的频繁使用有很大关系。名词化结构词汇密集度高，组合方式多，信息容量大，适宜表达法律文体复杂且精确的思想概念。

【例 6】It appears that the <u>admission</u> for the <u>prosecution</u> of a conviction of a person other than the accused under Section 2 in the context of the proper exercise by the judge of his exclusionary discretion and the <u>giving</u> of an appropriate discretion by the judge to the jury in circumstances in which the accused could have called the person whose conviction was admitted under Section 2 to give defense evidence will not give rise to a <u>violation</u> of human rights.

这个长句子分别用了 admit, prosecute, give, violate 等动词的名

词化形式，让人初看很难弄明白它的意思。仔细分析一下，整个句子的主干其实就是 It appears that the admission will not give rise to a violation of human rights，其他所有的词句都是限制 admission 这个词的。

【例7】The mortgagor shall pay to the mortgagee or to its order, on demand, all costs and expenses whatever (including, without limitation, legal costs, registration fees, VAT, stamp duties) incurred by the mortgagee in connection with the <u>negotiation</u>, <u>preparation</u>, <u>completion</u>, <u>registration</u> and <u>perfection</u> of the Mortgage and the <u>maintenance</u>, <u>protection</u> and <u>enforcement</u> of the security created by or intended to be created by or pursuant to the Mortgage or any of the mortgagee's rights whatever under this Mortgage.

这个句子中使用名词 negotiation, preparation, completion, registration, perfection 以及 maintenance, protection, enforcement 列明了抵押人在何种情况下应该负担抵押权人发生的支出和花费。一是在为达成抵押协议，抵押权人在谈判、起草、定稿、备案及完成该抵押手续过程中的花费和支出；二是为维护、保护、实现该抵押担保利益时，抵押权人的花费和支出。这样用名词并列的方式表达比用动词更加专业和严谨。

D. 陈述句

由于法律文书是为了进一步确定法律关系以及陈述法律法规当中所规定的权利义务和法律后果的专用公文，所以需要用陈述的口吻肯定的语气进行描述，从而使所表述的内容抛开些许的引申或者加工，达到精准、严谨、客观和规范的目的。因此，其句式结构主要是陈述句结构，很少用到疑问句、祈使句和感叹句。

【例8】The National People's Congress authorizes the Hong Kong Special Administrative Region to exercise a high degree of autonomy and enjoy executive, legislative and independent judicial power, including that of final adjudication, in accordance with the provisions of this Law.

【例9】As one of the youngest of the international organizations, the WTO is the successor to the General Agreement on Tariffs and Trade (GATT) established in the wake of the Second World War.

E. 被动句

法律语言的精确性和客观性决定了被动句在英文法律文书中的广泛使用。因为如果在法律法规中出现过多的第一、第二人称，会给人以一种主观臆断的印象，无法体现出法律语言客观公正的行文风格。使用被动句不仅仅是为了强调动作的承受者，而更侧重于通过隐藏和弱化法律主体对所涉事实以及相关规定的客观描述，从而避免主观色彩的出现，突出主题维护法律的严肃性和庄重性。

【例 10】No money shall <u>be drawn from</u> the treasury but in consequence of appropriations made by law; and a regular statement and account of the receipts and expenditures of all public money shall <u>be published</u> from time to time.

【译文】除了依照法律的规定拨款之外，不得自国库中提取任何款项；一切公款收支的报告和账目，应经常公布。

【例 11】The carrier <u>is entitled to</u> carry the goods on deck only if such carriage is in accordance with an agreement with the shipper or with the usage of the particular trade or <u>is required by</u> statutory rules or regulations.

【译文】承运人只有在依据和托运人签订的协议或该特定贸易的习惯，或为法规或条款所要求时，才有权在舱面载运货物。

【例 12】A sale of goods <u>is not prevented from being a sale by</u> description by reason only that, <u>being exposed</u> for sale or hire, they <u>are selected by</u> the buyer.

【译文】货物的买卖可以转变成为凭说明进行的货物买卖，因为它们由买方来选择。

F. 条件句

在英文法律文书中，一项规定或条款通常由事实情景和法律陈述组成。前者比较显性，法律英语常用条件状语从句来表达；后者则较为隐性，一般用主句来表达。二者合并一起，经过法律起草人对词句的再三推敲，形成了一个法律逻辑结构，往往以"If X, then Y shall do Z."的句式出现。文体学上把这种带有条件句的复合句称作圆周句（periodic sentence），是一种正式的书面句型，在法律英语中应用尤其普遍。需要注意的是，英文法律法规中一般只采用有条件的、符合逻辑推理的并且能出现或产生真实结果的条件句，而很少使用虚拟语气，尽管有时律师在陈述或辩状及案情的推测中也偶尔用到虚拟语气的句子。

【例 13】用人单位自用工之日起满一年不与劳动者订立书面劳动合同<u>的</u>，视为用人单位与劳动者已订立无固定期限劳动合同。

【译文】<u>If</u> the employer fails to sign a written labor contract with an employee after the lapse of one full year from the date when the employee begins to work, it shall be deemed that the employer and the employee have concluded a labor contract without a fixed term.

【例 14】<u>If</u>, ant any time during the execution of the Works, the Engineer requires the Contractor to make boreholes or to carry out exploratory excavation, such requirement shall be the subject of an instruction in accordance with Clause 51, unless an item or a Provisional Sum in respect of such work is inclued in the Bill of Quantities.

【译文】如果在工程施工过程中的任何时间内工程师要求承包人钻孔或进行勘探性开挖，<u>则</u>应根据第 51 条规定以指示形式下达这一要求，但工程量报价表中已经包括涉及此类工作的项号或暂定金额项号的除外。

除 if 之外，法律英语中还有许多其他词汇可以引导条件句来对事实情况加以限定，例如：where, when, provided that, in case that, in the event that 以及 should 等。在英文法律文书中，where 引导的条件句用得非常普遍，甚至远远超过了用 when 引导的条件句。就句式正式程度而言，前者一般超过后者，因为后者在某些情况下还用于时间状语成分，而以 where 引导的状语，几乎纯粹是法律条款中的一个条件。

【例 15】<u>Where</u> there is an unconditional contract for the sale of specific goods in a deliverable state the property in the goods passes to the buyer when the contract is made, and it is immaterial whether the time of payment or the time of delivery, or both, be postponed.

【译文】<u>凡属</u>无条件的特定物买卖合同，如果该物已处于可交付状态，则货物所有权于合同订立时转移，而不问付款日期或交付日期（或二者兼有）是否延迟。

【例 16】采取招标、拍卖、协议等出让方式设立建设用地使用<u>权的</u>，当事人应当采取书面形式订立建设用地使用权出让合同。

【译文】<u>When</u> construction land use rights are created through auction, invitation to tender, or agreement, etc., the related parties shall draw up a written contract on the transfer of such rights.

法律文书中另一个广泛出现的条件句引导词是 provided that，其在法律英语中的用法与 if，when 或 where 非常类似，没有本质上的差异，可译为"如"。

【例 17】<u>Provided that</u> the acceptance of rent or mesne profits by the Landlord after the expiration of the term of the tenancy hereby created shall not be deemed to operate as a waiver or breach of any of the terms hereof nor as a new periodic tenancy by way of holding over or otherwise.

【译文】<u>如</u>在本合约规定的租期届满后业主接受租金或中间收益，不应被认为是起了或违背本合约的任何条件的作用，也不应认为是起了作为继续租用或者其他的新租期的作用。

另外两个常见的引导词是 in case 和 in the event that，包括它们的短语变种 in the case of 和 in the event of，通常表示不大可能或不大容易发生的事情。区别在于两个介词短语后面只能接名词短语，而前二者是需要引导条件句的。在规范的法律英语中，in case 后直接引导从句而不可跟 that，而 in the event that 中的 that 是不可以省略的。

【例18】业主转让建筑物内的住宅、经营性用房,其对共有部分享有的共有和共同管理的权利一并转让。

【译文】In case an owner transfers his residential premises or premises used for business purposes within the building, the common ownership and management right held by him over the common parts shall be transferred at the same time.

【例19】In the event that either party hereto fails to comply with the terms or conditions of this Agreement, and, within 90 days after the written notice is issued by the other Party hereto, fails to remedy such failure, the Party giving notice may, forthwith, notify the other Party of the matter in question and terminate this Agreement.

【译文】如任何一方未能履行本协议规定的条款或条件,并在收到另一方书面通知之后90天内,未对其不履行进行补救,发出通知的一方可立即通知另一方终止本协议。

【例20】In the case of any actual or apprehended loss or damage the carrier and the consignee must give all reasonable facilities to each other for inspecting and tallying the goods.

【译文】遇有任何实际的或预料可能发生的天灾或损坏时,承运人和收货人须为检验和清点货物而相互提供一切合理的便利。

【例21】拾得漂流物、发现埋藏物或者隐藏物的,参照拾得遗失物的有关规定。

【译文】In the event of finding a drift item, an item buried underground or a hidden item, the relevant provisions on the finding of a lost property shall apply as reference.

英文法律文书中只有假设的是违背当事人意志的不利情况时才用should引导的条件句,而且一般将should从句置于句首,表示一种较强的虚拟或假设语气,甚至有时可以指不希望发生的天灾人祸。

【例22】Should no settlement be reached through negotiation, the case shall then be submitted for arbitration to the China International Economic and Trade Arbitration Commission (Beijing) and the rules of this Commission shall be applied.

【译文】如协商不能解决争议，则应将争议提交中国国际经济贸易仲裁委员会（北京），依据其仲裁规则进行仲裁。

3.2.3 审美特征

任何一种文体都具有其内在的审美价值。法律文书是非常正式的一种文体，其语言是经过起草人反复斟酌和再三推敲之后形成的，使用起来非常严谨，几乎不可更改哪怕一个字，具有接近完美的风格。英文法律文书中虽然少有文学修辞中的音韵美，然而正是其独特的文体功能带有一种别具一格的庄重美。

A．大词美

英文法律文书中的大词既包括那些冗长艰涩的书面词汇，又包括某些难词和生僻词。它们的正式程度都高于普通词汇，在法律英语特定的语言环境下，传递出大气、庄重、高贵、严肃、保守或委婉等别样美感，产生出一种义正词严之效果。

【例23】In carrying out its functions, the United States Patent and Trademark Office shall be <u>subject to</u> the policy direction of the Secretary of Commerce, but otherwise shall <u>retain responsibility</u> for decisions regarding the management and administration of its operations and shall <u>exercise independent control</u> of its <u>budget allocations</u> and <u>expenditures</u>, <u>personnel decisions</u> and processes, <u>procurements</u>, and other administrative and management functions <u>in accordance with</u> this title and applicable provisions of law.

这句话选自《美国专利法》（*Patent Laws*），使用了较多的大词或正式用语，例如：subject to, retain responsibility, exercise independent control, budget allocations, expenditures, personnel decisions, procurements, in accordance with 等。虽然这使整个句子略显累赘，但是这些带有浓厚书卷气的词汇给法律文书这种庄严肃穆

的文体定了调。大词的相互连动有力地传达了法律本身固有的神圣和尊严。

B. 逻辑美

英文法律文书的语言非常注重逻辑的缜密。这种严谨的表达形成了一种逻辑美，主要表现在通过形合手段构造出来的非常合乎语法及逻辑关系的完整句的使用上，产生出独到的修辞功能。由于法律文书结构的完整性和表意的严密性，法律英语中的各种句子成分比较完整，几乎很少有省略情况出现。句子中有许多修饰成分和限定语，以便更加精确地表达完整的意思，避免由于省略或者缺省而带来的歧义。

【例24】The WTO set up reference centres in over 100 trade ministries and regional organizations in capitals of developing and least-developed countries, providing computers and Internet access to enable ministry officials to keep abreast of events in the WTO in Geneva through online access to the WTO's immense database of official documents and other material.

【译文】WTO 集中对位于发展中国家和最不发达国家首都的100多个政府的贸易部门和地区组织提供参考资料。WTO 为这些政府官员提供计算机和网络，以使他们能够进入包含无数官方文件和其他资料的 WTO 数据库，从而使他们及时了解在日内瓦总部所发生的事情。

这个句子对 WTO 所能提供的技术协助及其目的做了详细的表述，整个句子结构完整，主、谓、宾、定、状、补所有成分完全出现，同时还使用了一个非常大的现在分词短语，短语中的逻辑成分也非常完整。这种大主谓加小动宾结构的使用体现了法律英语的严谨性和规范性，有效地将法律文书所要表述的内容完整地体现出来，形成一种大气和周全的完整美。

C. 冗长美

句子冗长、结构复杂是英文法律文体的显著特征。正式的法律法规由于对中心词的限定过多，对某一法律概念成立的条件限定很多，所以法律英语的长句多短句少。完整的长句一般由主干结构后附加多个修饰成分、并列成分、同位成分或者插入成分，甚至是多个分句以及复合句，形成一种层层限定、环环相扣、步步为营的冗长美，显示出法律英语句子的独特魅力。

【例25】Where a person having bought or agreed to buy goods obtains, with the consent of the seller, <u>possession of the goods or the documents of title to the goods or documents of title</u>, under any sale, pledge, or other disposition thereof, to any person receiving the same in good faith and without notice of any lien or other right of the original seller in respect of the goods, <u>has the same effect</u> as if the person making the delivery or transfer were a mercantile agent in possession of the goods or documents of title with the consent of the owner.

【译文】已购买或已同意购买货物的买方，如果得到了卖方的同意而取得占有货物或货物所有权凭证，并且买方或买方代理人在占有期间将货物或货物所有权凭证以买卖、质押或其他方式处分并交付或转移给买方之外的第三人，只要第三人是善意取得，并对原始卖方就货物所拥有的任何留置权或其他权利不知情，该处分行为同经征得货物所有人同意后由商务代理人做出的交付或转移货物或所有权凭证有着同样的效力。

再冗长的句子只要找到主干，分析起来就容易了，也能更好地促进对法律条文的准确理解。这个句子选自《英国货物买卖法》(*Sale of Goods Act*)，共有英文词汇99个，修饰语较多，给人一种连绵不断和盘根错节的感觉。画线部分是句子的主干，带有一个where引导的省略谓语动词的条件句和as if引导的虚拟条件句，以及under, to 和without 三个介词宾语结构，各种修饰语使用灵活，层层叠加，但句子的内涵却严谨分明，体现出一种紧凑的冗长美。

D. 平行美

平行（parallelism）是英语中一种非常具有表现力的修辞手法，由结构相同、意义关联、语气一致的短语或句子并列组成，广泛应用在英文法律文书中。法律英语中的平行结构追求语言的整体美，目的在于增强法律的固有气势，使枯燥的法律条文行文清楚、富有节奏感、更具有说服力。美国宪法的序言部分就是典型的例子。

【例 26】We the people of the United States, in order to <u>form a more perfect union, establish justice, insure domestic tranquility, provide for the common defense, promote the general welfare, and secure the blessings of liberty to ourselves and our posterity</u>, do ordain and establish this Constitution for the United States of America.

【译文】我们合众国人民，<u>为建立更完善的联盟，树立正义，保障国内安宁，提供共同防务，促进公共福利，并使我们自己和后代得享自由的幸福</u>，特为美利坚合众国制定本宪法。

这个句子状语部分的不定式用6个并列的动宾结构组成了一个平行结构，以一种带有韵律的语气非常明晰地呈现出了美国宪法的制定目的，语义紧凑，结构平衡，体现出了内容和形式的完美结合，给枯燥的法律语言增添了几分音乐美。

3.3 法律文书翻译的原则与解析

3.3.1 法律文书翻译的原则

"法律翻译是一种法律转换和语言转换同时进行的双重工作。"[①] 由于法律文体要求语气的庄重严肃、语义的清晰确凿，而且法律文书自身具有高度严谨性，所以法律翻译必须在符合法律文书的文体特征基础上，准确无误地译出原文的内容并追求译文语句的顺畅通达。针对以上对法律文书文体特征的分析，在实施法律文书翻译的过程中，焦点应放在交际功能的对等，而不是语言形式结构的对等，同时还应该注意文化因素对词汇内涵的影响，以求得最大限度的功能对等，这是法律文书翻译的总体原则。在实际翻译操

---

① Susan Sarcevic. *New Approach to Legal Translation*. The Hague: Kluwer Law International, 1997, p.12.

作的层面上，一词一句都要紧扣原文，遣词造句要仔细斟酌，谋篇布局要前思后想，不能像文学翻译那样有意地追求"达"和"雅"。本书把法律翻译的原则归纳为四项，即"精确性""简明性""规范性"和"一致性"。

3.3.2 法律文书汉译解析

【例27】An unenforceable contract is one for the breach of which neither the remedy of damages nor the remedy of specific performance is available, but which is recognized in some other way as creating a duty of performance, though there has been no ratification.

解析：本句选自 *Restatement (Second) of Contracts*（《美国合同法第二次重述》）。这句话看似简单，实则不然，其基本结构是 An unenforceable contract is one…。作为对 an unenforceable contract 进行解释的 one 后面带有两个互为转折关系的定语从句，尽管略显复杂，但却属于非常地道的法律英语用法，逻辑性很强。这里的关系代词 which 指的是 contract。前一个定语从句可以还原为：Neither the remedy of damages for the breach of the contract nor the remedy of specific performance for the breach of the contract is available。其中 remedy for the breach of contract 是固定短语，意为"因违反合同而要求赔偿"，而从句的主语是两个否定的并列成分。后一个定语从句是被动语态，并被 though 引导的状语从句修饰，作为语义的准确补充，可以还原为：Though there has been no ratification, the contract is recognized in some other way as creating a duty of performance。翻译时为了简洁规范，同时又完整无误地传达出法律原句的语气和语义，可以采用断句方法，把两个定语从句拆开分别对 contract 进行复指，给 an unenforceable contract 做一个法律意义上的严谨的解释。

【译文】不可强制执行的合同是指这样一种合同，即因违反该合同而要求的损害赔偿和特定履行救济均不适用，但是却被认为是以其他方式创设了并没有获得认可的履行义务。

【例28】Nothing contained in the present Charter shall authorize the United Nations to intervene in matters which are essentially within the domestic jurisdiction of any state or shall require the Members to submit such matters to settlement under the present Charter; but this principle shall not prejudice the application of enforcement measures under Chapter VII.

解析：本句选自 *Charter of the United Nations*（《联合国宪章》）。这句话以分号为间隔，是一个并列句。前一个分句由 or 连接两个并列谓语，其基本结构为 Nothing…shall authorize sb. to do sth. or shall require sb. to do sth.。前一个谓语中的 to do sth.为 to intervene in matters，后面带有一个限制性定语从句，可以直接译成 matters 的定语，即"干涉在本质上属于任何国家国内管辖之事件"。后一个谓语中"Members"指联合国的会员国，"settlement"和"application"属于名词化用法。句中"jurisdiction""submit""settlement""prejudice"以及"enforcement"属于法律英语中经常出现的"大词"。总体来说，该句结构相对工整，前后两个分句都是标准的主谓结构。按照各种逻辑关系，整个句子并不难译。

【**译文**】本宪章不得认为授权联合国干涉在本质上属于任何国家国内管辖之事件，且并不要求会员国将该项事件依本宪章提请解决；但此项原则不妨碍第七章内执行办法之适用。

【**例 29**】Everyone is entitled to all the rights and freedoms set forth in this Declaration, without distinction of any kind, such as race, color, sex, language, religion, political or other opinion, national or social origin, property, birth or other status. Furthermore, no distinction shall be made on the basis of the political, jurisdictional or international status of the country or territory to which a person belongs, whether it be independent, trust, non-self-governing or under any other limitation of sovereignty.

解析：本句选自 *Universal Declaration of Human Rights*（《世界人权宣言》）。这两句话的特点就是都带有相当长的状语，而且状语中心词使用了很多并列修饰语。很明显，两句话的 distinction 含义一样，第二句是对第一句中 distinction 的补充说明。前一句的基本结构为 Everyone is entitled to all the rights and freedoms…, 过去分词短语 set forth in this Declaration 为后置定语，句子的状语由 without distinction of 引出，翻译时可保留原文顺序，把这个中心词带有并列成分修饰语的状语放在后面。后一句同样是被动语态，distinction 是谓语动词 made 的宾语，后面由 on the basis of 引出长状语。the country or territory 作为定语修饰 the political, jurisdictional or international status，而同时又带有定语从句，该从句可以还原为 A person belongs to the country or territory。这种情况下可以采用倒序法把前半句译为 "不得因一人所属的国家或领土的政治的、行政的或者国际的地位之不同而有所区别"。这里的 "之不同" 采用了增词法，做到了 "增词不增意"，使法律含义更加准确。该句的后半部分是两个并列状语，前一个状语是 whether 引导的状语从句，句中的谓语用了 "(should) do" 结构，表示一种较弱的虚拟语气，主语 it 指的是 the country or territory，汉译时可采用复指的方法。后一个状语是介宾短语，两个状语由 or 连接，因为状语较长翻译时也可以保留原文的语序。

【译文】人人有资格享受本宣言所载的一切权利与自由，不分种族、肤色、性别、语言、宗教、政治或其他见解、国籍或社会出身、财产、出生或其他身份等任何区别。并且不得因一人所属的国家或领土的政治的、行政的或者国际的地位之不同而有所区别，无论该领土是独立、托管领土、非自治领土或者处于其他任何主权受限的情况下。

【例 30】If the bill of lading contains particulars concerning the general mature, leading marks, number of packages or pieces, weight or quantity of the goods which the carrier or other person issuing the bill of lading on his behalf knows or has reasonable grounds to suspect do not accurately represent the goods actually taken over or, where a "shipped" bill of lading is issued, loaded, or if he had no reasonable means of checking such particulars, the carrier or such other person must insert in the bill of lading a reservation specifying these inaccuracies, grounds of suspicion of the absence of reasonable means of checking.

解析：本句选自 *United Nations Convention on the Carriage of Goods by Sea, 1978*（《联合国 1978 年海上运输公约》）。这句法律条文的句子结构给人一种连绵不断、盘根错节的感觉，整个句子修饰语套修饰语，一个接一个叠加，一环扣一环相连。该句带有三个用 or 连接的条件句，其中第一个较长，主句又带有一个长宾语。主句属于 SVOC 结构，主干是 The carrier or such other person must insert a reservation in the bill of lading。由于宾语后面带有一个相当长的现在分词短语 specifying these inaccuracies, grounds of suspicion of the absence of reasonable means of checking 做后置定语，则把宾语补足语 in the bill of lading 放到了宾语的前面，以保持句子结构的平衡，也突出显示出了法律英语句子自身的逻辑性。翻译时可依然采用断句法按照原句顺序直接译出，在汉语译文中把英语中的动名词 specifying 动词化，对"保留的内容"进行补充说明，因此主句可以译为"承运人或上述其他人必须在提单中做出保留，说明这些不符之处、怀疑的根据或无适当核对手段等"。

第一个条件句的基本结构是 If the bill of lading contains particulars…，后面由 contains 引出了一个相当长的定语，其中还套着一个结构相对复杂的定语从句。介宾短语 concerning the general mature, leading marks, number of packages or pieces, weight or quantity of the goods 修饰 particulars，说明这些"殊项"的内容。后面的定语从句可以还原为：The carrier or other person issuing the bill of lading on his behalf knows or has reasonable grounds to suspect (that) the (above) particulars do not accurately represent the goods actually taken over. 很明显，这个定语从句的主干为：The carrier or other person knows or has reasonable grounds to suspect sth.，这里的 sth. 是一个省略 that 的宾语从句。而定语从句的主语 the carrier or other person 又带有两个定语，issuing the bill of lading 和 on his behalf；

宾语从句的宾语 the goods 又带有定语 actually taken over。这个条件句的特点是层层相扣，用非常复杂的句式体现出英文法律文书的多层含义。

后两个条件句则比较短小，句式简单，但为了增加语气，更加准确地表达法律文书的精确内容，翻译时可以采用重复法，在汉语中再现上面宾语从句的内容，既做到汉语句子的结构整齐，同时又避免歧义的发生。三个条件句加在一起可以翻译如下："如果承运人或代其签发提单的其他人，得知或有合理根据怀疑提单中所载有关货物的品类、主要标志、包数或件数、重量或数量等项，并不能准确地代表其实际接管的货物，或在签发'已装船'提单时，上述各项并不能准确地代表实际装船的货物，或者他没有核对这些项目的适当手段……"

【译文】如果承运人或代其签发提单的其他人，得知或有合理根据怀疑提单中所载有关货物的品类、主要标志、包数或件数、重量或数量等项，并不能准确地代表其实际接管的货物,或在签发"已装船"提单时，上述各项并不能准确地代表实际装船的货物，或者他没有核对这些项目的适当手段，则承运人或上述其他人必须在提单中做出保留，说明这些不符之处、怀疑的根据或无适当核对手段等。

归纳上述解析，英文法律文书主题庄重严肃，含义深刻丰富，结构严谨且样式多变，往往用长句表达相当复杂的法律关系。翻译时要逐步分析原文的语法结构，弄清各个句子成分的深层关系，准确地把握每一个词汇的法律含义，抓住该法律文书的文体特征，按照各意群之间的逻辑关系逐层翻译，然后根据汉语句式并比对英文原文进行逻辑综合，确保语言通顺、层次分明、意思连贯、内涵精确。

3.3.3 法律文书英译解析

【例31】为了维护国家基本经济制度，维护社会主义市场经济秩序，明确物的归属，发挥物的效用，保护权利人的物权，根据宪法，制定本法。

解析：本句摘自《中华人民共和国物权法》（Real Rights Law of the People's Republic of China）的总则部分，其句式在我国大多数法律的总则部分广泛出现，具有一定的代表性。本句虽短，但出现了"维护""明确""发挥""保护"和"制定"五个动词，其中"维护"便出现两次，所以动词的选用是翻译此句的关键。两个"维护"的内容不一样，程度也不一样，所以分别用"maintain"和"safeguard"来加以区分。"根据"一词在法律文书里应用十分广泛，译成英语宜采用正是说法"in accordance with"。"国家"和"宪法"都是特指，英文的首字母应该大写。为了突出主题并维护法律的严肃性，弱化法律主体对事实的客观描述，英语译文应使用被动句。

【译文】 This Law is formulated in accordance with the Constitution, in order to maintain the basic economic system of the State, to safeguard the socialist market economic order, to clearly define the attribution of specific properties, to promote the utilities of properties and to protect the real rights of rights holders.

【例32】 1982年8月23日第五届全国人民代表大会常务委员会第二十四次会议通过，根据1993年2月22日第七届全国人民代表大会常务委员会第三十次会议《关于修改〈中华人民共和国商标法〉的决定》第一次修正，根据2001年10月27日第九届全国人民代表大会常务委员会第二十四次会议《关于修改〈中华人民共和国商标法〉的决定》第二次修正

解析： 本句选自《中华人民共和国商标法》（Trademark Law of the People's Republic of China）。这是我国所有法律正文前的说明用语，强调法律颁布或修正的时间，具有很强的代表性。在这类语句中，为了表达法律的规范性和统一性，通常把"通过"译为adopt，"修正"译为amend，"修改"译为revise，译成英文用过去分词短语突出客观性。"第×届全国人民代表大会常务委员会第×次会议"已有官方的正式翻译，直接套用即可。汉语中"根据"引导的长状语英

译时可以放到从此后面。

【译文】Adopted at the 24th Meeting of the Standing Committee of the Fifth National People's Congress on August 23, 1982, amended for the first time in accordance with *The Decision on Revising the Trademark Law of the People's Republic of China* adopted at the 30th Meeting of the Standing Committee of the Seventh National People's Congress on February 22, 1993, and amended for the second time in accordance with *The Decision on Revising the Trademark Law of the People's Republic of China* adopted at the 24th Meeting of the Standing Committee of the Ninth National People's Congress on October 27, 2001

【例33】香港特别行政区应自行立法禁止任何叛国、分裂国家、煽动叛乱、颠覆中央人民政府及窃取国家机密的行为，禁止外国的政治性组织或团体在香港特别行政区进行政治活动，禁止香港特别行政区的政治性组织或团体与外国的政治性组织或团体建立联系。

解析：本句选自《中华人民共和国香港特别行政区基本法》(*The Basic Law of the Hong Kong Special Administrative Region of the People's Republic of China*)。本句的特点是目的状语的并列，即三个"禁止"。香港特别行政区有独立的立法权，所以"自行立法"可以译为enact laws on its own，后面用不定式跟上"禁止"的内容。翻译时内容中所有的动词都进行名词化，并且按照汉语原文顺序依次出现，作为"禁止"的宾语，或直接选用英语中的名词，或用prohibit sb. from doing sth.结构来翻译汉语中"禁止"后面的主谓短语。这样，三个"禁止"大并列，其他名词化的动词小并列，层次分明，结构均衡，译成的英文既保留了汉语原文的句式结构，又用地道的语言忠实地传达出了全部信息，做到了功能对等，突出了法律英语的庄重美。

【译文】The Hong Kong Special Administrative Region shall enact laws on its own to prohibit any act of treason, secession, sedition, subversion against the Central People's Government, or theft of state secrets, to prohibit foreign political organizations or bodies from conducting political activities in the Region, and to prohibit political organizations or bodies of the Region from establishing ties with foreign political organizations or bodies.

【例34】用人单位在制定、修改或者决定有关劳动报酬、工作时间、休息休假、劳动安全卫生、保险福利、职工培训、劳动纪律以及劳动定额管理等直接涉及劳动者切身利益的规章制度或者重大事项时，应当经职工代表大会或者全体职工讨论，提出方案和意见，与工会或者职工代表平等协商确定。

解析：本句选自《中华人民共和国劳动合同法》(*Labor Contract Law of the People's Republic of China*)。本句中"制定""修改""决定"的"制度"或"事项"很多，这一部分内容可以译成条件句，法律英语中这种情况通常由 where 来引导。而这些"事项"的性质是"直接涉及劳动者切身利益"，可以译成非限制性定语从句。所有这些内容都"应当经过讨论"，然后由用人单位"提出方案和意见"并与讨论者"协商"，所以译成的英文句子主要结构应该是 such rules or important events shall be discussed at the meeting…and the employer shall put forward proposals and opinions to the employees and negotiate with…。这样，翻译时把各个动作的执行者加上，采用一个大的主从复合句进行翻译，并在英文中加上不定式短语 to reach agreements on these rules or events，说明"讨论""提出"和"协商"的目的，以便更加清晰地传达出汉语原文的隐藏含义，做到万无一失，避免歧义，这也是法律文书的文体要求。

【译文】Where an employer formulates, amends or decides rules or important events concerning the remuneration, working time, break, vacation, work safety and sanitation, insurance and welfare, training of employees, labor discipline, or management of production quota, which are directly related to the interests of the employees, such rules or important events shall be discussed at the meeting of employees' representatives or the general meeting of all employees, and the employer shall also put forward proposals and opinions to the employees and negotiate with the labor union or the employees' representatives on an equal basis to reach agreements on these rules or events.

从上述解析可以看出，法律的特殊性决定了法律文书中动词词义的范围比较狭窄，这在中文法律法规中体现得尤为明显。汉语法律文书中的动词使用非常频繁，可以充当多种成分，而译成英文往往要多加考虑。同时汉语法律文书可以连贯地表达语义递进的结构，而英语却需要用不同的从句或介副词短语来表达，所以进行法律文书英译时首先要分析汉语表达的层次关系，找出隐藏的逻辑信息，挖掘出潜在的深层结构。在选词用语准确的同时需要尤其注意英汉法律文书文体特征的异同，最大限度地做到等效翻译。

3.4 法律文书翻译实例

3.4.1 英译汉实例：THE CONSTITUTION OF THE UNITED STATES OF AMERICA

美国宪法是世界上第一部成文法，其遣词造句是英语立法语言的典范，是法律英语的必修内容。迄今我国有多种不同的《美利坚合众国宪法》的中译本发表，但国内美国史界和法律界公认的中文译本是已故著名美国政治学研究专家李道揆先生的译本[①]。本书将李先生的译本配上英文原文摘录如下，供读者研究法律文书翻译时参考。

THE CONSTITUTION OF THE UNITED STATES OF AMERICA

March 4, 1789

---

① 参见李道揆：《美国政府和美国政治》，北京：商务印书馆，1999年，第775-799页。

美利坚合众国宪法

1789 年 3 月 4 日

Preamble

We the people of the United States, in order to form a more perfect union, establish justice, insure domestic tranquility, provide for the common defense, promote the general welfare, and secure the blessings of liberty to ourselves and our posterity, do ordain and establish this Constitution for the United States of America.

序言

我们合众国人民,为建立更完善的联盟,树立正义,保障国内安宁,提供共同防务,促进公共福利,并使我们自己和后代得享自由的幸福,特为美利坚合众国制定本宪法。

Article I
第一条

Section 1 All legislative powers herein granted shall be vested in a Congress of the United States, which shall consist of a Senate and House of Representatives.

第一款 本宪法授予的全部立法权,属于由参议院和众议院组成的合众国国会。

Section 2 The House of Representatives shall be composed of members chosen every second year by the people of the several states, and the electors in each state shall have the qualifications requisite for electors of the most numerous branch of the state legislature.

No person shall be a Representative who shall not have attained to the age of twenty five years, and been seven years a citizen of the United States, and who shall not, when elected, be an inhabitant of that state in which he shall be chosen.

Representatives and direct taxes shall be apportioned among the several states which may be included within this union, according to their respective numbers, which shall be determined by adding to the whole number of free persons, including those bound to service for a term of years, and excluding Indians not taxed, three fifths of all other Persons. The actual Enumeration shall be made within three years after the first meeting of the Congress of the United States, and within every subsequent term of ten years, in such manner as they shall by law direct. The number of Representatives shall not exceed one for every thirty thousand, but each state shall have at least one Representative; and until such enumeration shall be made, the state of New Hampshire shall be entitled to choose three, Massachusetts eight, Rhode Island and Providence Plantations one, Connecticut five, New York six, New Jersey four, Pennsylvania eight, Delaware one, Maryland six, Virginia ten, North Carolina five, South Carolina five, and Georgia three.

When vacancies happen in the Representation from any state, the executive authority thereof shall issue writs of election to fill such vacancies.

The House of Representatives shall choose their speaker and other officers; and shall have the sole power of impeachment.

第二款 众议院由各州人民每两年选举产生的众议员组成。每个州的选举人须具备该州州议会人数最多一院选举人所必需的资格。

凡年龄不满二十五岁，成为合众国公民不满七年，在一州当选时不是该州居民者，不得担任众议员。

众议员名额和直接税税额，在本联邦可包括的各州中，按照各自人口比例进行分配。各州人口数，按自由人总数加上所有其他人口的五分之三予以确定。自由人总数包括必须服一定年限劳役的人，但不包括未被征税的印第安人。人口的实际统计在合众国国会第一次会议后三年内和此后每十年内，依法律规定的方式进行。每三万人选出的众议员人数不得超过一名，但每州至少须有一名众议员；在进行上述人口统计以前，新罕布什尔州有权选出三名，马萨诸塞州八名，罗得岛州和普罗维登斯种植地一名，康涅狄格州五名，纽约州六名，新泽西州四名，宾夕法尼亚州八名，特拉华州一名，马里兰州六名，弗吉尼亚州十名，北卡罗来纳州五名，南卡罗来纳州五名，佐治亚州三名。

任何一州代表出现缺额时，该州行政当局应发布选举令，以填补此项缺额。

众议院选举本院议长和其他官员，并独自拥有弹劾权。

Section 3 The Senate of the United States shall be composed of two Senators from each state, chosen by the legislature thereof, for six years; and each Senator shall have one vote. Immediately after they shall be assembled in consequence of the first election, they shall be divided as equally as may be into three classes. The seats of the Senators of the first class shall be vacated at the expiration of the second year, of the second class at the expiration of the fourth year, and the third class at the expiration of the sixth year, so that one third may be chosen every second year; and if vacancies happen by resignation, or otherwise, during the recess of the legislature of any state, the executive thereof may make temporary appointments until the next meeting of the legislature, which shall then fill such vacancies.

No person shall be a Senator who shall not have attained to the age of thirty years, and been nine years a citizen of the United States and who shall not, when elected, be an inhabitant of that state for which he shall be chosen.

The Vice President of the United States shall be President of the Senate, but shall have no vote, unless they be equally divided.

The Senate shall choose their other officers, and also a President pro tempore, in the absence of the Vice President, or when he shall exercise the office of President of the United States.

The Senate shall have the sole power to try all impeachments.

When sitting for that purpose, they shall be on oath or affirmation. When the President of the United States is tried, the Chief Justice shall preside: And no person shall be convicted without the concurrence of two thirds of the members present.

Judgment in cases of impeachment shall not extend further than to removal from office, and disqualification to hold and enjoy any office of honor, trust or profit under the United States: but the party convicted shall nevertheless be liable and subject to indictment, trial, judgment and punishment, according to law.

第三款 合众国参议院由每州州议会选举的两名参议员组成，任期六年；每名参议员有一票表决权。参议员在第一次选举后集会时，立即分为人数尽可能相等的三个组。第一组参议员席位在第二年年终空出，第二组参议员席位在第四年年终空出，第三组参议员席位在第六年年终空出，以便三分之一的参议员得每二年改选一次。在任何一州州议会休会期间，如因辞职或其他原因而出现缺额时，该州行政长官在州议会下次集会填补此项缺额前，得任命临时参议员。

凡年龄不满三十岁，成为合众国公民不满九年，在一州当选时不是该州居民者，不得担任参议员。

合众国副总统任参议院议长，但除非参议员投票时赞成票和反对票相等，无表决权。

参议院选举本院其他官员，并在副总统缺席或行使合众国总统职权时，选举一名临时议长。

参议院独自拥有审判一切弹劾案的权力。为此目的而开庭时，全体参议员须宣誓或作代誓宣言。合众国总统受审时，最高法院首席大法官主持审判。无论何人，非经出席参议员三分之二的同意，不得被定罪。

弹劾案的判决，不得超出免职和剥夺担任和享有合众国属下有荣誉、有责任或有薪金的任何职务的资格。但被定罪的人，仍可依法起诉、审判、判决和惩罚。

Section 4 The times, places and manner of holding elections for Senators and Representatives, shall be prescribed in each state by the legislature thereof; but the Congress may at any time by law make or alter such regulations, except as to the places of choosing Senators.

The Congress shall assemble at least once in every year, and such meeting shall be on the first Monday in December, unless they shall by law appoint a different day.

第四款 举行参议员和众议员选举的时间、地点和方式，在每个州由该州议会规定。但除选举参议员的地点外，国会得随时以法律制定或改变这类规定。

国会每年至少开会一次，除非国会以法律另订日期外，此会议在十二月第一个星期一举行。

Section 5 Each House shall be the judge of the elections, returns and qualifications of its own members, and a majority of each shall constitute a quorum to do business; but a smaller number may adjourn from day to day, and may be authorized to compel the attendance of absent members, in such manner, and under such penalties as each House may provide.

Each House may determine the rules of its proceedings, punish its members for disorderly behavior, and, with the concurrence of two thirds, expel a member.

Each House shall keep a journal of its proceedings, and from time to time publish the same, excepting such parts as may in their judgment require secrecy; and the yeas and nays of the members of either House on any question shall, at the desire of one fifth of those present, be entered on the journal.

Neither House, during the session of Congress, shall, without the consent of the other, adjourn for more than three days, nor to any other place than that in which the two Houses shall be sitting.

第五款 每院是本院议员的选举、选举结果报告和资格的裁判者。每院议员过半数，即构成议事的法定人数；但不足法定人数时，得逐日休会，并有权按每院规定的方式和罚则，强迫缺席议员出席会议。

每院得规定本院议事规则，惩罚本院议员扰乱秩序的行为，并经三之二议员的同意开除议员。

每院应有本院会议记录，并不时予以公布，但它认为需要保密的部分除外。每院议员对于任何问题的赞成票和反对票，在出席议员五分之一的请求下，应载入会议记录。

在国会开会期间，任何一院，未经另一院同意，不得休会三日以上，也不得到非两院开会的任何地方休会。

Section 6 The Senators and Representatives shall receive a compensation for their services, to be ascertained by law, and paid out of the treasury of the United States. They shall in all cases, except treason, felony and breach of the peace, be privileged from arrest during their attendance at the session of their respective Houses, and in going to and returning from the same; and for any speech or debate in either House, they shall not be questioned in any other place.

No Senator or Representative shall, during the time for which he was elected, be appointed to any civil office under the authority of the United States, which shall have been created, or the emoluments whereof shall have been increased during such time; and no person holding any office under the United States, shall be a member of either House during his continuance in office.

第六款 参议员和众议员应得到服务的报酬，此项报酬由法律确定并由合众国国库支付。他们除犯叛国罪、重罪和妨害治安罪外，在一切情况下都享有在出席各自议院会议期间和往返于各自议院途中不受逮捕的特权。他们不得因在各自议院发表的演说或辩论而在任何其他地方受到质问。

参议员或众议员在当选任期内，不得被任命担任在此期间设置或增薪的合众国管辖下的任何文官职务。凡在合众国属下任职者，在继续任职期间不得担任任何一院议员。

Section 7 All bills for raising revenue shall originate in the House of Representatives; but the Senate may propose or concur with amendments as on other Bills.

Every bill which shall have passed the House of Representatives and the Senate, shall, before it become a law, be presented to the President of the United States; if he approve he shall sign it, but if not he shall return it, with his objections to that House in which it shall have originated, who shall enter the objections at large on their journal, and proceed to reconsider it. If after such reconsideration two thirds of that House shall agree to pass the bill, it shall be sent, together with the objections, to the other House, by which it shall likewise be reconsidered, and if approved by two thirds of that House, it shall become a law. But in all such cases the votes of both Houses shall be determined by yeas and nays, and the names of the persons voting for and against the bill shall be entered on the journal of each House respectively. If any bill shall not be returned by the President within ten days (Sundays excepted) after it shall have been presented to him, the same shall be a law, in like manner as if he had signed it, unless the Congress by their adjournment prevent its return, in which case it shall not be a law.

Every order, resolution, or vote to which the concurrence of the Senate and House of Representatives may be necessary (except on a question of adjournment) shall be presented to the President of the United States; and before the same shall take effect, shall be approved by him, or being disapproved by him, shall be repassed by two thirds of the Senate and House of Representatives, according to the rules and limitations prescribed in the case of a bill.

第七款 所有征税议案应首先在众议院提出，但参议院得像对其他议案一样，提出或同意修正案。

众议院和参议院通过的每一议案，在成为法律前须送交合众国总统。总统如批准该议案，即应签署；如不批准，则应将该议案同其反对意见退回最初提出该议案的议院。该院应将此项反对见详细载入本院会议记录并进行复议。如经复议后，该院三分之二议员同意通过该议案，该议案连同反对意见应一起送交另一议院，并同样由该院进行复议，如经该院三分之二议员赞同，该议案即成为法律。但在所有这类情况下，两院表决都由赞成票和反对票决定；对该议案投赞成票和反对票的议员姓名应分别载入每一议院会议记录。如任何议案在送交总统后十天内（星期日除外）未经总统退回，该议案如同总统已签署一样，即成为法律，除非因国会休会而使该议案不能退回，在此种情况下，该议案不能成为法律。

凡须由参议院和众议院一致同意的每项命令、决议或表决（关于休会问题除外），须送交合众国总统，该项命令、决议或表决在生效前，须由总统批准，如总统不批准，则按照关于议案所规定的规则和限制，由参议院和众议院三分之二议员重新通过。

Section 8 The Congress shall have power to lay and collect taxes, duties, imposts and excises, to pay the debts and provide for the common defense and general welfare of the United States; but all duties, imposts and excises shall be uniform throughout the United States;

To borrow money on the credit of the United States;

To regulate commerce with foreign nations, and among the several states, and with the Indian tribes;

To establish a uniform rule of naturalization, and uniform laws on the subject of bankruptcies throughout the United States;

To coin money, regulate the value thereof, and of foreign coin, and fix the standard of weights and measures;

To provide for the punishment of counterfeiting the securities and current coin of the United States;

To establish post offices and post roads;

To promote the progress of science and useful arts, by securing for limited times to authors and inventors the exclusive right to their respective writings and discoveries;

To constitute tribunals inferior to the Supreme Court;

To define and punish piracies and felonies committed on the high seas, and offenses against the law of nations;

To declare war, grant letters of marque and reprisal, and make rules concerning captures on land and water;

To raise and support armies, but no appropriation of money to that use shall be for a longer term than two years;

To provide and maintain a navy;

To make rules for the government and regulation of the land and naval forces;

To provide for calling forth the militia to execute the laws of the union, suppress insurrections and repel invasions;

To provide for organizing, arming, and disciplining, the militia, and for governing such part of them as may be employed in the service of the United States, reserving to the states respectively, the appointment of the officers, and the authority of training the militia according to the discipline prescribed by Congress;

To exercise exclusive legislation in all cases whatsoever, over such District (not exceeding ten miles square) as may, by cession of particular states, and the acceptance of Congress, become the seat of the government of the United States, and to exercise like authority over all places purchased by the consent of the legislature of the state in which the same shall be, for the erection of forts, magazines, arsenals, dockyards, and other needful buildings;

To make all laws which shall be necessary and proper for carrying into execution the foregoing powers, and all other powers vested by this Constitution in the government of the United States, or in any department or officer thereof.

第八款 国会有权：

规定和征收直接税、进口税、捐税和其他税，以偿付国债、提供合众国共同防务和公共福利，但一切进口税、捐税和其他税应全国统一；

以合众国的信用借款；

管制同外国的、各州之间的和同印第安部落的商业；

制定合众国全国统一的归化条例和破产法；

铸造货币，厘定本国货币和外国货币的价值，并确定度量衡的标准；

规定有关伪造合众国证券和通用货币的罚则；

设立邮政局和修建邮政道路；

保障著作家和发明家对各自著作和发明在限定期限内的专有权利，以促进科学和工艺的进步；

设立低于最高法院的法院；

界定和惩罚在公海上所犯的海盗罪和重罪以及违反国际法的犯罪行为；

宣战，颁发掳获敌船许可状，制定关于陆上和水上捕获的条例；

招募陆军和供给军需，但此项用途的拨款期限不得超过两年；

建立和维持一支海军；

制定治理和管理陆海军的条例；

规定征召民兵，以执行联邦法律、镇压叛乱和击退入侵；

规定民兵的组织、装备和训练，规定用来为合众国服役的那些民兵的管理，但民兵军官的任命和按国会规定的条例训练民兵的权力，由各州保留；

对于由某些州让与合众国、经国会接受而成为合众国政府所在地的地区(不得超过十平方英里)，在任何情况下都行使独有的立法权；对于经州议会同意、由合众国在该州购买的用于建造要塞、弹药库、兵工厂、船坞和其他必要建筑物的一切地方，行使同样的权力；

以及制定为行使上述各项权力和由本宪法授予合众国政府或其任何部门或官员的一切其他权力所必要和适当的所有法律。

Section 9 The migration or importation of such persons as any of the states now existing shall think proper to admit, shall not be prohibited by the Congress prior to the year one thousand eight hundred and eight, but a tax or duty may be imposed on such importation, not exceeding ten dollars for each person.

The privilege of the writ of habeas corpus shall not be suspended, unless when in cases of rebellion or invasion the public safety may require it.

No bill of attainder or ex post facto Law shall be passed.

No capitation, or other direct, tax shall be laid, unless in proportion to the census or enumeration herein before directed to be taken.

No tax or duty shall be laid on articles exported from any state.

No preference shall be given by any regulation of commerce or revenue to the ports of one state over those of another: nor shall vessels bound to, or from, one state, be obliged to enter, clear or pay duties in another.

No money shall be drawn from the treasury, but in consequence of appropriations made by law; and a regular statement and account of receipts and expenditures of all public money shall be published from time to time.

No title of nobility shall be granted by the United States: and no person holding any office of profit or trust under them, shall, without the consent of the Congress, accept of any present, emolument, office, or title, of any kind whatever, from any king, prince, or foreign state.

第九款 现有任何一州认为得准予入境之人的迁移或入境，在一千八百零八年以前，国会不得加以禁止，但对此种人的入境，每人可征不超过十美元的税。

不得中止人身保护状的特权,除非发生叛乱或入侵时公共安全要求中止这项特权。

不得通过公民权利剥夺法案或追溯既往的法律。

除依本宪法上文规定的人口普查或统计的比例,不得征收人头税或其他直接税。

对于从任何一州输出的货物,不得征税。

任何商业或税收条例,都不得给予一州港口以优惠于他州港口的待遇;开往或开出一州的船舶,不得被强迫在他州入港、出港或纳税。

除根据法律规定的拨款外,不得从国库提取款项。一切公款收支的定期报告书和账目,应不时予以公布。

合众国不得授予贵族爵位。凡在合众国属下担任任何有薪金或有责任的职务的人,未经国会同意,不得从任何国王、君主或外国接受任何礼物、俸禄、官职或任何一种爵位。

Section 10 No state shall enter into any treaty, alliance, or confederation; grant letters of marque and reprisal; coin money; emit bills of credit; make anything but gold and silver coin a tender in payment of debts; pass any bill of attainder, ex post facto law, or law impairing the obligation of contracts, or grant any title of nobility.

No state shall, without the consent of the Congress, lay any imposts or duties on imports or exports, except what may be absolutely necessary for executing it s inspection laws: and the net produce of all duties and imposts, laid by any state on imports or exports, shall be for the use of the treasury of the United States; and all such laws shall be subject to the revision and control of the Congress.

No state shall, without the consent of Congress, lay any duty of tonnage, keep troops, or ships of war in time of peace, enter into any agreement or compact with another state, or with a foreign power, or engage in war, unless actually invaded, or in such imminent danger as will not admit of delay.

第十款 任何一州都不得：缔结任何条约，参加任何同盟或邦联；颁发捕获敌船许可状；铸造货币；发行纸币；使用金银币以外的任何物品作为偿还债务的货币；通过任何公民权利剥夺法案、追溯既往的法律或损害契约义务的法律；或授予任何贵族爵位。

任何一州，未经国会同意，不得对进口货或出口货征收任何税款，但为执行本州检查法所绝对必需者除外。任何一州对进口货或出口货所征全部税款的纯收益供合众国国库使用；所有这类法律得由国会加以修正和控制。

任何一州，未经国会同意，不得征收任何船舶吨位税，不得在和平时期保持军队或战舰，不得与他州或外国缔结协定或盟约，除非实际遭到入侵或遇刻不容缓的紧迫危险时不得进行战争。

Article II
第二条

Section 1 The executive power shall be vested in a President of the United States of America. He shall hold his office during the term of four years, and, together with the Vice President, chosen for the same term, be elected, as follows:

Each state shall appoint, in such manner as the Legislature thereof may direct, a number of electors, equal to the whole number of Senators and Representatives to which the State may be entitled in the Congress: but no Senator or Representative, or person holding an office of trust or profit under the United States, shall be appointed an elector.

The electors shall meet in their respective states, and vote by ballot for two persons, of whom one at least shall not be an inhabitant of the same state with themselves. And they shall make a list of all the persons voted for, and of the number of votes for each; which list they shall sign and certify, and transmit sealed to the seat of the government of the United States, directed to the President of the Senate. The President of the Senate shall, in the presence of the Senate and House of Representatives, open all the certificates, and the votes shall then be counted. The person having the greatest number of votes shall be the President, if such number be a majority of the whole number of electors appointed; and if there be more than one who have such majority, and have an equal number of votes, then the House of Representatives shall immediately choose by ballot one of them for President; and if no person have a majority, then from the five highest on the list the said House shall in like manner choose the President. But in choosing the President, the votes shall be taken by States, the representation from each state having one vote; A quorum for this purpose shall consist of a member or members from two thirds of the states, and a majority of all the states shall be necessary to a choice. In every case, after the choice of the President, the person having the greatest number of votes of the electors shall be the Vice President. But if there should remain two or more who have equal votes, the Senate shall choose from them by ballot the Vice President.

The Congress may determine the time of choosing the electors, and the day on which they shall give their votes; which day shall be the same throughout the United States.

No person except a natural born citizen, or a citizen of the United States, at the time of the adoption of this Constitution, shall be eligible to the office of President; neither shall any person be eligible to that office who shall not have attained to the age of thirty five years, and been fourteen Years a resident within the United States.

In case of the removal of the President from office, or of his death, resignation, or inability to discharge the powers and duties of the said office, the same shall devolve on the Vice President, and the Congress may by law provide for the case of removal, death, resignation or inability, both of the President and Vice President, declaring what officer shall then act as President, and such officer shall act accordingly, until the disability be removed, or a President shall be elected.

The President shall, at stated times, receive for his services, a compensation, which shall neither be increased nor diminished during the period for which he shall have been elected, and he shall not receive within that period any other emolument from the United States, or any of them.

Before he enter on the execution of his office, he shall take the following oath or affirmation: "I do solemnly swear (or affirm) that I will faithfully execute the office of President of the United States, and will to the best of my ability, preserve, protect and defend the Constitution of the United States."

第一款 行政权属于美利坚合众国总统。总统任期四年,副总统的任期相同。总统和副总统按以下方法选举:

每个州依照该州议会所定方式选派选举人若干人,其数目同该州在国会应有的参议员和众议员总人数相等。但参议员或众议员,或在合众国属下担任有责任或有薪金职务的人,不得被选派为选举人。

选举人在各自州内集会,投票选举两人,其中至少有一人不是选举人本州的居民。选举人须开列名单,写明所有被选人和每人所得票数;在该名单上签名作证,将封印后的名单送合众国政府所在地,交参议院议长收。参议院议长在参议院和众议院全体议员面前开拆所有证明书,然后计算票数。得票最多的人,如所得票数超过所选派选举人总数的半数,即为总统。如获得此种过半数票的人不止一人,且得票相等,众议院应立即投票选举其中一人为总统。如无人获得过半数票,该院应以同样方式从名单上得票最多的五人中选举一人为总统。但选举总统时,以州为单位计票,每州代表有一票表决权;三分之二的州各有一名或多名众议员出席,即构成选举总统的法定人数,选出总统需要所有州的过半数票。在每种情况下,总统选出后,得选举人票最多的人,即为副总统。但如果有两人或两人以上得票相等，参议院应投票选举其中一人为副总统。

国会得确定选出选举人的时间和选举人投票日期，该日期在全合众国应为同一天。

无论何人，除生为合众国公民或在本宪法采用时已是合众国公民者外，不得当选为总统；凡年龄不满三十五岁、在合众国境内居住不满十四年者，也不得当选为总统。

如遇总统被免职、死亡、辞职或丧失履行总统权力和责任的能力时，总统职务应移交副总统。国会得以法律规定在总统和副总统两人被免职、死亡、辞职或丧失任职能力时，宣布应代理总统的官员。该官员应代理总统直到总统恢复任职能力或新总统选出为止。

总统在规定的时间，应得到服务报酬，此项报酬在其当选担任总统任期内不得增加或减少。总统在任期内不得接受合众国或任何一州的任何其他俸禄。

总统在开始执行职务前，应作如下宣誓或代誓宣言："我庄严宣誓（或宣言）我一定忠实执行合众国总统职务，竭尽全力维护、保护和捍卫合众国宪法。"

Section 2 The President shall be commander in chief of the Army and Navy of the United States, and of the militia of the several states, when called into the actual service of the United States; he may require the opinion, in writing, of the principal officer in each of the executive departments, upon any subject relating to the duties of their respective offices, and he shall have power to grant reprieves and pardons for offenses against the United States, except in cases of impeachment.

He shall have power, by and with the advice and consent of the Senate, to make treaties, provided two thirds of the Senators present concur; and he shall nominate, and by and with the advice and consent of the Senate, shall appoint ambassadors, other public ministers and consuls, judges of the Supreme Court, and all other officers of the United States, whose appointments are not herein otherwise provided for, and which shall be established by law: but the Congress may by law vest the appointment of such inferior officers, as they think proper, in the President alone, in the courts of law, or in the heads of departments.

The President shall have power to fill up all vacancies that may happen during the recess of the Senate, by granting commissions which shall expire at the end of their next session.

第二款 总统是合众国陆军、海军和征调为合众国服役的各州民兵的总司令。他得要求每个行政部门长官就他们各自职责有关的任何事项提出书面意见。他有权对危害合众国的犯罪行为发布缓刑令和赦免令，但弹劾案除外。

总统经咨询参议院和取得其同意有权缔结条约，但须经出席参议员三分之二的批准。他提名，并经咨询参议院和取得其同意，任命大使、公使和领事、最高法院法官和任命手续未由本宪法另行规定而应由法律规定的合众国所有其他官员。但国会认为适当时，得以法律将这类低级官员的任命权授予总统一人、法院或各部部长。

总统有权委任人员填补在参议院休会期间可能出现的官员缺额，此项委任在参议院下期会议结束时满期。

Section 3 He shall from time to time give to the Congress information of the state of the union, and recommend to their consideration such measures as he shall judge necessary and expedient; he may, on extraordinary occasions, convene both Houses, or either of them, and in case of disagreement between them, with respect to the time of adjournment, he may adjourn them to such time as he shall think proper; he shall receive ambassadors and other public ministers; he shall take care that the laws be faithfully executed, and shall commission all the officers of the United States.

第三款 总统应不时向国会报告联邦情况，并向国会提出他认为必要和妥善的措施供国会审议。在非常情况下，他得召集两院或任何一院开会。如遇两院对休会时间有意见分歧时，他可使两院休会到他认为适当的时间。他应接见大使和公使。他应负责使法律切实执行，并委任合众国的所有官员。

Section 4 The President, Vice President and all civil officers of the United States, shall be removed from office on impeachment for, and conviction of, treason, bribery, or other high crimes and misdemeanors.

第四款 总统、副总统和合众国的所有文职官员，因叛国、贿赂或其他重罪和轻罪而受弹劾并被定罪时，应予免职。

Article III
第三条

Section 1 The judicial power of the United States, shall be vested in one Supreme Court, and in such inferior courts as the Congress may from time to time ordain and establish. The judges, both of the supreme and inferior courts, shall hold their offices during good behaviour, and shall, at stated times, receive for their services, a compensation, which shall not be diminished during their continuance in office.

第一款 合众国的司法权，属于最高法院和国会不时规定和设立的下级法院。最高法院和下级法院的法官如行为端正，得继续任职，并应在规定的时间得到服务报酬，此项报酬在他们继续任职期间不得减少。

Section 2 The judicial power shall extend to all cases, in law and equity, arising under this Constitution, the laws of the United States, and treaties made, or which shall be made, under their authority; to all cases affecting ambassadors, other public ministers and consuls; to all cases of admiralty and maritime jurisdiction; to controversies to which the United States shall be a party; to controversies between two or more states; between a state and citizens of another state; between citizens of different states; between citizens of the same state claiming lands under grants of different states, and between a state, or the citizens thereof, and foreign states, citizens or subjects.

In all cases affecting ambassadors, other public ministers and consuls, and those in which a state shall be party, the Supreme Court shall have original jurisdiction. In all the other cases before mentioned, the Supreme Court shall have appellate jurisdiction, both as to law and fact, with such exceptions, and under such regulations as the Congress shall make.

The trial of all crimes, except in cases of impeachment, shall be by jury; and such trial shall be held in the state where the said crimes shall have been committed; but when not committed within any state, the trial shall be at such place or places as the Congress may by law have directed.

第二款 司法权的适用范围包括：由于本宪法、合众国法律和根据合众国权力已缔结或将缔结的条约而产生的一切普通法的和衡平法的案件；涉及大使、公使和领事的一切案件；关于海事法和海事管辖权的一切案件；合众国为一方当事人的诉讼；两个或两个以上州之间的诉讼；一州和他州公民之间的诉讼；不同州公民之间的诉讼；同州公民之间对不同州让与土地的所有权的诉讼；一州或其公民同外国或外国公民或国民之间的诉讼。

涉及大使、公使和领事以及一州为一方当事人的一切案件，最高法院具有第一审管辖权。对上述所有其他案件，不论法律方面还是事实方面，最高法院具有上诉审管辖权，但须依照国会所规定的例外和规章。

除弹劾案外，一切犯罪由陪审团审判；此种审判应在犯罪发生的州内举行；但如犯罪不发生在任何一州之内，审判应在国会以法律规定的一个或几个地点举行。

Section 3 Treason against the United States, shall consist only in levying war against them, or in adhering to their enemies, giving them aid and comfort. No person shall be convicted of treason unless on the testimony of two witnesses to the same overt act, or on confession in open court.

The Congress shall have power to declare the punishment of treason, but no attainder of treason shall work corruption of blood, or forfeiture except during the life of the person attainted.

第三款 对合众国的叛国罪只限于同合众国作战，或依附其敌人，给予其敌人以帮助和鼓励。无论何人，除根据两个证人对同一明显行为的作证或本人在公开法庭上的供认，不得被定为叛国罪。

国会有权宣告对叛国罪的惩罚，但因叛国罪而剥夺公民权，不得造成血统玷污，除非在被剥夺者在世期间，也不得没收其财产。

Article IV
第四条

Section 1 Full faith and credit shall be given in each state to the public acts, records, and judicial proceedings of every other state. And the Congress may by general laws prescribe the manner in which such acts, records, and proceedings shall be proved, and the effect thereof.

第一款 每个州对于他州的公共法律、案卷和司法程序，应给予充分信任和尊重。国会得以一般法律规定这类法律、案卷和司法程序如何证明和具有的效力。

Section 2 The citizens of each state shall be entitled to all privileges and immunities of citizens in the several states.

A person charged in any state with treason, felony, or other crime, who shall flee from justice, and be found in another state, shall on demand of the executive authority of the state from which he fled, be delivered up, to be removed to the state having jurisdiction of the crime.

No person held to service or labor in one state, under the laws thereof, escaping into another, shall, in consequence of any law or regulation therein, be discharged from such service or labor, but shall be delivered up on claim of the party to whom such service or labor may be due.

第二款 每个州的公民享有各州公民的一切特权和豁免权。

在任何一州被控告犯有叛国罪、重罪或其他罪行的人,逃脱法网而在他州被寻获时,应根据他所逃出之州行政当局的要求将他交出,以便解送到对犯罪行为有管辖权的州。

根据一州法律须在该州服劳役或劳动的人,如逃往他州,不得因他州的法律或规章而免除此种劳役或劳动,而应根据有权得到此劳役或劳动之当事人的要求将他交出。

Section 3 New states may be admitted by the Congress into this union; but no new states shall be formed or erected within the jurisdiction of any other state; nor any state be formed by the junction of two or more states, or parts of states, without the consent of the legislatures of the states concerned as well as of the Congress.

The Congress shall have power to dispose of and make all needful rules and regulations respecting the territory or other property belonging to the United States; and nothing in this Constitution shall be so construed as to prejudice any claims of the United States, or of any particular state.

第三款 新州得由国会接纳加入本联邦;但不得在任何其他州的管辖范围内组成或建立新州;未经有关州议会和国会的同意,也不得合并两个或两个以上的州或几个州的一部分组成新州。

国会对于属于合众国的领土或其他财产,有权处置和制定一切必要的条例和规章。对本宪法条文不得作有损于合众国或任何一州的任何权利的解释。

Section 4 The United States shall guarantee to every state in this union a republican form of government, and shall protect each of them against invasion; and on application of the legislature, or of the executive (when the legislature cannot be convened) against domestic violence.

第四款 合众国保证本联邦各州实行共和政体,保护每州免遭入侵,并应州议会或州行政长官(在州议会不能召开时)的请求平定内乱。

Article V
第五条

The Congress, whenever two thirds of both houses shall deem it necessary, shall propose amendments to this Constitution, or, on the application of the legislatures of two thirds of the several states, shall call a convention for proposing amendments, which, in either case, shall be valid to all intents and purposes, as part of this Constitution, when ratified by the legislatures of three fourths of the several states, or by conventions in three fourths thereof, as the one or the other mode of ratification may be proposed by the Congress; provided that no amendment which may be made prior to the year one thousand eight hundred and eight shall in any manner affect the first and fourth clauses in the ninth section of the first article; and that no state, without its consent, shall be deprived of its equal suffrage in the Senate.

国会在两院三分之二议员认为必要时，应提出本宪法的修正案，或根据各州三分之二州议会的请求，召开制宪会议提出修正案。不论哪种方式提出的修正案，经各州四分之三州议会或四分之三州制宪会议的批准，即实际成为本宪法的一部分而发生效力；采用哪种批准方式，得由国会提出建议。但在一千八百零八年以前制定的修正案，不得以任何形式影响本宪法第一条第九款第一项和第四项；任何一州，不经其同意，不得被剥夺它在参议院的平等投票权。

Article VI
第六条

All debts contracted and engagements entered into, before the adoption of this Constitution, shall be as valid against the United States under this Constitution, as under the Confederation.

This Constitution, and the laws of the United States which shall be made in pursuance thereof; and all treaties made, or which shall be made, under the authority of the United States, shall be the supreme law of the land; and the judges in every state shall be bound thereby, anything in the Constitution or laws of any State to the contrary notwithstanding.

The Senators and Representatives before mentioned, and the members of the several state legislatures, and all executive and judicial officers, both of the United States and of the several states, shall be bound by oath or affirmation, to support this Constitution; but no religious test shall ever be required as a qualification to any office or public trust under the United States.

本宪法采用前订立的一切债务和承担的一切义务,对于实行本宪法的合众国同邦联时期一样有效。

本宪法和依本宪法所制定的合众国法律,以及根据合众国的权力已缔结或将缔结的一切条约,都是全国的最高法律;每个州的法官都应受其约束,即使州的宪法和法律中有与之相抵触的内容。

上述参议员和众议员、各州州议会议员,以及合众国和各州所有行政和司法官员,应宣誓或作代誓宣言拥护本宪法;但决不得以宗教信仰作为担任合众国属下任何官职或公职的必要资格。

Article VII
第七条

The ratification of the conventions of nine states, shall be sufficient for the establishment of this Constitution between the states so ratifying the same.

Done in convention by the unanimous consent of the states present the seventeenth day of September in the year of our Lord one thousand seven hundred and eighty seven and of the independence of the United States of America the twelfth. In witness whereof We have hereunto subscribed our Names.

Signitures (omitted)

经九个州制宪会议的批准,即足以使本宪法在各批准州成立。

本宪法于耶稣纪元一千七百八十七年,即美利坚合众国独立后第十二年的九月十七日,经出席各州在制宪会议上一致同意后制定。我们谨在此签名作证。

签名(略)

3.4.2 汉译英实例:《中华人民共和国婚姻法》

婚姻法是社会主义法律体系中的一个独立部门。《中华人民共和国婚姻法》,虽然条文不多,内容也较简要,但确是全面规定婚姻家庭制度的独立法律,在法律文书的撰写方面占有极其重要的地位。全国人大常委会法制工作委员会组织翻译的婚姻法英文版[①]是我国法律文献翻译的经典之作,是研究法律翻译的必读版本。本书将此译本对照中文原文摘录如下,供读者研究法律文书翻译时参考。

中华人民共和国婚姻法
Marriage Law of the People's Republic of China

(1980年9月10日第五届全国人民代表大会第三次会议通过,根据2001年4月28日第九届全国人民代表大会常务委员会第二十一次会议《关于修改〈中华人民共和国婚姻法〉的决定》修正)

(Adopted at the Third Session of the Fifth National People's Congress on September 10, 1980, and amended on the basis of *The Decision on the Amendment to the Marriage Law of the People's Republic of China* made at the 21st Meeting of the Standing Committee of the Ninth National People's Congress on April 28, 2001)

第一章 总则
Chapter I General Provisions

第一条 本法是婚姻家庭关系的基本准则。

Article 1 This Law is the fundamental code governing marriage and family relations.

第二条 实行婚姻自由、一夫一妻、男女平等的婚姻制度。

[①] 参见《中华人民共和国婚姻法》,载《中华人民共和国涉外法规汇编(2001)》。

保护妇女、儿童和老人的合法权益。

实行计划生育。

Article 2 A marriage system based on the free choice of partners, on monogamy and on equality between man and woman shall be applied.

The lawful rights and interests of women, children and old people shall be protected.

Family planning shall be practised.

第三条 禁止包办、买卖婚姻和其他干涉婚姻自由的行为。禁止借婚姻索取财物。

禁止重婚。禁止有配偶者与他人同居。禁止家庭暴力。禁止家庭成员间的虐待和遗弃。

Article 3 Marriage upon arbitrary decision by any third party, mercenary marriage and any other acts of interference in the freedom of marriage shall be prohibited. The exaction of money or gifts in connection with marriage shall be prohibited.

Bigamy shall be prohibited. Anyone who has a spouse shall be prohibited to cohabit with another person of the opposite sex. Family violence shall be prohibited. Maltreatment and desertion of one family member by another shall be prohibited.

第四条 夫妻应当互相忠实，互相尊重；家庭成员间应当敬老爱幼，互相帮助，维护平等、和睦、文明的婚姻家庭关系。

Article 4 Husband and wife shall be loyal to each other and respect each other; family members shall respect the old and cherish the young, help each other, and maintain the marriage and family relationship characterized by equality, harmony and civility.

第二章 结婚

Chapter II   Marriage Contract

第五条 结婚必须男女双方完全自愿，不许任何一方对他方加以强迫或任何第三者加以干涉。

Article 5 Marriage must be based upon the complete willingness of both man and woman. Neither party may use compulsion on the other party, and no third may interfere.

第六条 结婚年龄，男不得早于二十二周岁，女不得早于二十周岁。晚婚晚育应予鼓励。

Article 6 No marriage may be contracted before the man has reached 22 years of age and the woman 20 years of age. Late marriage and late childbirth shall be encouraged.

第七条 有下列情形之一的，禁止结婚：
（一）直系血亲和三代以内的旁系血亲；
（二）患有医学上认为不应当结婚的疾病。

Article 7 No marriage may be contracted under any of the following circumstances:
（1）if the man and the woman are lineal relatives by blood, or collateral relatives by blood up to the third degree of kinship; or
（2）if the man or the woman is suffering from any disease which is regarded by medical science as rending a person unfit for marriage.

第八条 要求结婚的男女双方必须亲自到婚姻登记机关进行结婚登记。符合本法规定的，予以登记，发给结婚证。取得结婚证，即确立夫妻关系。未办理结婚登记的，应当补办登记。

Article 8 Both the man and the woman desiring to contract a marriage shall register in person with the marriage registration office. If the proposed marriage is found to conform with the provisions of this Law, the couple shall be allowed to register and issued marriage certificates. The husband-and-wife relationship shall be established as soon as they obtain the marriage certificates. A couple shall go through marriage registration if it has not done so.

第九条 登记结婚后，根据男女双方约定，女方可以成为男方家庭的成员，男方可以成为女方家庭的成员。

Article 9 After a marriage has been registered the woman may become a member of the man's family or vice versa, depending on the agreed wishes of the two parties.

第十条 有下列情形之一的，婚姻无效：

（一）重婚的；

（二）有禁止结婚的亲属关系的；

（三）婚前患有医学上认为不应当结婚的疾病，婚后尚未治愈的；

（四）未到法定婚龄的。

Article 10 The marriage shall be invalid if:

（1）either of the marriage parties commits bigamy;

（2）there is the prohibited degree of kinship between the married parties;

（3）before marriage either of the parties is suffering from a disease which is regarded by medical science as rending a person unfit for marriage and which has not yet been cured after marriage; or

（4）one of the marriage parties has not reached the statutory age for marriage.

第十一条 因胁迫结婚的，受胁迫的一方可以向婚姻登记机关或人民法院请求撤销该婚姻。受胁迫的一方撤销婚姻的请求，应当自结婚登记之日起一年内提出。被非法限制人身自由的当事人请求撤销婚姻的，应当自恢复人身自由之日起一年内提出。

Article 11 Where marriage is contracted by coercion, the coerced party may appeal to the marriage registration office or the People's Court for annulment of such marriage. Such an appeal for annulment of marriage made by the coerced party shall be submitted within one year from the date of marriage registration. Where the party concerned whose personal freedom is illegally restrained, such an appeal for annulment of marriage shall be submitted within one year from the date of the restoration of the personal freedom.

第十二条 无效或被撤销的婚姻，自始无效。当事人不具有夫妻的权利和义务。同居期间所得的财产，由当事人协议处理；协议不成时，由人民法院根据照顾无过错方的原则判决。对重婚导致的婚姻无效的财产处理，不得侵害合法婚姻当事人的财产权益。当事人所生的子女，适用本法有关父母子女的规定。

Article 12 Any marriage that is invalidated or annulled is null and void from the very beginning. The parties concerned are devoid of any rights or duties of a husband and a wife. The property acquired by them during the period of their cohabitation shall be disposed of by agreement between the parties; if they fail to reach an agreement, the People's Court shall make a judgment on the principle of giving consideration to the unerring party. Where property is to be disposed of because marriage is invalidated as a result of bigamy, the rights and interests in respect of the property enjoyed by the party under lawful contract of marriage may not be encroached on. With regard to the children born by the party concerned, the provisions of this Law on parents and children shall apply.

第三章 家庭关系
Chapter III Family Relations

第十三条　夫妻在家庭中地位平等。

Article 13 Husband wife shall have equal status in the family.

第十四条　夫妻双方都有各用自己姓名的权利。

Article 14 Both husband and wife shall have the right to use his or her own surname and given name.

第十五条　夫妻双方都有参加生产、工作、学习和社会活动的自由，一方不得对他方加以限制或干涉。

Article 15 Both husband and wife shall have the freedom to engage in production and other work, to study and to participate in social activities; neither party shall restrict or interfere with the other party.

第十六条　夫妻双方都有实行计划生育的义务。

Article 16 Both husband and wife shall have the duty to practise family planning.

第十七条 夫妻在婚姻关系存续期间所得的下列财产,归夫妻共同所有:

（一）工资、奖金；

（二）生产、经营的收益；

（三）知识产权的收益；

（四）继承或赠与所得的财产,但本法第十八条第三项规定的除外；

（五）其他应当归共同所有的财产。

夫妻对共同所有的财产,有平等的处理权。

Article 17 The following property acquired by the husband and the wife during the period in which they are under contract of marriage shall be in their joint possession:

（1）wages and bonuses;

（2）proceeds of production and business operation;

（3）incomes of intellectual property rights;

（4）property acquired from inheritance or presentation, with the exception of such property as stipulated by the provisions of the third item of Article 18 of this Law; and

（5）other property which should be in their joint possession.

Husband and wife shall enjoy equal rights in the disposition of their jointly possessed property.

第十八条 有下列情形之一的,为夫妻一方的财产:

（一）一方的婚前财产；

（二）一方因身体受到伤害获得的医疗费、残疾人生活补助费等费用；

（三）遗嘱或赠与合同中确定只归夫或妻一方的财产；

（四）一方专用的生活用品；

（五）其他应当归一方的财产。

Article 18 The property in the following cases shall belong to one party of the couple:

（1）the property that belongs to one party before marriage;

（2）payments for medical expenses receive by one party who suffers physical injury, subsidies for living expenses granted to the disabled subsidies, etc.;

（3）the property to be in the possession of one party as determined by will or by an agreement on gift;

（4）articles for daily use specially used by one party; and

（5）other property which should be in the possession of one party.

第十九条　夫妻可以约定婚姻关系存续期间所得的财产以及婚前财产归各自所有、共同所有或部分各自所有、部分共同所有。约定应当采用书面形式。没有约定或约定不明确的，适用本法第十七条、第十八条的规定。

夫妻对婚姻关系存续期间所得的财产以及婚前财产的约定，对双方具有约束力。

夫妻对婚姻关系存续期间所得的财产约定归各自所有的，夫或妻一方对外所负的债务，第三人知道该约定的，以夫或妻一方所有的财产清偿。

Article 19 The husband and the wife may conclude an agreement that the property acquired by them during the period in which they are under contract of marriage and the property acquired before marriage shall be in their respective possession separately or jointly or part of the property shall be in their possession separately and the other part jointly. Such an agreement shall be in written form. Where such an agreement is lacking, or the provisions in the agreement are not clear, the provisions of Articles 17 and 18 of this Law shall apply.

The agreement concluded by the husband and the wife with regard to the property acquired during the period in which they are under contract of marriage and the property acquired before marriage shall be binding on both parties.

Where the husband and the wife agree that the property acquired by them during the period in which they are under contract of marriage shall be in their possession separately, debts contracted by the husband or the wife shall be paid off with the property in the possession of the party of the husband or the wife, if the third person knows that there is such an agreement.

第二十条 夫妻有互相扶养的义务。

一方不履行扶养义务时，需要扶养的一方，有要求对方付给扶养费的权利。

Article 20 Husband and wife shall have the duty to maintain each other.

If one party fails to perform this duty, the party in need of maintenance shall have the right to demand maintenance payments from the other party.

第二十一条 父母对子女有抚养教育的义务；子女对父母有赡养扶助的义务。

父母不履行抚养义务时，未成年的或不能独立生活的子女，有要求父母付给抚养费的权利。

子女不履行赡养义务时，无劳动能力的或生活困难的父母，有要求子女付给赡养费的权利。

禁止溺婴、弃婴和其他残害婴儿的行为。

Article 21 Parents shall have the duty to bring up and educate their children; children shall have the duty to support and assist their parents.

If parents fail to perform their duty, children who are minors or are not capable of living on their own shall have the right to demand the costs of upbringing from their parents.

If children fail to perform their duty, parents who are unable to work or have difficulty in providing for themselves shall have the right to demand support payments from their children.

Infanticide by drowning, abandonment of infants and all other acts causing serious harm to infants shall be prohibited.

第二十二条　子女可以随父姓，可以随母姓。

Article 22 Children may adopt either their father's or their mother's surname.

第二十三条　父母有保护和教育未成年子女的权利和义务。在未成年子女对国家、集体或他人造成损害时，父母有承担民事责任的义务。

Article 23 Parents shall have the right and duty to protect and educate their children who are minors. If children who are minors cause damage to the State, the collective or individuals, their parents shall have the duty to bear civil liability.

第二十四条　夫妻有相互继承遗产的权利。

父母和子女有相互继承遗产的权利。

Article 24 Husband and wife shall have the right to inherit each other's property.

Parents and children shall have the right to inherit each other's property.

第二十五条　非婚生子女享有与婚生子女同等的权利，任何人不得加以危害和歧视。

不直接抚养非婚生子女的生父或生母，应当负担子女的生活费和教育费，直至子女能独立生活为止。

Article 25 Children born out of wedlock shall enjoy the same rights as children born in wedlock. No one may harm or discriminate against them.

The natural father or mother who does not directly bring up a child born out of wedlock shall bear the child's living and educational expenses until the child can live on his or her own

第二十六条　国家保护合法的收养关系。养父母和养子女间的权利和义务，适用本法对父母子女关系的有关规定。

养子女和生父母间的权利和义务，因收养关系的成立而消除。

Article 26 The State shall protect lawful adoption. The relevant provisions of this Law governing the relationship between parents and children shall apply to the right and duties in the relationship between foster-parents and foster-children.

The rights and duties in the relationship between a foster-child and his natural parents shall terminate with the establishment of his adoption.

第二十七条 继父母与继子女间，不得虐待或歧视。

继父或继母和受其抚养教育的继子女间的权利和义务，适用本法对父母子女关系的有关规定。

Article 27 Maltreatment and discrimination shall not be allowed between step-parents and step-children.

The relevant provisions of this Law governing the relationship between parents and children shall apply to the rights and duties in the relationship between step-fathers or step-mothers and their step-children who receive care and education from them.

第二十八条 有负担能力的祖父母、外祖父母，对于父母已经死亡或父母无力抚养的未成年的孙子女、外孙子女，有抚养的义务。有负担能力的孙子女、外孙子女，对于子女已经死亡或子女无力赡养的祖父母、外祖父母，有赡养的义务。

Article 28 Grandparents and maternal grandparents who can afford it shall have the duty to bring up their grandchildren and maternal grandchildren who are minors and whose parents are dead or have no means to bring them up. Grandchildren and maternal grandchildren who can afford it shall have the duty to support their grandparents and maternal grandparents whose children are dead or have no means to support them.

第二十九条 有负担能力的兄、姐，对于父母已经死亡或父母无力抚养的未成年的弟、妹，有扶养的义务。由兄、姐扶养长大的有负担能力的弟、妹，对于缺乏劳动能力又缺乏生活来源的兄、姐，有扶养的义务。

Article 29 Elder brothers and elder sisters who can afford it shall have the duty to maintain their younger brothers and sisters who are minors, if their parents are dead or have no means to bring them up. Younger brother or sisters who are brought up by their elder brothers or sisters and can afford it shall have the duty to maintain their elder brothers or sisters who lack not only the ability to work but also source of income.

第三十条 子女应当尊重父母的婚姻权利，不得干涉父母再婚以及婚后的生活。子女对父母的赡养义务，不因父母的婚姻关系变化而终止。

Article 30 Children shall respect their parent's right of marriage, they are not allowed to interfere in the re-marriage of their parents or their life after re-marriage. The duty of the children for supporting their parents shall come not to an end with the change in the marriage contract of their parents.

第四章 离婚
Chapter IV Divorce

第三十一条 男女双方自愿离婚的，准予离婚。双方必须到婚姻登记机关申请离婚。婚姻登记机关查明双方确实是自愿并对子女和财产问题已有适当处理时，发给离婚证。

Article 31 Divorce shall be granted if husband and wife both desire it. Both parties shall apply to the marriage registration office for divorce The marriage registration office, after clearly establishing that divorce is desired by both parties and that appropriate arrangements have been made for the care of any children and the disposition of property, shall issue the divorce certificates.

第三十二条 男女一方要求离婚的，可由有关部门进行调解或直接向人民法院提出离婚诉讼。

人民法院审理离婚案件，应当进行调解；如感情确已破裂，调解无效，应准予离婚。

有下列情形之一，调解无效的，应准予离婚：

（一）重婚或有配偶者与他人同居的；

（二）实施家庭暴力或虐待、遗弃家庭成员的；

（三）有赌博、吸毒等恶习屡教不改的；

（四）因感情不和分居满二年的；

（五）其他导致夫妻感情破裂的情形。

一方被宣告失踪，另一方提出离婚诉讼的，应准予离婚。

Article 32 If one party alone desires a divorce, the organization concerned may carry out mediation or the party may appeal directly to a People's Court to start divorce proceedings.

In dealing with a divorce case, the People's Court shall carry out mediation; divorce shall be granted if mediation fails because mutual affection no longer exists.

In one of the following cases divorce shall be granted if mediation fails:

（1）where one party commits bigamy or cohabits with another person of the opposite sex;

（2）where one party indulges in family violence or maltreats or abandons family members;

（3）where one party indulges in the gambling, drug taking, etc. And refuses to reform after repeated persuasion;

（4）where both parties have separated from each other for two full years for lack of mutual affection;

（5）other cases which lead to the shattering of affection between husband and wife.

Where one party is declared to be missing and the other party starts divorce proceedings, divorce shall be granted.

第三十三条 现役军人的配偶要求离婚，须得军人同意，但军人一方有重大过错的除外。

Article 33 If the spouse of a soldier in active service desires a divorce, the matter shall be subject to the soldier's consent, unless the soldier has made grave errors.

第三十四条 女方在怀孕期间、分娩后一年内或中止妊娠后六个月内，男方不得提出离婚。女方提出离婚的，或人民法院认为确有必要受理男方离婚请求的，不在此限。

Article 34 A husband may not apply for a divorce when his wife is pregnant, or within one year after the birth of the child, or within six months after the termination of her gestation. This restriction shall not apply in cases where the wife applies for a divorce, or where the People's Court deems it necessary to accept the divorce application made by the husband.

第三十五条 离婚后，男女双方自愿恢复夫妻关系的，必须到婚姻登记机关进行复婚登记。

Article 35 If, after divorce, both parties desire to resume their husband-and-wife relationship, they shall apply for registration or remarriage with the marriage registration office.

第三十六条 父母与子女间的关系，不因父母离婚而消除。离婚后，子女无论由父或母直接抚养，仍是父母双方的子女。

离婚后，父母对于子女仍有抚养和教育的权利和义务。

离婚后，哺乳期内的子女，以随哺乳的母亲抚养为原则。哺乳期后的子女，如双方因抚养问题发生争执不能达成协议时，由人民法院根据子女的权益和双方的具体情况判决。

Article 36 The relationship between parents and children shall not come to an end with the parent' divorce. After divorce, whether the children are directly put in the custody of the father or the mother, they shall remain the children of both parents.

After divorce, both parents shall still have the right and duty to bring up and educate their children.

In principle, the mother shall have the custody of a breast-fed infant after divorce. If a dispute arises between the two parents over the custody of their child who has been weaned and they fail to reach an agreement, the People's Court shall make a judgment in accordance with the rights and interests of the child and the actual conditions of both parents.

第三十七条　离婚后，一方抚养的子女，另一方应负担必要的生活费和教育费的一部或全部，负担费用的多少和期限的长短，由双方协议；协议不成时，由人民法院判决。

关于子女生活费和教育费的协议或判决，不妨碍子女在必要时向父母任何一方提出超过协议或判决原定数额的合理要求。

Article 37 If, after divorce, one parent has been given custody of a child, the other parent shall bear part or the whole of the child's necessary living and educational expenses. The two parents shall seek agreement regarding the amount and duration of such payment. If they fail to reach an agreement, the People's Court shall make a judgment.

The agreement or court judgment on the payment of a child's living and educational expenses shall not prevent the child from making a reasonable request, when necessary, to either parent for an amount exceeding what is decided upon in the said agreement or judgment.

第三十八条　离婚后，不直接抚养子女的父或母，有探望子女的权利，另一方有协助的义务。

行使探望权利的方式、时间由当事人协议；协议不成时，由人民法院判决。

父或母探望子女，不利于子女身心健康的，由人民法院依法中止探望的权利；中止的事由消失后，应当恢复探望的权利。

Article 38 After divorce, the father or the mother who does not directly bring up the child shall have the right to visit his or her child, and the other party shall have the duty to cooperate.

The manner and time for exercising the right to visit a child shall be decided by the parties through consultation; if they fail to reach an agreement upon in this regard, the People's Court shall make a judgment.

Where the visit to a child paid by the father or the mother is not conducive to the physical and mental health of the child, the People's Court shall terminate the right to visit; after the cause of such termination disappears, the right to pay visit to the child shall be resumed.

第三十九条 离婚时,夫妻的共同财产由双方协议处理;协议不成时,由人民法院根据财产的具体情况,照顾子女和女方权益的原则判决。

夫或妻在家庭土地承包经营中享有的权益等,应当依法予以保护。

Article 39 At the time of divorce, the husband and the wife shall seek agreement regarding the disposition of their jointly possessed property, If they fail to reach an agreement, the People's Court shall, on the basis of the actual circumstances of the property and on the principle of taking into consideration the rights and interests of the child and wife, make a judgment.

The rights and interests enjoyed by the husband or the wife in contracting land management on a household basis shall be protected in accordance with law.

第四十条 夫妻书面约定婚姻关系存续期间所得的财产归各自所有,一方因抚育子女、照料老人、协助另一方工作等付出较多义务的,离婚时有权向另一方请求补偿,另一方应当予以补偿。

Article 40 Where the husband and the wife agree in writing that the property acquired by them during the period in which they are under contract of marriage is in their separate possession, if one party has performed more duties in respect of bringing up the child, taking care of the old and assisting the other party in work, it shall, at the time of divorce, have the right to request the other party to make compensation for the above and the other party shall do so accordingly.

第四十一条 离婚时，原为夫妻共同生活所负的债务，应当共同偿还。共同财产不足清偿的，或财产归各自所有的，由双方协议清偿；协议不成时，由人民法院判决。

Article 41 At the time of divorce, debts incurred jointly by the husband and the wife during their married life shall be paid off jointly by them, Where their jointly possessed property is insufficient to pay the debts, or the property is in their separate possession, the two parties shall discuss alternative ways of payment; if they fail to reach an agreement, the People's Court shall make a judgment.

第四十二条 离婚时，如一方生活困难，另一方应从其住房等个人财产中给予适当帮助。具体办法由双方协议；协议不成时，由人民法院判决。

Article 42 If, at the time of divorce, one party has difficulty in supporting himself or herself, the other party shall render appropriate assistance with his or her own property such as his or her residential house. Specific arrangements shall be made by both parties through consultation. If they fail to reach an agreement, the People's Court shall make a judgment.

第五章 救助措施与法律责任
Chapter V Salvage Measures and Legal Liability

第四十三条 实施家庭暴力或虐待家庭成员，受害人有权提出请求，居民委员会、村民委员会以及所在单位应当予以劝阻、调解。

对正在实施的家庭暴力，受害人有权提出请求，居民委员会、村民委员会应当予以劝阻；公安机关应当予以制止。

实施家庭暴力或虐待家庭成员，受害人提出请求的，公安机关应当依照治安管理处罚的法律规定予以行政处罚。

Article 43 Where a person indulges in family violence or maltreats a family member, the victim shall have the right to advance a request;

the neighborhood committee, villagers committee or the unit where they belong to shall persuade the person to stop doing it and conduct mediation.

Where a person is committing family violence, the victim shall have the right to advance a request; the neighborhood committee or the villagers committee shall persuade the person to stop doing it; the public security organ shall stop such violence.

Where the victim advances a request, the public security organ shall, in accordance with the legal provisions on administrative penalties for public security, impose an administrative penalty on the person who commits family violence or maltreatment of a family member.

第四十四条 对遗弃家庭成员，受害人有权提出请求，居民委员会、村民委员会以及所在单位应当予以劝阻、调解。

对遗弃家庭成员，受害人提出请求的，人民法院应当依法作出支付扶养费、抚养费、赡养费的判决。

Article 44 The family member who is abandoned shall have the right to advance a request and the neighborhood committee, villagers committee or the unit where they belong to shall persuade the person to stop doing it and conduct mediation.

Where the abandoned family member advances a request, the People's Court shall, in accordance with law, make the judgment on payment by the person who abandons the family member to the victim for the costs of maintenance, upbringing or support.

第四十五条 对重婚的，对实施家庭暴力或虐待、遗弃家庭成员构成犯罪的，依法追究刑事责任。受害人可以依照刑事诉讼法的有关规定，向人民法院自诉；公安机关应当依法侦查，人民检察院应当依法提起公诉。

Article 45 The person who commits bigamy, family violence, maltreatment or abandonment of a family member, if it constitutes a crime, shall be investigated for criminal responsibility in accordance with law. The victim may, in accordance with relevant provisions of the Criminal Procedure Law, lodge a private prosecution with the People's Court; the public security organ shall investigate the case in accordance with law, and the People's Procuratorate shall institute public prosecution in accordance with law.

第四十六条 有下列情形之一，导致离婚的，无过错方有权请求损害赔偿：

（一）重婚的；

（二）有配偶者与他人同居的；

（三）实施家庭暴力的；

（四）虐待、遗弃家庭成员的。

Article 46 Where one of the following circumstances leads to divorce, the unerring party shall have the right to claim compensation:

（1）bigamy is committed;

（2）one party who has a spouse cohabits with another person of the opposite sex;

（3）family violence is committed; or

（4）a family member is maltreated or abandoned.

第四十七条 离婚时，一方隐藏、转移、变卖、毁损夫妻共同财产，或伪造债务企图侵占另一方财产的，分割夫妻共同财产时，对隐藏、转移、变卖、毁损夫妻共同财产或伪造债务的一方，可以少分或不分。离婚后，另一方发现有上述行为的，可以向人民法院提起诉讼，请求再次分割夫妻共同财产。

人民法院对前款规定的妨害民事诉讼的行为，依照民事诉讼法的规定予以制裁。

Article 47 If, at the time of divorce, one party conceals, transfers, sells off or destroys the property in the joint possession of the couple, or forges debts in an attempt to encroach upon the property of the other party, the former may get less or no property when the property in the joint possession of the couple is partitioned. After divorce, if the other party discovers the above, it may bring a suit in the People's Court to demand re-partition of the property in the joint possession of the couple.

With respect to acts that hinder civil procedures as mentioned in the preceding paragraph, the People's Court shall mete out sanctions in accordance with the provisions of the Civil Procedure Law.

第四十八条 对拒不执行有关扶养费、抚养费、赡养费、财产分割、遗产继承、探望子女等判决或裁定的,由人民法院依法强制执行。有关个人和单位应负协助执行的责任。

Article 48 Where a person refuses to abide by the judgment or ruling on the costs of maintenance, upbringing or support payments, or on the partitioning or inheritance or property, or visit to a child, the People's Court shall enforce the execution of the judgment or ruling in accordance with law. The individuals and unit concerned shall have the duty to assist such execution.

第四十九条 其他法律对有关婚姻家庭的违法行为和法律责任另有规定的,依照其规定。

Article 49 Where there are other provisions by other laws on illegal acts against marriage or family and on legal liability for the acts, such provisions shall apply.

第六章 附则
Chapter VI　　Supplementary Provisions

第五十条 民族自治地方的人民代表大会有权结合当地民族婚姻家庭的具体情况,制定变通规定。自治州、自治县制定的变通规定,报省、自治区、直辖市人民代表大会常务委员会批准后生效。自治区制定的变通规定,报全国人民代表大会常务委员会批准后生效。

Article 50 The people's congresses of national autonomous areas shall have the power to formulate adaptations in the light of the specific conditions of the local nationalities in regard to marriage and family. Adaptations formulated by autonomous prefectures and autonomous counties shall go into effect only after approval by the standing committee of the people's congress of the relevant province, autonomous region, or municipality directly under the Central Government. Adaptations formulated by autonomous regions shall go into effect only after approval by the Standing Committee of the National People's Congress.

第五十一条 本法自1981年1月1日起施行。

Article 51 This Law shall go into effect as of January 1, 1981.

第四章 新闻报道

新闻是人们了解外部世界的重要途径,而新闻语言是受到新闻学、社会学、政治学、经济学等多种学科和语体的综合影响所形成的应用语言,具有诸多的研究价值。新闻语言与具有劝说功能的广告语言不同,又与讲求生动、追求各种艺术效果和意蕴内涵的文学语言有所区别,具有自身鲜明的文体特点。新闻语言鲜明的文体特色增加了其翻译的难度。新闻要求向大众实事求是地传递信息,其向社会负责的特点要求新闻翻译必须通俗而且准确,但是新闻语言鲜明的文体特色和层出不穷的新词又使得译者在翻译新闻时应该灵活处理,因此在进行新闻翻译时必须将灵活性和原则性相结合,有针对性地具体对待。

4.1 新闻报道文体概述

新闻这个词对于大众来说并不陌生,但是关于新闻仍然没有一个十分确切的定义。新闻(news)是由 new 这个单词演变而来的,因而对于新闻来说,核心就在于"新"字,新闻应该是读者所不知道的信息。对于受众来说,新闻还应该是相对来说比较重要或者比较新奇的事情,所以西方有人将新闻定义为"狗咬人不是新闻,人咬狗才是大新闻"(If a dog bites a man, it is not news; if a man bites a dog, that is news.)。此外,中国有学者将新闻定义为"已经或正在或将要发生的事实的最及时的报道"[1]。

---

[1] 方梦之、毛忠明:《英汉—汉英应用翻译综合教程》,上海:上海外语教育出版社,2008 年,第 51 页。

新闻文体的功能主要由以下几个方面构成：

1. 传递信息。传递信息是新闻最主要最基本的文体功能，它是由新闻本身的时效性特点决定的。新闻传递信息的功能使得它能交流情况，沟通联系，对增强人类社会的联系和交往具有重大的作用，同时它也是其他功能所得以实现的基础。

2. 引导舆论。新闻对于舆论有着巨大的引导作用，一方面新闻通过反映符合社会主流价值观的舆论来扩大和强化社会的主流价值观和价值判断，另一方面新闻也会对不符合社会主流、不被社会大众接受的负向舆论进行控制，同时新闻本身还可以设置议题，影响社会舆论。新闻通过用事实说话的方式驳斥错误舆论，坚持正确的舆论导向。

3. 释疑解惑。新闻在传播知识、释疑解惑方面有范围广、层次多、知识新、选择性强、形式灵活等诸多优点。新闻运用灵活多样的传播手段和传播形式，使受众不受任何约束和限制地自由选择自己所需要的新知识、新技术、新观点，是一所"没有围墙的学校"。

4. 社会教育。新闻一方面通过正面报道宣扬符合社会价值观的真善美的信息来教育和引导受众，另一方面通过鞭挞和揭露社会丑恶现象来警醒和告诫受众，使得大众在新闻的监督下维护并遵守法律和道德规范，实现新闻社会教育的功能。

5. 提供娱乐。新闻可以提供娱乐，丰富人们的精神生活，它通过多层次、多品种、多样式的形式，满足受众多方面的需求，新闻在提供娱乐的同时也是一种文化观念的传播和意识形态的渗透。

4.2　英文新闻报道的语言特征

新闻与普通文体相比，具有真实性、简明性、及时性等特点。新闻英语与普通英语文体相比，也具有自身的鲜明特色。本书将从新闻英语的标题特点、词汇特点、篇章特点和语法特点进行逐一分析。

4.2.1 英文新闻报道的标题特点

标题是新闻的重要组成部分，对新闻起引导、概括和提示的作用。英文新闻标题遵循准确、简明和清晰的原则，而且还经常借助词法、句法和修辞等手段，以简单扼要、立意新颖、精辟动人的文字形式浓缩新闻的基本内容，使读者能如管中窥豹般一览而知其大概。标题不仅要高度概括新闻的基本内容，更要有画龙点睛的作用，而且标题要尽量标新立异并富有文采，以达到吸引读者的目的。

A. 省略虚词

众所周知，各种新闻报纸的版面极为有限，新闻从业者总是力图以最小的版面容纳最大的信息量，并且避免移行情况的出现，因此各种在语言结构中起次要作用的虚词，如冠词、助动词、系动词、人称代词、连词和介词往往就被省略了。例如：

【例1】China Demands U.S. Stop "Provocations" in South China Sea (*Beijing Review* Nov 21, 2015)

（=China Demands U.S. to Stop "Provocations" in South China Sea，省略了 to do 不定式的 to）

【译文】中国要求美国停止在南海挑衅

【例2】3 Chinese citizens killed in Mali hotel siege, 4 rescued: embassy (*People's Daily Online* Nov 21, 2015)（省略系动词 were）

【译文】大使馆消息：3名中国公民在马里酒店袭击中丧生，4人获救

【例3】China, U.S. attend drill on disaster relief operations in Seattle(*Xinhua News Agency* Nov 21, 2015)（省略连词 and）

【译文】中美在西雅图举行联合救灾演习

【例4】80 hostages freed as Mali special forces start clearing hotel (*People's Daily Online* Nov 20, 2015)（省略 are）

【译文】马里特种部队清理酒店80名人质获释

当然在某些情况下，冠词等一些虚词也会得到保留。例如：

【例5】The First Chinese to Present Tibet to the West (*China Today* Nov 10, 2015)

【译文】第一个把西藏介绍给西方的中国人

【例6】To buy or not to buy is the question for homebuyers

【译文】买还是不买是购房人的大心事

在上面的两个例子中，第一个标题保留了定冠词 the 是因为"西方"作为一个专有名词需要加 the，若省去则可能使读者无法理解到底标题所指"west"到底是何处。而第二个例子则是模仿了莎士比亚的名剧 *Hamlet* 中的 To be or not to be—that is the question，该表达已经固定下来被人们所接受，若去掉其中的 the 则难以达到原来的模仿效果。

B. 多用现在时，少用过去时

新闻报道的消息一般为已经发生了的事情，按照英语的语法规则，应该使用过去时态，但是这样很容易给人产生一种陈旧的感觉，因此英文报纸的新闻标题一般不用过去时态，当然更不用过去完成时等时态，而采用现在时态，使读者有一种身临其境的感觉，叫做"新闻现在时态"（journalistic present tense）。一般现在时在新闻中应用最为广泛，不仅省去了过去时的-ed 两个字母，而且增强了报道的新鲜感、现实感和直接感，因此在报道过去发生的事情时，新闻标题广泛使用一般现在时。例如：

【例7】Premier Li meets Indian PM in Malaysia (*People's Daily Online* Nov 21, 2015)

【译文】李克强总理在马来西亚会见印度总理

【例8】"Young Marshal" Dies at 101

【译文】少帅张学良仙逝

可见，新闻的要旨在于新，一般现在时在新闻标题中的应用极为普遍，为了造成一种仍然在发生的现实感，即使是某人死亡的新闻仍然可以用一般现在时来表达。此外，对于未来要发生的事情，英文新闻标题除了用"will+动词原形"的表达方式以外，还经常使用动词不定式，并且将前面的 be 省略。例如：

【例9】China to Reinforce IPR Protection: Vice Premier (*Beijing Review* Nov 21, 2015)

【译文】副总理：中国将加强知识产权保护

而对于眼下正在发生的事情，英文新闻标题习惯于以去掉 be 的"ing 分词"来表示正在进行或者发生的事件，例如：

【例10】Tempering the Warming Earth (*Beijing Review* Dec 1, 2015)

【译文】给日益变暖的地球降温

总体来说，在英文新闻标题中，一般现在时适用范围最广，既可以表示现在，还可以表示过去发生的或者未来要发生的事情，而动词不定式往往用来表示未来要发生的情况，对于眼下正在发生的事情则习惯于用去掉 be 的"ing 分词"表示。过去时和完成时由于会对读者产生一种陈旧感，在英文新闻标题中一般不用。

4.2.2 英文新闻报道的词汇特点与审美

新闻的目的是传递信息，而在当今社会，新闻媒体的数目极为繁多，为了能在有限的版面内尽最大可能吸引读者，满足读者的需求，新闻从业者在新闻词汇的选择上下了很大的功夫，也使得英文新闻的词汇与其他文体的词汇相比具有显著的区别。本书将从英文新闻词汇的简洁美、创新美、借用美、通俗美和模糊美几个方面来分析和欣赏英文新闻的用词。

A. 简洁美

新闻的价值就在于它的时效性和传播速度，为了达到更快的传播速度，一些过于冗长、不易识记的词汇需要被替换为短小精悍的小词。以下是英文新闻中经常使用的一些简短小词：

assail=denounce 谴责

balk=impede 阻碍

bar=prevent 防止，阻止

bid=attempt 企图，开始

dip=decline or decrease 下降

nix=deny/disapprove 否决/拒绝

pledge=make a solemn promise 发誓

poise=ready for action 做好准备

此外，英文新闻中为了节约篇幅，避免重复，往往会将一些专有名词或者术语以首字母缩略法的形式表达出来，这些缩略语用词简洁，生命力强，是英文新闻中重要的构词手段。例如：

TCM= Traditional Chinese Medicine 中医

WHO= World Health Organization 世界卫生组织

SARS= Severe Acute Respiratory Syndromes 非典型性肺炎

SCO= Shanghai Cooperation Organization 上海合作组织

KMT=Kuo Min Tang 国民党

此外，英文新闻中还有一些在原来的单词基础上通过截短或者拼缀而形成的缩略语，例如：

bath—bathroom 浴室

batt—battery 电池

ave.—avenue 大街

hi-tech—high technology 高科技

Dem—Democratic Party 民主党

encl—enclosure 信中的附件

govt—government 政府

通过使用以上这些简洁明了的词汇，英文新闻的传播速度得以加快，并且大大节省了英文新闻的版面。某些缩略词汇在英文新闻的传播中获得了强大的生命力，得以广泛流传，这些简单快捷的词汇也使得英文新闻形成了一种简洁明快的美感。

B. 创新美

英语是世界上最活跃、最有生命力的语言之一，英语以其独特的包容性和接纳性吸收了来自各种语言的词汇，并且其本身也具有极强的新词创造能力，所以在现代英语中各种创新的词汇层出不穷，让人耳目一新。而新闻是反映社会日新月异发展变化的一个最快捷、最有效的手段，新闻的核心就在于新，许多新闻都借用一些新词来显示其消息的时效性,同时许多新词也通过新闻的传播得以发扬光大,最终进入了正式的英语之中。许多这种词汇都是原来不为人所知的科技或者某一方面的术语,通过新闻媒体进入了大众的视野,为大众所熟知,例如:

genetic code 遗传密码

picornabirus 换心人

artificial intelligence 人工智能

transcription 信使核糖核酸

coedism 男女同校教育

prime time 黄金时间

除此之外,英文新闻中有许多生造词,也叫做仿词,指的是根据英语中原有的一些词缀、词根或其他成分通过类比或联想的方式创造出来的。例如:

sit-in 静坐示威

be-in 颓废派的社交集会

Black Power 黑色权利

Red Power 红色权利

green power 金钱魔力

environmental pollution 环境污染

在英文新闻中,这种仿词的大量使用极大地丰富了新闻的词汇,而且对于读者来说使用仿词可以联系起其来源词的含义,有助于理解作者的意思。除此之外,英文新闻中还有许多来自其他语言的外来语,甚至于平时习以为常的一些词汇也是外来语。例如:

dollar 美元(德语)

booze 豪饮(荷兰语)

bungalow 平房(印地语/孟加拉语)

tomato 番茄(阿兹台克那瓦特语)

zombie 僵尸(西非经加勒比海盗方言)

vampire 吸血鬼(匈牙利语)

shampoo 洗发水(印地语)

由此可以看出，英文新闻中出现的创新词汇极其繁多。一方面，这些层出不穷的新词是不断发展的人类社会的必然结果，而新闻作为消息传播的主要手段，自然会出现大量的新词；而另一方面，各个新闻媒体为了吸引读者，也竞相使用和创造新词。英语中这些创新词汇的广泛使用给读者一种耳目一新的愉悦感受，同时也使得英文新闻有一种创新的美感。

C. 借用美

英文新闻的受众极其广泛而文化程度又不一，为了使所有的受众都能准确理解新闻所指的内容，英文新闻中常常用某个事物的一个特点来代指事物整体，比如使用首都或总统府来代替政府，使用建筑物或地点来代替某个机构，使用一些特征词来代指某个地方或某人等，以便所有的读者都能明白新闻的含义，并且使得新闻更加生动活泼和形象，例如：

Big Board （纽约证券交易所的）大行情板——纽约股市
Fleet Street （曾经是英国媒体总部）舰队街——英国新闻界
Scotland Yard 苏格兰场——伦敦警方
White House 白宫——美国政府
Elysee 爱丽舍宫——法国政府
Downing Street No.10 唐宁街10号——英国政府
Donkey 美国民主党
Elephant 美国共和党

由此可见，在英文新闻中，借用词的应用极为普遍，这种借用词的使用使得英文新闻能够以多种手段间接地指出所要说明的事物，一方面表达了所指事物的鲜明特征，另一方面又增加了一种委婉的借用美。

D. 通俗美

作为一种应用文体，除外宣时政类外的一般新闻有别于用词文艺、追求艺术效果的文学文体，又区别于追求严谨、行文滴水不漏的法律文体。一般新闻所追求的是要在最短的时间内吸引最多的读者，这种定位决定了英文新闻在用词方面不可能是阳春白雪的书面和正式词汇，而倾向于使用大众喜闻乐见的通俗词汇。尤其对于一些不太严肃的通俗小报来说，通俗口语的广泛使用是吸引读者的一个重要手段。

【例 11】Florida court <u>Oks</u> proposed office smoking ban.

【译文】佛州法院通过办公室禁止吸烟提案。

句中的 Oks 原本是日常生活中极其常见的口语词汇，在句中做的是动词的成分，相当于 agrees，使得该新闻标题十分新奇生动和活泼。

【例 12】Loopholes in the proposed tax law could mean that is in for <u>a bumpy ride</u> when it goes before the Senate, and may even be quashed by a presidential vote.

【译文】提交的税法漏洞百出，被参议院通过的<u>前景十分艰难</u>，甚至还有可能被总统否决。

bumpy ride 在英语中原本的含义是指路程十分颠簸，但是在本句中指的是这个税法获得通过的路程将十分艰难，十分生动形象。

E. 模糊美

新闻报道本应该要求真实和准确，但是新闻本身也是在不断发展变化的，尤其是面对一些错综复杂的突发事件，信息来源往往不十分确定和可靠，获得的信息也往往不十分精确，而如果等到事实清楚之后再报道则会错失先机，失去时效性，因此英文新闻中往往会出现一些模糊性的词汇。

【例 13】<u>Intelligence obtained by European security agencies</u> indicates ISIS is aiming to attack the United Kingdom as a follow-up to its attacks in Paris last month, <u>a senior European counterterrorism official</u> told CNN. （*CNN* Dec 6, 2015）

【译文】<u>一位欧洲反恐部门高官</u>告诉 CNN 说，<u>欧洲安全部门获得的情报</u>显示伊斯兰国继上月在巴黎发动恐怖袭击后将英国列为下一个目标。

文中的 Intelligence obtained by European security agencies 和 a senior European counterterrorism offical 都是模糊性的用语，在本条

新闻中因为不能确切判断情报获得的来源或者出于保密考虑，所以只能用一些模糊词语来表示。

除此之外，英文新闻中在阐述一些消息来源可疑或者不确定的新闻时，出于严谨的考虑，特别会使用一些模糊的词语来交代新闻的来源，这样一方面可以体现出此新闻的客观性，另一方面万一新闻被证明不实，也可借此推脱逃避责任。英文新闻中常用的表示消息来源的模糊词语有：

experts　专家
financial quarters　金融界方面
it is reported　据报道
rumors say　据谣传
it is authoritatively learned　自权威方面获悉
according to an anonymous source　据一位不愿透露姓名的消息灵通人士说

由此可以看出，英文新闻中模糊词语的应用十分广泛。一方面，模糊词汇的使用可以在情况并不明了或不太确定的情况下，尽最大可能保证新闻的客观性，避免误导受众，而且形成一种模糊美；另一方面，这些模糊词语的运用也可以使新闻媒体本身逃避消息不实的责任，避免引火烧身。

4.2.3　英文新闻报道的语法特征

英文新闻作为一种功能独特的文体，为了达到信息传递等功能，在语法上也显现出了自身独特的特点。

A．时态的使用不一致

在英语中，一个句子内的谓语动词原则上要保持一致，叫做时态的一致或呼应。但是在英文新闻中，为了更合理、更真实地阐述实际情况，往往在一个句子中使用不同时态的谓语动词。

【例14】So, two days after one of the deadliest mass shootings in the United States, authorities <u>are</u> still left wondering what <u>motivated</u> the couple to mow down dozens of people at a holiday luncheon in San Bernardino, California. （*CNN* Dec 4, 2015）

【译文】所以，在这起美国历史上伤亡最惨重的枪击案之一发生两天后，官员们仍然十分不解到底是什么驱使着这对夫妻在加州圣贝纳迪诺市的一个节日午餐会上射杀了数十人。

在句中 are 是一般现在时，表示这种情况对于官员和政府来说至今仍然是难以置信的；而 motivated 则是过去时，表示凶手在凶案发生前便已经有了发动袭击的动机，是一个过去已经发生的情况。

【例 15】Police <u>released</u> no information about the man's identity or possible motive, but the United Kingdom <u>is facing</u> stepped-up threats from ISIS——especially after British fighter planes <u>began</u> flying sorties against ISIS targets in Syria this week. （*CNN* Dec 6, 2015）

【译文】警方没有透露此人的身份和可能的动机，但是英国目前正面临着来自伊斯兰国迫在眉睫的威胁，尤其是本周英国展开在叙利亚打击伊斯兰国目标的行动之后。

在本句中 released 使用的是过去时，说明警方在新闻报道以前并没有公布嫌疑人的信息；而 is facing 使用的是现在进行时，表示英国现在正在面临来自伊斯兰国的威胁；但是随后 began 又变为了过去时，表示打击伊斯兰国的行动已经发生了。

B. 较多使用被动语态

在英文新闻中，被动语态使用要比普通英语文体偏多，尤其对于灾难、战争类的新闻往往最重要的信息来自动作的承受者，因而使用被动语态能够使读者对于相关事实一目了然。

【例 16】Two bodies were found in a van the same day, on a back road in remote farmlands in Sinaloa——home of the Sinaloa drug cartel. （*CNN* Dec 5, 2015）

【译文】同一天，在锡那罗亚州的一个偏僻的乡村道路上的一辆面包车上发现了两具尸体，而锡那罗亚州则是锡那罗亚贩毒集团的老巢。

本条新闻报道了两名澳大利亚游客在墨西哥遇害的事件，而使用被动态更好地表达和证实了两名游客已经遇害的事实。

【例 17】The concern was discussed this week by FBI Director James Comey in testimony on Capitol Hill.（*CNN* Dec 11, 2015）

【译文】在本周举行的国会听证会上联邦调查局局长詹姆斯·可米讨论了这一顾虑。

C. 直接引语和间接引语的广泛使用

英文新闻的另一个特点便是引语的广泛使用。使用引语可以使新闻报道更有说服力，同时又能显示新闻的客观性，以示新闻是有客观依据，而不是记者主观臆想的。

【例 18】Sixteen people have been killed in the Egyptian capital, Cairo, after firebombs were thrown into a restaurant, officials say.（*BBC News* Dec 4, 2015）

【译文】官员声称在埃及首都开罗发生的餐馆爆炸案中有 16 人丧生。

【例 19】"It is possible that this was terrorist-related, but we don't know. It's also possible that this was workplace-related," Mr Obama said.（*BBC News* Dec 4, 2015）

【译文】"（这次枪击案）可能与恐怖袭击有关，但仍不确定。同时也有可能是由于职场矛盾造成的。"奥巴马说。

在以上两则新闻中都使用了引语。在例 18 中，使用了一名埃及官员的话作为间接引语，而例 19 则使用了奥巴马的发言作为直接引语。这种引语的使用使得以上两条新闻读起来真实可信，富有感染力，能够使得读者通过引语直接体会到新闻事实。

4.2.4　英文新闻报道的篇章特征

英文新闻从结构上来说可以分为倒金字塔形和金字塔形。所谓倒金字塔形指的是那种将最重要的信息前置于新闻的开头，让读者在新闻的开头就看到最为重要的信息这样一种布局模式。而金字塔形新闻正好相反，基本上是按照时间或逻辑顺序一步一步层层推进来揭露事实,给读者留下悬念。一般来说倒金字塔形结构适用于含有重大消息、时效性强的"硬新闻",而金字塔结构则适用于记叙色彩浓厚、趣味性强的"软新闻"。

【例20】**Straight hair is back**

Let's get one thing perfectly straight: If you want one of the hottest looks this season you have to get perfectly straight. Hair, that is.

Among the celebrities who've sported it recently on red carpets and elsewhere are Reese Witherspoon, Nicole Kidman, Beyonce, Gwyneth Paltrow, Queen Latifah and Jada Pinkett-Smith.

It's a trend that clearly has legs into summer and even fall. Major design houses are on board with print campaigns featuring straight hair, including advertisements for Valentino, Fendi, Hermes, Burberry, Prada, Versace, DKNY, Calvin Klein, Chanel and Gucci.

"It's a recycle, but it's definitely happening." Celebrity hairstylist Oscar Blandi said. "Straight is coming back strongly. It's straight, but it's a different straight." How?

It has body. Unlike the trend about six or seven years ago for stick-straight hair, this season's straight has body, movement and shine.

"The key thing is that the hair is phenomenally shiny. It is very glossy, shiny hair," Redken stylisst Kaz Amor said. "If you look at Gwyneth (at the Oscars), the hair was moving. It was not stiff, straight-down hair."

Blandi said the previous straight-hair trend dictated almost no movement.

"It's not spaghetti. Before, the hair was almost attached to the skull," he said. "Now, it's got a silky texture. It's not flat. There's much more body."

Today's straight styles are parted on the side and pulled away from the face, said Tim Rogers, stylist and spokesman for Charles Worthington hair products and salons.

【译文】　时尚：直发再掀流行风

直说吧！如果你想拥有本季最热的造型，就应该打造一头直发！

在近年来现身红地毯及其他仪式的名人中，瑞斯·威瑟斯彭、妮可·基德曼、碧昂斯、格温妮丝·帕特洛、奎因·莱提法和贾达·平科特·史密斯都是一袭直发亮相。

这一潮流必将席卷今夏甚至今秋。几大设计公司即将推出的宣传画都是以直发为主，其中包括华伦天奴、芬迪、爱马仕、伯百利、普拉达、范哲思、DKNY、卡尔文·克莱恩、香奈儿和古奇的广告。

名人造型师奥斯卡·布兰迪说："这是一次再循环，但这一潮流却是实实在在地开始了。直发正在强力回归，但如今它已是另一种'直'的理念了。"为什么这样说呢？

直发开始有了"形"。与六七年前笔直的头发不同，本季的直发更加有型、动感十足而且光彩盈亮。

Redken的造型师卡兹·阿莫说："关键在于头发一定要非常有光泽；要十分光滑闪亮。如果留意一下参加奥斯卡颁奖典礼的格温妮丝，你会发现她的头发很具动感，并不是那种呆板、笔直的直发。"

布兰迪说，此前的直发潮流几乎没有动感的概念可言。

他说："我们要的不是意大利面式的直发。之前，直发几乎都是紧贴着头皮的。而现在，直发则有了丝般的质感，不再扁平单调，变得更加有型了。"

查尔斯·沃兴顿美发产品及沙龙的造型师、发言人蒂姆·罗格斯说，如今的直发造型以偏分为主，这样就不会遮住脸了。

本条新闻的篇章结构属于金字塔形，在前两段作者首先提出了以直发示人的明星们，第三段又说明了推出直发宣传画的著名设计公司，吊起了读者的胃口，使得读者十分好奇直发今年颇为流行的原因，而文章的后半段则揭开了直发流行的原因，使整条新闻产生一种层层递进的效果，逐条阐述事实。

在当前快节奏的生活方式下，人们一般不会花太多时间阅读报纸，对于一些重大消息往往只求了解最主要的信息便一扫而过，而倒金字塔形的结构使得新闻把最重要的信息呈现在最前面方便读者阅读，因而适用于时效性强的"硬新闻"。但是这种结构的缺陷在于把最重要的信息放在开头部分，以至于后半部分没有悬念，造成一种虎头蛇尾的感觉。而金字塔形的结构则逐层叙述事实，给读者留下想象的空间，吸引读者继续向下去读，因而适用于娱乐和趣味性较强的"软新闻"。

4.3 新闻报道翻译策略

新闻是人们了解外部世界的一扇窗户，对于中国人来说，英文新闻是人们接触世界政治经济变化、跟上世界发展步伐的一个主要手段，因此英文新闻的翻译也扮演着一个越来越重要的角色。就新闻面向大众传递消息的文体功能而言，新闻翻译中准确和通俗是最重要的，因此从原则上来说新闻翻译要忠实于原文，坚持原则性。但是另一方面，新闻语言本身又有其鲜明特点，这些特点决定了在新闻翻译中又必须做到灵活处理，要有针对性地对待每一种不同的情况。

4.3.1 新闻报道标题的翻译

标题对于一则新闻来说至关重要，标题是一则新闻的浓缩和精华，起到引导和概括的作用。一个好的标题不仅能够吸引读者去阅读，更能够给读者一种美的享受；同样，把新闻标题翻译的传神也能达到同样的效果，翻译好新闻标题是翻译新闻的第一步。

A. 直译法

如果英文新闻的标题含义明白，内容直接，直接译成汉语不会使人产生误解，则基本上可以采取直译的方式加以译出。例如：

【例21】Turkey Shoots down Russian Plane to Protect Oil Trade with IS: Putin

【译文】普京：土耳其为了保住与伊斯兰国的石油贸易而击落俄国战机（*People's Daily Online* Dec 1, 2015）

【例22】 China's Alibaba opens branches in Germany, France

【译文】中国阿里巴巴集团在德国和法国开设分公司（*Xinhua News Agency* Dec 1, 2015）

以上三个例子都是典型的直译，英文新闻中的内容和形式几乎与翻译之后的汉语标题完全相同。像这种结构简单、内容直白的标题适于使用直译方法译出。对于某种形式的标题来说采取略带意译的直译手段还可以取得一定的修辞美感，例如：

【例23】Looking back to look ahead

【译文】回首往昔　展望未来

【例24】Ugly Duckling N-ship at Last Gets Happy Home

【译文】丑小鸭核动力船终于找到安乐窝

在例23中，汉语译文不仅把英文中的含义完全翻译了出来，而且还用两个四字结构起到了一定的对仗效果，富有美感。而例24中，原文中将核动力船比作丑小鸭，汉语译文索性将其翻译为"丑小鸭"，不仅在字面意思上完全吻合，而且在内涵意义上完全贴切，使读者能够生动形象地明白整个新闻的含义。

B. 意译法

对于大部分的新闻标题，直译并不能够完整地表达原文的含义，或者直译之后可读性较差，不被读者所接受，则应该采取意译法进行翻译。例如：

【例25】Surgeon saves gorilla from the mist

【译文】医生妙手回春，猩猩"重见天日"

【例26】Cushioning a Hard Landing

【译文】避免经济硬着陆（*Beijing Review* Dec 1, 2015）

【例27】Senior: a gold mine of wisdom

【译文】走过岁月沧桑，凝成智慧宝藏

以上三例中标题的翻译属于典型的意译法，例25中saves被翻译为"妙手回春"，from the mist 被译为"重见天日"，不仅恰当地体现了原标题中的含义，而且还使用了汉语中的四字结构，形成了一个对仗工整的标题，富有修辞美。例26中原意是为硬着陆铺上一个垫子，但是直译过来反而使读者不知所云，而结合原文可以得出硬着陆指的是中国经济形势，因此可以译为避免经济硬着陆。例27中汉语标题也是采用意译的方式，译为一个对仗工整的句子，形象地表达出了原文中 Senior 的含义。有时候，英语标题中会使用一些修辞手法，在不损害意思的情况下，将修辞手法一同译出更好。例如：

【例28】Middle East: A Cradle of Terror
【译文】中东：恐怖主义的摇篮
【例29】After the Booms Everything Is Gloom
【译文】繁荣不再 萧条即来

这两个例子都典型地翻译出了原文中的修辞手法。例28中使用了暗喻的修辞手法，将 Middle East 比作 cradle，而汉语译文中将这个暗喻完整地翻译了出来。例29则是含有尾韵的修辞，原文中 boom 和 gloom 押韵，而译文中"再"和"来"押韵。不过需要说明的是，像这种修辞性的标题如果能将含义和修辞手法一同翻译出来自然最好，如若不能求全，则应以含义为重，切不可求"形"而损"意"。

C. 增译法

一些新闻标题由于各种各样的原因，往往省略一些背景信息，对于母语读者来说可能无伤大雅，但是对于译入语读者来说，由于语言习惯、思维方式以及文化背景等原因，直接将原文的意思翻译过来往往使他们不知所云。因此，对于一些省略了重要背景信息的标题，在翻译时，应该采用增译法。例如：

【例30】No mentality of zero-sum game in climate talks: Xi
【译文】习近平：气候对话中不应有零和博弈的心态
（*Xinhua News Agency* Dec 1, 2015）
【例31】Japanese dash to US to say "I do"
【译文】日本情侣蜂拥美利坚，牧师面前誓言"我愿意"

上文中例30译文增添了人名，因为在英语中人们习惯于使用姓氏来代指某人，而中文则习惯于以全名来指人，仅仅一个姓氏容易让人产生误解，而且使用单个姓氏指人显得不正式，不符合中文新闻的文体特色。而例31则对"I do"进行了增译，say"I do"在英语中含有双方喜结连理的意思，因为在教堂婚礼中双方会以"I do"来回答牧师的提问作为婚姻的誓言。但是"I do"的中文翻译"我愿意"没有特殊含义，因此需要增译出"情侣"这一词，使得中国读者能够明白"我愿意"的真正含义。

4.3.2 新闻报道新词的翻译

上文中也提及，英文新闻中有许多新词，这些新词的翻译对于新闻的信息传递功能至关重要。在翻译新词时，应该根据词形和上下文判断词义，并在词典等资料求证的基础上通过直译、意译、音译或者增译等方法确切地翻译出词语的含义。

A 直译法

直译法是新闻新词中最常见的一种翻译方式，只要在直译过程中新词原有的意思可以得到保留、不产生误解和歧义的话，都可以采取直译的方式。例如：

carpet-bomb 地毯式轰炸
bloodless coup 不流血政变
foreign exchange reserve 外汇储备
intercontinental missile 洲际导弹
active capital 流动资金
working graduate 在职研究生
conductorless bus 无人售票车

B. 意译法

如果说直译法要求在形式和内容上都与原文相符合的话，那么意译则只是在内容上与原文保持了一致。有一些词汇的翻译无法做到形和意兼得，只好舍形取义，采用意译法翻译。例如：

fresh-air sports 户外运动
ceiling price 最高限价
hit film 大片；巨片
carrier rocket 运载火箭
hit-and-run accident 交通事故逃逸案

issue an IOU　打白条

jerrybuilt project　"豆腐渣"工程

C. 音译法

音译法也是新闻新词翻译中一种常见的方法，使用音译法的最大优势是给读者一种洋味时髦的感觉，使读者得到一种新鲜感，而且相当多的音译法翻译过来的单词被广为流传和接受，最后成为了汉语中的有机组成部分。例如：

El Nino　厄尔尼诺现象

La Nina　拉尼娜现象

Dengue fever　登革热

Ebola virus　埃博拉病毒

clone　克隆

mousse　摩丝

talk show　脱口秀

D. 增译法

由于英汉两种语言的思维方式、文化背景等差异，一些词经过翻译之后需要加上一定的解释性的语言才能让读者明白其真正含义，这类词适用于使用增译法进行翻译。例如：

ghost examinee　（考试）替考者；枪手

Earth Day　地球（保护）日（每年4月22日）

head-on collision　（车辆等）迎面相撞（事故）

Richter scale　（地震震级的一种数值标度）里氏震级

suicide hotline　自杀救助热线

atomic veteran　原子退伍老兵（受到核武器或核辐射的退伍兵）

golden hello　专门给新员工的见面礼

green card　绿卡（允许外国人进入美国工作的许可证）

增译法并不是绝对的，而是要根据读者的具体情况来确定。例如 green card，在改革开放初期，中国人对于绿卡往往一无所知，在翻译时一般需要加上注释，否则"绿卡"一词使人完全无法联想到其真正的含义，但是现如今绿卡在中国已经人尽皆知，就没有必要再十分啰嗦地加上注释了。同样，对于 Richter scale 来说，如果读者的科学文化素质相对较高，则没有必要加上注释，但是如果新闻的读者是普通大众，则宜加注释为妙。对于那种不加注释就会使人产生误解的词语，如 atomic veteran，注释一般来说是必不可少的。

4.3.3　新闻报道中修辞的翻译

新闻除了要遵循真实的原则，另一个重要的原则便是吸引读者，所以新闻的语言在准确反映事实的基础上还要尽可能吸引读者，使读者有继续读下去的欲望，所以各种形式的新闻都大量使用了修辞手法来表达意思，增加语言的艺术效果，达到传播消息的目的。比较常用的修辞手法有比喻、委婉语、双关、用典和仿拟等。

A. 比喻

比喻是新闻中出现频率颇多的一种修辞手段，包含明喻、暗喻和借喻等。一个比喻中包含本体和喻体，所谓本体指的是被比喻者，即要表达和描绘的对象，喻体指的是比喻者，即用来表达和描绘的对象。对于比喻的翻译来说，如果喻体的形象及内涵在汉语中可以得到对应，则可以采用保留喻体的方式予以翻译，这样保留了原文中的表现力和感染力，使译文和原文在形式和内容上都得到了统一。

【例 32】Indeed, networks have washed over corporate America <u>like a tsunami</u>, dramatically altering the architecture of computing.

【译文】确实，电脑网络已<u>如海啸般</u>横扫美国企业界，大大改变了电脑业的结构。

以上例子是将英文原文中的比喻保留喻体直接翻译而来。该新闻旨在说明电脑网络对于美国企业界的影响，而 tsunami（海啸）这一词在英语和汉语中都生动形象地反映出了网络所带来的巨大而迅猛的影响。在此例中，英文喻体可以直译为汉语而不损害原有的比喻意义和效果，所以对于这种喻体可以予以保留。但是这种完全保留喻体的情况并不多，有时候英语中的喻体在汉语中无法完全对应，如果直译照搬，不但起不到原来喻体的效果，反而会造成理解上的困难，在这种情况下，需要替换喻体。

【例33】"We have a PR mountain to climb," says Willy de Greef, head of regulatory and government affairs at Novartis Seeds in Basel, Switzerland.

【译文】"要让大家接受转基因食物，我们还有漫长的路要走，"瑞士巴塞尔市诺瓦提斯种子公司管理与政府事务部主管威利·德·格里夫如是说。

以上例子中，英语喻体在翻译成汉语后全部被替换了，a PR mountain 指的是 Public Relation mountain，意思是要说服公众们接受转基因食品的任务十分艰巨，就像攀登一座大山一样，但是"公众关系的大山"并不符合汉语的表达习惯，也体现不出原有的隐喻意义，反倒是汉语中的"漫长的路"与英语原文中的隐喻有异曲同工之妙，所以原文中的喻体宜做替换。但是英汉两种语言之间的巨大差异也产生了一种情况，那就是原喻体在译入语中完全找不到合适的喻体来翻译，对于这种喻体，只能舍形取义，放弃原来的喻体形象，只将意思翻译出来。

【例34】But country vs. country team competition begins losing its luster among USA pros in recent years as big purses, which brought bigger endorsement deals, became available to grand slam tournament champions.

【译文】但是对于美国职业赛手来说，国际的团体竞赛近年来已渐趋式微，因为只要能赢得锦标赛大满贯冠军，赞助大赛的大奖是不愁不到手的。

【例35】The research finds that young women are heading for an early grave through smoking and lack of exercise.

【译文】这项研究发现，由于抽烟和减少运动，一些青年女性正踏上一条减寿之途。

以上两例中，原文中的喻体在汉语中都无法得到对应，只得舍弃喻体，翻译内容。例34 中 big purses 代指的是赞助大赛的大奖及其带给选手的诱惑力,但是 big purses 在中文中找不到合适的喻体,如果直译为"大钱包"不但不能起到原文中喻体的效果,反而使人感到莫名其妙,因此只好译出意思,舍弃喻体。而例 35 中,an early grave 代指的是人的寿命变短,但是直译过来"更早的坟墓"造语不通,完全不符合汉语的表达习惯,此外在汉语中也难以找到合适的喻体来代替"early grave",因此只好作罢,翻译为"减寿之途"。

B. 委婉语

委婉语是间接地表达某种意思或者思想,以相对和谐礼貌的方式来代替粗鲁野蛮或者令人不快的用词,它的主要作用是减少语言上给人带来的不适或不快,起到一种安慰或美化的作用。在新闻报道中,往往涉及战争、政治、犯罪、性、贫穷等人类社会的阴暗面,为了在报道这些内容时不对读者造成太强烈的刺激,新闻报道中往往采用许多委婉语,因此委婉语的翻译也是新闻翻译中的一个重要组成部分。

【例 36】Officials dismissed Henry Kissinger's public suggestion in mid-August the U.S. should consider a "surgical" strike to remove Iraq's most dangerous weapons if sanctions are too uncertain and diplomacy unavailing.

【译文】政府官员拒绝考虑亨利·基辛格在 8 月中旬提出的公开建议:如果制裁的功效不能肯定,外交解决无法奏效,美国应该考虑进行一次"外科手术式"的打击,以消除伊拉克最危险的武器。

【例 37】These Olympic Games, for once, were supposed to be all play and no sportsmanship, or good journalism, for news commentators in the United States to put a political gloss on the opening-day parade?

【译文】大家曾经期望这些奥运会只有竞技,不搞政治:不要什么超级大国的抵制或可悲的恐怖暴行,既然如此,美国的新闻评论员,给开幕那天的入场仪式,添加政治色彩,算是表现出最好的运动精神或良好的新闻道德吗?

以上两例都是委婉语在新闻英语中的应用。例 36 中外科手术式的打击指的是定点破坏伊拉克的大规模杀伤性武器,因为打击方式很像外科医生专门对某一部位做手术的方式,所以以"外科手术式"的打击来委婉地说明打击的方式。例 37 中添加政治色彩指的是把政治话题扯入奥运会中,借此干涉别国内政。以上两例中的委婉语在汉语和英语中意思接近,而且委婉色彩可以得到保留,能够实现功能对等,因此在翻译过程中都使用了直译的方式。但是由于文化语言等因素,英语和汉语中往往存在大量的委婉语不对等现象,此时,如果直译往往起不到委婉语应有的效果,反而会产生误解,应该采用意译的方式译出。

【例 38】Responding to the crisis, Ghanaian Foreign Secretary Obed Asamoah told the BBC in London that it's time the peace-keeping force <u>showed its teeth</u>.

【译文】在回答有关这一危机的问题时,加纳外长阿萨莫阿在伦敦对英国广播公司说,维和部队该是<u>强硬表态</u>的时候了。

【例 39】Since 1971, the Aechdiocese of New York and donors to <u>Inner-City</u> Scholarship Fund have invested in futures: the talents of the most <u>under-resourced</u> neighborhoods in New York.

【译文】1971 年以来,纽约大主教区和<u>贫民区</u>奖学金基金会的捐献者一直在投资"期货",即帮助居住在纽约一些最<u>贫穷</u>社区的成千上万的天才少年。

以上两个例子是委婉语意译的典型。例 38 中 showed one's teeth 在英语中有表达愤怒的意思,但是如果直译过来"显露牙齿"则毫无意义可言,所以翻译成"强硬表态"为宜。例 39 中 inner-city 和 under-resourced 都是"贫穷"的委婉语,但是如果直译过来,则完全偏离了原意,所以应该翻译成"贫民区"和"贫穷"。

C. 双关

所谓双关就是利用一个词或一个表达方式的多义或同音等因素来表达双重含义的修辞手法,使用双关使文章的语言生动有趣。

【例 40】I finally figured out how government works. The senate gets the <u>bill</u> from the House. The President gets the <u>bill</u> from the Senate. And we get the <u>bill</u> for everything.

【译文】我终于弄懂了政体是如何运行的。议会的<u>提案</u>由众议院转到参议院再从参议院转到总统。于是轮到我们支付一切<u>账单</u>。

【例41】Women have a wonderful sense of <u>right</u> and wrong, but little sense of <u>right</u> and left.

【译文】女人对<u>善恶</u>感觉惊人，而对<u>左右</u>感觉麻木。

例40是典型的谐音双关，同一个单词bill在句中不同的位置分别有"提案"和"账单"的不同含义。例41中的第一个right表示"对的"，但第二个right表示的是"右"这个方向。除了谐音双关之外还有语义双关，指的是利用一词多义的特点构成明暗双重意义。

【例42】A new harvest of troubles

【译文】农产品丰收，新问题成堆

上面的例子就是语义双关，"harvest"不仅表示农产品的丰收，也表示问题的大量出现。

D. 用典和仿拟

用典指的是不注明来源或者出处地引用典故、谚语、成语、格言等，将其融合在新闻报道之中，使语言深刻含蓄，富有启发性，而仿拟则是对这些典故加以模仿。

【例43】24 years a slave ... for doctor and his wife in suburbs

【译文】为奴24载……郊区医生夫妇涉嫌非法拘禁

【例44】Israel is a "Catch-22" problem for the Iranian regime.

【译文】以色列问题对于伊朗政府而言，有如"第二十二条军规"一样，令人左右为难。

以上两例都引用了典故。例43中24 years a slave 仿拟自所罗门·诺瑟普在1853年所著传记体小说 12 years a slave（《为奴十二载》），将受害人的遭遇比作美国内战前的黑奴的遭遇。例44中Catch-22来源于小说《第二十二条军规》，指的是无论如何也不可能走出的死循环，以此代指以色列问题给伊朗政府带来的困扰。

E. 巧用汉语四字结构

英汉两种语言的差异明显地体现在句式上。英语句子逻辑清楚，层次分明，如同一棵树一样，有着主干和分枝，但是汉语句子行文略显松散，习惯于用隐含性的逻辑关系连接句子，因此汉语句子被称为流水句或者竹节句。由于汉语的这一特点，在翻译英文新闻时，往往可以把英语中的一些句子成分处理成汉语四字结构，不仅使得行文流畅，而且使读者喜闻乐见，增加新闻的可读性。

【例45】A staggering 16 out of the serving 24 committee members from the year the tournaments were granted are now being investigated or have been punished for misconduct.

【译文】在当年涉及世界杯申办的24名执委中已有16名被调查或者除名，这一数字让人瞠目结舌。

【例46】The present-day American society is disfigured by huge blemishes: entrenched poverty, persistent racial tension, the breakdown of the family and staggering budget deficits.

【译文】当今美国社会污迹斑斑，面目全非：贫困现象难以消除，种族对立由来已久，家庭关系支离破碎，预算赤字骇人听闻。

以上两个例中都广泛使用了四字结构。例45中staggering原意是"极其让人惊讶的，难以置信的"，而汉语中"瞠目结舌"这一四字结构正好表达了这一含义。例46中运用的四字结构则突出反映出了美国社会当前遇到的社会问题和困境。这种四字结构不仅很好地处理了一些英语中难以翻译的词语，而且大大缩短了句子的长度，节省了版面，更赋予了一种汉语独特的美感，使整个文章行文流畅。

4.3.4 新闻报道中文化因素的处理

新闻作为一种信息传播的工具，不可避免地会带有来源语文化的烙印，所以在进行新闻翻译的过程中，文化差异也是需要译者注意的重要因素。在翻译与文化有关的表达方式时，一般有两种策略可以选择，即归化和异化策略。所谓归化策略就是尽可能地用符合译入语思维和表达习惯的方式进行翻译；而异化正好相反，则是以保留原文的文体色彩为主。在新闻翻译中，异化和归化需要根据实际情况灵活运用。

【例47】Glasnost unleashed, like <u>Prometheus unbound</u>, can ignite a holocaust as easily as it can warm a conversation, and the shift from a planned economy to a market economy may work only if the central government is willing to loosen its stranglehold on commerce.

【译文】"开放"的力量一旦敞开发挥，就会像<u>解放了的普罗米修斯</u>一样，既可以鼓励对话，也可能同样轻而易举地引起一场大灾难。同时，要从计划经济转入市场经济，中央政府必须愿意解除对商业的严格管制。

【例48】Surely Prime Minister Thatcher was advised that public voicing of "what-we-have-we-hold" position (on Hong Kong) would wound Chinese pride; and that a bold public declaration which amounted to her pledging to take the interests of the people of Hong Kong—people whom Peking regards as her own—into account would <u>rub salt into the wound</u>.

【译文】撒切尔首相公开宣称"我们不放弃我们已拥有的（香港）"的立场，无疑伤害了中国人的自尊心：她鲁莽的做法就等于答应香港人考虑他们的利益问题（北京认为他们是中国人），这无异于<u>在伤口上撒把盐</u>。

以上两例中与文化因素有关的表达方式都是采取的异化的表达方式。例47中普罗米修斯原来是希腊神话中偷盗天火而被宙斯绑在高加索山上的神祇，后来被英雄赫拉克勒斯救出，所以解放了的普罗米修斯可以用来代指一些曾经被压抑或困住很久的事物突然间获得了自由，由于中国人对于普罗米修斯的形象已经颇为了解，其在汉语中也有了相似的语义，所以在翻译的过程中完全可以直译过来。例48中 rub salt into the wound 也采用了异化的策略，翻译为"在伤口上撒盐"，因为"在伤口上撒盐"这一表达方式已经为中国人所接受，它在汉语中含有和英语中相似的含义，不会引起误解。类似的由英语传入的表达方式还有"武装到牙齿 armed to the teeth""连锁反应 chain reaction""冷战 cold war""跳蚤市场 flea market"等。

但是对于一些采取异化策略容易使读者不知所云、产生误解的情况，还是要适当地进行归化处理。

【例 49】 Nelson Mandela urges the international community to carry its pariah treatment of Pretoria. That line may be hard to sell in Europe, where many believe easing sanctions could be <u>a constructive carrot</u> to dangle before a reformist Pretoria.

【译文】曼德拉敦促国际社会继续采取唾弃南非当局的行动，这条路线在欧洲或许不容易让人接受，因为很多欧洲人士认为，放宽制裁对于有心改革的南非当局可能成为<u>一个有积极意义的诱因</u>。

【例 50】 I will give aid the day when I <u>skate in hell</u>.

【译文】<u>太阳从西边出来</u>的那天我就会给你帮助。

以上两例采取的是归化的策略。例 49 中 a constructive carrot 直译过来是"有积极意义的胡萝卜"，虽然英语中的胡萝卜加大棒这一说法已在汉语中得到了认可，但是如果完全异化地翻为"有积极意义的胡萝卜"还是会让人感到莫名其妙，所以在这一句中还是采取了归化的方式，翻译为"有积极意义的诱因"。例 50 中 skate in hell 这一说法与西方的文化密切相关，在西方文化中地狱里充满了火和硫磺来惩罚罪人，因此 skate in hell 是永远不可能发生的事情，但是如果翻译为"在地狱中滑冰"不仅莫名其妙，而且其内涵引申意义顿时全无，反而用归化的方式译为"太阳从西边出来"完美地保存了其引申意义。

4.3.5　中文新闻报道英译的注意事项

中文新闻英译的过程中，除了注意语言上的差别之外，更要注意两种文化思维方式的差别、受众的差别，而且还要提高译者自身的政治敏感性。

【例 51】为进一步扩大对外开放，加快招商引资步伐，促进我市经济持续、快速、健康发展，根据上级有关文件规定，结合我市实际，经市委、市政府研究，就鼓励外商来本市投资提出如下意见。

【译文】In order to open wider to the outside world and promote the foreign investment for the city's economic development, the municipal government has put forward the proposals for the foreign investment as follows:

上面例子中的汉语原文在政治性较强的中文新闻中具有典型特征。中文政治外宣新闻的一个特点便是使用大量的并没有具体实际含义的套话,对于中国人的思维方式和中文的行文习惯来说这是一种普遍而且正常的事情,但是对于外国人来说这种行文方式太冗长多余,因此在翻译过程中应该删除冗长多余的文字,将文章中的精髓翻译出来,使读者一目了然,明白文章的大概含义,这样的翻译便是忠于原文的。原文中的"根据上级有关文件规定,结合我市实际,经市委、市政府研究"对于外国人来说毫无意义,在翻译中应该删除,使行文流畅。

【例52】中国有两点是靠的住的,一是讲原则,二是说话算数。

【译文】China can be accounted on. Among other things, first, it upholds principle and second, it honors its words.

此例中增译出了 among other things,这一句十分有必要,因为如若不加上这一句,会给人一种中国只有两点可以靠得住的感觉,歪曲了原意。

由以上两点可以看出,译者在翻译中文政治外宣类新闻时,不仅要有良好的语言功底,更要体会到受众的差别,增强自己的政治敏感性和政治基本功,切不可生搬硬套,犯下低级错误。

第五章 商贸文本

随着改革开放的进一步深化、社会主义市场经济的不断发展和完善，我国的对外贸易发展迅速。中国现在已经正式加入了世贸组织，对外经贸交流必将得到前所未有的发展。而商贸英语作为一种特殊的专门用途英语（English for Special Purposes），将发挥更加重要的经济效益和社会效益。商贸英语涉及国际贸易进出口业务，包括各种实用文体，如商业信函、合同、协议、各种文件、通则、惯例以及商业谈判等等。商贸英语由于涉及的范围广、内容复杂、形式多样，因而翻译不同的商贸文书有一定困难。一篇好的商贸文本翻译，不仅要准确地表达原文的内容，传达原文的信息，还要再现原文语体功能，从而区别于文学文体或科技文体。本章就商贸英语的功能和特征进行分析，以探求其翻译方法和原则。

5.1 商贸文本的文体类型及功能

5.1.1 文体类型

商贸英语是一种实用性很强的功能语体。商贸英语文本涉及面广，体中有体，类型多样。大体上说商贸文本主要有以下三种类型。

固定格式型：合同、信用证、汇票、提单、保险单、装运通知、商业发票、报关单等。这些文本措辞严谨，常用术语，逻辑性强，结构缜密，多长难句，语体格式化且行文规范。

传递信息型：询盘、报盘、还盘、订货单、电报、传真、电邮等。这类文本大都具有语气委婉、语言简洁明了、语法简明易懂等特点。

劝说诱导型：推销信、产品广告、商标、产品说明书、索赔函等。这类文本充分发挥语言的诱导功能，措辞严谨，修辞多变，以劝说读者为目的。

5.1.2　文体功能

语言的第一重要功能是"信息功能"，也就是传递信息。这也是商贸英语的最重要的一个功能。商贸信函首先要准确地传达信息。在进出口实务中，准确地传达信息对于双方都至关重要。任何在表达上或理解上的疏忽和差错都可能造成难以弥补的重大损失。商贸英语的信息功能的另一个重要方面是传递信息的时效性，也就是以最快的速度交换信息。只有迅速传递或获得信息，才能抢占贸易先机。除"信息功能"外，商贸英语还具有重要的"社交功能"。商贸信函中经常包含具有固定格式的客套语，这些客套语所传递的信息内容已降到次要地位，其主要作用是做出礼节性的表示，帮助贸易双方建立一定的社会关系，从而起到交际应酬功能。商贸文本的最终目的是促成双方的贸易往来，即使交易不能达成，也必须和对方保持良好的业务关系，便于以后业务的开展。此外，有些商贸文书具有明显的"呼唤功能"，如为建立业务关系的商贸信函及推销信，由于常向客户介绍己方企业的基本业务状况和产品经营情况而带有广告文体特色，语言亲切活泼，从而达到吸引客户的目的。

5.2　英文商贸文本的文体特征

商贸英语广泛应用于商业领域，是决定谈判能否成功的决定性因素。作为英语语言系统的一个分支，商贸英语特指服务于国际商贸活动的专门用途英语。商贸活动中特有的信息传递方式赋予了商贸英语极具特色的特征。因此，相比于其他非文学文体，商贸文本具有不同的语言规范和特殊的文体特征。作为一种专用英语，经贸英语是随着世界经济和国际贸易的不断发展而形成的一种学术英语。商贸文本通常语言简洁、用词准确、语气正式、语体格式化、行文规范且注重礼貌原则。

5.2.1 词汇特征

A. 缩略语

缩略语简洁明了，信息容量大，使用方便。使用缩略语既能节省篇幅，又能节省时间、提高效率。缩略语通常用较少的语言表达丰富而复杂的内容，传达更多的信息，因此在商贸英语文本中，特别是一些文书文本中得以广泛运用。通常采用首字母缩写，组成缩略语。商贸英语中缩略语的使用主要表现在以下几个方面。

（1）机构、组织、公司等名称

商贸英语中，常常涉及或重复出现国际、组织、公司名称，而其全称往往过于冗长。因此，一些广为人知的机构、组织和世界著名公司名称通常使用缩略语。例如：

APEC=Asia-Pacific Economic Cooperation 亚太经合组织
ASEAN=Association of Southeast Asian Nations 东南亚国家联盟公约
CMEA=Council for Mutual Economic Aid 经互会
EEC=European Economic Community 欧共体
EU=European Union 欧洲联盟
G20 =Group of Twenty 20 国集团
IATA=International Air Transport Association 国际航空运输协会
ICC =The International Chamber of Commerce 国际商会
IDA =International Development Association 国际开发协会
IFA=International Franchise Association 国际特许经营加盟协会
IFC=International Finance Corporation 国际金融公司
IMF=International Monetary Fund 国际货币基金组织
IMC=International Maritime Committee 国际海事委员会
IMO=International Maritime Organization 国际海事组织
ITT=International Telephone and Telegraph 国际电话电报公司

OPEC=The Organization of Petroleum Exporting Countries 石油输出国组织
PNOC=Philippine National Oil Company 菲律宾国家石油公司
UNDP=United Nations Development Program 联合国开发计划署
WFP=World Food Program 世界粮食计划署
WHO=World Health Organization 世界卫生组织
WIPO=World Intellectual Property Organization 世界知识产权组织
WTCA=World Trade Center Association 世界贸易中心协会
WTO=World Trade Organization 世界贸易组织

（2）货币和度量衡

商贸活动中，询盘、发盘、合同签订、装运货物，无不涉及货币和度量衡的名称。相较于其他文体的语言，商贸文本使用货币和度量衡的频率最高。在商贸英语文本中，它们通常以缩略语的形式出现。例如：

AUD	AUstralian Dollar	澳大利亚元
BEF	BElgischer Franc	比利时法郎
CAD	CAnadian Dollar	加拿大元
CHF	sCHweizer Franken	瑞士法郎
CNY	ChiNese Yuan	人民币
DEM	DEutsche Mark	德国马克
FRF	FRench Franc	法国法郎
GBP	Great Britain Pound	英镑
HKD	Hong Kong Dollar	港元
JPY	Japanese Yen	日元
NLG	NetherLandish Guilder	荷兰盾
USD	United States Dollar	美元
Kg	Kilogram	千克
Gal	Gallon	加仑
In	Inch	英尺
Q.ty	Quantity	数量

PCTG	Percentage	百分比
Min	Minimum	最小
Max	Maximum	最大

（3）贸易术语

贸易术语是商贸英语所特有的，也是固定的表达方式。商贸英语中有种类繁多的贸易术语，往往以缩略语的形式出现，有时短短的一句话甚至会出现几个缩写名称。如：

AAR	against all risks	一切险
A/O	account of	进某账户
A/P	authority of purchase	委托购买证
B/C	bill for collection	托收票据
B/L	bill of lading	提单
C/N	credit note	收款通知
CIF	cost, insurance and freight	成本、保险加运费（到岸价）
CFR	cost and fright	成本加运费
D/A	document against acceptance	承兑交单
D/D	demand draft	即期汇票
D/P	document against payment	付款交单
FOB	free on board	离岸价
F.P.A.	free from particular average	平安险
L/C	letter of credit	信用证
M/O	money order	汇款单
P/L	packing list	装箱单、明细表
S/C	sales contract	销售确认书
TT	telegraphic transfer	电汇
W.A.	with particular average	水渍险

【例1】We are prepared to accept payment by confirmed irrevocable L/C available by draft at sight instead of T/T reimbursement.

【译文】我们不接受电汇付款，只接受保兑的不可撤销的即期信用证。

【例2】The Bank of China declined to negotiate the payment because the B/L weight differs from that as stipulated in the L/C.

【译文】中国银行拒绝议付，因为提单重量和信用证规定不符。

B. 专业词汇

专业词汇常常用来表达某些特定的功能，阐释各种各样的条款。商贸业务中的专业词汇可分成两类：一类是源于普通英语的词汇，在语言发展过程中逐渐丰富了自身的含义。除了通常的含义外，这些词汇还具备与贸易相关的某些特殊意义。经过频繁使用后，它们成为贸易领域惯用的词汇。另一类是针对性强、语意准确的专业词汇，这类词汇很难引起任何误解，具有权威性。例如：

accept	承兑
charter (the chartered ship)	租船
collect	托收
consignee	收货人
coverage	险别
customs duty	关税
delivery	交货
document	单证
dumping	商品倾销
export credit	出口信贷
forward	发货
freight	运费
inquiry	询盘
landing charges	卸货费
literature	书面材料
negotiation	议付
net price	净价
offer	要约

protest	拒付
retirement	赎单
shipment	装运、装船
shipper, consignor	托运人
special preferences	优惠关税
stamp duty	印花税
total value	总值
wharfage	码头费

C. 古体词

在商贸英语中，古体词也广泛用于商贸法律合同或文件。古体词能避免重复，使句子结构紧凑精炼，体现商贸文体规范正式的特征。例如：

hereby	特此，因此
hereof	关于此点、在本文件中
hereto	对此，至此
herein	此中，于此
hereinafter	以下，在下文
hereunder	在本合约内
thereof	它的，其
whereas	鉴于，然而，尽管
whereby	由此
whereof	关于那个
wherein	在那方面
wheresoever	无论何处
thereafter	此后
thereto	向那里

D. 词语叠用

商贸英语的另一个词汇特征是同义词或近义词的叠用，这一特点在商贸合同中尤为明显。这种叠用确保了合同文本中词语的含义不被曲解，并使原文意思高度完整、准确，更好地体现出合同的严肃性。例如：

alter and change	变更
agent or representative	代表
before and on	在……之前
bind and oblige	承担
claim or allegation	主张
covenants and agreements	契约
in full force and effect	生效
final and conclusive	唯一的
force and effect	效力
from and above	上述
fulfill or perform	履行
furnish and provide	提供
goods and chattels	个人动产
lose or damage	灭失或损坏
make and enter into	达成
power and authority	权利
procure and ensure	确保
release and discharge	弃权
right and interest	权益
save and except	除了
sole and exclusive	唯一的
terms and conditions	条款
when and as	当……时候

【例 3】It is the intent of the parties that all documents and annexes forming part hereof shall be read and taken together and that <u>each and every</u> <u>provision or stipulation</u> hereof be given <u>full force, effect and applicability</u>. However, in the event that one or more <u>provisions or stipulations</u> herein be declared <u>null and void</u> by the courts, or otherwise rendered ineffective, the remaining <u>provisions and stipulations</u> shall not be affected thereby.

上述例句中，近义词或同义词叠用达七处之多。由此可见，词语叠用的确是商贸合同文本的语言特征之一。

5.2.2 句法特征

A. 句型多变

商贸函电的交流极其注重表达效果的准确性、时效性和逻辑性。因此，商贸函电英语句式最突出的特点是语句简洁连贯，多使用短句、简单句、并列句以达到省时和清楚的目的。

【例4】As requested, we are now offering you as follows subject to our final confirmation.

【译文】应贵方要求，现报盘如下，以最终确认为准。

【例5】Partial shipments and transshipment allowed.

【译文】允许分批装运和转运。

然而，贸易合同或条款却频繁使用结构复杂的长句、复合句、并列复合句或包含许多分词短语、从句，从而使句子显得更加正式，避免歧义。

【例6】Any dispute, controversy or claim arising out of or relating to this Contract, or the breach, termination or invalidity thereof, shall be settled through amicable negotiation, in case no settlement can be reached through negotiation, the case shall then be submitted for arbitration.

【译文】由于本合同或者由于违反本合同、终止本合同或者本合同无效而发生的或与此有关的任何争端、争议或索赔，双方应通过友好协商解决；若协商不能解决，应提交仲裁。

【例7】The parties are considered, unless otherwise agreed, to have impliedly made applicable to which in international trade is widely known to, and regularly observed by, parties to contracts of the type involved in the particular trade concerned.

【译文】除非另有约定，应是双方当事人为默认地同意对他们的合同或合同订立双方当事人已知或理应知道的惯例，而这种惯例在国际贸易中已受有关特定行业所设计同类合同的当事人广为知道并遵守。

B. 规范正式

商贸领域是一个非常严谨的领域，因此商贸英语也就必须严谨而规范。在商贸英语中，尤其是对双方具有法律约束力的商贸合同中，其句式规范严谨，以避免产生误解和歧义，也为了显示合同的严肃性。

【例8】<u>Should</u> you desire, we would <u>be pleased to</u> send you catalogs together with export prices and estimated shipping costs for these items.

【译文】若贵方需要，本公司将乐意邮寄目录以及这些项目的出口价格以及预估的运输费。

【例9】If the credit does not so stipulate, banks will accept such documents as presented, <u>provided that</u> their data content makes it possible to relate the goods and/or services referred to <u>therein</u> to those referred to, in the commercial invoice(s) presented or to those referred to in the credit if the credit does not stipulate presentation of a commercial invoice.

【例10】If <u>either</u> of the Parties <u>fails to</u> fulfill its obligations under this Contract, <u>it shall</u> compensate the other party for all its economic losses resulting <u>thereof</u>.

解析：例10中，either 的使用指明了应该承担责任的一方，意思明确。it shall 解释了在何种情况下双方应该承担责任，表述规范严谨，不存在含糊其辞。而 fails to，thereof 这些词通常只出现在正式文体中，这些词汇的使用使句子更加正式规范。

【例11】Documents against Acceptance: After shipment, the Seller shall draw <u>a sight bill of exchange</u>, <u>payable 10 days</u> after the Seller delivers the document through Sellers bank to the Buyer against acceptance (D/A 10 days). The Buyer shall make the payment on date of the bill of Exchange.

解析：本句中，a sight bill of exchange 后使用短语 payable 10 days 来代替一个定语从句（which can be paid），而在这个短语后还用 after 引导了一个介宾从句，短语加从句的结构使句子结构清晰、简洁明了、严谨而规范。shall 这个词通常适用于正式文体中，它的使用使句子显得更加规范。规范严谨的构句能更加准确地传递商贸英语的信息，同时能避免商贸交易中不必要的损失。例如：

C. 使用套话

经贸文本具有程式化的显著特点，不管是信函还是合同都有固定的格式，使用类似的套话。同时，商贸文本作为信息型文本既要简明直接，又要礼貌得体。商贸信函涉及买卖双方的权利、义务和利害关系，因此礼貌是商贸信函的基本原则，但同时又要避免过于亲密。商贸英语信函类文本在交往中形成了一套国际上通用并认可的公式化句型，多用情态动词构成礼貌性的套话。例如：

Always pleasure at your service. 竭诚为您服务。

Best wishes. 致以真诚问候。

I am looking forward to… 期待着您的……

In reply to your letter of…, we … 兹复贵方……来函，我方……

Please accept my sincere appreciation for… 请接受我方的真挚谢意。

Thank you in advance for… 承蒙……谨先致谢。

Through the courtesy of… 承蒙好意……

We are sorry for the inconvenience that may have caused you. 对给贵方造成的不便我方深表歉意。

We have/ take pleasure in informing you that… 兹欣告贵方……

We hope to receive your favor at an early date/a favorable reply per return mail. 盼复/即复为盼。

We shall appreciate your…若能……我方将不胜感激。

We thank you for your letter of…contents of which have been noted/have had our careful attention. 谢谢贵方……月……日来信，内

容已悉。

We have duly received your letter dated... 我方已及时收到贵方……信函。

D. 被动句

商贸英语中被动语态比较常见，除了由动词构成的被动结构，还经常使用 it 引导的被动结构，表达含蓄委婉的语气。有时也使用表示被动意义的形容词，以达到和被动语态类似的修辞效果。

【例 12】We have been informed that you are in the market of textiles.

【例 13】The two arbitrators shall be selected within thirty (30) days after giving or receiving of the request for arbitration.

【例 14】This Agreement is executed in Chinese. If necessary, it may be translated into other languages.

【例 15】It should be recognized that the intent of this agreement is to benefit both participants.

5.2.3 语篇特征

从语言层面看，商贸文本的语篇体现出内容全面、结构分明和纲目完整等特征。从形式层面看，商贸文本具有格式化的显著特征，并且可以依据文本功能划分成具有不同固定格式的范本，有些只需在原有的文本格式上填入相应的具体内容即可，比如信用证、商贸信函以及商贸合同等等。

A. 信用证

信用证是指开证银行应申请人（买方）的要求并按其指示向受益人开立的载有一定金额的、在一定的期限内凭符合规定的单据付款的书面保证文件。它是贸易商最重要的信用保证方法。从意义上讲，信用证是一项约定，它对双方均有约束力。其用词正规、严谨、专业性强，具有法律文书的语言特色。以下是一份不可撤销信用证范文。

IRREVOCABLE LETTER OF CREDIT

Irrevocable Credit No. _____ Date:

All drafts drawn must be marked: "Drawn under Credit No. _____"

Messrs. _____ (Beneficiary)

Gentlemen:

You are hereby authorized to value on the (bank), of the City of _____, State of _____, for any sum or sums up to the aggregate of _____ ($) dollars.

For the account of _____ available by your drafts at (specify) days sight.

Drafts are to be accepted only against delivery of the following documents: _____

Documents of title must be dated not later than _____, 20___. All drafts against this credit are to be drawn and negotiated before (date).

We hereby agree with the drawers, endorsers, and bona fide holders of drafts drawn in compliance with the terms of this credit that they shall be honored on presentation.

Yours faithfully,

Signature _____

B. 商贸信函

商贸信函属于商务礼仪文书，指企业间在各种商务场合或商务往来过程中所使用的简便书信。商贸信函的格式主要包括信头、日期、收信人姓名和地址、正文、结尾客套语、签名等等。从语篇风格层面看，英汉商贸信函应做到正确（correctness）、全面（completeness）、具体（concreteness）、清楚（clearness）、简洁（conciseness）、礼貌（courtesy）、体谅（consideration），也称 7C

原则。下面是一封报价信函范文。

Dear Sirs,

    We are pleased to make you an offer regarding our "Swinger" dresses and trouser suits in the sizes you require. Nearly all the models you saw at our fashion show are obtainable, except trouser suits in pink, of which the smaller sizes have been sold out. This line is being manufactured continuously, but will only be available again in February, so could be delivered to you in March.

    All other models can be supplied by the middle of January, subject to our receiving your firm order by 15th November. Our CIF prices are understood to be for sea/land transport to Chicago. If you would prefer the goods to be sent by air freight, this will be charged extra at cost.

① Trouser suits sizes 8-16 in white, yellow, red, turquoise, navy blue, black.

    Sizes 12-14 in pink .　　　　　　　per 100 US $ 2,650.00

② Swinger dresses sizes 8-16 in white, yellow, red, turquoise, black.

    Per 100 US $ 1,845.00

    Price: valid until 31st December

    Delivery: CIF Chicago

    Transport: sea freight

    Payment: by irrevocable letter of credit, or check with order.

    You will be receiving cuttings of our materials and a color chart. They were airmailed to you this morning.

    We hope you agree that our prices are very competitive for these good quality clothes, and look forward to receiving your initial order.

Yours faithfully,
(Signature)

C. 商贸合同

商贸合同在性质上属于法律文献，规定了买卖双方之间的权利和义务，给出争议的解决方式，预防双方的漏洞。因此，商贸合同内容缜密，结构完整，语气正式，措辞严谨，以免产生歧义、误解或纠纷。商贸合同由合同名称、合同前文、合同正文和结尾条款组成。

5.3 商贸文本翻译的原则与解析

5.3.1 商贸文本翻译的原则

作为中国与世界其他国家商贸交流纽带和桥梁的商贸翻译，近年来需求与要求的矛盾更加突出。中国的国际交流与合作的领域不断扩大，商贸汉英互译的任务日趋繁多，令各行各业译者应接不暇。没接触过商贸英语、也缺乏商贸业务知识的译者，恐怕难以有效地从事商贸英汉互译工作。然而，译者具备了英语技能和国际商贸知识之后，还必须掌握商贸汉英翻译的原则和技巧。商贸文本词汇专业性强，语体规范正式，语句简洁，翻译过程中必须遵循"忠实、准确和统一"的原则。另外，商贸活动的参与者文化背景不尽相同，译者需要时刻牢记文化差异对语言各层面的影响，翻译不仅要关注语言信息的忠实和准确，更要关注文化信息的对等。

"忠实"是商贸汉英翻译工作者坚守的第一条翻译原则。与文学翻译的"忠实"标准相比，商贸汉英翻译的"忠实"不涉及原文与译文之间的结构、寓意、正反与反正表达、词汇的轻重程度，只要求译文正确传递原文信息，要求原文读者获得的信息与译文读者获得的信息等值。这是翻译起码应该做到的。商贸汉英翻译缺乏"忠实"，就会曲解原义，误导译文读者，最终造成双方误解，引发商贸纠纷。

商贸翻译的"准确"原则，主要是规定原文与译文术语概念上的准确传递，而并不要求表面用词和结构的对应。要做到翻译的"准确",译者就应扎实地学习汉英语言知识和商贸专业知识。同样一个概念在不同的语言环境中需要不同的表达。译者把握翻译的"准确",就等于使原文的文字在译文中顺利而贴切到位,依靠照抄汉英字典的释义来做翻译,是不可能做好商贸翻译的,更不可能达到"准确"的标准。商贸汉英翻译的"统一"原则,就是汉英翻译过程中译名、概念、术语在任何时候都应保持统一,不允许将同一概念或术语随意变换译名。

商贸英语翻译者不仅要有扎实的汉语和英语知识基础以及高超的英汉互译技巧,而且必须具备较好的国际商贸知识,同时还需要有较好的本民族文化和英语文化知识。尽管文化信息传递过程中可能会出现这样或那样的信息流失,翻译对不同文化的传递、介绍起了至关重要的作用。只有通过翻译才有可能使一国的文化遗产为全世界的人所共享。文化信息的传递是完全可能的。我们了解他国文化,主要是通过翻译。文化信息的对等也是可能的,人类文明发展到今天,除了本民族文化的自身发展,还有一个很大的因素就是不同民族文化的互相渗透,加上人类思维的共性,使我们对周围大千世界的认识有不谋而合的相似点。为了达到文化上的对等,译者必须在翻译中做调整。在以下情况下,可以做出调整:(1)原文可能引起译文读者误解;(2)原文在译文读者看来可能毫无意义;(3)译文"语义过载"而不能为一般读者看懂。

5.3.2 商贸文本汉译解析

【例 16】 A confirmed irrevocable letter of credit shall be established within 30 days after the conclusion of the contract and such letter of credit should be maintained at least 30 days after the month of shipment for the negotiation of the relative draft. If the Buyers fail to provide such letter of credit in the Seller's favor as prescribed above, the Seller shall have the option of reselling the contracted goods for the account of the Buyers or delaying any shipment and/or canceling any orders at any time on the Buyers' account and risk.

解析：这段文字仅有两个句子，但与商贸英语相关的词 confirmed, irrevocable letter of credit, conclusion of the contract, shipment, negotiation, draft, in the Seller's favor, reselling the contracted goods and for the account of the Buyers 却占了这段文字的绝大部分。在商贸文本中，这些词语具有完全不同于其普通意义的特殊意义。例如，我们熟知的"negotiation"的含义为"协商、谈判"，而在本句的意思是"议付"；"confirm"的一般含义为"确认"，而在本句中的意思是"保兑"，"a confirmed letter of credit"为"保兑信用证"；"draft"的含义也不再是"草稿"，而是"提单"。在翻译过程中，译者必须把握住原文的语义信息和文体信息，确保能正确识别出这些区别于其普通含义的专业术语，并找到与之语义对等的词，从而做到准确无误地传递信息，实现文本的功能。

【译文】保兑的和不可撤销的信用证必须在合约签订之后三十天内开立。而且，该信用证必须在货物付运之后至少三十天内继续有效，以便议付有关汇票。如果买方未能向卖方提供如上规定的信用证，卖方有权选择转售合约规定为买方的货物，或推迟付运和(或)随时撤销任何订单，损失和风险由买方承担。

【例 17】The Buyer shall have the right to claim against the Seller for compensation of losses within 45 days after arrival of the goods at the port of destination, should the quality of the goods be found not in conformity with the specifications stipulated in the Contract after re-inspection by the China Commodity Inspection Bureau. The Buyer shall have the right to claim against the Seller for compensation of short weight within 45 days after arrival of the goods at the port of destination, should the weight be found not in conformity with that stipulated in the Bill of Lading after re-inspection by CCIB.

解析：这段话包含两个句子，每个句子由相同的从句结构组成：主句在前，后面加一个由"should"引导的条件状语。这两个条件状语又有一个时间状语"within 45 days after arrival of the goods at the port of destination"，形成从句套从句的结构。翻译过程中，译者调整了句子结构，将"should"引导的条件状语放在前，主句在后，并将时间状语融入主句中。以功能文体学为指导的翻译原则注重译入语读者的接受程度，此番调整符合汉语的表达习惯，更利于中文读者理解。这就要求译者不仅要传达原文的信息，做到信息对等，还要迎合读者的语言习惯，让读者充分接受原文的信息。

【译文】若货物经中国商品检验局复检后发现质量与本合同之规定不符，买方有权与货物抵达目的港后的 45 天向卖方提出索赔。若货物经中国商品检验局复检后发现货物重量与提单所示重量不符，买方有权于货物抵达目的港后的 45 天向卖方提出短重索赔。

【例 18】Know-how shall mean all the manufacturing technology and process engineering to manufacture the contract products which are required by Party A and which Party B possesses. Such technology engineering shall include technical details of all designs, operation drawings, technical documentations, manufacturing engineering, procedure and techniques.

解析：这段文字来源于一份商贸合同。在这个句子中包含多个分词短语、连词，组成了复杂的句子结构。商贸合同通常使用长句以显示其句法特征和文体正式。在翻译过程中，译者应尽量保留这些特征，以实现译文和原文在功能和文体方面的统一。

【译文】专有技术指所有乙方拥有甲方需要的用于生产本合同产品的生产技术和工艺技术。该技术应包括具体设计、操作图纸、技术文件、生产工艺、流程和方法。

【例 19】The easiest way to establish credit is to open checking and savings accounts at your local bank. Then apply for a gasoline or store credit card. These cards are fairly easy to get because retailers want you to buy their goods and services. The third step, and the most dangerous one, is obtaining a major credit card like Visa, MarsterCard, or American Express.

解析：从逻辑关系来看，读者会以为要取得信贷，必须经过三个步骤，缺一不可，即先到银行开户，然后申请加油信用卡或商店信用卡，第三步才是获得主流信用卡。这样的理解是由于缺乏英语国家的信贷知识。实际上通过任何一个都可以获得信贷。原文中的衔接性词语 The easiest way，Then，The third step 并不是指获得信贷的三种不同的途径。语言是文化的载体。商贸英语在交易双方交流过程中蕴含着特定文化信息的传递。由于不同民族有着不同的历史背景、风俗习惯和文化传统，这种文化差异的客观存在对商贸活动必然产生影响。有了足够的背景知识，就能更容易地呈现出原文衔接词语所传达的语义，进而实现译文与原文文化信息的对等。

【译文】取得信贷最便捷的途径是在当地银行开立支票账户和储蓄账户。第二个途径是申请一张加油信用卡或商店信用卡，由于零售商希望出售他们的商品或服务，这类信用卡极易获得。第三个途径是风险最大的途径，即申请一张主流信用卡，如维萨卡、万事达信用卡或美国运通卡。

5.3.3 商贸文本英译解析

【例 20】对外开放取得新进展。2006 年共批准"三资"企业 200 家，全省"三资"企业已达到 550 家。

解析："三资"是中国特色的表达方式，是指侨资、外资、中外合资的合称。翻译过程中，如果按字面直译成"Three Ventures"，英文读者从中无法获得任何信息，甚至会引起困惑。因此，译者需要对这一特有的文化意象进行解释："Three Forms of Ventures" (Sino-foreign joint ventures, cooperative enterprises and wholly foreign-funded enterprises)，括号中的解释性文字能有效地帮助译语读者获得充分的信息，也帮助译者在商贸英语翻译中传递文化意象，保证文化信息的对等，以促成贸易的顺利进行。如果在形式上贴近的译文对所指文化意象可能产生误解的话，必须对译文文字做某些变通；可以保留直译，但必须加上脚注来解释可能产生的误解。上述通过直译加注的方法，既对词语的指称意义做了说明，又巧妙地保持了原文的语言风格，文化意象也得到了传递。

【译文】New progress has been made in the process of opening to

the outside world. In 2006, the province approved 200 "Three Forms of Ventures" (Sino-foreign joint ventures, cooperative enterprises and wholly foreign-funded enterprises), the total number of the "Three Forms of Ventures" reached 550.

【例21】贵公司迫切要求我方早日安排直达轮船以确保及时交货,我们对此已进行详细讨论。但令人遗憾的是,由于最近订不到上海至利物浦之间的直达货船,因此有必要在香港转运,但我们仍会抓紧办理。

解析:该例句是卖方针对买方有关装运问题做出的回复。按照原文的句式,第一个句子包含两个主语"贵公司"和"我们",而第二个句子是无主句。显然,这不符合英语的表达习惯。按照英语的表达思路,"贵公司迫切要求"后面可以跟一个宾语从句从而作为主语:"Your urgent request for early shipment to ensure prompt delivery";"我方对此已进行详细讨论"可以理解为"我方已经详细地讨论了这些事情",把"讨论"用作动词,整个句子使用完成时;"因此有必要在香港转运"可以译成一个含有结果原因从句的主句,并适当地增补主语"我们"。要体现商贸文本精简的特征,能够用短语者应优先使用短语,而非小句和长句。

【译文】Your urgent request for early shipment to ensure prompt delivery has been given every consideration. To our regret there is no shipping direct from Shanghai to Liverpool, it is necessary to ship first to Hongkong and then to Liverpool. Nevertheless, we will do all we can to expedite immediate shipment and do not anticipate late delivery.

【例22】按贵方要求改变包装另需不少时间,港口装卸业务繁忙导致该单卸货延迟,所有货品检验又得等候数日,我们因此未能在合同的规定的日期完成交货。

解析:该例句是卖方对未能及时交货做出的一个合理的解释。从原文来看,前三个小句是原因状语,卖方要承担不能及时交货的后果。据此,用"我们"做主语,将主句译成"we were therefore unable to have the goods delivered within the contracted period",这不失为一种译法。但是，换个角度，将句子中前三个小句视作一个主语部分，是导致卖方不能及时交货的行为者。据此，译者将原文的长句拆分成了四个简单句，分别采用主语"Changing the packing of the products""Considerable congestion in the port""Testing and examining the cargo"和"These combined factors"，实现了句子的表达功能。同时，第二种译法表达相对缓和，让读者了解到是由于前面三个客观原因才导致交货不及时，可以有效避免卖方处于首当其冲的境地，对实现商贸文本的社交功能起到一定作用。

【译文】Changing the packing of the products in accordance with your instructions required a lot of time. Considerable congestion in the port delayed unloading your order. Testing and examining the cargo needed several more days. These combined factors resulted in our failure to have the goods delivered with in the contracted period.

【例23】双方均已同意，至于目前洽谈的补偿贸易方案，将由甲方全面负责在规定限期内完成机器设备的安装调试任务，至该厂在生产质量上和数量上都能达到规定的标准时，乙方应当接收并以上述机器生产的产品偿还该机器的价款。

解析：该例句来自于贸易合同中的补偿条款。例句由一个长句子组成，是典型的商贸文本。中文句式常常采用"竹"结构，在本句中，主语相对模糊，较难确定。翻译过程中，译者重组了句子结构，使之成为了英语惯用的"树"结构。"双方均已同意"由汉语的完整句子降为了英语中的条件从句；"甲方"做了第一个句子的主语，采用主动态；"乙方"为第二个句子的主语，句式为被动态，主语成为动作的承受者，强调了责任的最终承受者，表达更为客观，语气更加委婉。由此可见，译者采用将主动语态与被动语态相结合加条件从句的句式，完整再现了原文的信息。同时，被动语态的使用体现出该文本正式规范的特征，实现了文体的对等。英国翻译家Peter Newmark（2001）的观点值得借鉴，他认为，最有效的翻译步骤就是首先发现句子的逻辑主语，然后是具体的动词，最后其他成分才好各归其位。

【译文】Under the present compensation plan we mutually agreed upon, Party A should assume full responsibility for the installation and pilot runs of the plant equipment and machinery within stipulated periods; Party B shall not be required to accept the plant until it can meet the specified qualitative and quantitative production standards and repayment of the cost of the machine will be made with the products produced with the said machine.

另一方面,语义信息对等和文体信息对等必须服从于文化信息对等。换言之,在语义信息对等和文体信息对等与文化信息对等出现矛盾时,必须以文化信息对等为大局,以商贸功效对等为目的。必须说明,文化信息并不总是由语言承载。换言之,原文中有时没有承载文化信息。这时,译者自然不必考虑文化信息对等。但是,任何时候,译者都必须以商贸功效对等为最高标准,因为所有商贸文本都承载商贸信息。若译文中的语义信息或文体信息或文化信息(如果有的话)没有与原文中这三个方面达到对等,商贸功效对等就将大打折扣。商贸功效对等是以前面三个方面的对等为前提条件的。从另外一个角度来看,译者在翻译商贸文本时,必须时刻牢记译文有其商贸目的。

5.4 商贸文本翻译实例

5.4.1 英译汉实例:International Rules for the Interpretation of Trade Terms (INCOTERMS)[①]

INCOTERMS—FREE ON BOARD
国际贸易术语解释通则——船上交货

FOB (insert named port of shipment)
船上交货(……指定装运港)

---

① 参见:《国际贸易术语解释通则 2010》,第 88-93 页,第 29-32 页。

GUIDANCE NOTE

This rule is to be used only for sea or inland waterway transport.

"Free on Board" means that the seller delivers the goods on board the vessel nominated by the buyer at the named port of shipment or procures the goods already so delivered. The risk of loss of or damage to the goods passes when the goods are on board the vessel, and the buyer bears all costs from that moment onwards.

The seller is required either to deliver the goods on board the vessel or to procure goods already so delivered for shipment. The reference to "procure" here caters for multiple sales down a chain ("string sales"), particularly common in the commodity trades.

FOB may not be appropriate where goods are handed over to the carrier before they are on board the vessel, for example goods in containers, which are typically delivered at a terminal. In such situations, the FCA rule should be used.

FOB requires the seller to clear the goods for export, where applicable. However, the seller has no obligation to clear the goods for import, pay any import duty or carry out any import customs formalities.

序言

该术语仅适用于海运或内河运输。

船上交货是指当卖方在指定的装运港将货物运至买方指定的船上或取得已按此送交的货物，即完成交货。当货物已运至船上时，货物灭失或损坏的风险发生转移，买方自那时起承担一切费用。

卖方必须将货物运到船上或取得已按此送交准备发运的货物。这里的"取得"适合于多层次链条式销售（线性销售），在商品销售中尤为普遍。

FOB不适用于货物在装船之前移交给承运人的情况，比如集装箱内的货物通常在目的地交付。在这种情况下，应使用FCA术语。

FOB要求在需要办理海关手续时由卖方负责货物出口清关。然而，卖方并没有义务办理货物进口清关、负担任何进口关税或办理任何进口海关手续。

A. THE SELLER'S OBLIGATIONS 卖方义务
A1. General obligations of the seller

The seller must provide the goods and the commercial invoice in conformity with the contract of sale and any other evidence of conformity that may be required by the contract. Any document referred to in A1-A10 may be an equivalent electronic record or procedure if agreed between the parties or customary.

A1. 卖方基本义务

卖方必须提供符合销售合同规定的货物和商业发票以及按照合同约定必需的有同等作用的其他任何凭证，以及经当事人同意或根据交易习惯在A1-A10中提到的任何有同等作用的电子记录或程序的凭证。

A2. Licenses, authorizations, security clearances and other formalities

Where applicable, the seller must obtain, at its own risk and expense, any export licence or other official authorization and carry out all customs formalities necessary for the export of the goods.

A2. 许可、授权、安全许可和其他正式手续

在需要办理清关手续时，卖方必须承担风险和费用获得任何出口许可或其他官方授权，办理货物出口所需的一切海关手续。

A3. Contracts of carriage and insurance

a) Contract of carriage

The seller has no obligation to the buyer to make a contract of carriage. However, if requested by the buyer or if it is commercial practice and the buyer does not give an instruction to the contrary in due time, the seller may contract for carriage on usual terms at the buyer's risk and expense. In either case, the seller may decline to make the contract of carriage and, if it does, shall promptly notify the buyer.

b) Contract of insurance

The seller has no obligation to the buyer to make a contract of insurance. However, the seller must provide the buyer, at the buyer's request, risk, and expense (if any), with information that the buyer needs for obtaining insurance.

A3. 运输合同和保险合同

a) 运输合同

卖方没有义务为买方订立运输合同。但若买方要求，或者如果是商业惯例而买方未适时给予卖方相反指示，则卖方可按照通常条件订立运输合同，费用和风险由买方承担。在任何一种情况下，卖方都可以拒绝订立此合同；如果拒绝，则应立即通知买方。

b) 保险合同

卖方没有义务为买方订立保险合同。但应买方要求并由其承担风险和费用，卖方必须提供给买方办理保险所需的相关信息。

A4. Delivery

The seller must deliver the goods either by placing them on board the vessel nominated by the buyer at the loading point, if any, indicated by the buyer at the named port of shipment or by procuring the goods so delivered. In either case, the seller must deliver the goods on the agreed date or within the agreed period and in the manner customary at the port.

If no specific loading point has been indicated by the buyer, the seller may select the point within the named port of shipment that best suits its purpose.

A4. 交货

卖方必须将在买方指定的装运港，在买方指定的装运地点，在约定日期或期限内，按照该港习惯方式将货物交至买方指定的船上或取得已交运的货物。

若买方没有指定具体交货点，那么卖方可选择指定装运港内最适合其目的的交货点。

A5. Transfer of risks

The seller bears all risks of loss of or damage to the goods until they have been delivered in accordance with A4 with the exception of loss or damage in the circumstances described in B5.

A5. 风险转移

除B5规定者外,卖方必须承担货物灭失或损坏的一切风险,直至已按照A4规定交货为止。

A6. Allocation of costs

The seller must pay:

a) all costs relating to the goods until they have been delivered in accordance with A4, other than those payable by the buyer as envisaged in B6; and b) where applicable, the costs of customs formalities necessary for export, as well as all duties, taxes and other charges payable upon export.

A6. 费用划分

卖方必须支付:

a) 除按照B6规定应由买方支付的费用外,卖方必须支付与货物有关的一切费用,直至已按照A4规定交货为止;在需要办理海关手续时,货物出口应办理的海关手续费用及出口应交纳的一切关税、税款和其他费用。

A7. Notices to the buyer

The seller must, at the buyer's risk and expense, give the buyer sufficient notice either that the goods have been delivered in accordance with A4 or that the vessel has failed to take the goods within the time agreed.

A7. 通知买方

在货物已按照A4规定交付或在约定时间内船舶未能接收货物时,卖方必须给予买方充分通知,由买方承担风险和费用。

A8. Delivery document

The seller must provide the buyer, at the seller's expense, with the usual proof that the goods have been delivered in accordance with A4. Unless such proof is a transport document, the seller must provide assistance to the buyer, at the buyer's request, risk and expense, in obtaining a transport document.

A8. 交货凭证

卖方必须自担费用向买方提供证明已按照A4规定交货的通常单据。如果这些凭证不是运输单据，应买方要求并由其承担风险和费用，卖方必须给予买方协助以取得运输单据。

A9. Checking-packaging-marking

The seller must pay the costs of those checking operations (such as checking quality, measuring, weighing, and counting) that are necessary for the purpose of delivering the goods in accordance with A4, as well as the costs of any pre-shipment inspection mandated by the authority of the country of export. The seller must, at its own expense, package the goods, unless it is usual for the particular trade to transport the type of goods sold unpackaged. The seller may package the goods in the manner appropriate for their transport, unless the buyer has notified the seller of specific packaging requirements before the contract of sale is concluded. Packaging is to be marked appropriately.

A9. 查对、包装、标记

卖方必须支付按照A4规定为了将货物交给买方处置所需进行的查对费用（如查对货物品质、丈量、过磅、点数的费用）以及出口国有关当局在装运前强制检验的费用。卖方必须自付费用包装货物，除非按照相关行业惯例，所售类型的货物通常无需包装发运。卖方应该按照有关货物运输所要求的方式包装货物，除非买方在订立合同前已经通知卖方特殊的包装要求。包装应作适当标记。

A10. Assistance with information and related costs

The seller must, where applicable, in a timely manner, provide to or render assistance in obtaining for the buyer, at the buyer's request, risk and expense, any documents and information, including security-related information, that the buyer needs for the import of the goods and/or for their transport to the final destination. The seller must reimburse the buyer for all costs and charges incurred by the buyer in providing or rendering assistance in obtaining documents and information as envisaged in B10.

A10. 信息协助及相关费用

应买方要求并由其承担风险和费用，在需要办理清关手续时，卖方必须给予买方一切及时的协助，以帮助其取得包括买方为进口货物和/或为使货物运输到最终目的地所需的有关货物安全信息在内的任何凭证和信息。卖方必须偿付买方按照B10规定在卖方获得相关凭证和信息时给予协助所发生的费用。

B. THE BUYER'S OBLIGATIONS 买方义务

B1. General obligations of the buyer

The buyer must pay the price of the goods as provided in the contract of sale.

Any document referred to in B1-B10 may be an equivalent electronic record or procedure if agreed between the parties or customary.

B1. 买方基本义务

买方必须按照销售合同规定支付价款。

以及经当事人同意或根据交易习惯在B1-B10中提到的任何有同等作用的电子记录或程序的凭证。

B2. Licenses, authorizations, security clearances and other formalities

Where applicable, it is up to the buyer to obtain, at its own risk and expense, any import license or other official authorization and carry out all customs formalities for the import of the goods and for their transport through any country.

B2. 许可、授权、安全许可和其他正式手续

在需要办理清关手续时，由买方自担风险和费用获得任何进口

许可或其他官方授权，并负责办理货物进口和从他国过境的一切海关手续。

B3. Contracts of carriage and insurance

a) Contract of carriage

The buyer must contract, at its own expense, for the carriage of the goods from the named port of shipment, except where the contract of carriage is made by the seller as provided for in A3 a).

b) Contract of insurance

The buyer has no obligation to the seller to make a contract of insurance.

B3. 运输合同和保险合同

a) 运输合同

买方必须自付费用订立自指定装运港运输货物的合同，卖方按照A3 a）订立了运输合同时除外。

b) 保险合同

买方没有义务为卖方订立保险合同。

B4. Taking delivery

The buyer must take delivery of the goods when they have been delivered as envisaged in A4.

B4. 受领货物

买方必须在卖方按照A4规定交货时，受领货物。

B5. Transfer of risks

The buyer bears all risks of loss of or damage to the goods from the time they have been delivered as envisaged in A4.

If a) the buyer fails to notify the nomination of a vessel in accordance with B7; or

b) the vessel nominated by the buyer fails to arrive on time to enable the seller to comply with A4, is unable to take the goods, or closes for cargo earlier than the time notified in accordance with B7; then, the buyer bears all risks of loss of or damage to the goods:

(i) from the agreed date, or in the absence of an agreed date,

(ii) from the date notified by the seller under A7 within the agreed period, or, if no such date has been notified,

(iii) from the expiry date of any agreed period for delivery, provided that the goods have been clearly identified as the contract goods.

B5. 风险转移

买方必须承担自按照A4规定交货之时起货物灭失或损坏的一切风险。

a) 如果买方未按照B7规定就指定的船只给予卖方相应通知；

b) 或当自约定的交货日期或并未约定日期；自买方按照A7规定指定的约定期限内的日期起或买方并未指定该日期；或自交货期限届满之日起（但以该项货物已正式划归合同项下为限），买方指定的船只未能按时到达致使卖方未能按照A4规定交货，或未能接收货物或较按照B7通知的时间提早停止运输货物，买方承担货物灭失或损坏的一切风险。

B6. Allocation of costs

The buyer must pay:

a) all costs relating to the goods from the time they have been delivered as envisaged in A4, except, where applicable, the costs of customs formalities necessary for export, as well as all duties, taxes and other charges payable upon export as referred to in A6 b);

b) any additional costs incurred, either because:

(i) the buyer has failed to give appropriate notice in accordance with B7, or

(ii) the vessel nominated by the buyer fails to arrive on time, is unable to take the goods, or closes for cargo earlier than the time notified in accordance with B7, provided that the goods have been clearly identified as the contract goods; and

c) where applicable, all duties, taxes and other charges, as well as the costs of carrying out customs formalities payable upon import of the goods and the costs for their transport through any country.

B6. 费用划分

买方必须支付：

a) 自按照A4规定交货之时起与货物有关的一切费用，以及在需要办理海关手续时，货物出口所需办理海关手续的费用和按照A6 b)规定在货物出口时应交纳的一切关税、税款和其他费用。

b) 在买方未能按照B7规定给予卖方适当通知，或买方指定的船只未能按时到达，或未能接收货物，或较按照B7通知的时间提早停止运输货物时，买方应承担所发生的一切额外费用，但以该项货物已正式划归合同项下为限。

c) 在需要办理海关手续时，货物进口应交纳的一切关税、税款和其他费用，以及办理海关手续的费用和从他国过境的费用。

B7. Notices to the seller

The buyer must give the seller sufficient notice of the vessel name, loading point and, where necessary, the selected delivery time within the agreed period.

B7. 通知卖方

买方必须就指定船只名称、装运点和必要时约定期限内的指定交货时间给予卖方充分通知。

B8. Proof of delivery

The buyer must accept the proof of delivery provided as envisaged in A8.

B8. 交货证明

买方必须接受卖方按照A8规定所提供的交货证明。

B9. Inspection of goods

The buyer must pay the costs of any mandatory pre-shipment inspection, except when such inspection is mandated by the authorities of the country of export.

B9. 货物检验

买方必须支付任何装运前强制检验的费用，出口国有关当局强制进行的检验除外。

B10. Assistance with information and related costs

The buyer must, in a timely manner, advise the seller of any security information requirements so that the seller may comply with A10.

The buyer must reimburse the seller for all costs and charges incurred by the seller in providing or rendering assistance in obtaining documents and information as envisaged in A10.

The buyer must, where applicable, in a timely manner, provide to or render assistance in obtaining for the seller, at the seller's request, risk and expense, any documents and information, including security-related information, that the seller needs for the transport and export of the goods and for their transport through any country.

B10. 信息协助及相关费用

买方必须及时通知卖方以便其按照A10规定提供任何必要的安全信息。

买方必须偿付卖方按照A10规定在买方获得相关凭证和信息时给予协助所发生的费用。

应卖方要求并由其承担风险和费用，在需要办理清关手续时，买方必须给予卖方一切及时的协助，以帮助其取得包括卖方为货物运输和出口和必要时从他国过境所需的有关货物安全信息在内的任何凭证和信息。

5.4.2 汉译英实例：

合同

Sales Contract

合同编号：_____

签订日期：_____

签订地点：_____

买方：_____

地址：_____

电话：_____

传真：_____

电子邮箱：_____

卖方：_____

地址：_____

电话：_____

传真：_____

电子邮箱：_____

Contract No.: _____

Date: _____

Signed at: _____

The Buyer: _____

Address: _____

Tel: _____

Fax: _____

E-mail: _____

The Seller: _____

Address: _____

Tel: _____

Fax: _____

E-mail: _____

买卖双方同意按照下列条款签订本合同：

The Seller and the Buyer agree to conclude this Contract subject to the terms and conditions stated below:

1. 货物名称、规格和质量

1. Name, Specifications and Quality of Commodity

2. 数量

允许_____的溢短装

2. Quantity

_____ % more or less allowed

3. 单价

3. Unit Price

4. 总值

4. Total Amount

5. 交货条件

5. Terms of Delivery

6. 原产地国与制造商

6. Country of Origin and Manufacturers

7. 包装及标准

货物应具有防潮、防锈蚀、防震并适合于远洋运输的包装,由于货物包装不良而造成的货物残损、灭失应由卖方负责。卖方应在每个包装箱上用不褪色的颜色标明尺码、包装箱号码、毛重、净重及"此端向上""防潮""小心轻放"等标记。

7. Packing

The packing of the goods shall be preventive from dampness, rust, moisture, erosion and shock, and shall be suitable for ocean transportation/multiple transportation. The Seller shall be liable for any damage and loss of the goods attributable to the inadequate or improper packing. The measurement, gross weight, net weight and the cautions such as "Do not stack up side down", "Keep away from moisture", "Handle with care" shall be stenciled on the surface of each package with fadeless pigment.

8. 唛头

8. Shipping Marks

9. 装运期限

9. Time of Shipment

10. 装运口岸

10. Port of Loading

11. 目的口岸

11. Port of Destination

12. 保险

由_____按发票金额110%投保_____险和_____附加险。

12. Insurance

Insurance shall be covered by the _____ for 110% of the invoice value against _____ Risks and _____ Additional Risks.

13. 付款条件

（1）信用证方式：买方应在装运期前/合同生效后_____日，开出以卖方为受益人的不可撤销的议付信用证，信用证在装船完毕后_____日内到期。

（2）付款交单：货物发运后，卖方出具以买方为付款人的付款跟单汇票，按即期付款交单（D/P）方式，通过卖方银行及____银行向买方转交单证，换取货物。

（3）承兑交单：货物发运后，卖方出具以买方为付款人的付款跟单汇票，付款期限为____后____日，按即期承兑交单（D/A____日）方式，通过卖方银行及_____银行，经买方承兑后，向买方转交单证，买方在汇票期限到期时支付货款。

（4）货到付款：买方在收到货物后____天内将全部货款支付卖方（不适用于FOB、CRF、CIF术语）。

13. Terms of Payment

(1)Letter of Credit: The Buyer shall, _____ days prior to the time of shipment/after this Contract comes into effect, open an irrevocable Letter of Credit in favor of the Seller. The Letter of Credit shall expire ____ days after the completion of loading of the shipment as stipulated.

(2) Documents against payment: After shipment, the Seller shall draw a sight bill of exchange on the Buyer and deliver the documents through Sellers bank and _____ Bank to the Buyer against payment, i.e D/P. The Buyer shall effect the payment immediately upon the first

presentation of the bill(s) of exchange.

(3) Documents against Acceptance: After shipment, the Seller shall draw a sight bill of exchange, payable _____ days after the Buyers delivers the document through Seller's bank and _____ Bank to the Buyer against acceptance (D/A ___ days). The Buyer shall make the payment on date of the bill of exchange.

(4) Cash on delivery (COD): The Buyer shall pay to the Seller total amount within _____ days after the receipt of the goods (This clause is not applied to the Terms of FOB, CFR, CIF).

14. 单据

卖方应将下列单据提交银行议付/托收：

（1）标明通知收货人/受货代理人的全套清洁的、已装船的、空白抬头、空白背书并注明运费已付/到付的海运/联运/陆运提单。

（2）标有合同编号、信用证号（信用证支付条件下）及装运唛头的商业发票一式____份；

（3）由_____出具的装箱或重量单一式____份；

（4）由_____出具的质量证明书一式____份；

（5）由_____出具的数量证明书一式____份；

（6）保险单正本一式____份（CIF 交货条件）；

（7）_____签发的产地证一式____份；

（8）装运通知：卖方应在交运后____小时内以特快专递方式邮寄给买方上述第____项单据副本一式一套。

14. Documents Required

The Seller shall present the following documents required to the bank for negotiation/collection:

(1) Full set of clean on board Ocean/Combined Transportation/Land Bills of Lading and blank endorsed marked freight prepaid/ to collect;

(2) Signed commercial invoice in _____ copies indicating Contract No., L/C No. (Terms of L/C) and shipping marks;

(3) Packing list/weight memo in _____ copies issued by _____;

(4) Certificate of Quality in _____ copies issued by _____;

(5) Certificate of Quantity in _____ copies issued by _____;

(6) Insurance policy/certificate in _____ copies (Terms of CIF);

(7) Certificate of Origin in _____ copies issued by _____;

(8) Shipping advice: The Seller shall, within _____ hours after shipment effected, send by courier each copy of the above-mentioned documents No. _____.

15. 装运条款

（1）FOB 交货方式　　卖方应在合同规定的装运日期前 30 天，以_____方式通知买方合同号、品名、数量、金额、包装件、毛重、尺码及装运港可装日期，以便买方安排租船/订舱。装运船只按期到达装运港后，如卖方不能按时装船，发生的空船费或滞期费由卖方负担。在货物越过船弦并脱离吊钩以前一切费用和风险由卖方负担。

（2）CIF 或 CFR 交货方式　　卖方须按时在装运期限内将货物由装运港装船至目的港。在 CFR 术语下，卖方应在装船前 2 天以_____方式通知买方合同号、品名、发票价值及开船日期，以便买方安排保险。

15. Terms of Shipment

(1) The Seller shall, 30 days before the shipment date specified in the Contract, advise the Buyer by _____ of the Contract No., commodity, quantity, amount, packages, gross weight, measurement, and the date of shipment in order that the Buyer can charter a vessel/book shipping space. In the event of the Seller's failure to effect loading when the vessel arrives duly at the loading port, all expenses including dead freight and/or demurrage charges thus incurred shall be for the Seller's account.

(2) The Seller shall ship the goods duly within the shipping duration from the port of loading to the port of destination. Under CFR terms, the Seller shall advise the Buyer by _____ of the Contract No., commodity, invoice value and the date of dispatch two days before the

shipment for the Buyer to arrange insurance in time.

16. 装运通知

一旦装载完毕，卖方应在＿＿＿＿小时内以＿＿＿＿方式通知买方合同编号、品名、已发运数量、发票总金额、毛重、船名/车/机号及启程日期等。

16. Shipping Advice

The Seller shall, immediately upon the completion of the loading of the goods, advise the Buyer of the Contract No., names of commodity, loading quantity, invoice values, gross weight, name of vessel and shipment date by ＿＿＿＿ within ＿＿＿＿ hours.

17. 质量保证

货物品质规格必须符合本合同及质量保证书之规定，品质保证期为货到目的港＿＿＿个月内。在保证期限内，因制造厂商在设计制造过程中的缺陷造成的货物损害应由卖方负责赔偿。

17. Quality Guarantee

The Seller shall guarantee that the commodity must be in conformity with the quatity, specifications and quantity specified in this Contract and Letter of Quality Guarantee. The guarantee period shall be ＿＿＿＿ months after the arrival of the goods at the port of destination, and during the period the Seller shall be responsible for the damage due to the defects in designing and manufacturing of the manufacturer.

18. 检验

（1）卖方须在装运前＿＿＿＿日委托＿＿＿＿检验机构对本合同之货物进行检验并出具检验证书，货到目的港后，由买方委托＿＿＿＿检验机构进行检验。

（2）发货前，制造厂应对货物的质量、规格、性能和数量/重量作精密全面的检验，出具检验证明书，并说明检验的技术数据和结论。货到目的港后，买方将申请中国商品检验局（以下简称商检局）对货物的规格和数量/重量进行检验，如发现货物残损或规格、数量与合同规定不符，除保险公司或轮船公司的责任外，买方得在货物到达目的港后_____日内凭商检局出具的检验证书向卖方索赔或拒收该货。在保证期内，如货物由于设计或制造上的缺陷而发生损坏或品质和性能与合同规定不符时，买方将委托中国商检局进行检验。

18. Inspection

(1) The Seller shall have the goods inspected by _____ days before the shipment and have the Inspection Certificate issued by ____. The Buyer may have the goods reinspected by _____ after the goods arrival at the destination.

(2) The manufacturers shall, before delivery, make a precise and comprehensive inspection of the goods with regard to its quality, specifications, performance and quantity/weight, and issue inspection certificates certifying the technical data and conclusion of the inspection. After arrival of the goods at the port of destination, the Buyer shall apply to China Commodity Inspection Bureau (hereinafter referred to as CCIB) for a further inspection as to the specifications and quantity/weight of the goods. If damages of the goods are found, or the specifications and/or quantity are not in conformity with the stipulations in this Contract, except when the responsibilities lies with Insurance Company or Shipping Company, the Buyer shall, within _____ days after arrival of the goods at the port of destination, claim against the Seller, or reject the goods according to the inspection certificate issued by CCIB. In case of damage of the goods incurred due to the design or manufacture defects and/or in case the quality and performance are not in conformity with the Contract, the Buyer shall, during the guarantee period, request CCIB to make a survey.

19. 索赔

买方凭其委托的检验机构出具的检验证明书向卖方提出索赔（包括换货），由此引起的全部费用应由卖方负担。若卖方收到上述索赔后_____天未予答复，则认为卖方已接受买方索赔。

除合同第 21 条不可抗力原因外，如卖方不能按合同规定的时间交货，买方应同意在卖方支付罚款的条件下延期交货。罚款可由议付银行在议付货款时扣除，罚款率按每____天收____%，不足____天时以____天计算。但罚款不得超过迟交货物总价的____%。如卖方延期交货超过合同规定____天时，买方有权撤销合同此时，卖方仍应不迟延地按上述规定向买方支付罚款。

买方有权对因此遭受的其他损失向卖方提出索赔。

19. Claim

The buyer shall make a claim against the Seller (including replacement of the goods) by the further inspection certificate and all the expenses incurred therefrom shall be borne by the Seller. The claims mentioned above shall be regarded as being accepted if the Seller fail to reply within _____ days after the Seller received the Buyer's claim.

Should the Seller fail to make delivery on time as stipulated in the Contract, with the exception of Force Majeure causes specified in Clause 21 of this Contract, the Buyer shall agree to postpone the delivery on the condition that the Seller agree to pay a penalty which shall be deducted by the paying bank from the payment under negotiation. The rate of penalty is charged at _____% for every _____ days, odd days less than _____ days should be counted as _____ days. But the penalty, however, shall not exceed _____% of the total value of the goods involved in the delayed delivery. In case the Seller fail to make delivery _____ days later than the time of shipment stipulated in the Contract, the Buyer shall have the right to cancel the Contract and the Seller, in spite of the cancellation, shall nevertheless pay the aforesaid penalty to the Buyer without delay.

The buyer shall have the right to lodge a claim against the Seller for the losses sustained if any.

20. 不可抗力

凡在制造或装船运输过程中，因不可抗力致使卖方不能或推迟交货时，卖方不负责任。在发生上述情况时，卖方应立即通知买方，并在____天内，给买方特快专递一份由当地民间商会签发的事故证明书。在此情况下，卖方仍有责任采取一切必要措施加快交货。如事故延续____天以上，买方有权撤销合同。

20. Force Majeure

The Seller shall not be responsible for the delay of shipment or non-delivery of the goods due to Force Majeure, which might occur during the process of manufacturing or in the course of loading or transit. The Seller shall advise the Buyer immediately of the occurrence mentioned above and within _____ days thereafter the Seller shall send a notice by courier to the Buyer for their acceptance of a certificate of the accident issued by the local chamber of commerce under whose jurisdiction the accident occurs as evidence thereof. Under such circumstances the Seller, however, is still under the obligation to take all necessary measures to hasten the delivery of the goods. In case the accident lasts for more than _____ days the Buyer shall have the right to cancel the Contract.

21. 争议的解决

凡因本合同引起的或与本合同有关的任何争议应协商解决。若协商不成，应提交中国国际经济贸易仲裁委员会深圳分会，按照申请仲裁时该会现行有效的仲裁规则进行仲裁。仲裁裁决是终局的，对双方均有约束力。

21. Arbitration

Any dispute arising from or in connection with the Contract shall be settled through friendly negotiation. In case no settlement is reached, the dispute shall be submitted to China International Economic and Trade Arbitration Commission (CIETAC), Shenzhen Commission for arbitration in accordance with its rules in effect at the time of applying for arbitration. The arbitral award is final and binding upon both parties.

22. 通知

所有通知用＿＿＿文写成，并按照如下地址用传真/电子邮件/快件送达给各方。如果地址有变更，一方应在变更后＿＿＿日内书面通知另一方。

22. Notices

All notice shall be written in ＿＿＿ and served to both parties by fax/courier according to the following addresses. If any changes of the addresses occur, one party shall inform the other party of the change of address within ＿＿＿ days after the change.

23. 本合同使用的 FOB、CFR、CIF 术语系根据国际商会《2000年国际贸易术语解释通则》。

23. The terms FOB, CFR, CIF in the Contract are based on INCOTERMS 2000 of the International Chamber of Commerce.

24. 本合同用中英文两种文字写成，两种文字具有同等效力。本合同共＿＿＿份，自双方代表签字（盖章）之日起生效。

24. This Contract is executed in two counterparts each in Chinese and English, each of which shall deem equally authentic. This Contract is in ＿＿＿ copies, effective since being signed/sealed by both parties.

买方代表（签字）：

Representative of the Buyer

(Authorized signature):

卖方代表（签字）：

Representative of the Seller

第六章　影视字幕

作为一种传媒介质，电影是文化交际的重要载体。近年来，越来越多的英文电影传入我国，成为中国人接触并了解欧美文化的一个重要途径，而英文电影的翻译问题也引起越来越多的翻译者的重视。如果说英文电影本身是一个蕴含丰富欧美文化内涵的宝库的话，那么其片名也就是能够展现这座宝库绚丽多姿景象的窗口。随着经济的发展，现代生活的快节奏使人们更加追求高品质的精神享受，更乐意欣赏影视作品的原声效果，正因为如此，影视作品的字幕翻译才又备受青睐，拥有广阔的研究空间。尽管技术的突飞猛进和跨文化交流的深入使字幕翻译发展很快，但是对它的研究还局限于译者的实践经验，很少有学者从更深的理论层次来研究。基于此，本书从功能翻译理论的角度来探讨影视字幕的翻译，并提出相应的翻译方法和策略。

如上所述，和把大量的英文电影介绍给中国观众的市场相比，相关方面的研究人员实在少得可怜。影视翻译属于应用型翻译。作为在应用翻译领域被广泛接受的引领性的理论，德国功能翻译理论试图从其自身角度解析影视翻译，并将影视字幕翻译视为一种行为。其主要目的是在时空限制下，通过再现源语信息，传递电影内容，以期在目观众中激发与源语观众类似或相同的观影感受。为了实现上述目的，影视翻译人员应当遵从相应的翻译原则，采用相关的翻译策略。本书拟在这一方面做些探索，以期对提高影视字幕翻译实践水平有所裨益，填补相关领域的空白。

6.1 影视字幕的特点

字幕翻译的对象主要是电影、电视剧和所有需加字幕的视频节目或文件等。字幕是基于观众对原节目的需要，在后期通过技术手段加在屏幕上的图片文字，是对原节目的一种解释性的说明。电影的字幕翻译是指电影在播放中，通常显示在屏幕下方，对片中人物的对白和其他相关信息的一种解释性的补充说明。

影视字幕翻译从不同的角度出发，可以有不同的分类。从语言学的角度看，字幕翻译可分为语内字幕（intra-lingual subtitling）和语际字幕（inter-lingual subtitling）。语内字幕翻译是把话语转换成文本，这样改变了说话的方式，但语言没有改变。有时也把这种字幕翻译称为"垂直字幕翻译"（vertical subtitling translation）。语际字幕翻译是在保留原声的情况下，把源语译为目的语，并将目的语同步地叠印在屏幕或图片下端的过程，有时也把这种字幕翻译称为"对角字幕翻译"（diagonal subtitling translation）。通常所说的字幕翻译即为语际字幕翻译。

从字幕的内容上看，电影的字幕翻译由于原文本的内容与性质不同，分为显性影视字幕翻译和隐性影视字幕翻译。从字幕的形式上看，字幕翻译可以是双语影视字幕，字幕的形式分为两行；一行为源语字幕；另一行为译语字幕。另外字幕翻译也可以是单语影视字幕，其特点是只显示一种语言。影视字幕翻译也根据电影作品的类别而异，比如说故事片、纪录片、文献片等有不同的特点，字幕翻译也会因此有不同的类别和策略。

6.1.1 通俗化

影视文学与书面文学语言不同，英文影片字幕的翻译不单纯是文字翻译的问题。影视语言绝大部分是由人物的对白组成，对白的内容是整个作品核心。优秀的对白翻译要遵从其通俗化的特点。通俗化是指绝大部分影视剧所使用的语言都是浅显易懂的日常口语。

所以，字幕中常出现 Um，Yeah，Yup，Gosh，Damn it，Dude 等只在口语中存在的词；出现 So What，After you，Anything else，You owe me one 等短句和不完整句；并且大量出现 all wet，hot number，have a ball 之类的俚语。再如"Got a minute？"译为"有空吗？"，"You'll be the first to know."译为"我会第一时间告诉你"，"Why the long face？"译为"干嘛拉着个脸？"。以上的英文对白充分体现了直接、简洁的语言特点，所以翻译成汉语时也要求用最简单的词句和非正式用语才能传达出原文的生动度。

6.1.2 时空制约

不同于书面创作，影视文学中的语言是有声语言，转瞬即逝。对于文学作品读者可以反复阅读，难以理解之处还可以用注解加以说明。而观众在看电影时间，精彩瞬间转瞬即逝，如果听不懂只能放弃。所以要求字幕的翻译应该贴近观众、易于理解，只要能表明原片中的内容就可以了，不要使用过多的另外的字幕。

6.1.3 文化差异

影视作品作为文化传播的主要媒介之一，是一种大众化的艺术，是供人们欣赏的。因此，译文要靠近大众，通俗易懂，特别是注意原文和译文之间的文化差异，应该尽量使用通俗的、和人们日常生活密切相关的语言，使广大观众能直接越过文化障碍，达到良好的理解效果。

例如：*Shakespeare in Love*（《莎翁情史》）中，"Follow me close. I will speak to them."译为"跟我来，我去跟他们理论"。这句英文非常简练，但是字里行间表达了说话人的态度。将"speak"翻译成"理论"，很贴切地传达了人物的情感。

6.1.4 主体对象

译者主体性主要表现为译者对原作进行能动的转述和转换，如有意识地编译、节译、改编等，以及有目的地对原文进行取舍或增删。读者通过阅读台词可以填补对剧情理解的"空白",文本的接受过程就是对文本的再创造过程。不同的电影字幕和配音具有不同的翻译要求。字幕翻译是一种特殊的语言转换类型,要照顾到电影中特定的主体对象。

6.1.5 信息容量

台词担负着传播影视剧信息的功能,其翻译的好坏直接影响影片的价值,所以台词翻译是影视翻译的基础和核心,台词翻译对于译制片的重要性是毫无疑问的。影视台词翻译不同于文学翻译,与其说是一种艺术的再创造,不如说它更侧重真实地再现影片的内涵表达,在电影传播方面起着举足轻重的作用。

6.1.6 人物情感化

电影主要运用人物语言塑造形象,剧情片更是如此,常常借助对话表现思想、刻画性格、推进情节等。电影中的人物语言富有性格化的特征。性格化是电影人物语言艺术的最高审美价值体现。影视翻译的重要任务之一就是要忠实地传达原片的这一审美特质,在译制片中再塑人物形象。

6.2 影视字幕翻译策略

根据功能文学体理论,翻译是一个过程,而达到过程的目的则是最为重要的。所有的翻译过程都要有一个明确目的。在特定的翻译过程中,根据特定的目的选择相适应的翻译技巧。不仅如此,所有的翻译版本都应该忠于原作。同翻译的原则相比,翻译技巧则更有实用导向性。一方面,翻译技巧有赖于大量实践,另一方面,它们又超脱于实践并企图更好地引领实践。因此,整理梳理影视字幕翻译策略,对于得到更好的字幕翻译效果而言是非常必要的基础性工作。

6.2.1 注重语言的艺术性

这个技巧是指根据语言的发音特点将源语言翻译成目标语言。用这种方法翻译的词语和短句不仅应该保持旧的发音特点和形式，而且要包含新的意思，传达出语言本身独有的技术性。在源语言中它们的本来意思丢失，而且承担了和源语言中的本来意思截然不同的新含义。例如一些最寻常的外语词语的用法：cool（酷）、disco（迪斯科）、TOEFL（托福）等等。语言之间的不同是不可否认的难题。合理的翻译能成功架起语言沟通之间的桥梁，并且有很多这方面成功的例子。可能许多单词或短语最初出现的时候都被视为异类，但在一段时间后会被目标语言群体慢慢接受。例如"芭蕾"，现在中国人已经接受了这个词而且都对这个表达很熟悉，能立马就知道它的意思。

电影是人类生活的影子，而且是多国文化的混合体，因此注重语言的艺术性显得十分必要。所以所有被译者选择的词都是翻译者精挑细选的结果。例如下面的例子：

【例1】—What's the artist's name?
　　　　—Something Picasso. (*Titanic*)
【译文】——画家叫什么？
　　　　——好像叫毕加索。（《泰坦尼克号》）

毕加索是一位世界知名的艺术家，为其选择的中国名字为"毕加索"，这个中文名字已经深入中国人的心中。也就是说，他的中文名字已经融入了中国的文化之中，对这三个汉字的任何翻译都会令人们心中浮现出他的形象，因此很好地传递了该词所含的艺术气息。下面的两个例子来自电影《阿凡达》。

【例2】Venezuela that was some mean bush.
【译文】委内瑞拉是个险象坏生的地方。
【例3】Grace Augustine is a legend.
【译文】格瑞斯·奥古斯丁是个传奇人物。

人名或者地名已经通过音译的方式表达了其意思。电影是对真实生活的反映，并根植于特定的文化土壤之上。在影视字幕翻译中，总是会有许多的名字，或者是人名，或者是地名、项目名称等等。通过翻译，许多外国的事物被介绍进目标文化，并且大大丰富了词语的种类。

此外，有时候在翻译的过程中免不了会产生某一类词，这些词能解释外来语的含义。对于这种类型的音译，很容易就把其归纳进内化的行列。例如：

【例 4】But there is a sign from Eywa. (*Avatar*)

【译文】可是艾娃女神有启示了。(《阿凡达》)

外来词"Eywa"在电影中被翻译成了"艾娃女神"。不同于根据语义进行翻译的"毕加索"，Eywa 这个外来词被加上了女神的解释，扩大了 Eywa 的含义。看另一个例子：

【例 5】You are on Pandora ladies and gentlemen. (*Avatar*)

【译文】这里是潘多拉星球，女士们、先生们。(《阿凡达》)

古希腊和古罗马是欧洲文化的发源地。罗马人征服了希腊人，但是却被希腊人的文化所征服。罗马帝国的扩张以及持续的交流使得古希腊神话为古大不列颠人所熟知。更有甚者，在文艺复兴时期，来自古希腊和古罗马的许多文学著作被介绍进英国，对他们的文学有了深远的影响。Pandora 这个词即来自一个古希腊神话，在古希腊神话中它代表邪恶和希望。而在《阿凡达》这部电影中，Pandora 是一个星球，它正在面对来自人类的威胁，当地人是这个星球微小的希望。"潘多拉"这个词在中国已经被广泛引用，选择该词还保留了原来的发音。这就是音译的一种技巧。但是由于 Pandora 这个词本来代表的是一个故事，而且被用于很多场合，所以译者加了一个分类词"星球"，让该词的意思更为清晰。这种翻译就是一个合理的形式，因为它不仅包含了词语的意思，也有清晰的类别意思。

对于语言的艺术性这一技巧的使用并没有一个统一的格式，它对于译者来说是一个很好的方式。

6.2.2 正确处理文化信息

对于翻译策略来说正确处理文化信息是比较重要的，但是其定义也不是如大家所愿的很清晰。很多人认为对台词的翻译就是字对字的翻译，显然这是错误的。这种硬翻译其实是翻译的一种错误途径，因此自然不能被当成电影台词翻译的一种选择。

正确处理文化信息在翻译中应保持原文的形式和内容，但是不排斥在整个句子中，进行词语顺序、短语顺序方面轻微的调整。同硬翻译相比，在处理句型问题上直译显然更具有灵活性。成功的翻译是那些具有流畅的目标语言句型的翻译。但是由于译入语保留了源语言的表达思想的方式，而且每种语言都有其固定的魅力所在，当原文的内容可以使用旧句型表达时，直译就是最佳而且最简单的翻译方式。更具针对性地讲，直译一方面可以保留源语言的本来风味，也就是鲁迅说的异域风味，另一方面它可以通过更新更具体的单词、短语和句型丰富目标语言，将目标语言引入更具色彩、更完整和更细致的境界。因此，如果直译能被目标语言观众轻易理解、在时间和空间约束下成功实施的话，对于成功的电影台词翻译实践来说是一种相对简单的方式。见下面的例子：

【例6】Well, you really shouldn't **have said that.** (*Twilight*)

【译文】你真不该这么说。(《暮光之城》)

《暮光之城》这部电影是讲一个在17岁的女孩Swan Bella 和食素的吸血鬼 Edward Cullen 之间发生的爱情故事。这个例子选自一个相对缓慢的情节。在Bella说"我不怕你"之后，Edward缓慢地又说了一次，然后很快地将女孩放在他的背上，飞出了窗户之外。值得一提的是，第一个词"Well"是一个语气词，说明了Edward心中孕育了一个小把戏，所以不应该被省略。翻译成"哦，你真不该那么说"可能更好。尽管不是最理想的翻译，但这个例子已经足够解释直译是一种相对简单和容易出彩的翻译方式。

【例7】Back on Earth these guys were Army dogs, Marines. Fight for freedom. (*Avatar*)

【译文】在地球上他们只是为了自由而战的普通士兵和战士。(《阿凡达》)

电影是由连续闪过的画面构成的，在这些动画之间确实存在时间的差别，在字幕上反映的信息不能忽视这一点。上述例子是选自电影《阿凡达》的连续的画面，而且我们看到其中文翻译在句子片段上并不具有对称性。但是在句子层面，这两段文字可以被看成是同源的。尽管词语顺序有微调，但这种翻译仍属于直译。而且由于字幕翻译提供信息是以不连贯的方式进行的，此处的微调是一种保持可理解性的良好方式。但是，"Army dogs"是一种表达士兵意思的非常粗放的方式，因此建议使用"兵仔"代替"普通士兵和战士"。该句翻译为"回到地球，这些家伙只是为了自由而战的普通兵仔"会更好。

【例8】She's the largest moving object ever made by the hand of man in all history. And our master shipbuilder, Mr. Andrews, here, designed her from the keel plates up. (*Titanic*)

【译文】她是史上最大的交通工具，完全是由安德鲁先生设计的。(《泰坦尼克号》)

这是对泰坦尼克这艘船的一句评价，我们可以看到前半句"ever made by the hand of man"和后半段的"our master shipbuilder"在翻译中被省略。所以此处的例子首先使用了删减的策略，目的是节省时间和空间。"designed her from the keel plates up"被翻译为"完全"，不仅如此，"Mr. Andrews"被译为"安德鲁先生"，是直译策略的一种很好的表现。由于时间和空间在特定的例子中并不能展现什么问题，所以此句可以更恰当地被译为："她是史上人造的最大的可移动物体，是我们的造船大师安德鲁先生一手设计的。"

6.2.3 展译与缩译

在翻译实践中最普遍的问题是目标语言的语法系统与源语言不同。译者需要采取或者发明另一种形式以表达同样的内容。因此，译者有可能会忽视原先的句子，以另一种更革新的方式表达意思，也就是采用展译与缩译的方法,尽管在词语和句子顺序上允许微调,但是能创造一种全新的方式表达原意。

展译与缩译,如其名字所示,对于原文存在一些调整。在相似性方面,这种翻译方式类似于直译。其不同之处仅存在于语言代码方面。

【例9】Her name was Rose Dawson back then. Then she married this guy named Calvert.

They move to Cedar Rapids and she punches out a couple of kids.

Now Calvert's dead, and from what I hear, Cedar Rapids is dead.

(*Titanic*)

【译文】她当时叫萝丝·道森,后来她嫁给卡维特先生

搬到柏湍镇,生了几个孩子

现在卡维特死了,柏湍镇也没落了。(《泰坦尼克号》)

这段字幕来自著名的电影《泰坦尼克号》,讲的是在沉船之后女主角的生活。在这个例子中,对于"Cedar Rapids"的翻译采取了直译加类别词的方式,因此我们得知它是一个小镇。因此,在下一个句子中,"Cedar Rapids is dead"译为"这个镇子不再像以前那么繁华了"。在英语中,一个小镇可以死去,但是在中文中只有活着的东西可以用"死"这个词,所以,译者选择了保持原意,创造了另一种表达方式。也就是说,译者使用了展译与缩译的方法。当然,这种翻译也不是完美的。单词"guy"是一种表达成年男子的比较随意的方式,因此"Then she married this guy named Calvert"应该译为"后来她嫁给了一个叫卡维特的家伙"。

此外,展译与缩译被广泛用于揭示外国文学形象的隐含意。它将意思融入到目标语言中,在图画和字幕两者之间建立较为简单的联系。此外,它可以在一定程度上美化源电影较为粗俗的语言。

6.2.4 释译与化译

在翻译电影对白时,必须处理好不同文化下源语言和目标语言的相互转换。主要是词法和句法上的语言转化,要多采用释译与化

译的技巧。首先要注意的是避免语句直译。因为中西方在语言的表达和文化上存在差异，翻译时尽量在不改变源语言意思的情况下，向目标语言的表达方式靠拢，就是我们所说的"化译"。其次，合理处理语言和文化空缺。在对白翻译过程中我们会遇到一些语言和文化空缺，这是翻译最大的阻碍之一。当遇到这种情况的时候，就要求译者通过理解和加工进行合理的翻译，让目标语言观众理解其背后意思，这时就需要使用释译。

【例 10】Lizzy: You actually think this is you, Nana?
　　　　Rose: It is me, dear.
　　　　Rose: Wasn't a dish？(*Titanic*)
【译文】莉西：奶奶，真的是你吗？
　　　　萝丝：是我呀，亲爱的。
　　　　萝丝：我那时很美吧？（《泰坦尼克号》）

在许多年之后，萝丝在容貌上已经改变了太多，她的孙女看到图片里的她感到非常的惊奇：太美太漂亮了。所以她问萝丝，想确定问题的答案。她的奶奶很快给了一个肯定性的答复。萝丝此刻也包含着许多感情，所以她问道："Wasn't a dish？"不仅是在问她的孙女，也是在问自己。dish 本意为美味的食物，在此处指的是年轻萝丝的美貌。为了达到易于理解的目的，译者此刻使用了该词的隐含意，并翻译为"我那时很美吧？"。但是笔者却觉得翻译成"难道不美？"可以更好地体现出原文的情感意味。

【例 11】You're so full of shit, boss. (*Titanic*)
【译文】老板，你也太废话了吧？（《泰坦尼克号》）

原文是一段非常粗俗的表达，因为 shit 是指动物排出的废物。电影观众整体上认为台词应该和电影整体的文化保持一致。译者使用了化译的方式，是一种非常恰当的解决方式。

【例 12】Let's nobody be dead today！Looks very bad on my report. (*Avatar*)
【译文】但愿今天不要死人，不然我的报告就不好写。（《阿凡达》）

上校告诉新来的人戴上面具,句子"Looks very bad on my report"原意为"报告看上去会很糟糕",听起来翻译与该意思不符合。人们需要知道什么样的不好的报告会让上校感到进退两难。直到字幕出现,人们才知道意思是不想让任何一个新来的人牺牲。同新员工的生命相比,他更关心的是报告,这反映出他是一个邪恶的角色。为了让观众用更少的工夫更快地理解剧情,译者使用了展译与缩译的方式,将上句翻译为"不然我的报告就不好写了"。

6.2.5 删译与弃译

这里说的删译与弃译,是指影视语言的翻译在字数上有一定的局限性,其翻译要简洁明了,不能拖泥带水。在电影台词翻译过程中要注意声音与口型的同步配合,因此影视翻译人员若是不注意字数方面的限制,会使配音人员陷入困境:源语短、译语长,给人的感觉是"赶"。因此,要十分注意删译与弃译技巧的使用,达到台词与电影画面的和谐统一。

【例 13】Bus-driver: Are you coming alone?

Forrest: No, Mister, I'm not to be taking rides from strangers.

Bus-driver: This is the bus to school. (*Forrest Gump*)

【译文】司机:要上来吗?

阿甘:"不,我不上陌生人的车。

司机:车是去学校的。(《阿甘正传》)

译文中大家可以看到,"you""mister""this"这三个词都没有必要翻译出来。因为司机在和阿甘对话的时候脸也转过来对着他,并且一个在车上一个在车下,所指非常明显。当然省略成分多并不意味着翻译可以随便乱删对白中的内容,所指的删译与弃译只能建立在不影响原内容的基础上。

6.2.6 在目标语言中寻找替代

在电影台词翻译中,在目标语言中寻找替代是一种很好的解决中西方文化差异的方法。在翻译电影台词时，既要做到自身的自主性、灵活性，又要有创造性。使用这一技巧能解决台词中带有浓厚地方特色的词汇、短语、方言、俗语和句子等翻译难题。如《浮华世家》(*The Colbys*)中有这么一句话："Is Camille so lovely—even on her death bed?"，译者将其翻译为"天上的仙女临终时有这么美吗？"，既简单又不失原意，是一种高明的寻找目标语言中替代的方法。

6.3　电影《功夫熊猫》的翻译策略赏析

电影《功夫熊猫》是梦工厂在 2008 年推出的首部以中国功夫为题材的 3D 电影。自上映以来，《功夫熊猫》在票房与批评界均获得了巨大的成功，登陆中国后广受好评，成为中国首部票房过亿的动画片。就本质而言，《功夫熊猫》依然是一部典型的好莱坞式英雄电影，然而电影中大量的中国功夫元素使这部电影在同类型电影中脱颖而出。国内版本的翻译工作是由上海电影译制片厂完成的。译制方在翻译过程中对翻译策略与技巧灵活运用，在保持台词原有风貌的同时添加中国本土特色，为这部电影增色不少。而要想做出好的字幕翻译，译者必须把握字幕翻译的目的。字幕翻译的最终目标就是要使影片观众能够借助字幕跨越语言和文化的障碍，看懂影片所要表达的意义，欣赏到国外的影视作品，实现跨文化交流的目的。

6.3.1　《功夫熊猫》中的异化与归化

在《功夫熊猫》这部电影中，将师父翻译成 Shi Fu 或者是 Master Shi-Fu，把乌龟翻译成 Wu-Gui，冰棒为 Bing Bang 等。采用异化策略，就是让观众直面异域文化的不同，从而扩展其经验视野。

再如，"There is a saying, yesterday is a history, tomorrow is a mystery, but today is a gift, that is why it is called the present"，这是《功夫熊猫》中"乌龟"大师的另一句经典台词。原句中涉及了押

韵与双关。若采取简单直译的方法，译作"俗语说昨天是历史，明天是谜团，只有今天是天赐的礼物""过去的，已经过去了；未来的，还未可知；现在，却是上苍的礼赠，那就是什么今天是present（现在／礼物）"或"昨天已经过去，明天一切未知，但'今天'是上帝赐给我们的'礼物'"，这样的处理似乎丧失了这句话隐含的美感，读起来十分平淡。但是如果用归化的方法，考虑译者的再创造力加以处理，译为"昨日之日不可留，明日之日不可知，今日之日胜现金。好好把握现在吧"或者"逝者长已矣，来者犹可追"，感觉截然不同，起到发人深省的效果。

6.3.2 《功夫熊猫》中的关联政策

《功夫熊猫》中有一段旁白：Legend takes of legendary warrior whose Kung Fu skills with the stuff of legend. He travelled the land in search of worthy foes（传说中有个传奇侠客，他的武功出神入化，浪迹江湖。一路行侠仗义）。原文中几处如"stuff""in search of"及"worthy foes"等，如果精确直译，只能译为"东西""寻找"和"值得一战的敌人"，这样会使原文韵味尽失。译文中避开了这几个词的精确之意，将"stuff of legend"关联到"出神入化"，而"in search of worthy foes"则译为"行侠仗义"。现译文不但符合影片背景，而且"出神入化"和"行侠仗义"两个成语也很有侠味，和整个影片的"中国功夫"相一致。可以说，此译文看似不忠实原文，却是和原文对等的译文，实为神来之笔。

6.3.3 《功夫熊猫》中的文化差异

《功夫熊猫》中出现了一些近年来被西方大众认可的翻译，功夫为Kongfu而不是Shadow Boxing，豆腐为tufou，麻将为majiang等等。这些词汇的英文翻译都涉及东西方文化方面的差异，但是影片放映之后在美国国内取得了巨大的成功，放映当天票房居首位，可见这些词汇还是为大众所接受。

再如浣熊师傅的开场白："Let the tournament begin. Citizens of

valley of peace, it's my great honor to present to you…"这是一段典型的主持人语篇,在称呼完在场的观众后用套话介绍到场的各位嘉宾。那么汉译时要注意哪些和文化语境相关的因素呢?有译文是这样的:"比武大会现在开始!和平谷的父老乡亲们,今日,老夫有幸向诸位介绍……"这一段文字不长,但却考虑到了中西方文化的差异。首先,译者用了三个符合中国文化的表达"比武大会""父老乡亲们""老夫",这些表达在中国古代很常用。其次,"tournament"不仅可以指现在的锦标赛,还可以指中世纪的骑士较量勇气和技艺的比武大会,与中国侠文化中的比武很相似,所以译为"比武大会"很贴切。"citizens"翻译成"居民""公民"都不符合中文的习惯表达,"父老乡亲们"就拉近了和中国观众的距离。在翻译"my great honor"时,用"我很荣幸"就现代感十足,"今日,老夫有幸"就把观众带到了中国古代。因此,从文化因素的角度考量,这几句的翻译也是相当成功的。

总之,若要使影片字幕翻译准确而传神,其一,要以正确的理论为指导,又要保持影片原来的风格,具体策略可归纳为:准确地理解原文,从而正确地传达语意;掌握源语所处的文化背景,从而恰当翻译;了解专有名词,使之符合翻译规范。其二,在理论的指导下采用合理的翻译方法,具体策略为:注重语言的艺术性、展译与缩译、正确处理文化信息、释译与化译、删译与弃译、在目标语言中寻找替代。如果译者能正确运用以上策略,定能让观众更好地观看外国影片,也能更体现出原作所蕴涵的艺术效果。

6.4 影视片名翻译

6.4.1 英文电影片名汉译中存在的问题

全球化时代的来临使得英文电影作为文化爆炸的一个代表越来越多地传播到我国。然而,由于语言习惯、社会制度、文化背景、生活方式等因素的客观存在,这些电影的中文译名出现很多问题,

"一片多名"屡见不鲜,翻译界对电影片名的翻译标准也不统一,造成一种混乱状态的出现。我们通过研究大量英文电影的中文译名发现这种混乱问题主要由三个原因所引起。

第一,中国大陆、中国香港及以中国台湾的文化差异造成同一部英文电影出现不同的译名。翻译界没有达成一致的翻译标准,译者的翻译习惯和原则也不同,这就造成了"一片三名"的局面的出现。例如,电影 *Terminator Salvation* 中国在大陆译为《终结者2018》,在中国香港译为《未来战士2018》,在中国台湾译为《魔鬼终结者4:未来救赎》。值得一提的是,美国经典大片 *Ghost* 在中国香港的译名是《人鬼情未了》,在中国台湾译作《第六感之恋》,而中国大陆的译名《幽灵》则把一部充满柔情蜜意的爱情片当成了一部恐怖片,这是一种根本没有考虑剧情的误译。一般来说,中国大陆在翻译英文电影片名时往往比较忠实于英文原名,体现了中国大陆翻译家的严肃风格。港台译名则相对随意大方一些,商业色彩比较浓厚。

第二,由于缺乏统一的管理和协调,媒体广告等传播渠道本身不注意译名的统一和规范问题而各行其是,这也使译名的混乱愈演愈烈。例如,影片 *Do the Right Thing* 分别有《循规蹈矩》《为所欲为》以及《做一件事》等译名出现在中国大陆的媒体上。21世纪以来,随着网络媒体的盛行,一部新片刚刚上映甚至即将上映时各路媒体便纷纷加以宣传,使用的译名也是不尽相同。有时在一些小的报纸杂志上,同一篇电影评论文章中也会出现不同译名同时并存的混乱局面。

第三,由于文化交流渠道的增多和力度的加大,一些英文电影通过不同的途径涌入我国,使得电影市场竞争激烈。一些电影商和发行机构为了追求商业利益不惜大肆炒作,另辟蹊径推出其他译名,这也是造成译名混乱的原因之一。例如,电影 *Robocop* 在中国香港译为《铁甲威龙》,中国内地一开始译作《机器警探》,放映时便改用《威虎争雄》。这种"公映译名"的出现往往是在译名上大做手脚,使原本通过其他渠道已被引进的电影在放映时用全新陌生的译名欺骗观众,造成的影响岂能仅仅用"混乱"二字来表达?

通过上面的分析我们可以看到，三种原因互相交错，最主要的要属"一片多名"的现象。这种混乱不仅使观众由于遭到经济或欣赏上的损失而深恶痛绝，同时严重破坏了广大翻译者和影视工作人员的形象，所以我们强烈呼吁相关规范或整治办法的出现。

6.4.2 英文电影片名汉译的四项基本原则

有些英文电影的中文译名会使观众感觉韵味十足，而有些译名却令人感到云里雾里、迷惑不解。中文译名往往最多只有五六个字的空间，却"既要符合语言规范，又要富有艺术魅力，既要忠实于原片名的内容，又要体现原名的语言特色，力求达到艺术的再创造……起到很好的导视和促销作用"。尽管当前在英文电影片名汉译上存在很多问题，但仔细思考之后笔者发现，英文电影的片名汉译涉及文化和语言两个方面的转换，可以遵循如下的四项基本原则。

A. 信息传递原则

翻译最主要的功能是做到信息传递的等值，所以英文电影片名的中文译名要做到忠实于原电影的内容，实现信息的等值。捕风捉影、偏离原电影内容的翻译是英文电影片名汉译的大忌。例如，中国台湾曾经将 *The Sound of Music*（中国大陆译为《音乐之声》）译作《仙乐飘飘何处闻》，这种标题简直适用于各类音乐片。更有甚者，将 *True Lies*（中国大陆译为《真实的谎言》）译作《魔鬼大帝》，将 *Anna Karenina*（中国大陆译为《安娜·卡列尼娜》）译作《爱比恋更冷》，这些译名都与影片的内容风马牛不相及，既令人费解，还误导观众，引起他们错误的心理预期。

翻译英文电影片名时要尽可能直译，保持其英文名的"原汁原味"，例如 *A Christmas Carol*（《圣诞颂歌》）和 *Dance with Wolfs*（《与狼共舞》）等。如果不好直译，可以另辟蹊径稍加转换，译出其应有的意境，例如 *Ghost*（《人鬼情未了》）、*Madison County Bridge*（《廊桥遗梦》）、*Garfield*（《加菲猫》）等。这些译名为原英文影片增色不少，令人耳目一新。当然无论采用什么方法，译者必须遵循最大限度地忠实于原电影内容的原则。

B. 文化等值原则

在翻译中体现文化价值、促进文化交流和理解，是英文电影片名汉译的重要任务。由于中西方在社会发展历程、习惯信仰、价值观念、伦理道德、历史政经等方面存在着很大差异和不同，文化价值的实现首先表现在充分理解、准确传递原电影片名所负载的文化信息、情感，避免出现误译这一方面。只有忠实于原英文电影及其片名的语言文化特征，用生动的汉语文字符号来传递源语文化的丰富内涵，才能保证英文电影与其中文电影片名所传递信息的一致性。这是一种创造性的融合，也是一种忠实性与艺术性兼备的翻译。

英文电影片名的"汉译过程中，巧妙地结合中国文化，因地制宜，就好比'西餐中吃'，经常能引起观众联想，起到出奇制胜的效果"[①]。例如，好莱坞大片 *Gone with the Wind* 在中国大陆被传神地译为《乱世佳人》，而不是直译《随风而逝》，因为前者更能激活观众大脑中诸如"乱世出英雄""美酒配佳人"等文化因素，也更符合中国传统的文化背景。还有，英文电影 *The Spiderman* 的中译名《蜘蛛侠》以及 *Transformer* 的中译名《变形金刚》中的"侠"和"金刚"，都为西洋电影艺术增添了一股东方的侠气和阳刚之气，这便把英文电影的丰富内涵与中国的文化精髓巧妙地结合起来。

C. 美学鉴赏原则

任何美的事物都是形式美和内容美的辩证统一体，电影片名具有独特的美学特征。实际上，英文电影片名汉译是一种特殊的文学翻译，因此在进行电影片名汉译的过程中要考虑美学鉴赏的价值问题，深入挖掘电影作品的美学内涵和艺术性，将电影中的美感传递给观众。"翻译美学既关注审美感性在翻译中的关键作用，又重视审美理解在翻译中的引导作用。"[②]电影片名汉译的美学鉴赏原则最主要的是由英汉两种语言的差异来体现的。英语片名常用名词短语，

[①] 郑玉琪、王晓东.《小议电影片名的英汉翻译原则》，《中国翻译》2006 年第 3 期，第 66 页。

[②] 刘宓庆、章艳.《翻译美学理论》，北京：外语教学与研究出版社，2011 年，第 XXV 页。

而汉语多采用带有动词的四字成语。例如 *Bathing Beauty* 译为《出水芙蓉》，*Enemy at the Gates* 译为《兵临城下》，*Moon Light* 译为《披星戴月》等等。这些汉语译名短小精悍，却动感十足，读起来朗朗上口，既包含丰富的中国风味，又体现出意味深长的意境，给人以极大的感染力。

D. 商业推广原则

电影本身就是一种商业行为，从某种意义上来讲，票房收入是其最大的目的。因此，除了以上三个原则之外，英文电影片名汉译还必须遵循商业推广原则。电影片名其实就是一种广告，而广告的目的通常只有一个，就是促销，增加客户的利润，所以谁管得着翻译出来的标语文稿跟原文关系是否理想？要想引发观众的观看欲望和心理认同感，就必须在电影片名的翻译上下大力气，既要符合电影本身的实际需求，又要迎合观众的口味、期待和审美情趣。票房高升才能说明电影获得了一定程度上的成功。例如，惊险大片 *Speed* 最初在我国译为《速度》，让人不可捉摸，后来改译为《生死时速》才迎合了观众的期待和好奇感，这便是商业利益的驱使所为。

因此，英文电影片名的汉译看似雕虫小技，但要做到雅俗共存、不失韵味绝不是一件易事。好的译名能够画龙点睛，使原版电影脱颖而出，对是否能使其成为佳片或者精品起着不可小觑的作用。英文电影片名汉译是一项重要而富于创造性的工作，不是简单的照搬，而是需要遵循一定的翻译原则，在忠实于原片的基础上，做到符合汉语文化特征，达到文字优美，生动传情，富于吸引力。翻译者在英文电影片名汉译的问题上要发扬翻译大师严复所言的"一名之立，旬月踟蹰"精神，敢于打破原电影片名的桎梏，从我国观众的接受性和欣赏性出发进行变通，争取译出令人难忘、耐人回味的佳名来。经典的电影和绝佳的片名相结合，是可遇而不可求的。

第七章 广告语

英语单词"advertise"源自拉丁语"advertere",意思是唤起大众对某一事物的注意并诱导于一定的方向所使用的一种手段。广告类文体属于一种独特的应用性文体,按照纽马克的划分,应该属于"呼唤型"文体①。广告是一种微型劝说文,撰稿者需要在有限的篇幅内使用各种手法增强语言的感染力,使人认识和理解某种商品或服务,从而产生购买欲望。广告语的这一文体功能定位决定了广告语具有语言简明、活泼、生动、形象、富有感染力的特点,更重要的是广告语对人的心理产生一种诱导功能,这种功能的效果直接影响着广告的实际效果。因此,在广告语的翻译中,不能仅仅做到语言上的对等,更要做到在广告问题呼唤诱导功能上的对等,这样的广告语翻译才是成功的。

7.1 广告语的文体功能

从总体上来说广告语的文体功能主要是劝说诱导功能,即劝说消费者去购买某一种服务或者商品,但是从过程来说,广告语的文体功能可以分为5大类:报道功能、唤起需要功能、说服功能、促使行动功能、扶持信誉功能。

报道功能(informative function)。这是广告文体最基本的功能,一个广告的首要任务便是将自己的产品和服务广而告之,让尽可能多的潜在消费者了解有关信息,才能为后续文体功能的实现做好铺垫。

唤起需要功能(evocative function)。广告不仅需要让消费者

---

① 贾文波.《应用翻译功能论》.北京:中国对外翻译出版公司,2004年,第157页。

了解自己的商品和服务，更重要的是向消费者灌输一种消费理念，让消费者产生一种需要感，使消费者产生一种好奇心理和消费的兴趣。

说服功能（persuasive function）。在产生消费需要之后，广告需要说服消费者认定自己的产品和服务才是最好的，广告引导消费者的态度和行为趋向于广告预定的方向变化，促进消费者对特定的产品和服务产生积极的态度和购买行为，这就是说服功能。

促使行动功能（prompting function）。消费者在被说服后并不一定立刻会有购买行为，消费者可能会有各种各样的顾虑，这时候广告的功能便是促使行动功能，通过罗列事实或者情感攻势来消除消费者的顾虑和犹豫，促使其抓紧行动。

扶持信誉功能（credit-winning function）。所谓扶持信誉功能指的是在消费过程以外，广告可以通过大范围长时间的传播，使大众熟悉某一产品或者服务，对其产生亲切感和信任感，不仅巩固已有的消费群体，而且可以增加潜在的消费者。

7.2 英文广告语的语言特征

7.2.1 英文广告语的词汇特点

A. 多用复合词

在英语中，复合词的构成可以是任何词类，其组合不受英语词序排列的限制，具有极大的灵活性和表现力，而广告的一个特点就是在尽可能短的篇幅内以最大的可能性展现出产品的魅力，因而英文广告语为复合词提供了广阔的舞台。

adj. + n.	first-class, top-quality, excellent-craftsmanship
adv. + n.	up-to-date, up-to-the-minute, must-haves
v. + -ing + adj.	shinning-clean, piping-hot
adv. + v. + ed	perfect-textured, carefully-designed
n. + n.	economy-size, a state-of-the-wheat color

n. + adj.	brand-new, sugar-crisp, line-dry, feather-light
n. + v. + ed	home-made, honey-coated
adj. + infinitive	easy-to-dress, easy-to-do, hard-to-reach
adj. + v.+ -ing	fresh-tasting, innocent-looking
adv. + v.+ -ing	best-selling, hard-working

B. 使用简短动词和形容词

在广告中，为了使广告语言更加简洁生动，内容一目了然，广告撰稿人往往采用一些最简洁易懂的词汇。G. N. Leech 在他的 *English in Advertising* 中列出了一些英文广告语中使用最为频繁的词汇，如动词中的 make, get, give, have, do 等，以及形容词中的 new, good, fine, free, great 等。

【例 1】 Time is what you make of it. （Swatch）

【译文】天长地久。（斯沃琪手表）

【例 2】 Good teeth, good health. （Colgate toothpaste）

【译文】牙齿好，身体就好。（高露洁牙膏）

【例 3】 The taste is great. （Nestle）

【译文】味道好极了。（雀巢咖啡）

【例 4】 Just do it （Nike）

【译文】想做就做。（耐克）

以上几个例子中的动词和形容词都是日常生活中极为常见的词汇，这种简单易懂的词适用性广，同时也是人们生活中使用频率最高的词汇，可以在最短的时间内吸引受教育程度不同的消费者，最大程度地贴近潜在消费者。

C. 灵活使用代词

在广告中，为了更加贴近消费者，增强消费者的参与感，广告中往往使用大量的人称代词和物主代词，通常来说第一人称用来指示生产厂家，第二人称指代消费者，而第三人称往往用来指消费者所熟悉或喜欢的某个人或者商品本身。

【例 5】 Exceed Your Vision.

【译文】梦想让视野无限。（爱普生）

【例6】 I am what I am.
【译文】我就是我。（锐步）
【例7】 Catch that Pepsi spirit. Drink it in.
【译文】喝百事可乐，感受百事精神。（百事可乐）

上述的广告都使用了人称代词或者物主代词，这种代词的使用拉近了厂商和消费者之间的距离。除了人称或者物主代词以外，广告中还经常出现一些不表示特定范畴的不定代词，以此利用消费者的从众心理或者宣传产品的非凡特性。

【例8】 All good things come in pears.
【译文】好梨天天吃，好礼天天来。
【例9】 Everyone needs the sun.
【译文】人人需要阳光。（阳光保险）

D. 多语并用

在广告中，尤其是介绍外国产品的广告中，往往会加入一些外语词汇，这样不仅显示出产品的特质，更给消费者带来一种异域的风味，吸引消费者的注意。

【例10】 Yoplait yogurt est fanastique. （Yoplait 牌酸奶）

法语"est fanastique"等同于英语"is fantastic"，在表示酸奶品质的同时更标示了其产地，带来一股异域色彩。

【例11】 Order it in bottles or in canes.
　　　　　Perrier…with added je ne sais quoi.

法语"je ne sais quoi"相当于"I don't know"，这句简单的法语不但表示了它的法国风味，而且增加了人们对于饮料的好奇。

【例12】 Start in Downtown London and in 3 hours
　　　　　Arrivez au centre de paris.
【译文】从伦敦闹市启程3小时抵达巴黎市中心。

这是一则旅游广告，这一广告用语言的转换巧妙地表达出了地点的转换，同时还使人感到交通的便利，仿佛两地之间用一句广告就连接起来，不同的只有语言而已。值得注意的是，由于法国的食品、酒类、服饰、旅游在世界都享有盛誉，并且英语国家的读者大多懂得法语,所以一些英文广告语中会加入法语,正如中国的一些商品包装上会有日语一样,因为日语含有汉字,可以给消费者联想猜测的空间。

E. 创造新词

一些广告为了吸引消费者往往标新立异,突出产品的新、奇、特,满足消费者追求新潮的心理。

【例 13】The orangemostest drink in the world.

orange 本来就是橙子的意思,而这则广告在 orange 之后又加了一个 most,并且在 most 之后又加了一个表示最高级的后缀 est,仿佛橙子已经变成了一种属性,而这种橙汁恨不得成为世界上橙子属性最重的东西。可以想见,当消费者看到这则广告时很难不动心。

【例 14】Give a Timex to all, and to all a good time.

【译文】拥有一块天美时表,拥有一段美好时光。

在这则广告中,厂商将自己的产品取名为 Timex,对于一款手表产品而言,很容易让人联想起 time 和 excellent 两个单词,以此来提升产品在消费者心中的形象。此外,英文广告语中还经常故意使用一些拼错了的词汇来创造一些新词,产生意想不到的效果。

【例 15】We know eggsactly how to tell eggs.

这是一则鸡蛋的广告,在广告中"exactly"被错拼为"eggsactly",故意将"鸡蛋"(egg)嵌入广告之中,在使读者明白其含义的同时,又绝妙地突出了自己的专业性和质量,让人拍案叫绝。

【例 16】TWOGETHER

The Ultimate All Inclusive One Brice Sunkissed Holiday

这则旅馆的广告故意把"together"拼错为"twogether",将"two"加入广告中,以一种十分新奇的手段吸引外出度假的情侣。值得注意的是,这种创新手段虽然在广告应用中可以取得出奇制胜的效果,但是在翻译时却往往找不到合适的译法而使得其在源语言中的效果丧失殆尽。

7.2.2　英文广告语的句法特点

A. 常用简单句

简单句简洁明了，对于广告这种需要在短时间内吸引读者的文体来说非常合适，可以很快地吸引读者的视线，达到宣传效果。

【例17】Fresh up with Seven-up.

【译文】君饮七喜，提神醒脑。（七喜）

【例18】We integrate, you communicate.

【译文】我们集大成，您超越自我。（三菱电工）

【例19】Going East, Staying Westin.

【译文】到东方，住威斯汀酒店。（威斯汀酒店）

上述广告语都使用了颇为简单的句式，但是并没有影响广告的宣传效果，反而寥寥数语便将产品的优势和特点表达出来，吸引了人们的视线，激发起了购买欲。

B. 常用祈使句

祈使句本身就含有请求、命令和号召的含义，这与广告的文体功能不谋而合，因此祈使句在发挥广告的劝说和诱导功能时具有得天独厚的优势，也是广告英语中相当常用的一种句式。

【例20】Stop in a store near you, take a look
　　　　 Go ahead compare
　　　　 See for yourself
　　　　 So step in and take a look
　　　　 Visit an authorized IBM Personal Computer.（IBM 电脑）

【例21】Buy one pair, get one free.

【译文】买一送一。（强力蚊香）

【例22】So come in McDonald's and enjoy big mac sandwich.

【译文】走进麦当劳，享用大三明治。（麦当劳）

上述广告中都是以祈使句为主。值得注意的是，在这些祈使句中并没有一般英语祈使句中表示委婉和礼貌的"please"等词，反而多是以命令式的口吻为主，但是在广告语境中这种祈使句非但没有一种冒犯感，反而给人一种欲罢不能的感觉。

C. 使用疑问句

疑问句在广告中也有着独特的功能。疑问句不仅简化了语法结构，而且从心理学上来看，疑问句先提出问题后提供答案，符合语言的合作原则，更重要的是疑问句包含预设（presuppositions），这种预设一般是有利于广告所宣传的产品的，从而在心理上给消费者一种好的印象，使消费者产生购买的欲望。

【例 23】Are you going grey too early?

【译文】问君早生白发乎？（新新染发剂）

这则广告中的预设就是你不应该过早地有白头发，你应该想办法去遮住它，而这时候出现的染发剂对消费者来说吸引力不言而喻，颇有一种只可意会不可言传之妙。此外，英文广告语中还经常使用反义疑问句，给读者造成更强的心理冲击。

【例 24】Wouldn't you really want to have a Buick?

【译文】难道你不愿意拥有一辆别克车吗？（别克汽车）

这则广告巧妙地使用了一个反问句。如果说使用疑问句的话消费者还可能给予否定回答的话，那么使用这种反问句则彻底使消费者不忍心拒绝广告所宣传的产品。

D. 使用省略句与分离句

分离句是英文广告语中所特有的一种语言现象，指的是一个长句被分割为若干短句，而每个短句都包含有自己独特的信息点，从而增大信息量的一种现象。在广告中使用分离句，可以把需要用一个长句表达的内容用若干分离句表达出来。信息隐藏在长句中不易被消费者注意，但是分离句的使用恰到好处地解决了这一问题。

【例 25】Talk global. Pay local.

【译文】全球通信，就近付款。

【例 26】First across the Pacific; first across the Atlantic; first throughout Latin America.

【译文】首跨太平洋，首跨大西洋，首跨拉丁美洲。（航空公司）

以上两个广告中都使用了分离句，把一个完整的长句分离为两个短句,突出了要宣扬的产品信息,如若将其合为一个句子,则信息量大为缩小,远不如使用分离句。此外,为了达到节省版面甚至标新立异的效果,一些广告还使用省略句,将一些句子成分省略甚至仅仅使用一个单词组成独词句。

【例27】Every time a good time.

【译文】分分秒秒,欢聚欢笑。(麦当劳)

【例28】Intel inside.

【译文】给电脑一颗奔腾的"芯"。(英特尔奔腾)

【例29】Think

【译文】思索(IBM)

以上三则广告如果从英语语法上来讲都不能属于句子,因为一些句子成分被省略了,但是这种省略句做广告却妙用无穷,尤其是例29中只有一个单词,给消费者留下了无限遐想的空间。

7.2.3 广告语的语域特点

语域理论是系统功能语言学的一个重要理论,以韩礼德为代表的系统功能学派特别强调语境的作用,即语言发生的环境。他们将语境分为两类:文化语境和情景语境。所谓文化语境指的是语言使用者生活在其中的社会文化或者文化背景,而情景语境指的是语言正在使用时的场合,即语言使用的实际环境。文化语境的差异导致语言产生了基于语言使用者的变体,即由于方言、社会地位、性别等语言使用者的因素所产生的语言变体。而情景语境的差异则使得语言产生了基于语言运用的变体,比如不同类别广告用语之间的差异,所谓语域就是语言使用的功能变体,即因情景语境的变化而产生的语言形式的变化。系统功能派的语言学家进一步将语域概括为三个部分:话语范围、话语基调和话语方式,即语场、语旨和语式。所谓语场指的是实际发生的事情,或者说语言发生的环境及语言的话题;语旨指的是语言参与者之间的关系,包括参与者之间的社会地位和他们的角色关系;而语式指的是语言交际的渠道或者媒介,比如说是口头的还是书面的,是即兴的还是有准备。在不同的语场中，广告所使用的词汇和术语完全不同，如食品广告和化妆品广告的词汇就千差万别。在不同的语旨情况下，广告的语言特征就完全不同，面向儿童的广告和面向成人的广告其语言完全不同。而语式则在外部环境中改变了广告的形态，一则报纸广告和户外展牌广告的语言可以说大相径庭。

A. 语场不同

【例 30】

Vaeshartelt is an exceptional castle located in Maastricht. It is set in seven hectares of <u>magnificent parkland</u> graced by <u>quiet ponds</u> and <u>ancient trees</u>. Its <u>elegant drive</u> is lined with <u>lime trees</u>. King William Ⅱ of the Netherlands was once the proud owner of this estate and endowed the castle with <u>royal glamour</u>. Veashartelt castle is known today for its <u>unique style</u>, which combines <u>historical elements and modern architecture</u>. It is pleasingly different, striking and full of character.

Guests' wishes are paramount here, with attention to detail, professionalism and continuous innovation defining our approach. Whether you are here for business, leisure or for a party, Vaeshartelt is the right choice.

这是一则度假宾馆的广告，文中画线部分的词汇都是用来修饰宾馆景色的，如"magnificent parkland""quiet ponds""ancient trees""elegant drive""royal glamour""unique style""historical elements and modern architecture"。这些词汇符合宾馆广告这一语场的需要，充分体现出了宾馆环境的优雅、舒适，因而广泛出现。与此相对，其他种类的广告也因语场的不同而有着特殊的词汇。

【例 31】　　　　　**李锦记 XO 酱**

李锦记 XO 酱，食出创意！

李锦记 XO 酱选用上等干贝、虾米等食材精制而成，食法千变万化。XO 酱既为餐前或伴酒小食之极品，亦适合伴食各款佳肴、中式点心、粉面、粥品及日本寿司，更可用于烹调肉类、蔬菜、海鲜、豆腐、炒饭等等。

滋味小食　变化无穷

李锦记XO酱，<u>香浓惹味</u>，将XO酱配以各类材料，如饼干、鸡蛋、番茄、青瓜或其他蔬菜，发挥您的创意，自制小食，简单方便，<u>随时享用</u>，<u>滋味无穷</u>。

蘸食点心　蘸出特色

李锦记XO酱，蘸食点心、肠粉等传统中式美食，为美点锦上添花，<u>味美无比</u>！

调拌粉面　惹味倍添

李锦记XO酱，采用精选干贝秘制，最宜调拌即食面、日本乌冬面及各类粉面，加倍惹味之余，平凡粉面顿变<u>精彩美食</u>！

创意炒饭　色香味美

李锦记XO酱炒饭，不但色香味美，更能为传统美食加添新意，领您<u>口味一新</u>！

品味最尊贵的酱料美食——李锦记XO酱首屈一指！

本则广告作为一则典型的食品广告，使用了大量的与饮食滋味有关的词汇，这种词汇使得整篇广告十分出彩，使人流涎三尺，仿佛只看广告便已经尝到了这种酱料的美味。所以，在不同的语场下，不同种类的广告使用词汇截然不同，这样才能达到突出自身特色、吸引消费者的目的。

B. 语旨不同

【例32】Hi, <u>my</u> name is Messy Marvin.

<u>I</u> got that name because no matter how hard <u>I</u> tried <u>my</u> room and <u>my</u> clothes are always messy. But the one day, Mom brought home thick, rich, yummy Hershey's Syrup in the no mess squeeze bottle. And before <u>I</u> knew it, <u>I</u> was making the best chocolate milk <u>I</u>'d ever had. But <u>I</u> wasn't making a mess. It's fun, too. <u>I</u> just pull the cap and squeeze. Nothing drips, nothing spills.

这是一则面向儿童的广告。这则广告中广泛使用了第一人称的代词，因为对于儿童来说，同伴之间的影响力是最大的，甚至大于

他本身的感受。儿童往往是看到别的儿童的零食或者玩具时才产生了拥有欲望的，因此在面向儿童的广告中使用这种第一人称代词往往会给其他儿童一种同伴间的压力，促使他们不断向父母索要这种商品。与儿童相反，成年人懂得用自己的角度来衡量一件商品，所以面向成年人的广告极少大量出现第一人称代词，反倒是出现大量的第二人称代词。

【例33】Sometimes nothing but pure indulgence will do. The nights are longer, the evening is your own…, and the perfect accompaniment to make <u>you</u> feel special is the delicious Terry's Chocolate Orange Bar.

And we really do mean indulgence. It's the unique blend of rich chocolate and deliciously orangey flavours, together with that melt-in-the-mouth quality, that gives the Terry's Chocolate Orange Bar its delectably decadent feel. And its convenient size makes it just right for <u>you</u> to eat alone…

So, picture the scene. It's <u>your</u> first evening in for weeks. <u>You</u>'ve kicked off your shoes, turned the lights down low and put on some slow music, perhaps a little soft soul or gentle jazz. The whole evening is a "me-time", a special time just for <u>you</u> to relax. Make it complete with a Terry's Chocolate Orange Bar…it's sumptuous, luxurious and delectable. Go on…indulge. <u>You</u> deserve it.

与上一则广告相反，本则广告中出现了大量的第二人称代词，主要是因为这一则广告面向成人。与儿童相比，成人判断力更强，更相信自己的感受，它通过大量的第二人称代词使广告直面顾客，针对性强，使读者相信这种巧克力确实能给人带来不一般的享受。

C. 语式不同

当今由于信息传播载体的极大丰富，广告种类也极为繁多，在不同媒介上刊登的广告由于语式的不同，其内容和形式也有着极大的差异性。

【例34】　　　　　北京恒基中心广告
　　　　　　　精雕细琢　京城瑰宝
　　位于北京东长安街黄金地段、地铁站上方的北京恒基中心，总建筑面积逾30万平方米，拥有甲级办公大楼3幢、酒店1幢及5层大型购物商场，并设有充足车位之特大停车场；规划完善，宏伟夺目。北京恒基中心与今日现代首都新貌互相辉映，俨如京城瑰宝。

　　这是一则典型的报纸广告，由于报纸是书面性媒体，所以报纸广告语言倾向于使用书面语。而且由于报纸在多媒体表现上的不足，所以报纸广告往往在文字上做足文章，尽可能靠文字吸引读者。

　　户外展牌广告则又是另一种情况。

　　【例35】Intelligence everywhere
　　【译文】智慧演绎，无处不在。（摩托罗拉）

　　上面的广告是一个户外展牌广告。与报纸广告不同，户外展牌广告可以有充分的空间和手段进行生动立体的视觉宣传，所以这种广告的语言以简短精悍为佳，往往与宣传图片互相呼应，形成一种复合效果。而在多媒体上播放的广告如电视和网络广告更侧重发挥多媒体的优势，创造一种交互性的模式，增强观众的参与感。

7.2.4　广告中的修辞与审美

A. 音韵美

　　对于一则广告来说，尽最大可能的吸引更多人的注意是它的主要任务。广告语言可用各种修辞手段来满足人的审美需求，吸引受众的注意力。语言最吸引人的地方便在于发音，所以具有音韵美的修辞在广告中极为常见。

　　【例36】Asking for More.
　　【译文】摩尔香烟，多多益善。（摩尔香烟）
　　【例37】Forget hot taste.
　　　　　　Only Kool, with pure menthol has the taste of extra coolness
　　　　　　Come up to Kool.

【译文】忘掉辛辣的感觉。

只有"酷"牌,纯正的薄荷口味带给你特别清凉的酷爽。

想"酷"你就来!(酷牌口香糖)

【例 38】OIC(眼镜广告)

【例 39】It's up to you.

【译文】由你做决定。(up2u 化妆品)

上述四则广告都使用了谐音双关的修辞手法。"More"和"KOOL"在表示原有普通含义的同时还是商标品牌。例 38 中 OIC 的发音与"oh, I see"相同,用于眼镜广告可谓恰到好处,而例 39 中"up to you"则是与品牌"up2u"谐音,很好地起到了宣传品牌的作用。

头韵也是英文广告语中常用到的一种修辞手段。

【例 40】Sea, sun, sand, seclusion, and Spain!

【译文】大海、阳光、沙滩、静谧,还有西班牙!(饭店)

【例 41】It's flavor wins flavor.

【译文】以我茗香,赢君品尝。(茶)

【例 42】Spare, shapely, sensational one step dressing

【译文】省料、匀称、激情——一步裙

【例 43】Health, humor and happiness. It's a gift we'd love to give.

【译文】健康、幽默、快乐,这就是我们给您的礼物。

【例 44】Safe and Sound.

【译文】安然无恙。(火灾保险)

上述广告都使用了头韵的修辞手法,如例 40 中的 s、例 41 中的 f、例 42 中的 s、例 43 中的 h、例 44 中的 s,这种头韵修辞手法的使用在完整地表达广告含义的同时,还形成了一种朗朗上口的音韵美。

除了头韵外,另外一种经常被用到的修辞手法是尾韵。

【例 45】My Goodness! My Guinness!

【译文】我的健力士,要爽由自己。(健力士啤酒)

【例 46】Workout without wearout.

【译文】鞋好运动好,耐穿不磨脚。

【例47】Flash dash. Classic Splash!

【译文】闪光、炫耀、经典的飞溅。(女士泳衣)

以上广告都使用了尾韵的修辞手法,值得注意的是例45和例46中不仅使用了尾韵,还使用了头韵的修辞手法。这种尾韵的修辞手法使得广告像诗歌一样富有一种押韵的美感。

除此之外,对偶的修辞手法也常出现在广告中,尤其是中文广告。

【例48】Once tasted. Always loved.

【译文】一朝品尝,爱恋不舍。

【例49】虽是毫末技艺,却是顶上功夫。(理发店广告)

【例50】Lose ounces. Save pounds.

【译文】失去几盎司,省下数英镑。(减肥广告)

上述几则广告都使用了对偶的修辞手法。尤其是例49,"毫末"和"顶上"在对偶的同时还使用了语义双关的修辞手法,"毫末"既可以指"头发"又可代指"微不足道的",而"顶上"既可指"头顶"又可以指"极好的",堪称绝妙至极。对偶的修辞手法给广告一种对称的音韵美,但是也要注意过于规整的对称会使广告显得呆板无趣。上述几种修辞手法都是典型的音美类修辞手法,通过这些修辞手法,广告获得了一种在短时间内吸引人的音韵美。

B. 重复美

除了在音韵上做文章外,广告还倾向于使用反复或排等修辞手法来增强气势。

【例51】每周七天,每天七点,七点直播。

【例52】Make up your mind before make up your face.

【译文】化妆前慎用化妆品。

【例53】Less space. Less noise. Less expense.

【译文】少空间,少噪音,少费用。(松下电器)

【例54】When you're sipping Lipton, you're sipping something special.

【译文】啜饮立顿茶,品尝独特味。(立顿袋装茶)

【例55】Finish the job in less time, with less fuel and less noise.

【译文】用更少的时间、更少的能源、更少的噪音,完成同样精彩的工作。

上述广告中都使用了重复的修辞手法,即某一单词反复出现,如例51中的"七"、例52中的"make up"、例53中的"less"、例54中的"sipping"和例55中的"less",这种反复修辞手法的使用使得这些广告读起来更有气势,更有说服力。

与重复效果相近的修辞手法是排比。

【例56】美来自内心,美来自美宝莲。(美宝莲化妆品)

【例57】You can buy everything
　　　　From perfume to pearls
　　　　From Watches to wallets
　　　　From radios to wraps

【译文】从香水到珠宝,
　　　　从手表到钱包,
　　　　从收音机到包装纸,
　　　　一应俱全。

【例58】金星电视,精心设计,精心生产,精心筛选,精心测试,金星精心,电视明星。(金星电视)

上述三则广告中都使用了排比的结构。反复修辞手法是某一单词或词语反复在句中出现的现象,而排比指的是几个结构相似、语义相关的短句反复使用来加强语气的语言现象,不刻意强调某一单词的反复出现。

C. 外形美

广告首先是一种语言,其次才是一种营销手段。作为一种语言,不仅有音美,更可以有形美,而且这种形美可以更好地为广告的文体功能服务。因此,形美类的修辞手法虽然不及音美类的多,但是在广告中,尤其是汉语广告中仍然占有一席之地。

【例59】The last fits, the fit lasts.

【译文】精湛合宜的工艺,永久舒适的产品。(鞋)
【例60】全球通,通全球。(中国移动全球通业务)
【例61】中国平安,平安中国。(中国平安集团)

以上数则广告都是用了顶真的修辞手法,即前半小句的结尾是后半小句的开头,这样使得广告在形式外观上有一种对称美。

此外,还有一种回文的修辞手法,可使广告打破语序的羁绊。

【例62】居然天上客,客上天然居。(天然居饭店)
【例63】可以清心也。(茶馆茶杯盖上的广告)
【例64】Red root put up to order(红菜头罐头)
【例65】Rise to vote sir. (大选广告)

例62中的"居然天上客"反过来便是"客上天然居",不仅夸赞了酒店,更夸赞了客人;例63中"可以清心也"不论从哪个字开始都可以成句,"可以清心也,以清心也可,清心也可以,心也可以清,也可以清心",构成了一个回环的效果;而例64和例65是英文广告语中的回文,正序和倒序所形成的词句完全一样。这种回文的修辞手法给广告赋予了极大的外观美,让人不禁赞叹人类语言的精妙绝伦。

D. 类比美

广告作为一种向消费者介绍新产品新事物的应用文体,其最大的任务便是让消费者认识、了解新产品的功效和作用,并产生消费欲望,而以类比的方式将消费者不熟悉的新产品与他们所熟知的事物联系起来,更有利于人们了解新事物,也符合人类认知的规律。因此,广告中常常可见各种类比性质的修辞。广告中最为常见的一类修辞手法便是比喻,其中又可以细分为明喻和暗喻。

【例66】这双鞋就像妈妈牵引宝宝的手。
【例67】帅哥牌牛仔裤,犹如第二层皮肤。(帅哥牌牛仔裤)
【例68】Breakfast without orange juice is like a day without sunshine.
【译文】没有橘汁的早餐犹如没有阳光的日子。(橘汁)
【例69】Light as a breeze, soft as a cloud.

【译文】轻如微风，柔若浮云。（丝绸女装）

以上四例广告使用的修辞手法便是明喻，使用明喻明确形象地指出产品的特征，给人一种强烈的联想感。明喻的特点是比喻词在句中显现，如"就像""犹如""as""like"等词都在句中出现，而暗喻则正好相反，比喻词是隐含的。

【例 70】Blessed by year round good weather, Spain is a magnet for sun worshipers and holiday makers.

【译文】西班牙蒙上帝保佑，一年四季天气晴朗，宛如一块磁铁，吸引着酷爱阳光、喜好度假的人们。（西班牙旅游广告）

【例 71】Pick an Ace from Toshiba.

【译文】东芝品牌，卓越超群。（东芝）

【例 72】四十岁是一条龙。

【例 73】The most sensational place to wear satin on your lips.

【译文】丝般柔滑的口红擦在唇上这最富有激情的地方。（口红）

【例 74】Wash the big city out of the hair.

【译文】洗去头发上大城市的污垢。（洗发水）

上述五则广告虽然也使用了比喻的修辞手法，但是并没有出现比喻词，所以是暗喻的修辞手法。例 70 中西班牙被比喻成了磁铁，例 71 中东芝被比喻成了 Ace 王牌，例 72 中四十岁的人被比喻为像龙一样有活力，例 73 中口红被比喻成了丝绸，而例 74 将污垢比作了 the big city。这种暗喻修辞手段虽然没有明确出现比喻词，但人们可以从文中明白其喻体，在不知不觉中相信广告的宣传。

此外，在广告中拟人的修辞手法也极为常见，尤其用在产品的宣传上，可以起到一种生动活泼、让人感到亲切的效果。

【例 75】Flowers by Interflora speak from heart.

【译文】"茵特"之花，表达肺腑之言。（茵特花店）

【例 76】Unlike me, my Rolex never needs a rest.

【译文】和我不一样，我的劳力士从不需要休息。（劳力士手表）

【例 77】Let Kelly work for you!

【译文】让凯莉为你服务！（凯莉咨询公司）

【例78】特快专递,当代神行太保。(中国邮政特快专递)

【例79】It handles the road as easily as it handles Mother Nature.

【译文】他能很轻松地对付道路。(福特汽车)

上述广告中都使用了拟人的修辞手法,将产品拟人化来突出有关特征和优势,如例75中将花比作人,仿佛他们花店里的花像人一样能够有情感;例76中则将手表比作人,而且是一个不需要休息的人;例77中整个公司都被比作人,随时准备为顾客服务;例78中将快递比作《水浒传》中的"神行太保",以突出快递之"快";例79中则将汽车比作人,以突出车的能力强大。

在广告之中模仿典故创作广告语也是一种常见的修辞手法,叫做仿拟。

【例80】衣衣不舍沫沫含情 (洗衣粉)

【例81】Where there is a way, there is a Toyota.

【译文】丰田汽车,风行天下。(丰田汽车)

【例82】To smoke, or not to smoke, that is a question.

【译文】烟,吸还是不吸,这是一个值得考虑的问题。

【例83】Give me Green world, or give me yesterday.

【译文】今日的风采,昨夜的"绿世界"(绿世界晚霜)

【例84】白菊蚊香,默默无蚊。(白菊蚊香)

例80中仿拟了"依依不舍脉脉含情"的语句,只不过把"依依"改成了"衣衣","脉脉"改成了"沫沫",突出了洗衣粉的产品特点。例81仿拟了成语"When there is a way, there is a will(有志者事竟成)",不仅在语言上让人感到熟悉,更突出了丰田车的销量之大。例82仿拟了《哈姆雷特》中著名的台词"To be, or not to be, that is a question",生动地描写出了消费者对于吸不吸烟的犹豫。例83仿拟了美国独立战争时期革命活动家 Patrick Henry 的名言"Give me liberty, or give me death(不自由毋宁死)",表明这种晚霜对于消费者来说如同自由一般重要。例84中的"默默无蚊"仿拟了成语"默默无闻",充分反映了蚊香在除掉蚊子后给人带来的惬意和宁静。这种仿拟的修辞手法可以给读者一种似曾相识的美感,更可以恰到好处地宣传自己产品的优点。不过要注意的是，在广告中广泛使用仿拟也是对语言的一种消费和侵蚀，使一些脍炙人口的词句都染上了商业气息。

E. 夸张美

与法律等其他应用文体不同，广告文体语言并不十分严谨。相反，过分呆板拘谨的语言往往使广告失去本来的色彩和宣传力，因此广告文体在尊重事实的基础上允许一定的夸张。一些广告文体通过描述一些近似荒谬的情景来说服消费者，达到一种剑走偏锋的效果。

【例 85】一夫当关，万夫莫开（制锁厂广告）

【例 86】We've hidden a garden full of vegetables where you'd never expect. In a pie.

【译文】小馅饼有大惊奇，满园蔬菜放饼里。（馅饼）

【例 87】The first ever, the last you'll need.

【译文】一朝拥有，别无所求。（精工手表）

以上几则广告都是用了夸张的修辞手法，尤其是例 86，宣称将满园蔬菜都放入一个馅饼里，让人感觉十分惊讶。但就是这种近似于荒谬的语句却极大地调动起了消费者的好奇心，让人不禁想走到店里看一下到底什么样的馅饼才能有这种神效，于是广告的目的也就达到了。不过在使用夸张修辞手段的时候也要掌握好分寸，如果夸张得离谱则会产生反效果，甚至被认为是虚假广告。

F. 内涵美

广告文体在描述产品的同时更要求吸引、说服和劝诱消费者，因此只是干巴巴地描述产品远远不够。优秀广告更应该在内涵上做功夫，在字里行间委婉含蓄地表达意思，使读者在短短的广告中读出新意，达到无声胜有声的效果。

【例 88】谁能惩治腐败——新飞牌电冰箱。（新飞牌冰箱）

【例 89】A deal with us means a good deal to you.

【译文】和我们做买卖意味着您做了一笔好买卖。（贸易公司）

【例 90】Give a SEIKO to all, and to all a good time.

【译文】精工表走时准确,戴表人心情愉悦。(精工手表)

【例91】Try out sweet corn. You'll smile from ear to ear.

【译文】品尝我们的甜玉米,穗穗令你欢乐开怀。(甜玉米广告)

【例92】Give your hair a touch of spring.

【译文】给你的头发一缕春色。(洗发水)

上述几则广告中都使用了语义双关的修辞手法。例88中的"腐败"不仅指官场腐败,更指的是食物腐败。例89中 a good deal 可以表示"好买卖",也可以表示"很多"。例90中 a good time 不仅指走时精准,更表示心情愉悦。例91中 ear to ear 可以指一穗一穗的玉米,如果指人则表示从耳朵到耳朵的面部表情。例92中 spring 既表示春天,也表示有弹力。

对比是把两个相反和相对的事物融入同一个句子之中,给人一种善与恶、丑与美的对比,更加突出了所宣传产品的优势和特点。

【例93】To the host it's half empty. To the guest it's half full.

【译文】主怕杯沿满,客恐瓶底干。(威士忌酒)

【例94】A mighty Mini.

【译文】高能微型录音机。

【例95】阳光下的绿荫。(美加净防晒广告)

【例96】Cancer is often curable. The fear of cancer is often fatal.

【译文】癌症常可治,惧癌会致命。(美国癌症协会公益广告)

【例97】We lead. Others copy.

【译文】我们领先,他人复制(理光复印机)

例93中主与客的对比形象表现出了酒的美味与珍贵。例94中短短的一小句却表现出了产品的两个特征:体积小和功能强大。例95将防晒霜比作阳光下的绿荫更是突出了其防晒作用。例96中通过对比癌症和惧癌的后果,警告人们恐惧癌症比癌症本身还可怕。而例97中通过对比,不仅将自己的产品抬高,更贬低了其他的竞争者。

除了仿拟经典的词句外,有些广告词直接将典故或一些著名的句子拿来做广告,这种手法叫做用典。

【例 98】Seeing is believing.

【译文】眼见为实。(眼镜广告)

【例 99】All work and no play.

【译文】连续运转，永不停息。(轴承)

【例 100】As you like it.

【译文】如你所愿。(针织品)

例 98 中的 Seeing is believing 原意是"看到的才是真实的"，用作眼镜的广告可谓名副其实，戴上这副眼镜，看到的就是真实的。例 99 中将"All work and no play makes Jack a dull boy"后半部分去掉，以显示出轴承的耐用。而例 100 中 As you like it 是莎士比亚的喜剧 *As You Like It*（《皆大欢喜》）的名称，用它做广告，显示出这种针织品的受欢迎程度。

此外，广告中还有一种反语的修辞手法，可以以一种十分幽默、以退为进的手法为自己的产品造势。

【例 101】If people keep telling you to quit smoking cigarettes, don't listen—they're probably trying to trick you into living.

【译文】如果有人苦口婆心地想劝你戒烟，不要理他——他想骗你活得更久。(美国防癌协会)

【例 102】实不相瞒，"天仙"的名声是吹出来的。(天仙电扇)

以上广告都使用了反语的修辞手段，用显而易见说反话的方式来强调正面的信息。例 101 中"trick you into living"虽然使用了"trick"（欺骗）这一词，但是所有人都明白让你活得更久是对你好，因而从另一个方面说明了吸烟的危害。而例 102 中的"吹"在使用反语的同时，也使用了双关的修辞手法："吹"不仅指吹嘘，更指的是使用电风扇来吹，意思是这个品牌的口碑和名声是建立在大众的体验之上的。

广告作为一种劝诱性的文体，不仅要吸引人，更要在含义上说服别人，以上各种修辞手段的使用使得广告增添了一种内涵意义上的美感，因而说服消费者的能力大为增强。

7.3 汉英广告语差异

汉语广告与英文广告语在文体色彩、写作手法上都有着突出的区别。一般来说，长篇汉语广告措辞夸张，气势豪壮，往往喜欢罗列产品所获得的各种权威认证或者荣誉，以此来打动消费者；在句法上倾向于堆砌产品特点及相关术语，形成一种冗长繁复近似于八股文的语式；而在文体上则往往严肃认真，通过严肃庄重的语气来给消费者一种信赖感和安全感。总体来说，长篇汉语广告的特点与中国人的审美有相当大的联系。

【例 103】

涡阳苔干——中国特产

涡阳苔干，名优特产，驰名中外，声震古今，翠绿、鲜嫩、可口，有"天然海蜇""健康食品"之称；清乾隆年间奉献皇宫，故又名"贡菜"。本品含蛋白质、可溶性糖、果胶、多种氨基酸、维生素B1、B2、C和胡萝卜素及钾钠钙铁磷锌等十余种矿物质，有清热降压、通经络、壮筋骨、去口臭、解热毒就毒及治疗心脏病、神经官能症、消化不良、贫血诸功效；畅销国内，远销日本等地，为厨下及馈赠佳品。

本品食前需水泡发开，去缨洗净，开水焯过，凉滤备用。单盘与拼盘均可，以肉配炒，风味尤佳。温凉自便，咸甜酸辣皆宜。

此则广告具有典型的中式广告的特点，罗列堆砌了大量关于产品的荣誉及功效信息，甚至出现了"清热降压、通经络、壮筋骨、去口臭、解热毒就毒及治疗心脏病、神经官能症、消化不良、贫血诸功效"等词语。此外，这则广告用语颇为正式，出现了汉语口语中不常见的四字结构，如"名优特产""驰名中外""声震古今"等，语气较为严肃庄重，与读者有一定距离。

英文广告语与汉语广告相比有显著差异：汉语广告注重描述产品的荣誉奖项，而英语长篇广告则倾向于描述产品本身的实际效果，符合崇尚实用、注重实效的西方文化。而在语气上则一改汉语广告的严肃认真，或平实简洁，或轻松幽默，随意性较强，善于从消费者的角度描述产品，注重消费者的情感需要，能够拉近与消费者之间的心理距离。同样是食品广告，下面这则巧克力广告就与例 103 的行文风格大相径庭。

【例 104】Sometimes nothing but indulgence will do. The nights are longer, the evening is your own ... and the perfect accompaniment to make you feel special is the delicious Terry's Chocolate Orange Bar.

And we really do mean indulgence. It's the unique blend of rich chocolate and deliciously orangey flavors, together with that melt-in-the-mouth quality, that gives the Terry's Chocolate Orange Bar its delectably decadent feel. And its convenient size makes it just right for you to ear alone...

So, picture the scene. It's your first evening in for weeks. You've kicked off your shoes, turned the lights down low and put on some slow music, perhaps a little soft soul or gentle jazz. The whole evening is a "me-time", a special time just for you to relax. Make it complete with a Terry's Chocolate Orange Bar ... it's sumptuous, luxurious and delectable. Go on ... indulge. You deserve it.

这则英文巧克力广告没有刻意宣传巧克力的口味品质，也没有宣传巧克力所获荣誉，仿佛只是一篇描述消费者本人享受巧克力过程的散文而已。尤其是最后一段，将消费者下班后回到家打开音乐享受夜晚的过程表现得淋漓尽致。当然在这过程中少不了一块"特利橘味巧克力"，于是在广告渲染的背景下，消费者会不由而然地在脑海中联想起这一浪漫场景。而广告在满足消费者精神需求的同时，以润物细无声的方式实现了对产品的推销，达到了广告的目的。

7.4 广告语翻译策略

不同于一般的应用文体，广告语在翻译过程中不仅要求将原文中的意思翻译出来，更要求译文与原文实现功能对等，即使得译文能够发挥原来译文中的各种文体功能。要做到这一点，仅仅将广告中的字面意思翻译过来是远远不够的，而应该根据译文的具体语境和文体功能采取多种翻译策略。

7.4.1 直接转换翻译

如果译文在翻译过程中没有比较大的语言文化障碍，直译过来不会对文本的含义及文体功能产生损害时，在广告语的翻译过程中便可以采用直译的策略进行翻译。直译在翻译中属于异化的手段，采用直译的方式更能够将原文中的文化因素保留下来，有利于中外文化的交流。

【例105】Making the most of the time. (Citizen)

【译文】充分利用时间。（西铁城手表）

【例106】The Choice of a new generation.

【译文】新一代的选择。（百事可乐）

【例107】非常可乐，非常选择。（非常可乐）

【译文】A Special Cola. A special Choice. (Future Cola)

上述几则广告的翻译都遵循了直接转换的方法，也就是直译的手段。由于上述广告在中文和英文中并没有大的语言障碍，直接将原文翻译过来便可以实现文体的功能对等，所以采用直译的方式翻译便可。但是对于大多数广告而言，采用直译的方式并不能够实现文体功能的完全对等。

7.4.2 意译

相对于直译，意译在广告语翻译中应用更为广泛，因为大部分的广告语仅靠直译无法发挥应有的宣传和劝诱功能，需要用意译的手段翻译才能与原文实现功能对等。

【例108】Connecting People.

【译文】科技以人为本。（诺基亚手机）

【例109】Mosquitoes. Bye! Bye! Bye!

【译文】蚊子杀！杀！杀！（雷达牌杀虫剂）

【例 110】Spoil yourself and not your figure.

【译文】尽情享受，美丽依旧。（冰激凌）

上述几则广告都使用了意译的翻译手段。例 108 中广告的原意是"把人们连接起来"，但是译文翻译成了"科技以人为本"，更加突出了企业的核心价值观念，起到了更好的宣传效果。例 109 中的 bye 本来是"再见"的意思，但是在汉语中翻译为了极有气势的"杀！杀！杀！"，这种意译非但没有损害意思，造成误解，反而给人一种大快人心的感觉，让人恨不得立刻去买一瓶雷达牌杀虫剂。例 110 原意是"放纵自己而不破坏体型"，这样直译固然可以，但是作为广告的美感已经荡然无存，远不如意译的译文吸引人。

7.4.3 灵活套译

在英语和汉语中都有一些相对固定的表达方式，或是词组，或是成语名句谚语，这种固定的表达方式是人民在长期的生活中形成的，为人们所喜闻乐见，易于被人们所接受。灵活套译这种固定结构可以最大程度地消除两种语言在内涵意义和形象上的不同和缺损，使人们能够接受译文，减少文化差异带来的心理冲突。

【例 111】百闻不如一尝（浙江粮油食品进出口公司）

【译文】Tasting is believing.

【例 112】Only your time is more precious than this Watch.

【译文】手表诚可贵，时间价更高。

【例 113】红梅相机新奉献。（红梅相机）

【译文】My love is like a Red Rose.

【例 114】速效救心丸

随身携带，有备无患，随身携带，有惊无险。

【译文】A friend in need is a friend indeed.

上述广告的翻译都是用了套译的方法。例 111 中广告原文套用了中文的"百闻不如一见"，于是英语译文索性也套用了"Seeing is believing"，形成了一种语言上的对等。例 112 中中文翻译套用了人们所熟知的词句"生命诚可贵，爱情价更高"。例 113 中英文翻译套用了苏格兰诗人彭斯的诗句"My love is like a red, red rose"。例 114 中汉语广告使用了反复和排比结构,突出了气势,而英译时套用了英语中常用的谚语,突出了这种药物的可信赖性。

除了套用一些名言警句外,汉语广告中常常使用的四字表达在英语中往往也有对应的习惯表达,如:

品质优良　fine in quality
安全可靠　safe and stable
用料上乘　excellent in quality
携带方便　convenient to carry
老幼咸宜　suitable for all ages
美味可口　sweet and delicious
芬芳香甜　sweet aroma

7.4.4　修辞化的翻译

为了宣传的需要,许多广告都使用了各种各样的修辞手法,在翻译的过程中如果能够在不损害原文内涵和字面意思的情况下恰当地运用修辞手段翻译出来,则能够起到锦上添花的作用,尽最大可能发挥广告的文体功能。

【例 115】Reliably solid, solidly reliable.
【译文】安如磐石,磐石之安。(汽车广告)
【例 116】It S-T-R-E-C-H-E-S and springs back.
【译文】拉—得—长—收得紧。(腰带)
【例 117】Outcleans, outpulls, outlasts.
【译文】更干净,更美观,更耐用。(轮胎)
【例 118】Born in 1820 … still going strong!
【译文】生于 1820 年的壮汉。(苏格兰威士忌)

以上广告在原文中都用了修辞手法。如例 115 中原文和译文都是用了顶真的修辞手法,而例 116 中为了表现腰带的性能,特地将单词拆开拉长使用,而译文也如法炮制,完整地表现了原文中的形象。例 117 中译文和原文都使用了反复的修辞手法来增强气势,而例 118 中则使用了拟人的修辞手法。值得注意的是，并不是所有带有修辞手法的广告在翻译过程中都要和原文对应，有一些广告不宜也不能以原修辞手法译出。

【例 119】人无我有，人有我新，人新我优

【译文】We're leading.

上面这则广告就不宜按照原修辞手法译出，如果照搬的话势必使译文十分冗长，失去号召力和美感，反而直接译为"We're leading"，做到了神似。

7.4.5 注意文化因素的影响

在广告翻译中，文化因素也起着很重要的影响。在广告创作过程中一些词汇往往带有比较浓重的文化烙印，对于这种词语在翻译时要注重转换视角，在目的语的文化中找到相对应的词汇。还有一些词汇可能在两种文化中含有相异甚至相反的内涵意义，如果直接翻译极容易引起误解，这种情况也要注意。

【例 120】衣食住行，有"龙"则灵。（建行龙卡）

【译文】Loong Card will make your busy life easy.

【例 121】冬天到了，是买寒衣的时候了。

【译文】With the winter coming in, it's time to buy warm clothes.

【例 122】所有顾客凭本券享受打折优惠，购买 50 瓶矿泉水可享七折优惠。凭此券每户限购一份。

【译文】All shoppers must present this coupon to receive discount 30% off toward the purchases of fifty bottles of Mineral Water. With this coupon, limit one per family.

以上广告的翻译中都注重了对一些文化词汇的处理。如例 120 中"龙"，在英语中直译过来是"dragon"，虽然近年来随着西方国家对中国文化了解的增强，越来越多的人了解到中国的"龙"和英语中的"dragon"不是一回事，但是"dragon"在英语中仍然是一个给人以负面联想的词汇，而"龙"如果照拼音音译的话又与英语中的"long"混淆，所以有译者提出用"loong"来翻译汉语中的"龙"，

也不失为一个解决文化冲突的好办法。例 121 中"寒衣"在汉语中表示冬天穿的衣服,但是在英语中却没有这样的说法,冬天的衣物是用来保暖的,所以英语中对应的说法是"warm clothes"。例 122 中也是同理,在汉语中表示商品打折通常以几折来表示,七折就是按原价的百分之七十出售,但是在英语中则正好相反,七折便是给予百分之三十的优惠,所以是"30% discount"。

同样需要注意的还有一些商标品牌的译名。如说"西子香皂"就不宜音译为"shitze",这与英语单词"shits"相近,使人产生不好的联想。而"白翎"牌金笔也不可直译为"white feather",因为"white feather"在英语中有"投降""胆小"的含义。

7.4.6 汉语篇章广告英译注意改写

前文也提到过,汉语篇章广告在文体风格上与英文广告有很大的不同。在汉语语境中,汉语篇章广告以繁复冗长为美,在行文上往往庄重严肃,文体正式,善于列举和论述自身的优势和特点,这些在中国人看来并没有问题,但是英文广告语侧重点和行文风格与汉语广告截然不同,英文广告语语气轻松活泼,善于从顾客的角度出发,满足顾客的精神需求。因此,汉语篇章广告在翻译为英语时不能直接原封不动地翻译过来,而应该做适当的改写,以适应英语读者的习惯和需求。

【例 123】……<u>诞生于 20 世纪 80 年代末的虎豹集团,坚守孜孜以求、永不言退的发展理念</u>,在市场经济的大潮中,任凭浊浪排空,惊涛拍岸,独有胜似闲庭信步的自信,处变不惊,运筹帷幄。<u>尽握无限商机于掌间,渐现王者之气于天地</u>。虎豹人以其特有的灵气,极目一流,精益求精,<u>集世界顶尖服装生产技术装备之大成</u>,裁天上彩虹,绣人间缤纷,<u>开设计之先河,臻质量之高峰,领导服装之潮流</u>,尽显领袖之风采……

【译文】Founded in the late 1980's, the Hubao Group has now well developed into a leading enterprise in garment-fashion manufacturing by its great efforts for continuous progress. Enhanced by the world's most advanced technologies and its ceaseless technical innovation, it is now taking the lead in the world fashion designs for its good quality productions.

这则广告具有典型的汉语篇章广告的特点,可以说除了画线部分之外,其余词汇都没有实际的含义,只不过是从各个角度壮大声势,为企业做宣传而已。这类词汇不仅翻译起来有相当的困难,而且翻译过来也严重不符合英语的表达习惯和英文广告语的行文方式,很难被英语读者所接受,所以在翻译时对于这类广告应该进行删减和改写。

第八章　旅游宣传

旅游首先是和大自然打交道，同时也是和人文景观打交道。前者足以"养眼"，后者足以"养心"。旅游宣传资料既宣传自然，也宣传文化，作为一种大众化的通俗读物，为人们传递信息、熟悉环境、了解自然、解读文化提供窗口，其主要目的是让游客读懂并喜闻乐见，从中获取一定的自然、文化、民俗等相关知识。因此，旅游宣传文体多使用鼓动性语言来激发受众对宣传对象的兴趣，在语言描述中留有许多意义空白的空间，供他们发挥自己的想象力，形成朦胧的心理意向。旅游翻译是一种目的性很强的跨文化交际活动，在理论上应以功能文体学和功能目的论为指导，在实践上已成为一项重要的国际性服务。在实施旅游翻译时，为有效传递信息并感染受众，译者应该保留这些意义空白的空间，考虑文化因素对人们思维方式的影响，同时尽可能地靠近受众的思维方式，尽可能地使译文获取近似于原文的读者效应。本章主要从分析旅游宣传文体的特色和风格出发，探讨旅游宣传的翻译原则和翻译策略，给中外游客的旅游活动提供一些语言层面的参考。

8.1　旅游宣传的文体功能

旅游宣传是一种典型的呼唤型文体，通常凝聚着自然景观、人文景观、文化积淀等丰富的信息，与异国情调、民俗文化不可分离。"从整体上来说，旅游文体具有以下特点：短小精悍，生动活波，通俗易懂，信息量大，又不失文学性、艺术性、宣传性和广告性"（伍峰等，2008：319）。很多情况下，旅游宣传是旅游指南和旅游广告的复合体，不仅可以为游客提供游览、食宿、交通等信息，同时也起到了广告宣传的作用。其语言表达必须准确通俗、简洁明了，并富有吸引力，利于不同层面的读者或游客理解和接受。

旅游宣传文体主要有三种功能：一是传递信息的功能，这是旅游宣传文体的首要功能。它需要把大自然的鬼斧神工、历史及人文的丰富传承以及本土的审美情趣等景点所承载的各种信息都传达给读者，激发他们的探究欲和猎奇心。闪亮且独特的旅游信息会产生意想不到的效果，所以旅游宣传文字的编排和翻译都是非常重要的。二是诱导行动的功能。旅游宣传的最终目的就是以其自身魅力和宣传效果诱发读者的旅游行动。因此，旅游宣传的文字必须顾及读者的心理接受能力和审美取向，尽量雅俗共赏，使读者通过文字介绍产生心向旅游目的地的心理，满足他们的文化认同感。这种诱导功能的实现必须以提供足够的信息为前提。三是提示警告的功能。这种功能主要是通过景点的公示语来实现的。旅游景点内的公示语用介绍性、指示性、提示性、警告性的简明语言或图示向游客提供一定信息，具有诱发他们前往参观、使用相关旅游服务、促发或阻止行动等作用。

8.2　旅游宣传的文体特征及风格

旅游宣传语言是一种不特别严格的书面语，既没有口语化，也没有正式化，它要求不同阶层和不同文化背景的人们都可以理解。由于中西语言文化、社会习俗、审美意识等都有各自的历史渊源，在旅游宣传文体上则反映出表达习惯和风格的不同。本书从行文用字习惯和语言审美标准对此进行分析，以便使译者在进行旅游宣传的翻译时能树立文化意识，通过翻译的手段更好地进行文化交流和沟通。

8.2.1　简约与华美——行文用字习惯不同

中英文旅游宣传的用词一般都倾向于正式，涉及历史、文化、政治、民俗、地理、宗教、经济、休闲等内容。这些词汇多带有很强的描述性质，力求体现艺术性或美感，如 breathtaking（叹为观止的）、snowcapped（积雪覆盖的）、picturesque（风景如画的）；有时会使用一些科学术语或带有特定文化内涵的专有名词，如喀斯特地貌（Kast topography）、哥特式（Gothic-style）、颐和园（the Summer Palace）、寒山寺（Hanshan Temple）、布达拉宫（Potala Palace）等。

英文旅游宣传文体大多风格简约，结构严谨而不复杂，行文用字简洁明了，考虑到接受者不同的教育背景，以实现明白晓畅地在更多的读者群中进行宣传的目的。因为西方哲学强调抽象理性注重分析，英文旅游宣传在行文上表现出重形式与写实，表达直观通俗，注重信息的准确性和语言的实用性。多数情况下，景物描写往往用客观的具象罗列来传达实实在在的景物之美，力求忠实再现自然，让读者有一个明确具体的印象。

【例1】The high Eiffel Tower, the colorful streets, the beautiful river Seine, the glorious palaces, the romantic people, the old history … Paris is a great place to all people in the world.

【译文】高耸入云的埃菲尔铁塔，流光溢彩的街道，美丽的塞纳河，金璧辉煌的宫殿，浪漫的民族，源远流长的历史……这就是伟大的巴黎，一个属于全世界所有民族的城市。

这句话看起来就像一张在巴黎上空拍下的照片，几乎全是景物的罗列："高耸入云的埃菲尔铁塔，流光溢彩的街道，美丽的塞纳河，金璧辉煌的宫殿"，构成了一副高贵典雅的巴黎城市风光图。

中文旅游宣传要显得"文采浓郁"一些，多仰仗华丽的辞藻而不是物象的明晰展示，不惜重复笔墨以渲染行文的语气或语势，加大语言的感染力。这与中国人传统的思维方式有很大关系。中国哲学中的"天人合一"理念强调客观融入主观，在文学艺术形式上往往借景抒情、托物言志，重神似而轻形似。由于历来受古典山水诗词及山水游记散文一类作品的影响，中文旅游宣传的语言表达常常伴有大量的对偶平行结构和连珠四字句，以使文意对比、行文工整、声律对仗，在语言表达形式上追求音形意皆美，以达到诗意盎然的效果。

【例2】苏州位于沪宁线上，地处太湖之滨，建成于公元前415年，是我国江南著名的古老城市之一。城内外遍布名胜古迹。寒山寺，诗韵钟声，脍炙人口；虎丘，千年古塔，巍然屹立；天平山，奇石嶙峋，枫林如锦；洞庭东山，湖光山色，花果连绵。别具匠心的园林驰名中外。沧浪亭、狮子林、拙政园、留园、网师园、怡园等，亭台楼阁，池石林泉，疏密适度，相映生辉；廊榭曲折，沟壑幽深，移步换景，引人入胜；布局结构，各显特色，表现了宋、元、明、清各个时期园林艺术的不同风格，反映了我国历代劳动人民的高度智慧和卓越的创造才能。

【译文】Located on the Shanghai-Nanjing railway and off Lake Taihu, Suzhou is a city of historical fame south of the Yangtze, which claims its founding in 514 B.C. The city abounds with fine scenery and historical interest. The popular haunt of Hanshan Temple, with its charming bell, has inspired many poetic mind. On Tiger Hill, a thousand-year-old pagoda stands in majesty; and while luxuriant fruit-trees add to the natural beauty of East Dongting Hills and lake around, Tianping Hill is featured by grotesque rock formations and red maple woods.

这段关于苏州的旅游宣传中大量使用了四字结构，浓缩了苏州园林的菁华：亭台楼阁以严谨均衡的几何图形空间布局的静态美与径缘池转、廊引人随、步移景换的立体动感美，将一幅美轮美奂的自然山水与人文景观在读者面前展露无遗。译文也应体现原文的动静之美，达到与原文形式美学等化的效果。翻译时将多个装饰性的四字结构整合为极具特色的英语单词，充分表现了这些景点的独特魅力之处，通过这些简单而不重复的词语再现了原文的美感功能。

【例3】环湖的山峰外观秀丽挺拔，势若骏马奔腾。在西湖风景区内，分布有苏堤春晓等名胜四十余处，以及六合塔等三十余处古迹。沿湖四周，花木繁茂；群山之中，泉溪竞流；亭台楼阁，交相辉映；湖光山色，千古风情，令多少人流连忘返。"上有天堂，下有苏杭"的赞语真是恰如其分。

【译文】The mountains towering around the lake look like galloping horses, presenting an imposing air. Over 40 scenic spots and 30 historical sites dot the West Lake, such as "The Early Spring at the Su Causeway" and the Pagoda of Six Harmonies. The causeways, bridges, pavilions, springs, trees and flower sin and around the West Lake make it a paradise on earth, where one cannot tear himself away.

文中"秀丽挺拔""花木繁茂""泉溪竞流""交相辉映""湖光山色"等修饰词语,从不同角度描写了西湖的环境特点,给读者留下强烈的印象。这类散文式的语言充满美感,帮助读者领略到了自然风光,同时还揭示了西湖丰富的文化,可谓是与自然景色相辅相成,珠联璧合。

当然并非所有中文旅游宣传都是这种散文风格,也有不少说明文体类型的。这类文体一般都文字简约,就事论事,信息型文本功能突出,不重情感诱导。

【例4】山西省五台山是闻名中外的佛教圣地,境内迄今为止仍保存着北魏、唐、宋、元、明、清及民国历朝历代的寺庙建筑47座。精美绝伦的古代建筑、稀世文物及博大雄伟的佛教文化充满了无限的神秘感。五台山是我国大佛教名山之一,是文殊菩萨的道场。五台山也是夏天避暑纳凉的好去处。

【译文】On Mt. Wutai, located in Shanxi Province, there are 47 temples built during the seven dynasties from Northern Wei (386-534) to the Republic of China (1912-1949). Splendid ancient architecture, rare relics and unparalleled Buddhist culture have all lent mystery to the mountain. It is one of China's well-known Buddhist mountains, where Wenshu (Manjusri) performs the Buddhist rites. The mountain is also highly recommended as an escape from the heat in summer.

【例5】浦东地区紧靠繁华的上海市区,背倚物阜民丰的长江三角洲,面对太平洋和东南亚发达国家和地区,有着得天独厚的地理优势。东方明珠广播电视塔位于黄浦江畔、浦东陆家嘴嘴尖上,塔高468米,三面环水,与外滩的万国建筑博览群隔江相望,是亚洲第一、世界第三的高塔。

【译文】Adjacent to Shanghai proper, backed by the rich and populous Yangtze River Delta and located vis-à-vis the Pacific and Southeast Asian developed countries and regions, Pudong Area enjoys a unique geographic advantage. Situated on the Huangpu River and at the point of Lujiazui in Pudong, the Oriental Pearl Radio and Television Tower is surrounded by waters on three sides and faces a row of buildings of variegated international architectural styles in the Bund across the river. This 468-meter-tall tower ranks first in Asia and third in the world in height.

8.2.2 文化渊源——语言审美标准不同

旅游宣传写作手法上的风格差异，反映出来的是不同的民族文化心理和审美意识，与各自不同的语言文化传统、社会历史背景、审美思维习惯等有深厚的历史渊源。西方传统哲学在主观与客观的物象关系上，主张"主客分离"，更多地强调摹仿和再现，在描绘外界自然美时，总是"站在自然之外"去欣赏自然之美。旅游英语表达客观、简约，语言上追求一种自然理性之美，行文用字最忌重复堆砌；另一方面，旅游英语也十分讲究句式结构的逻辑层次和有机组合，语法规则十分严格，反映出英语表达逻辑严谨、思想缜密的美学特点。

【例6】Australia is a land of exceptional beauty. It is the world's smallest continent and largest island, and a relatively young nation established in an ancient land. A series of geological and historical accidents has made Australia one of the world's most attractive counties from the tourist's viewpoint. This country has a land area of 7,686,850 square kilometers and its coastline is 36,735 kilometers. The vast movements of the earth's crust created a vast land of Australia, isolated it and positioned it across the tropical and temperate climatic zones. This land has a small population, which left enormous areas unspoiled.

Here you witness an astonishing variety of environments, from desert to rain forest, tropical beach to white snowfield, from big, sophisticated cities to vast uninhabited areas.

【译文】澳大利亚是一个异常美丽的国家。这是世界最小的洲，也是最大的岛，是在古老的土地上建立起来的较为年轻的国家。地质史上，这块土地的地貌形态发生了一系列变化，澳大利亚在旅游者眼中成了世界上最吸引人的国家之一。这个国家的陆地面积为7686850 平方千米，海岸线长达 36735 千米。地壳的剧烈运动使澳大利亚成了幅员辽阔，与大陆分离，地处温、热带地区的国家。由于澳大利亚可以观赏到各种地形风貌，从沙漠到热带雨林，从地处热带的海滩到白雪皑皑的田野，从扑朔迷离的大都市到人迹罕到的旷野，景观各异，令人叹为观止。

【例 7】迪庆藏族自治州位于云南省西北部滇、川、藏三省交界处，这里有冰山雪川、家河峡谷、湖泊草甸，美丽而宁静。州内以藏族居民为主，还居住着傈僳族、纳西族等 20 多个民族，长期以来，这里各民族和谐相处，创造了独特而灿烂的文化——山川秀美、民风淳朴、历史悠久、文化丰富，与詹姆斯·希尔顿笔下的香格里拉极其相似。

【译文】Located at the junction of Yunnan and Sichuan Provinces and the Tibet Autonomous Region, the scenery in picturesque Diqing, filled with glaciers, deep canyons, meadows, and lakes, remarkably resembles that of the Shangrila described in James Hilton's novel. Residents here are mainly Tibetans who coexist peacefully with over 20 other ethnic groups, including Lili and Naxi groups, thus creating a rich and unique culture.

为了突出英文旅游宣传句子结构的层次感和逻辑性，译文采用了篇章整合的方式，打乱了原文语序，将段末句子提前。全段按内容调整为两个逻辑层次分明的复合句，重点突出主题信息的表达，并将破折号后汉语惯用的评述性话语"山川秀美、民风淳朴、历史悠久、文化丰富"省去不译，这样，使译文结构更紧凑，信息更明确。

中国人喜欢抒发感情,尤其是描绘自然景色,往往佐以个人的联想,追求"三分像,七分想"。这种把人的情感植入语言描述中的手法使得自然景色充满了感情色彩,产生的效果是无法比拟的。在中文旅游宣传的语言描绘中,常常运用到比喻、拟人等修辞手法,使读者能产生具体的影像。因为汉语语言表达主观色彩浓厚,一贯强调"意与境混"的上乘境界,追求客观景物与主观情感高度和谐、融为一体的浑然之美,正所谓"一切景语皆情语也"。

【例 8】南溪山,双峰并列,峭拔挺立,烟翠凌空,山形似马鞍。每逢空山新雨,阳光映照,可见石色洁白如玉,恰似一幅浓淡相宜的山水丹青。

【译文】The Nanxi Hill, features a twin peak, thrusting abruptly into the sky, shaping like a saddle, whenever it rains, the hill under the sunshine is afresh with cliff washed white as a piece of jade, making the hill look as though it were an ink-washed picture.

在这段话中,"峭拔挺立,烟翠凌空"是作者对南溪山的印象,"山形似马鞍""可见石色洁白如玉,恰似一幅浓淡相宜的山水丹青"则把南溪山和"玉""山水丹青"相比拟,生动地展现了南溪山的秀美。

8.3 旅游宣传翻译的过程与原则

鉴于英汉旅游宣传文体特征和表达风格上的差异,在翻译的理解和表达过程中,译者必须准确理解原文实质,把握原文与译文间的社会、文化差异,结合考虑各种语境因素,对原文信息和内容进行判断和取舍,做到虚实互化、各展其长,突出译文"呼唤"功能,用符合译入语规范和文化标准的语言准确地传达旅游翻译的功能,让读者喜闻乐见。

8.3.1 推敲原文语境因素,弄清原文实质

在旅游宣传的翻译过程中,对原文语境因素进行正确分析推理是真正理解原文实际意义的关键。所以,读者除了利用自己的语言知识获取句子本身的意义之外,还必须根据原文语境中提供的各种信息进行思辨、推理,找出原作者隐于明说之后的交际意图和语用用意,以形成自己对原作者语篇意义的认知,进而考虑译文读者的需要,确定相应的翻译策略和译文形式。

【例9】这里三千座奇峰拔地而起,形态各异,有的似玉柱神鞭,立地顶天;有的像铜墙铁壁,巍然屹立;有的如晃板垒卵,摇摇欲坠;有的若盆景古董,玲珑剔透……神奇而又真实,迷离而又实在,不是艺术创造胜似艺术创造,令人叹为观止。

【译文】3000 crags rise in various shapes—pillars, columns, walls, shaky egg stacks and potted land scapes... —conjuring up unforgettably fantastic images.

这篇关于张家界武陵源风景区的宣传介绍用词华美、富于文采,给人以极美的感受,达到了吸引游客的目的。但翻译成英语时如果照搬直译,就会因语言冗长拖拉,让英语读者不得要领,而妨碍译文吸引观众的预期效果。所以该译文摒弃了汉语的行文形式,删减了有悖于英语读者阅读习惯的内容,采取符合他们习惯的表达方式,有效传达出原作意图。

【例10】(天然壁画)正中位置是一座典型的土家吊脚楼,一架梯子搭在屋边,屋角挂着成串的玉米和辣椒,楼的左边是小桥流水,楼的后边是良田美池,一农夫正在扶犁耕田。真是好一幅"小桥流水人家"的童话世界。

【译文】The middle of it is a typical Tujia suspended house, a ladder is against the wall of the house. Bunches of corns and hot peppers are hung on the corner of the house. There is a bridge with water running under it on the left, and fertile farmland and a pool are behind the house. A farmer is ploughing the land. What a beautiful landscape painting!

这段文字先写景，最后引用古诗感叹，很符合中国人的审美观点，但在翻译成英文时，对景物的描写自然能传达一种美感，勾起游客的兴趣，如果非要把古诗翻译过来，反而显得生硬。

8.3.2 体味字里行间意蕴，引申原文内涵

由于英汉旅游宣传文体修辞风格上的明显差异，英译文不会也不可能将汉语大段的华丽辞藻和平行结构全盘译出，汉译文也不会做到像英文那样简洁平白而句式紧凑。就旅游宣传文体功能而言，英语的简约风格并不是汉语旅游文本追求的理想形式。因为汉语的传统和习惯使其在描绘和展示自然美景时，往往更多借助言辞的渲染去烘托一种"诗情画意"，语言过于简约会使表达太显平白，达不到旅游翻译的目的。

【例11】The hub of public life is the "Piazza San Marco" (St. Mark's Square) where tourists and citizens sit on the terraces of the famous Florian and Quadri cafes to listen to the music, dream and see the mosaics of St. Mark's glow under the rays of the setting sun. The Quadri is more popular but the Florian is the best-known cafe: founded in 1720, it has received Byron, Goeth, Musset and Wagner within its mirrored and allegory-painted walls.

【译文】圣马可广场是公众的生活中心，游客和市民常坐在广场著名的佛洛里安和夸德里咖啡店里，聆听着店内的音乐，目睹着夕阳余晖下圣马可教堂熠熠生辉的马赛克墙面，恍然入梦。夸德里咖啡店虽名扬全城，却不及佛洛里安咖啡店声名显赫：自1720年以来，这家四壁明镜相嵌、壁画环绕的百年历史老店先后接待过拜伦、歌德、谬塞和瓦格纳等一大批文化名人。

【例12】Its subterranean world holds some of Europe's most magnificent underground galleries. Time losses all meanings in the formation of these underground wonders. Dripstones, stalactites, in different shapes—columns, pillars and translucent curtains, conjure up unforgettable images

【译文】这里的溶洞景观美如画廊，恢宏壮阔堪称欧洲之冠。洞中的奇观异景，其形成过程之漫长，使时光在这里也失去了意义。各种钟乳石形态各异——有的如玉柱浑圆；有的如栋梁擎天；有的如瀑布飞帘，晶莹剔透——大自然鬼斧神工，妙景天成，令人难忘。

8.3.3 发挥译语优势，注重读者效应

旅游宣传翻译作为实用文体翻译，自有其一定的功利性和商业意图，即要迎合译文读者的口味，唤起他们的美感共鸣。旅游宣传翻译所追求的应该是译文的读者效应，是源语和译入语间功能的传递，不应是语言形式上的对应。作为一种以译入语文化为归属的应用型文体翻译，旅游宣传译文更应顺从译语文化环境的规范和标准。从"目的论"原则出发，旅游宣传翻译应当充分考虑译语读者的认知能力和心理感受（即一种换位思考），在正确传达原文文本信息内容的前提下，有效发挥译文的优势以增强感染力。

【例13】峨眉山位于中国西南部的四川省，距成都156千米，走高速公路需1.5小时。主峰金顶绝壁凌空高插云霄，巍然屹立。登临其间，可西眺皑皑雪峰，东瞰莽莽平川。气势雄而景观奇，有云海、日出、佛光、圣灯四大奇观。中部群山峰峦叠嶂，含烟凝翠，飞瀑流泉，鸟语花香，草木茂而风光秀。是我国著名的游览胜地，1996年被联合国教科文组织列入"世界自然与文化遗产"。

【译文】156 kilometers (1.5-hour drive) away from Chengdu City in Sichuan Province, southwest of China, stands the Mt. Emei with its summit Jinding (the Golden Top) towering above range upon range of rolling mountains stretching westward, all covered with snow, and in an eastward distance lying a wide expanse of flat land. It boasts of its mountainous spectacles of clouds sea, sunrise, and the marvelous natural phenomena of "Buddha's Halo" and "Holy Lamp", as well as its natural landscapes filled with large green-woods, exuberant vegetation, flowers, streams, waterfalls, etc. As one of the best-known tourist attractions, Mt. Emei has been listed as a World Natural and Cultural Heritage Site by the UNESCO.

原文文辞优美，充满诗情画意，但英译文若照搬这种形式，行文必定臃肿，从而破坏英文的美感。这样，就有必要摆脱原文形式的束缚，对篇章结构进行有机整合，表达出译文读者期待的景点信息。译文按英语的逻辑层次将原文五个平行铺排的松散句式整合为三个结构紧凑的主从复合句，有增有减。另外，在原文的四大奇观之中，"云海""日出"为客观自然景象，"佛光""圣灯"则是由自然现象变化出的幻景，二者不属于同一类事物，因而译文采用增译的手法将其区别开来，逻辑上显得更加合理，表达也更清楚。

【例14】A fascinating city between sea and sky, like Venus rising from the waves, Venus welcomes tourists from the five continents drawn to her by the charm of her water and pellucid light, free from all dust and cooled by the sea breeze. She also offers the intellectual pleasures to be derived from her masterpieces which mark the meeting of East and West.

【译文】威尼斯水城海天相连，景色迷人，宛如碧波中涌现的维纳斯，吸引着五大洲的游客。她水色旖旎，波光澄澈，清风拂面而来，荡去你心中的不快与烦恼。而城中那些集东西方艺术之大成的艺术杰作，更给你以精神上的享受。

此句原文结构严谨，用词虽简但搭配巧妙，特别是短语"the charm of her water and pellucid light, free from all dust and cooled by the sea breeze"犹为精彩。英语"the charm of her water and pellucid light"搭配奇妙；如果用汉语说"水和澄清的光的魅力"却显生硬。"all dust"于英文读者通俗易懂，如果用汉语表达为"灰尘""尘土""尘念""倦容"等，恐都不适宜。翻译在透彻理解原文字里行间的意义后，利用拆译技巧，按事理推进关系，发挥汉语的四字结构、和谐节奏等优势，增强了广告的感染力，也加深了读者的喜好程度。

8.4　旅游宣传翻译技巧

旅游宣传翻译不像文学、科技和政治经济类翻译，它的功能重在"诱导"和"呼唤"受众，但旅游翻译同样有一个美学标准和文化观念的问题，同样需要考虑文本的功能特征和翻译策略，考虑形式与内容的关系，也同样需要完备的理论知识和翻译技巧。在旅游宣传的翻译实践中，译者可根据实际需要，运用适当的手法，如常用的音译加释义法、意译法、增译法、类比或转译法、删减法、改写法和再创造等，对译文进行调整，尽量做到言之有物，言之有理，言之有情，言之有趣。

8.4.1　音译加释义法

音译法是根据汉语读音，将旅游景点名称直接用拼音标注，目的是尽可能保留原风景名胜、旅游饭店的原汁原味和鲜明特色。如：

　　城隍庙　　Chenghuang Temple
　　民族饭店　Mingzu Hotel

景点名称多涉及本民族文化的专有名词，单纯的音译不能传递任何实际信息。这类名称应该在音译的基础上另作释义，在旅游宣传中对使用的某些词或习惯用语进行解释或注释。利用这种译法将名称与其含义联系起来，对旅游景点的名称进行解释，会给景点的外国游客留下深刻印象，便于他们记忆，增加他们的游览兴致。例如：

　　天安门　　Tiananmen (the Gate of Heavenly Peace)
　　大观园　　Daguanyuan (Grand View Garden)
　　花港观鱼　Hua Gang Guan Yu (Viewing Fish at Flower Harbor)
　　孤山　　　Gushan (Solitary Hill)
　　天涯海角　Tianya-Haijiao (the end of the earth and the edge of the sea)

由于中西文化有很大差异，不同的历史条件、地理环境、宗教信仰、社会习俗都会使两种语言出现不对应现象，有的只是词汇空缺（lexical gap）或词义空白（semantic zero）。在翻译旅游宣传资料中这类文化负载词（culture-loaded or culture-bound words）时也可以采用音译加释义的方法。一方面，这些词属典型的汉语文本，采取音译可以让译入语读者体会到独特的异国风味；另一方面，加入适当的释义能够使译文更通俗准确地传达源语信息，更好地实现其目的功能。例如：

粽子　　　zongzi (a kind of traditional Chinese food eaten on lunar May 5th which is made of glutinous rice wrapped in green reed leaves)

风水　　　fengshui (supposed influence on the fortune of a family from the location of a house or tomb)

8.4.2 意译法

一些中国特有的历史事物、历史上的典故、神话传奇、独特的民族传统节日以及一些文化内涵丰富的旅游景点名称采用音译不能把相应的文化含义翻译出来，此类名称翻译时要突出其内在含义或相应典故与传说，便于游客理解、记忆。对此类名称多采用意译，即用意义相同而形式不同的解释性文字来加以说明并翻译，以便更好地让国外游客理解。意译的特点在于能够填补文化空缺，消除文化差异。例如：

兵马俑　　Terra Cotta Warriors and Horses
十三陵　　Ming Tombs
故宫　　　the Imperial Palace
颐和园　　the Palace Museum

【例15】大乘寺坐北朝南，院墙按八卦建造。

【译文】The Great Vehicle Temple faes south with its walls shaped after the Eight Diagrams (combinations of the whole or broken lines formerly used in divination).

八卦是我国古代的占卜符号，是中国特色词汇，需要经过说明才能为外国游客所接受。

又如，杭州是我国著名的风景名胜旅游城市，有着丰富的旅游资源和各式各样的旅游景点名称。杭州有名的风景都有其历史渊源和文化背景，翻译时稍一不慎，便会产生错误。如人们往往将"虎跑泉"的"跑"字念成"pǎo"，结果便把"虎跑泉"错译成"Tiger Running Spring"。其实，这里的"跑"应该念成"páo"（意为兽用爪扒土）。相传唐代元和十四年（公元819年），有位法名性空的高僧云游至今日的虎跑寺，想栖禅于此，但一直苦于无水，准备迁走。夜里忽然梦见神仙相告："南岳有童子泉，当遣二虎移来。"次日清晨，性空果然见有二虎"跑地作泉"，泉水涌出。于是，他就建寺居住，并把此泉起名为"虎跑泉"。因此，虎跑泉可意译为"Tiger-clawed Spring"。

8.4.3 增译法

增译是指在翻译的时候，为了使译文更容易被外国游客了解，适当增加一些相关的背景知识或信息。在译文中，对一些朝代、社会状况、历史人物等若根据字面意思再略加注释，则让译入语读者易于理解，并加深印象、增添乐趣。但是翻译中的增添必须本着译入语读者对原文信息充分理解和接受的原则，所以增添的内容一定不能仅仅是文字的堆砌，必须言简意赅。例如：

秦始皇　　Qin Shihuang (the first emperor in Chinese history who unified China in the year 221 B.C.)

西域　　the Western Regions (a Han Dynasty term for the area west of Yumenguan Pass, including what is now Xinjiang Uygur Autonomous Region and parts of Central Asia)

【例16】元宵节那天，大红灯笼高高挂。

【译文】Duringthe Yuanxiao Festival, also called Lantern Festival, which falls on the 15th day of the first lunar month, red lanterns (Lantem Festival exhibition began in the Han Dynasty, about 2,000 years ago. Some people believe its origin to be related to Buddhism.) can be seen everywhere.

这份旅游宣传资料中对"元宵节"和"灯笼"的补充解释，便于外国游客对元宵节有个较为透彻的了解。

【例17】路左有一巨石，石上原有苏东坡手书"云外流春"四个大字。

【译文】To its left is a rock formerly engraved with four big Chinese characters Yun Wai Liu Chun (Beyond clouds flows spring) hand-written by SU Dongpo (1037-1101), the most versatile poet of the Northern Song Dynasty (960-1127).

中国拥有悠久的历史和古老的文化，在介绍文物古迹的时候，总会联系到大量的历史事件和朝代名称，而国外游客对我国的历史朝代并不熟悉，因此最好补充一个朝代的公元年份。在翻译国外游客不熟悉的历史名人时，可以添加相关的背景资料，补充这个人的身份、在历史上的地位和功绩等，以增加国外游客对此人的了解。译文增加了对苏东坡的说明，较好地表达了原文要想表达的意图："云外流春"四个字具有较高的文物价值。

8.4.4 类比或转译法

类比又称"文化替换"，指在翻译过程中，当在译入语文化中找不到与原文本对等的表达时，就用"以此比彼"的方法把译语读者对原文本不熟悉的事物替换成译入语情况下意思表达相近的事物。这种翻译策略尤见于在对历史人物和景点进行简明但精确的介绍时。更重要的是，译入语读者能在自身背景文化的基础之上深切感受异国的文化风味，有助于跨文化交际。例如：

青岛	Switzerland of Orient
清明节	Chinese Easter
苏州	Venice of China
澳门	Eastern Las Vegas
观音	Goddess of Mercy

【例18】故宫耗时14年，整个工程于1420年结束。

如果这份旅游宣传资料针对北美市场发行，可译为：The construction of the Forbidden City took 14 years, and was finished in 1420, 72 years before Christopher Columbus discovered the New World.

若这份资料的目标市场是欧洲，则可译为：The construction of the Forbidden City took 14 years, and was finished in 1420, 14 years before Shakespeare was born.

采取这样的类比手法能使外国人将他们陌生的中国历史年代与他们熟悉的历史或人物所处的年代联系起来，给他们留下深刻的印象。

8.4.5 删减法

删减即删去中文资料中对译文理解没有帮助的东西。中国人在写事状物时喜欢引用名人名言或古诗词加以验证，中国读者读了会加深印象，并从中得到艺术享受，而在外国人看来似乎是画蛇添足。译文中删去，反而干净利落，明白晓畅。在旅游宣传中，有些内容是中国传统文化特有的产物，若逐字逐句翻译，对理解原文没有任何帮助，甚至外国游客根本看不懂，这时就应该适当删改。

【例19】烟水苍茫月色迷，渔舟晚泊栈桥西。乘凉每至黄昏后，人依栏杆水拍堤。这是古人赞美青岛海滨的诗句。青岛是一座风光秀丽的海滨城市，夏无酷暑，冬无严寒。西起胶州湾入海处的团岛，东至崂山风景区的下清宫，绵延80多华里的海滨组成了一幅绚烂多彩的长轴画卷。

【译文】Qingdao is a beautiful coastal city. It is not hot in summer and not cold in winter. The 40-km-long scenic line begins from Tuan Island at the west end to Xiaqing Gong of Mount Lao at the east end.

译文把古诗全部删减，但不影响译入语读者对原文中其他部分的理解，而译文中的第一句正是对前面古诗简洁的概括。

8.4.6 改写法

由于历史发展的独特性和唯一性，汉语旅游宣传资料中对有些诸如历史古迹等重要信息的介绍都包含很多特定的古代术语，而这些复杂的术语根本无法使译入语读者领会原文所要传达的信息，故译入语文本的信息功能也就不可能实现。所以针对这类术语，在翻译中一般将其改写成内涵相同或相近的现代语表达方式。

【例20】刘备章武三年病死于白帝城永安宫，五月运回成都，八月葬于惠陵。

【译文】Liu Bei died of illness in 223 at present day Fengjie County, Sichuan Province, and was buried here in the same year.

这句话在中国人看来浅显易懂，因为中国人都深知三国历史，但如果直译过去要外国人读懂却并非易事。"章武三年""白帝城永安宫"等都是中国历史上的年代和地名，不加译注外国人是不可能理解的。并且刘备永安宫托孤一事也非一两句话就能说清楚。要是在其他读物里可以用译者注的办法来讲清楚这些中国历史知识，而成都武侯祠导游图，文字不足一千，类似这样的历史知识还很多，不可能加上比正文还长的译者注。译文只能在不改变原作原意的原则下，进行改译，把文本中的时间术语改写成了公元纪年"223"，把当时所处时代的地名改写成当代的地理位置"Fengjie County"。这样，译文表达既精确又流畅，可接受性自然也就增强。

8.4.7 创造性翻译

创造性翻译指在不损害源语信息的前提下，不拘泥于源语，对源语不符合译语习惯的词句、语序进行必要的改造和调整，以期更好地服务于读者。

【例21】江岸上彩楼林立，彩灯高悬，旌旗飘摇，呈现出一派喜气洋洋的节日场面。千姿百态的各式彩龙在江面游弋，舒展着优美的身姿，有的摇头摆尾，风采奕奕；有的喷火吐水，威风八面。

【译文】High-rise buildings ornamented with colored lanterns and bright banners stand out along the river banks. On the river itself, gaily decorated dragon-shaped boats await their challenge, displaying their individual charms to their hearts' content. One boat wags its head and tail; another spits fire and sprays water.

【例22】(龙舟赛)演历史于古今,生传说于纷纭,珠联爱国情操,悲壮色彩,璧合神秘气氛,拼搏精神,动如摧枯拉朽,轰轰烈烈,势若排山倒海,可歌可泣,此唯舟竞渡,无有出其左右者。

【译文】The Dragon Boat Race, a most exciting group event, is held in memory of Qu Yuan, patriotic stateman and poet in ancient China.

工整对仗的原文句式,华丽雍容的夸张辞藻,如果照字直译不符合旅游者的信息接受能力,对于不了解中国端午节历史的西方读者来说必定感觉不知所云。因此,为了更好地把龙舟节文化信息传递给观光者,只有对那些含晦涩不好理解的中国式典故加以缩并改写,才能更好地达到文化传递的效果。

第九章 公示语

公示语（public signs）是在公共场合面对公众的文字及图形信息，是与人们生活休戚相关、最常见的实用语言，广泛应用于公共设施、商业设施、旅游服务、公共机构、涉外机构、治安监督等，在生活中几乎随处可见。同"公示语"意义相近的术语有"标识语""标志语""标示语""警示语"等。这些术语的内涵和外延相对较小，隶属于"公示语"。因此，公示语这一文体具有告示、提示、指示、标示、显示、警示、解释等功能，语汇短小精悍、简练明了。

公示语是社会用语的重要类型，是城市社会开放程度和文化品位的重要体现。公示语以通俗易懂、简单明了的方式向公众传递各种各样的信息，是全球范围的通用语言。规范的公示语翻译具有美化城市环境的重要功能，对于提升一个城市的国际形象具有非常重要的意义。公示语翻译研究的重点是服务海外游客、常驻外籍人士等，涉及食、宿、行、游、娱、购等行为与需求的文字信息内容。公示语在使用中的功能不同，所展示的信息状态和意义也不同，而且公示语是全球性的，在目的语中一般都能找到对应的习惯说法。因此，探讨公示语的文体功能、研究英语公示语的语言特征，对公示语的翻译有着极其重要的价值。

9.1 公示语的文体功能

公示语的应用范围非常广泛，公共场所旅游外出者所到之处，所见的指示牌、路牌、标志、告示等具有持久性、固定性的信息都可称为公示语。在实际运用中，公示语具有指示性、提示性、限制性和强制性四种突出的应用示意功能。此外，像广州、上海这样的商业城市，公示语的设置重点主要是服务于城市商业和社会两大功能。

9.1.1 应用示意功能

公示语应用于日常生活的方方面面，提供的是一种信息服务，满足的是游客、社会公众的社会、行为和心理需求，根据其在实际应用中的示意功能主要划分为四类：指示性公示语、提示性公示语、限制性公示语、强制性公示语。

A. 指示性公示语

指示性公示语体现的是周到的信息服务，为公众提供指示性服务，对公众不产生任何限制或强制意义，其语言不要求公众采取何种行动，功能在于指示服务的内容。例如：

机场休息室 Airport Lounge

出口 Exit/Way out

存包处 Cloak Room

问询服务 Information

高速路入口 Freeway Entrance

B. 提示性公示语

提示性公示语没有任何特指意义，仅起提示作用，但用途广泛。例如：

小心轻放 Handle with Care

请在乘车前购买好车票

Please buy your ticket before you board the train

油漆未干 Wet Paint

易爆物品 Explosive

C. 限制性公示语

限制性公示语对公众的行为提出具体的限制、要求和约束。所用语言直接，但不会让人感到强硬甚至粗暴无理，不可接受。例如：

出租车上下乘客专用 Taxi Pick Up & Drop Off Only

私家路段 禁止通行 This Is a Private Path. No Admittance.

排队等候 Stand in Line

残疾人士专用 Handicapped Only

靠右行，只准从左边超车 Keep Right, Pass Left Only

D. 强制性公示语

强制性公示语要求公众必须或不能采取某种行动，语言强制、直白，多采用命令口气，没有任何商量的余地。常用词语有：Do not, No, …not permitted/allowed 等。例如：

严禁拍照 No Photography

禁止乱穿马路 Don't Jaywalk

禁止无照行车 It is forbidden to drive without license

禁止与驾驶员交谈 Conversation with driver prohibited

任何人不得越过此处 No person is allowed beyond this line

9.1.2 商务功能

公示语的商务功能主要体现在商业公示语的特定应用功能。商场内外设置的公示语根据消费者类别、消费行为和消费需求可分为激发兴趣、提供信息、加深理解、促进行动、巩固形象等营销功能。

A. 激发兴趣

此类公示语常用来引起消费者的注意，激发消费兴趣，或者以筛选特定的消费群体为目的，因此常见于商家门面、橱窗等处。例如：

削价处理 Price Crash

免费送货上门 Free Delivery

新货上市 New Arrivals

大甩卖 Big Sale

B. 提供信息

此类公示语常用于提供服务与消费信息，提示、导向消费者消费的区域或类别。例如：

女装 Women's Wear

免税店 Duty Free

日用必需品 Daily Necessities

本处销售伦敦塔门票与导游手册

Tickets and guide books on sale here for Tower of London

C. 加深理解

此类公示语旨在使消费者对商家的经营有更加深入的理解和更多的好感，为消费者采取消费行动打下基础。例如：

顾客至上 Customer Is Always Right

您的安全，我们的天责 Your Safety Is Our Priority

D. 促进行动

此类公示语旨在使消费者采取行动，实现消费。例如：

今日特价 Daily Special

六折优惠 40% Off

买一赠一 Buy One and Get One Free

E. 巩固形象

商业机构不仅要通过公示语促进消费者的即时消费，还要借公示语树立并巩固良好的企业形象，提高消费者满意度，提升企业的知名度，培养消费者的忠诚度。例如：

谢谢您到访伦敦伊克塞尔车站！

Thank you for visiting ExCel London!

我们关注！欢迎批评！We care! We want your comments!

9.2 英文公示语的语言特征

英文公示语的文本主要表现为信息功能和祈使功能两种语言功能。信息功能的文本主要是描绘、叙述或说明有关事物的情况；祈使功能的文本则是用语言来唤起他人的情感共鸣，促使他们采取某种行动。从语言学的角度来说，公示语是话语交际的一种特殊形式，目的就是要表达对受众的某个要求或引起受众的某种注意。话语交际既是一个信息交流的过程，也是一种社会交往活动。公示语的话语交际过程是指说话人（发布公示语的人或机构）根据社会规范和情景语境，用相应的言语（或非言语）的表达方式，向受话人（读者/社会公众）传达话语信息，实现交际目的。根据已经收集的英文公示语的语料汇总，我们发现英文公示语普遍具有以下的语言特征。

9.2.1 语言简约，措辞精确

公示语文体的特殊功能要求语言表达必须简练精确，能让公众迅速明白所指示的信息，具体可体现在以下几个方面。

A. 名词或名词性词组的大量使用

指示性英语公示语大量使用名词或名词性词组，直接、准确无误地提供特定的信息。例如：

Toll Gate 收费站

Information 问询服务

City Buses Only 市内公交车专用

Caution Automatic Door 小心自动门

B. 动词和动名词的使用

突出提示、限制、强制功能的公示语广泛应用于公共设施、公共交通、紧急救援等方面，更多地使用展现公示语信息的动态意义。表示动态意义的公示语（多为限制性、强制性公示语）大量使用动词和动名词，旨在把公众的注意力引向公示语发出者要求采取的行动上。例如：

Please Hold the Hand Rail 请紧握扶手

No Crossing 禁止横穿

Please Don't Leave Valuables Unattended 贵重物品，随身携带

Mind Your Head 小心碰头

C. 词组与短语的使用

词组与短语（多为动词短语、名词短语）结构简单、组合多样，广泛应用于英文公示语。例如：

Lift Out of Order 电梯故障

Construction in progress! Keep away 正在施工

Set Down & Exit 下客后驶离

Clean It Up 清理狗便

D. 省略

公示语因为文体简洁需要，只要不影响准确体现其特定的功能和意义，很多语法方面的成分可以省略，常见的有省略冠词、助动词、标点符号、状语从句或独立结构。例如：

Stand behind red line until summoned by inspector 红线后站立，等待检查员（the red line, the inspector 冠词省略；另外，until summoned by inspector 省略了状语从句，完整句子应该是 until you are summoned by the inspector）

No authorized access prohibited 未经许可，禁止入内（is prohibited 助动词省略）

英文公示语常使用分行的形式自然断句，标点可省略，不会引起歧义和混淆，如：

Caution

Noise hazard

Ear protectors

available on

E. 缩略语的使用

为使公示语看起来更加简洁，公共设施和服务的公示语可使用国际通用或大众约定俗成的缩略语表示。例如：

WC (Water Closet) 厕所

P (Parking) 停车场

YMCA (Young Men's Christian Association) 基督教青年会

BERWICK RD 伯尔威克大街

YHA (Youth Hotels Association) 青年旅舍

9.2.2 规范使用大写字母

英文公示语中常使用大写字母，以显示规范和庄重的文体风格，不必严格遵照"英文标题中英文单词首字母大小写的规定",可以根据版面和设计的需要决定字母的大小写。常见的做法如下。

A. 全部采用大写字母

英文公示语通常采用文档排版居中的排列形式,以使公示语整体紧凑、活泼、美观、浑然一体。我们看美国某城市大街上的公示语,很多都是全部采用大写字母,如:

DANGER

CONSTRUCTION

AREA

KEEP OUT

B. 全部单词首字母大写,如:

Please Be A Responsible Dog Owener

Clean After Your Dog

C. 英文文章标题大小写原则

英文公示语格式也可以遵循英文文章标题大小写原则,即首单词首字母大写,其他单词实词首字母大写,虚词小写,如:

Walk Bikes on Paths

Central Park Closed 1-6 am

D. 第一个单词首字母大写

Welcome to the Washington Square Park Dog Run

1. No people without dogs.
2. No dogs without people.
3. Not all dogs like kids.
4. No food or drink please!

Watch your dog. Be smart. Have fun!

9.2.3 一般现在时(时态)的应用

公示语给予所处特定区域范围的公众以现实行为的指示、提示、限制、强制等,为此英文公示语的时态广泛使用一般现在时。例如:

Keep Clear 保持通畅

Wait Till the Train Stops 火车未停，请勿下车

This road is closed to heavy motor traffic.

此路段禁止载重机动车辆通行。

Tickets are FREE from the admissions desk. Please ask a member of staff if you require assistance. Last admission: 5:30

门票在检票处免费索取，如需帮助，请找工作人员。5:30禁止入园。

9.2.4 祈使句的使用

英文公示语大量应用祈使句，因为公示语具有明确的目的性，使用祈使句能够引起公众的注意和反应，增加执行力。例如：

Watch Your Steps 当心脚下

Under Repair, Detour 马路翻修，车辆绕行

Please Show Your ID 请出示证件

Do Not Jaywalk 不准横穿马路

No Entry 禁止通行

9.3 城市公示语翻译现状的调查与研究

随着国际交往的日益广泛和深入，公示语翻译的重要性日益凸显。可以说，公示语翻译是国家对外宣传不可忽视的一个组成部分，是一个国家对外交流水平和人文环境建设的具体体现。

随着中国与世界的接轨，越来越多的国家希望了解中国，很多外国朋友来到了中国。在这种跨文化交际的过程中，作为国际通用语言，英语成为各国人民进行交流沟通的最便捷的语言工具。因此，对中国各大城市来说，汉英双语公示语成为国际化大都市、国际旅游目的地语言环境、国际人文环境中不可缺少的组成部分，成为城市对外的又一窗口。为提升城市形象、加速其国际化进程、创建良好的投资及旅游环境，全国大中小城市都致力于汉英双语公示语的建设。

9.3.1 城市汉英公示语的翻译现状

随着 2008 年北京奥运会的成功举办、2010 年上海世博会的成功举办，以及 2011 年西安世界园艺博览会的举办，社会各界对公示语翻译越来越关注，其中译界学者对公示语翻译的研究尤为引人瞩目，我国学术界已越来越感到公示语翻译规范化的必要性和紧迫性。

事实上，自 2005 年首届全国公示语翻译研讨会在北京召开以来，近十余年来许多译界学者对现行城市公示语翻译的许多问题提出了不同的观点。对城市公示语翻译现状的调查分析，主要集中于公示语的翻译失误，提出为了提高公示语翻译的指导作用，要编纂公示语汉英双语词典。网络是现代传媒的强力支持，北京第二外国语学院向全社会推出了"公示语翻译在线研究"，也是提高城市公示语质量的途径之一。近年来，对"公示语翻译"的文献逐年增多，从发表论文数量的增加，可以看到全国各地研究者对公示语的关注程度。京、津、沪等大城市在公示语翻译方面做得还是不错的，但在其他的许多城市中出现的问题，也是不容乐观或者说触目惊心的。根据我们的调查，我国城市公示语的汉英翻译仍存在一些问题，主要表现在以下几个方面。

A. 英文和汉语拼音混用

随着城市国际化步伐加快，公示语汉英翻译受到公众的足够重视。尽管如此，还是出现了令公众困惑的公示语，即英文与汉语拼音混用。城市的每条街、路都有具体的名称，如："和平街"，我们总会看到在其附近的道路公示语标牌出现不同版本的译文，像 HEPING STREET, HEPING AVENUE 或 HEPING JIE。再如，中国的高铁火车票也同样出现了英文与汉语拼音的混用。如：G13 次列车从北京南开往南京南，车票英文译文为 Beijing South→Nanjing Nan。south 的汉语含义为"南方""南部"，而同样表达"南京南"时却用到了中国汉字"南"的汉语拼音。此类问题一定会给外国友人带来困扰。目前，类似的英文公示语错误现象普遍存在，亟需国家出台统一的翻译标准，给公示语翻译工作者做出指导。

B. 拼写、大小写错误

拼写错误在各种翻译中都属于低级错误，责任往往不在译者，而在排版印刷环节中，但在公示语翻译中这种错误不能为人接受，因为公示语的受众是公众，天天受人检阅。这类错误会使场所的形象大打折扣，因此应极力避免。如：

禁止坐靠

Please Stard Clear

公示语"禁止坐靠"的译文"Please Stard Clear"出现了明显的拼写错误，应为"Please Stand Clear"（原译文中 Stand 拼写错误）。

C. 语言的失当与错误

译者的语言功底如果不扎实，翻译时就难免会出差错，很多公示语译文就存在着语言的失当问题。北京某候车室入口处有公示语标牌如下："警务工作站"，其译文是"Police Affairs Station"，"Affairs"此处用词不当，"警务工作站"译为"Police Station"即可。有些地方"公厕"的译文是"Public Toilet"；宾馆的前台被译成了"Front Desk"，出口被译成了"EXIT GATE"，这些都让人感觉画蛇添足。其实，用"Toile""Reception""EXIT"就能清楚地传达原文的意思。

再如，在"和谐号"动车组的车厢内，座椅背后附带可折叠的小茶几，便于书写或放置物品。这个可折叠的小茶几被掀起之后，旅客看到的最醒目的一行文字就是"到站的旅客请往前门下车"，而大大出人意料的是，其译文却是令人难以置信的"Arriving passengers, please forward door alight"，其中，"请往前门下车"的译文不仅是字字对应，而且还有用词不当和语法错误。根据英语语法规则，please 引导的祈使句应该在其后直接跟一个动词，而此译文却是在 please 之后出现了一个名词词组 forward door。alight 的释义是"从（交通工具上）下来"，虽然在概念意义上没有问题，但它是一个非常正式的用词，在日常英语中属于一个很不常用的单词。公示语因受时间和空间限制，不便于详读，因此通常以简单明确为主，英译时当然应遵循上述原则，其语言风格要求简洁。英语公示用语的词汇选择应考虑到广大公众和旅游者的文化水平，严格避免使用生僻词语、古语、俚语、术语。把"前门"翻译成 forward door 而不是 front door,是此译文的又一翻译失误。forward 虽然可以做形容词用,但这时候它只能修饰抽象名词,如 forward planning, forward thinking。此公示语建议改译如下:"Arriving passengers, please get off at the front door."

D. 生硬直译

生硬直译指的是按原文逐字直译,字字对译,造成译文不知所云或不符合译入语表达习惯,这些译文常被称为中式英语。这类错误的出现往往是由于译者没有查阅相关资料,没有掌握汉语原文的英语地道表达方式。东西方在思维方式和文化背景等方面的不同,导致汉语和英语在表达方式以及习惯上有很大差异。中式英语貌似正确,很多与中文原文字字对应,但却不符合英语的用语习惯和规范,常常让外国人一头雾水而不知所云。例如,提示性公示语"小心碰头",在很多商场和医院被译成"Take care of your head"。该公示语是提醒人们注意,不要粗心大意被楼梯或较低矮的门框等物体碰着头,在英语里有现成的说法,即"Mind Your Head"或者"Low Ceiling"。"收银台"在某商场被译成"Cash Desk",cash 对应"收银",desk 对应"台",这是典型的生硬直译的中式英语,其实在英语里"收银台"有与之对应的表达,"Cashier"即可。

E. 译名不统一

公示语的语义具有特定性和唯一性,同一个公示语出现在出版物、宣传品、路牌、交通标识等任何场合,均应是统一的,否则就会给来中国的外国人带来很多的困惑与不便。

译名不统一这一问题非常严重,尤其体现在道路指示牌和标识牌的翻译上。指示牌上大多用"汉语拼音+英文同名"的音意结合方式翻译,例如,MACHANG Rd(马场道)、JIULONG Rd(九龙路)、JINZHONGHE St(金钟河大街)、WEIJIN South Rd(卫津南路)。而道路标识牌往往直接用大写的汉语拼音字母书写,上面四条同样的马路在道路标识牌上则被写成 MACHANG DAO(马场道)、JIULONG LU(九龙路)、JINZHONGHE DAJIE(金钟河大街)、

WEIJIN NANLU（卫津南路）。在石家庄市，"中山路"在路牌上被译为"ZHONGSHAN LU"，在马路标识牌上则被译为"ZHONGSHAN ROAD"。来中国的外国人不懂汉字和拼音，不能理解拼音"LU"和英语"ROAD"指的是同一事物，会认为"ZHONGSHAN LU"和"ZHONGSHAN ROAD"是两条不同的街道。而且，不管这样翻译遵循的是什么原则，同一条马路应该只有一个英文名称。

除路名以外，同一地方的不同标识牌对于同一汉语公示语也出现不同的英文翻译。例如，位于天津华苑新技术产业园区的五星级酒店赛象酒店中的"赛象宴会厅"就有四种英文翻译："SAIXIANG Ballroom""Saixiang Ballroom""Saixiang Grand Ballroom"和"Grand Ball Room"。同样也在该酒店，"卫生间"被译为 Lavatory，"洗手间"被译为 Toilet。"卫生间"和"洗手间"并没有实质上的不同，对应的翻译也应当统一。同一酒店中的同一公示语不应该出现多个版本的英文译名，这足以给该酒店的形象乃至整个城市的形象造成不良影响。

在"和谐号"动车组车厢内可折叠的小茶几背后有四个中英文对照的警示标识语，其中的三个句子中都出现了"车厢"这两个字，但是译文的处理却有三种不同说法：1. 请保持车厢内整洁。译文：Please keep clean inside. 2. 请勿大声喧哗，以保持车厢安静。译文：Please do not make much noise, and to keep the train quiet. 3. 为了您的安全，请勿在车厢内奔跑。译文：For your safety, please do not run in the compartment. 同样是"车厢"，第一个句子没有译出，第二个句子译成了 train，而第三个句子则译成了 compartment。同一场景下的公示语译文应尽量保持一致，避免说法不一。很显然，上述公示语翻译未能体现这个原则。

9.3.2 问题分析和对策建议

A. 原因分析

经过分析发现，造成我国城市公示语翻译存在上述问题的原因主要有两个方面。

1. 公示语翻译工作无主管部门统筹

目前，某些城市在公示语翻译这一工作上，尚无专门的主管部门进行统一管理和规范。据调研了解，除公路、道路、桥梁是根据《中华人民共和国国家标准》和各城市《地名管理条例》统一命名和翻译外，其他公共场所的告示、指示、提示、显示、警示、标示等的英文翻译，均无统一规范和标准，均由主建单位自主决定，完全没有经过权威部门或专家进行审定和批准。有关行政部门只是对翻译语言的种类做出规定，但对翻译的内容并不做审核。

2. 公示语翻译工作无相关规范标准和法律规定

公示语的翻译既需要专门的部门进行主管，也需要统一的规范标准，更需要行政法规的引导。但调研显示，目前我国很多城市的公示语翻译工作既无统一的规范标准，又缺乏专门的管理办法和法律规定，从而造成公示语翻译的随意性和任意性，导致了滥用、误用的现象比比皆是，行政管理和监督工作更是纸上谈兵。

B. 提高我国城市公示语翻译水平的对策建议

1. 完善行政管理体制，成立主管部门

建议各城市借鉴北京、上海、广东等省市的成功经验，由政府牵头，并协调相关部门，由建交委和质量技术监督局联合成立公共场所双语标识规范工作办公室，负责公示语翻译的统一管理工作，包括对公示语翻译的申报、审批和监督。

2. 建立长效工作机制，成立专家委员会

建议由主管部门牵头，成立公共场所双语标识英译专家委员会，建立专家库，由翻译专家、外籍专家、语言文字专家、法律专家以及政府有关部门领导和专业人士组成，并建立相应的长效工作机制。以北京第二外国语学院公示语翻译研究中心开发研制的公益性质的公示语翻译语料库为依托，不断更新和完善公共场所的中英文标识。同时，可充分发挥高校的社会服务功能，组织成立国际化语言环境建设志愿者队伍。

3. 制定法律法规，规范统一标准

建议尽快制定《城市公共场所双语标识英文译法标准》，由专家委员会负责审定，确保其准确性和权威性。同时，出台相关的法律规定，以地方法规形式发布实施，严格公示语翻译的申请、审批、使用和监管程序，使公示语翻译工作规范化、标准化和制度化。

4. 提供资金支持，分步实施推进工作

建议政府对该项工作给予专项资金支持，协调相关单位落实所需资金，分步实施并有效推进工作。对建设相对稳定成熟的片区可先行推进，对正在建设和将要建成的片区暂缓推进，避免标识牌设置上的重复利用和不必要的浪费，对翻译没有任何问题的标识牌完全可以保留。

9.4 公示语翻译策略

9.4.1 功能文体学与公示语翻译

韩礼德功能文体学是指以系统功能语法为理论基础的文体学理论，其文体学的主要思想包括两个方面：（1）功能的思想；（2）文体就是前景化。其中，功能的思想是韩礼德功能文体学理论的核心。

语言以满足人们的需要求得发展，并通过满足人们需要的功能而形成语言结构。语言用来满足人们需要的功能多种多样，具有无限的可能性。韩礼德从无数具体的功能类别中归纳出语言的三种功能：概念功能、人际功能和语篇功能。概念功能是讲话者作为观察者的功能，表达人们的社会经历和内心的心理体验，同时也表达事物之间的逻辑关系。人际功能是讲话者作为参与者的功能，表达意见、态度、评价及与听话者的角色关系，包括社会角色关系和交流角色关系。语篇功能是讲话者作为组织者的功能，他把概念功能和人际功能，根据情景语境在语篇中组织成一个整体，共同在语境中起作用。三种功能组成三种意义资源。在语言的运用过程中，讲话者根据情景语境（语场、基调和方式）同时从这三种意义资源的系统网络中做出选择。从所有这三种意义中做出的选择都对语篇的文体有意义。

语言的文体都与它的功能密切相关。某一语言特征，如某一词汇、语法或修辞格，在某一语篇中出现时若与语篇的情景语境是一致的，那么在这一情景语境中它就是文体特征。各种语言形式和手段都有成为文体特征的潜势，但不是天生就是文体特征，只有在一定情景语境中具有一定功能的形式手段才可称为文体特征。韩礼德指出，语言功能在文体分析中起中介作用。语言形式，包括语法结构、语音结构等，自身不能表明是否与语篇文体相关，而是通过它在语言交流中的"价值"表现出来，也就是说，看它是否在语篇整体中起突出作用，具有"前景化"效应，有利于实现交际者的交际目的。

韩礼德的功能文体学理论对公示语翻译具有重要启示意义。文本的文体功能决定文本的语言形式，反之，语言形式能突显文体功能的文本才是好的译文。由此，译文的文体必须适合表达文本的功能。译者在动笔翻译之前的理解阶段要钻研原文，充分了解原文的文体功能、信息发出者的交际目的以及原文的前景化文体特征。表达阶段则要洞悉两种语言的文化差异，从汉语中跳出来，摆脱汉语形式束缚，遵循英文公示语的文体特征，创造出简洁准确的公示语译文。

9.4.2 汉英公示语的相似之处与差异

由于社会宣传功能是所有公示语的共性，所以汉英两种公示语在语言形式上有一定的相似性。根据上文我们对公示语的文体特征和语言风格的分析，不难得出，用词力求浅显，句式力求简洁明了、准确易懂，是汉英公示语最明显的共同之处。此外，在语言结构上，汉英公示语还有以下四个相似之处。

1. 以名词为中心

指示性公示语和提示性公示语旨在对公共基础设施、单位部门名称、功能设施等进行指示和说明，无论是汉语还是英语都大量使用名词或名词性短语。例如：

登记处 Registration　　　　地铁 Subway/Underground

问讯处 Information　　　　　美食街 Food Court

2. 以动词为中心

提示、限制、强制性公示语经常向公众发出号召或要求，并期望公众做出相应的反应，无论是英语公示语还是汉语公示语，都大量使用动词或动词短语。例如：

推杠报警 Push for Alarm　　　小心碰头 Mind Your Head
登记入住 Check In　　　　　　严禁手扶 Hands Off

3. "请"/Please 结构

有的公示语用于向公众提出请求或要求，期待公众的合作，所以语气不能过于生硬冷峻，需要用礼貌用语表示，汉语用"请"，英语用 please，易于被公众接受。例如：

请排队等候入场 Please Line Up

请给残障人士让座 Please offer your seat to the disabled

4. "严禁……""禁止……""请勿……"/Do not 结构

公示语还可用来对公众在公共场合的某些行为进行限制和禁止，这类公示语一般使用语气强烈肯定、严肃的词语。句型多为简洁的肯定句、否定句或祈使句，以体现其警示作用。例如：

禁止超车 Do Not Overtake

严禁酒后驾驶 Do Not Drive after Drinking

请勿打扰 Do Not Disturb

汉英公示语虽然有很多相似之处，但由于两种语言在文化背景、思维习惯和表达方式方面有很大的差异，这些差异必然也会影响到这两种语言公示语的表达形式和内容。汉英公示语的差异主要表现在两个方面。

第一、汉语和英语语言结构差异造成公示语表达方式的差异。汉语的"意合"特征使得汉语里常见结构对称、音韵铿锵的四字词语，汉语公示语也秉承了这一特征，多使用四字结构，形式对称工整；而英语的"形合"则要求句子结构之间大量使用介词、连词、冠词等虚词起连接作用（但在英语公示语里常省略），因此英语公示语尽量使用独词、名词或名词短语、动词或动词词组，避免选用句子。例如：市内公共汽车专用（City Buses Only），只需三个单词就表明了意义，"专用"用 only 表达恰到好处；再如"切勿回返（No reentry）""庭院摊市（Yard sale）""过街天桥（Overpass）"等。

第二、汉语公示语多使用主动语态，英语公示语则多使用被动语态。汉语很少使用被动语态，因为汉语被动形式通常用来表示事故或不幸，如"被害""挨骂"；而英语出于强调主语或避免言及动作的实施者，所以多使用被动语态，且系动词 be 常被省略，直接用过去分词表示被动。例如："车位已满（Occupied）""已预订（Reserved）""此门不通（This Entrance Closed）"等。

9.4.3 公示语的翻译原则

关于公示语翻译，著名翻译学者丁衡祁（2006）提出了"简洁、规范、统一、醒目和方便"的翻译标准。上海市公共场所名称英译专家委员会提出了"公共场所标识语翻译应遵循'信息准确、行文简练、语法规范'的原则，力求以最简洁的语言表述最精确的信息"的标准。陕西省《公共场所公示语中英文译写规范》提出了合法性原则、规范性原则、准确性原则、通俗性原则、文明性原则、针对性原则、简练性原则。北京第二外国语学院公示语研究中心的吕和发（2007）在其主编的《公示语汉英翻译》中提出"功能对等、情境相同、对象一致、目标明确、转换对应、触景传情是公示语汉英翻译所应遵循的原则标准"。

公示语具有独特的功能特色和语言风格，其社会功能主要是指示、提示、限制和强制。此外，鉴于汉英公示语在遣词造句和表达角度等方面都有很大的差异，且汉语公示语有其特色和特殊性，所以在英译汉语公示语时宜遵循以下三个原则。

1. 统一原则（Consistency）

统一原则就是直接借鉴（借译）英语国家现成的惯用公示语，统一到国际惯例。由于社会生活的共性，英语国家很多公示语与汉语公示语的语用目的是完全一致的，所以很多汉语公示语在英译时可直接借用现成的英语公示语。此外，虽然有些英语公示语和汉语公示语的形式和字面意思并不对应，但只要它们的语用功能一致，也可以借用。要尽量避免生造不符合英语公示语习惯的译文。例如："打六折"宜译为 40% Off，而不能译为 60% Discount；"爱护环境，从我做起，垃圾带走，不要残留"，直接采用现成的英语公示语 No Littering 或 Do Not Litter，即可达到相同的功能，没必要直译。

2. 简洁原则（Conciseness）

简洁原则要求译文简单、明了、扼要、表达自然。既要用词简洁，还要措辞精确。根据简洁这一原则，英语公示语往往可以省略不影响整体语言效果的词语，比如冠词、代词、助动词等虚词以及系动词，仅使用实词、关键词、核心词汇，同时大量使用无主句或短语。例如："贵宾候车室"可简洁地译为 VIP LOUNGE，而不必译为 Distinguished Guests Wait for the Train at the Place；"市公安局报警中心"可译为 Police Center，比 City Center of Reporting to the Police 更赫然入目。

3. 易懂原则（Comprehensibility）

易懂原则是指英文的可读性,易被英语国家游客或来访者理解,避免中式英语。例如，如果将"软席""硬席"直译为 Soft Seat, Hard Seat，会让外国旅客搞不清车上的软席到底有多"软"，硬席到底有多"硬"。如果译为 Cushioned Seat 和 Ordinary Seat，会让英语旅客看懂，起到指示作用。这种译法符合英语表达习惯和思维方式，可以达到对外交流和宣传的效果。

9.5 公示语翻译规范解析

9.5.1 城市公共信息导向系统

公示语可以理解为公众在公共场所活动需要了解的信息，包括场所地点信息、服务功能信息、行为提示信息等，如宾馆饭店、旅游场所、购物、教育、医疗、行路、驾车信息等等。城市公共信息导向系统是引导人们在某个城市内的任何公共场所进行活动的信息系统。系统在恰当的位置以最佳的方式为公众提供其所需要的公共信息。完善的城市公共信息导向系统可概括分为三个相互联系的子系统：城市出入口（机场、火车站、长途汽车站、码头等公共场所）导向系统，市内公共交通（地铁、地面公交客运、道路交通、街区）导向系统，和市内公共服务、娱乐设施（如宾馆、饭店、商场、医院、展览馆、旅游景点）导向系统。设置在各子系统内部的各个节点（道路、通道的交叉点、汇合点），以及系统与系统衔接处的公示语，可以为出行者提供准确的导向信息，是城市软环境必不可少的构成元素，同时也体现了一座城市的精神面貌。

这类公示语多为指示性公示语，通常由文字加上相关的图形标志、符号及指示方向的箭头等元素组成，其语言形式非常简洁，指示性强，多使用名词和名词词组，如服务和服务设施名称、地名、街区名称、建筑名称等加上指示方向的箭头，再配置上诸如卫生间、地铁、出租车、火车站、公共汽车等服务设施的统一、固定的图形标志。

城市公共信息导向系统内的公示语翻译多采用功能对等的翻译策略。中国特色地名、街区、道路、建筑名称等采用汉语拼音拼写，交通基础设施、公共服务设施等均采用国际上普遍使用的英文翻译。现行国际、国家、地方的公共信息、道路交通、旅游服务等规范是公示语翻译的标准和参照。

下面我们将选取英语国家（英国、美国）的相关场所或服务设施公示语示例，以及北京、天津公共信息导向系统内的一些公示语译例，供读者参考。

A. 道路名称

道路名称是公示语的重要组成部分。许多地区都已经意识到英语公示语在城市国际化道路建设中发挥的作用，因而纷纷出台相应的公示语英文书写的标准。下面将对北京市的标准进行描述分析，力求为城市道路名称公示语翻译的规范化提供一些参考与借鉴。作为最早开展公示语标准化工作的城市，北京市的《公共场所双语标识英文译法》对道路英文名称做了详细规定，具体内容见下表：

表 9.5-1　北京市《公共场所双语标识英文译法》
中有关道路名称英语书写的规定

	道路名称	专名	通名
定义	人们对各个地理实体（道路）赋予的专有名称	地名（路名）中用来区分各个地理实体的词	地名中用来区分地理实体类别的词
翻译策略	专名+通名	路名专名通常采用汉语拼音全部大写来标注	路名通名采用英文意译，英文单词首字母大写，其余小写

	通名翻译细则	
街	Avenue (Ave) 适用情况仅三例	长安街 CHANG'AN Ave
		平安大街 PING'AN Ave
		两广路 LIANGGUANG Ave
	大街、街译为 Street (St)	菜市口大街 CAISHIKOU St
		西单北大街 XIDAN North St
		惠新西街 HUIXIN West St
	小街、条、巷、夹道一般情况下译为 Alley，当路宽达到一定规模时可以为 St；斜街译为 Byway	东直门北小街 DONGZHIMEN North Alley
		横一条 HENGYITIAO Alley
		东四十条 DONGSI SHITIAO St
		后海夹道 HOUHAI Alley
		烟袋斜街 YANDAI Byway
路	路译为 Road (Rd)	白云路 BAIYUN Rd
	辅路译为 Side Road (Side Rd)	京石高速辅路 JINGSHI Expwy Side Rd
	高速公路译为 Expressway (Expwy)	京津唐高速 JINGJINTANG Expwy
	公路译为 Highway	京兰路 JINGLAN Highway

专名翻译细则	
专名为路名专名时，专名采用汉语拼音全部大写	白云观街 BAIYUNGUAN St
	天坛东路 TIANTAN East Rd
指示以地区名称命名的街道或立交桥时，地区名用汉语拼音，街道或立交桥用英文	牛街 NIUJIE St
方位词包括："东、西、南、北、前、后、中、上、内、外"。其对应的英文译法分别为 East (E.), West (W.), South (S.), North (N.), Front, Back, Middle, Upper, Inner, Outer。通常情况下，方位词含有指示方向的意义时应译成英文，特别是当一条街道按方位分为东西、南北或内外两段时，或多条街道在方位上构成平行等对应关系时，方位词应译成英文。	景山前街 JINGSHAN Front St
	马家堡东路 MAJIAPU East Rd
当方位词本身固化为地名的一部分时，方位词采用汉语拼音。	北纬路 BEIWEI Rd
	南池子大街 NANCHIZI St
通常情况下，方位词译成英文时位置不变；在一些较复杂的地名中，方位词的位置根据需要置于最后；当地名以方位词开头且需要译成英文时，英文方位词采用缩写形式。	和平里西街 HEPINGLI West St
	西直门外南路 XIZHIMEN Outer Rd South
	西三环北路 W. 3rd Ring Road North
	东长安街 E. CHANG'AN Ave

通过归纳可以看出，撇开通名部分需视具体情况选用 Ave，St，Alley，Rd，Expwy 等不同的对等词汇，以及专名部分的音译须全部采用大写形式等细节不谈，北京市道路名称英语书写的原则基本上可以概括为"专名音译，通名意译"。当然，标准中也有一些特殊的情况，就是对方位词的处理。如果方位词含有指示方向的意义时就意译，而如果方位词本身固化成为地名的一部分就采用汉语拼音。道路名称英语书写涉及对翻译目的和文体功能的认定。"专名音译，通名意义，方位词音、意译兼用"的目的在于帮助外国游客或在华

从业人士更好地理解地名的含义。Avenue，Street，Alley，Road，Expressway 等词汇的区别运用本身就体现出有关道路的属性信息，能够加强公众的理解效果。总的来说，北京标准对于专名及通名区分化的处理方法值得其他地区借鉴。

下面是天津市道路名称翻译的示例：

水产前街　　　SHUICHAN Front St
金钟河大街　　JINZHONGHE St/JINZHONGHE DAJIE
王串场五号路　WANGCHUANCHANGWUHAO Rd
乐园道　　　　LEYUAN Rd
大沽南路　　　DAGU South Rd
友谊北路　　　YOUYI North Rd
南京路　　　　NANJING Rd
广东路　　　　GUANGDONG LU
马场道　　　　MACHANG DAO

从上述示例我们可以发现天津市道路名称翻译存在的几个问题。同一道路"金钟河大街"的英文名称不一致，有些路名中的通名"大街"采用意译的处理方法，用 St 标注，而其他同一通名却采用的是音译（汉语拼音大写）。上述示例中道路名称通名"道""路""大街"的翻译属于音译和意译混用，这必然会给外国游客的理解带来困扰。

B. 机场

伦敦希思罗机场候机楼公示牌用不同的符号、箭头和图形标出以下内容：

登机口　Departure Gates
1-62 号登机手续办理处　Check-in Desks 1-62
201-210 号登机手续办理处　Check-in Desks 201-210
酒吧餐饮　Bar & Catering
英国边境管制　UK Border Control

C. 都市景点

导向牌的功能与传统的导向树一样，不过更为紧凑，更易于识别，如纽约都市景点导向牌。

i (information) 信息牌
CITY HALL 市政厅
9/11 MEMORIAL "9·11"国家纪念博物馆
WORLD FINANCIAL CENTER 世界金融中心
NY STOCK EXCHANGE 纽约证券交易所
FEDERAL HALL 联邦国家纪念堂
SOUTH STREET SEAPORT 南街海港
BROOKLYN BRIDGE 布鲁克林大桥

D. 博物馆

下例为美国纽约市"9·11"国家纪念博物馆，关于导游服务及租用讲解设备说明的信息牌。此信息牌设立在"9·11"国家纪念博物馆的大厅，位置醒目，对导游服务及讲解设备租用价格做了详细的说明，为参观者提供了便利。

博物馆导游服务

· 导游服务"带你了解'9·11'"

60分钟本馆工作人员全程向导：20美元

· "9·11"国家纪念博物馆语音讲解器

Robert De Niro 语音录制，提供三条主题路线

	非会员价	会员价
手持讲解器租金（带耳机）	7美元	免费
耳机式讲解器	2美元	免费

想了解更多信息和设备说明，请参见《会员资格手册》

租用设备请出示您的身份证件或护照

苹果或安卓系统可免费下载

WiFi: MEMORIAL.ORG

"9·11"国家纪念博物馆

9.5.2 公示语集锦

A. 指示性公示语

票务与旅游中心 Ticket & Travel Centre
地铁 Underground
威斯敏斯特站 Westminster Station
行人（绕行）Pedestrians
伦敦旅游咨询亭 City Information Kiosk
公共厕所 Public Toilet
问询服务 Information
婴儿换巾处 Baby Change
安全通道 Emergency Access
残障顾客专用坡道 Wheelchair Ramp

B. 提示性公示语

此门关闭，请走旁门 Out of Use, Please use the other doors
限高 3.3 米 RESTRICTED HEIGHT 3.3M
请勿践踏草坪 Please Keep Off the Grass
请右侧站立(自动扶梯) Please stand on the right
请在此交款 Please pay here
请沿站台过往 Pass along the platform please

C. 限制性公示语

施工现场 禁止入内 Construction Site Keep Out
勿靠两侧（电动扶梯）Keep clear of the edges
残疾人通道 Handicapped Only
导盲犬不限（厕所）Except Guide Dogs
请勿坐靠 Please Stand Clear
读者止步 No Admittance; Staff Only

D. 强制性公示语

警戒线勿超越 Police Line Do Not Cross
严禁拍照 No Photography

红线区内 严禁停车 RED ROUTE No stopping at any time
禁止通行 Don't Walk
禁止导游讲解 NO BRIEFING OF GROUPS
禁酒区 Alcohol Free Zone
禁止驶入 No Entry

E. 生态环保公示语

（1）召唤类公示语

尊敬自然 Respecting Nature
废物利用 能源再生 Recycle your rubbish, it's a resource.
立即行动，保护自然 Act now, save what's left!

（2）提示性公示语

请继续使用毛巾 Please reuse the towels
回收利用 Recycled

（3）指示性公示语

环保木材 Forest-friendly building timbers
完全无氯 Totally chlorine free
无汞（电池）Mercury free

（4）带强制意义的

请勿乱弃 Please don't litter

F. 商务性公示语

（1）经营服务信息

化妆品/香氛 Cosmetics/Fragrances
时装配饰 Fashion Accessories
礼服/套装 Dresses/Suits
纤体运动装 Petites Sportswear
牛仔精品 Status Denim
男装部 Men's Store
箱包 Luggage

（2）促销性公示语

买一送一 Buy 1 Get 1 Free

厂家特价直销 Deal Direct with Manufacturer at Special Prices
清仓 甩卖 3~4 折 CLEARANCE 60% to 70% off
免费进行珠宝清洗和检查 Free Jewelry Cleaning And Inspection

第十章　哲学文献

　　哲学是理论化、系统化的世界观。哲学文献运用高度抽象的语言表达人们对自然知识、社会知识、思维知识的概括和总结。哲学文献所描述的是自然界、社会和人类思维的普遍规律和一般问题。哲学文献是正式程度较高的一种文体，它的翻译涉及哲学、语言学、社会学、翻译学等学科，是一种跨学科的行为。

　　哲学文献以严谨的思辨、推理和逻辑分析著称。因此，翻译哲学文献对译者的要求很高。译者除了具备过硬的语言功底外，还要具备一定的哲学知识和思辨能力。

10.1　哲学文献的文体功能

　　所谓"功能文体"（functional style），指根据语言作为交际工具所行使的社会职能而划分的文体。语言应用于社会的各个领域，便产生了相应的不同类型的文体。例如，语言应用于商业及贸易活动，就形成了商贸文体；应用于法律，就形成了法律文体。人在社会中运用语言表现出多少种行为，就有多少种语言功能。

　　一直以来，哲学文献的文体形式比较单一，它既不像文学作品的文体功能是寄情，即抒发情感，也不像法律或科技文献的文体功能是为了表事，即传递信息，哲学文献以独特的视角传递非语言信息，旨在唤起读者的先验感官，激发读者深层次的反思。

10.2　英文哲学文献的语言特征

　　语言系统根据其表达对象的不同，可以分为三类：日常语言、科学语言及诗歌语言。日常语言是人类的基本语言形态，使用最为广泛普遍。日常语言以人类常识为基础，是人类把握和认识经验世界的基本方式。科学语言专注于事物本质规律的考察，因而追求准确性和清晰性。诗歌语言的主要功能是寄情，其特征是蔑视一切逻辑和语法，因而与讲"理"的哲学文献语言相距甚远。

哲学文献的语言不同于日常语言、科学语言及诗歌语言，它所侧重的是对真理、存在等超验事物的探究和思辨，因而具有如下几个特征。

10.2.1 超验性

哲学文献的语言具有超验性特征，是因为"超越经验的哲学理性总是面向无限的超验的存在，并以超验的无限性去看待有限的经验"[①]，因而表达有限经验的日常语言并不适用于表达超验的哲学文献思想。哲学文献的语言被赋予了超越日常经验和常识的意义，这导致了哲学文献的语言晦涩难懂，也给人们理解哲学家的思想理论带来了很大困难。

【例1】The "I think" as a logical condition of experience (i.e. the transcendental unity of apperception) is not the same as the I that is actually experienced, since the latter (the empirical ego that we introspect) has constantly changing contents. (David Couzens Hoy. "A History of Consciousness: From Kant and Hegel to Derrida and Focault", in *History of the Human Sciences*, 1991(4), p.264.)

【译文】作为经验逻辑条件的"我思"（如统觉的先验统一）不同于实际被经验的我，因为后者（我们反思的经验自我）拥有不断变化的内容。

【解析】康德认为，笛卡尔的"我思"概念指自我意识，它是先验的、不可知的、不带有任何感官印象的经验，而"经验自我"是可知的实体。"统觉"是指先验的我思，具有统一性。这些概念表

---

① 孙正聿：《简明哲学通论》，北京：高等教育出版社，2000年，第78页。

明哲学语言具有极强的超验性，如果不深入探究文本，在翻译时就会出现误译。

10.2.2 抽象性

哲学语言是抽象了的符号，因此哲学文献的语言具有抽象性特征。在翻译文献时，采用直译法将导致译文晦涩难懂，造成对原著的误解误译。只有从隐喻角度理解哲学文献的语言，深入语境，将原作者的思想理论和原作品所处的文化背景、社会状况、历史环境研究透彻，才能正确把握哲学文献的内涵。

【例 2】Deconstruction explores the <u>periphery</u> of a text's self-understanding in order to bring out the elements of uncertainty, <u>the unsaid</u> that decenters a discourse. The discourse that tries to be coherent and complete can be so only by ignoring <u>what it does not want to see</u>. (David Couzen Hoy. *Critical Resistance: From Poststructuralism to Post-Critique*. MIT Press, 2004, p.45.)

【译文】为了突出不确定性的因素，也就是使话语去中心化的<u>未说之物</u>，解构探索了文本自我理解的<u>边缘</u>。只有忽视那些<u>不想看到的</u>，话语才能试图保持连贯和完整。

【解析】"未说之物""边缘""不想看到的"都是被理性所忽视的，而后现代主义的解构策略就是要摧毁形而上学理性的根基，打破话语的连贯性和统一性，还原历史的本来面目。如果译者不了解文献的时代特征，只局限于文字的表层意义，就会误读甚至歪曲原文。

10.2.3 概念性

哲学文献的语言具有很强的概念性，它旨在用概念去构造人类经验的世界。上文指出，哲学文献的语言具有抽象性，并且其抽象性越强，概念化程度就越高。纵观各个时期、各个流派的哲学思想体系都是由不同的概念编织组合而成的。因此，译者在对哲学文献的思想理论进行梳理和翻译的过程中，要特别注意概念性词汇的处理。

【例3】For these reasons, then, Gadamer does not think that his <u>ontological</u> notions of the <u>facticity (situatedness)</u>, <u>historicity</u>, and <u>linguisticality</u> of understanding entail philosophical <u>relativism</u> or <u>nihilism</u>. (David Couzens Hoy. *The Critical Circle: Literature, History and Philosophical Hermeneutics*. University of California Press, 1978, p.72.)

【译文】由于这些原因，伽达默尔不认为他关于<u>事实性（情境性）</u>、历史性和理解的<u>语言性</u>的<u>本体论</u>观点会导致哲学<u>相对主义</u>或<u>虚无主义</u>。

10.2.4 隐喻性

哲学文献中常用到"隐喻"（metaphor）的手法。法国著名后现代哲学家雅克·德里达曾提出"隐喻是哲学的近邻"这个著名论断。古今中外的哲学家都热衷于运用隐喻的方式表达抽象的思想。只有通过隐喻，才能把抽象的哲学概念和经验的日常生活联系在一起。隐喻激发了人类想象力，使得人们更加自由开放地去理解晦涩难懂的哲学文献及著作的意义及内涵。

【例4】Historical beginnings are lowly: not in the sense of modest or discreet like the <u>steps of a dove</u>, but derisive and ironic, capable of undoing every infatuation. (Paul Rainbow. *The Foucault Reader*. Pantheon, 1984, p.79.)

【译文】历史的开端是卑微的，不是在如<u>鸽子脚步般</u>的谦逊或谨慎意义上的卑微，而是嘲笑的、讽刺的、足以瓦解一切痴迷的卑微。

【解析】人们普遍认为，"鸽子的脚步"谦虚而卑微，谱系学通过研究历史开端的细枝末节、偶然性等被忽略的因素，破除起源说的同一本质和高贵血统，还原历史开端的卑微基础。但这种卑微不像鸽子脚步那样轻微无力，而是足以摧毁形而上学根基。隐喻的手法使哲学家抽象晦涩的思想在人们脑海中呈现出清晰的画面。

10.2.5 开放性

纵观从古希腊到后现代的整个西方哲学史，哲学语言整体上是持续发展、不断前进的。哲学语言具有能动创造性和内在生命力，这表现为哲学语言的语义变化过程是流动的，它随着时代、社会环境的变化而不断演变，而非固定僵死的。尤其到了当今时代，后现代思想家们大胆颠覆西方形而上学的理性传统，毫不留情地批判"逻各斯中心主义"，主张用对话克服僵化，打破限定，从而使哲学语言具有更广泛的开放性。

【例5】Genealogy recognizes that it does not change the world, but it does prepare the world for change. By disrupting the fatalism resulting from resignation to the inevitability of oppressive social institutions, genealogy frees us for social transformation, even if it does not tell us precisely what to do or where to go. (David Couzens Hoy. *The Time of Our Lives: A Critical History of Temporality.* MIT Press, 2009, p.230.)

【译文】谱系学意识到它不能改变世界，但它的确能使世界为改变做好备。通过打破由屈从于压迫的社会机构的必然性而导致的宿命论，谱系学使我们自由地接受社会变革，即使它不能准确地告诉我们应该做什么或为我们指出前进的方向。

【解析】这段话选自美国著名后现代主义者大卫·霍伊的著作《我们生活的时间：时间性的批判历史》。谱系学反对"一元论""宿命论"等形而上学假设，坚持多元论的解释，主张向分歧和差异开放。

10.2.6 批判性

哲学家大都具有强烈的批判思维和意识，这也决定了哲学语言必然具有批判性特征。纵观西方哲学史，哲学思想的发展都是建立在对前人思想观念批判基础之上。批判的功能使哲学思想体系不断完善、哲学语言不断发展更新，新的哲学概念、词汇也随之涌现。

因而哲学文献的译者要善于捕捉原文本作者的批判思维，使译文能够传承并体现原文本的批判思想。可以说，哲学家在文献作品中表现出来的批判性思维更有利于人的自我反思和社会进步。

【例6】On the contrary, contemporary hermeneutics is based on a thoroughgoing criticism both of the Enlightment assumption that everyone everywhere thinks essentially alike and of Schleiermacher's and Dilthey's tendency to presuppose the universal validity of their own beliefs, interests and psychology. (David Couzens Hoy. "Forgetting the Text: Derrida's Critique of Heidegger", in *Boundary 2*, 1979(1), p.230.)

【译文】与此相反，当代解释学建立在彻底批判基础之上，既彻底批判无论何处所有人的思想在本质上都是相似的这种启蒙假设，又彻底批判施莱尔马赫和狄尔泰预设了他们自己的信念、兴趣和心理学的普遍有效性的倾向。

10.2.7　多元性

哲学文献的语言以抽象著称，词汇呈现出语义多元性特征，其意义是相对的、变化的并且受语境的影响。如王佐良先生所言："一个词不仅有直接的、表面的、词典上的意义，还有内涵的、情感的、牵涉许多联想的意义。"[①] 此外，奎因的"翻译不确定性"打破了译者为哲学词汇或术语寻求确定、统一译法的企图。根据奎因的观点，翻译不是简单地用一个词替换另一个词，也没有所谓"唯一正确"的翻译，因此很难为某个哲学词汇找到唯一确定不变的对等词。在哲学文献中很多看似简单的哲学词汇，其语义内涵丰富而复杂，哲学界对于其译法一直是争论不休。译者在翻译过程中既不能按照权威词典生硬地死译某个术语，也不能武断地生造"对等词"，而是要深入到哲学文献的语境中仔细探究、反复推敲。下面就举两个翻译实例来说明哲学文献用语的多元性特征。

---

① 王佐良：《翻译：思考与试笔》，北京：外语教学研究与出版社，1997年，第9页。

(1) being

being 一词在西方哲学界的译法主要包括 "是" "有" "存在" "存在者",如何准确把握这个词的译法,要看具体的语境。在英语语法中,being 是 to be 的分词形式,因此通常用作系动词译为 "是"。但在哲学文献中,being 更多情况下用作名词,它包含 "existence" 含义,因而不能按照英语语法规律将其简单地翻译为 "是"。如海德格尔的巨著 *Being and Time* 就不能翻译为《是与时间》,而要翻译为《存在与时间》。

【例 7】The purpose of starting with Dasein is, for Heidegger, not to posit man as the measure of all things, but instead to undermine the modern preoccupation with self and to shift philosophy back towards a concern with Being. (David Couzens Hoy. "A History of Consciousness: From Kant and Hegel to Derrida and Focault", *in History of the Human Sciences*, 1991(4), p.272.)

【译文】对海德格尔来说,始于此在的目的并不是将人假定为万物的尺度,而是瓦解现代自我占先的意识,进而使哲学关注的焦点转向存在。

【例 8】Rather than being nostalgic, interpretation opens up avenues for future action that carries out values and choices that have been forgotten. (David Couzens Hoy. *The Time of Our Lives: A Critical History of Temporality.* MIT Press, 2009, p.202.)

【译文】与其说解释是怀旧的,倒不如说解释开启了未来行动的大道,通过行动可以实现那些被遗忘的价值观和选择。

(2) idea

idea 这个词在 15 世纪左右进入英语词汇,最初表达抽象概念。译者对这个词的译法可谓五花八门,包括 "观念" "观点" "理念"。idea 在哲学文献中出现频率很高,因此译者要深入语境,在透彻理解原文的基础上把握精准的译法。

【例 9】Thought is only one such system, for its sole motive, idea and function is to produce belief, and whatever does not concern that purpose belongs to some other system of relations. (Charles S. Peirce. "How to Make Our Ideas Clear", in *From Modernism to Postmodernism: An Anthology*. Blackwell Publishers, 1996, p.147.)

【译文】思想只是这些体系中的一种,因为其唯一的动机、<u>观念</u>和功能就是产生信念,并且凡是与那个目的无关的都属于其他的关系体系。

【例 10】Basically, then, Hirsch's <u>idea</u> that the author's intention is the only basis for defining correct interpretation is a philosophical rather than a practical point. (David Couzens Hoy. *The Critical Circle: Literature, History and Philosophical Hermeneutics.* University of California Press, 1978, p. 33.)

【译文】那么基本上可以说,赫齐关于作者意图是定义正确解释的唯一基础的<u>观点</u>是哲学的而非实践的观点。

【例 11】God, free will, and an immortal soul are other such <u>Ideas</u> of Reason, unlike the categories of the Understanding, without which we could not have experience. (David Couzens Hoy. *The Time of Our Lives: A Critical History of Temporality.* MIT Press, 2009, p.144.)

【译文】上帝、自由意志和不灭灵魂是其他这种理性的<u>理念</u>,它们不同于理解的种类,如果没有后者我们就无法拥有经验。

10.3 哲学文献翻译的原则与解析

10.3.1 哲学文献翻译的原则

按照严复先生的"信""达""雅"标准,翻译要求译者把"信"放在首位,即译者要忠实于原著,如实表达原著的思想;此外,还要兼顾"达",即要求译文的语言通顺流畅、一目了然。

哲学文献的翻译不同于文学或其他非文学文体的翻译。哲学文献的主要文体功能是说明事理,以激起读者的反思。由于哲学文献的语言具有高度概括性和抽象性,因而如果译者一味追求忠实于原文本，将会使译文语言僵硬晦涩，这样更加不利于读者准确理解原文思想。因此，译者在理解哲学文献时要深入探究原著思想，在一词一字的译语选择上要精准，结合上下文语境，不能随意发挥。既要使译文通顺易懂，又不能过于通俗化，要体现出哲学文献文体语言的逻辑性和严谨性。上文总结了哲学文献语言的 7 个特点，由于哲学文献语言的特殊性，因而对译者也提出了更高的要求。

A. 翻译即解释

西方哲学语言具有"意在言中"的特点，哲学文献语言用词抽象、语义晦涩难懂，那么到底采用何种译法既能准确传达原文本的思想又能使译文语言清晰流畅呢？在哲学文献翻译过程中，译文并不是对原文的机械复制或等量替换。翻译是一个译者积极参与建构、解释的过程。换句话说，翻译哲学文献就相当于译者用译入语（TL）解释哲学文献源语（SL）。翻译既然是解释，那么也就是阅读、解读的过程。因此，在翻译任何一部哲学经典著作或论文之前，都要仔细研读原著，透彻理解原文，在翻译过程中要反复推敲上下文语境。

哲学文献的语境比较复杂，词义随语境的变化而变化，如王佐良所言："一词一句的意义有时不是从本身看得清楚的，而要通过整段整篇——亦即通过这个词这句话在不同情景下的多次再现——才能确定。"① 因此，哲学文献翻译并不是语词的简单替换，更不是原文思想的机械复制。译者翻译文献的过程本身就是一种解释，其中包含着译者自己对文献的理解。既然翻译就是解释，那么译者在翻译过程中，在力求忠实于原文思想的基础上，必须打破字对字的死板直译，必要时打破原文献的句法结构、调整语序、添加注释等，务必使译文语言流畅，思路清晰，浅显易懂。

B. 体现译者的主体性

上文提到，哲学文献的语言具有开放性特点，因而哲学文献的翻译也应该是开放的、创造的过程。伽达默尔的"视域融合"概念对于哲学文献的翻译具有重要的指导作用。"视域融合"是指解释者

---

① 王佐良：《翻译：思考与试笔》，北京：外语教学研究与出版社，1997年，第9页。

的视域与文本所包含的视域之间的相互重叠和融合。由于哲学文献的译者和文本之间存在着时间距离，因此译者在翻译时要与哲学文本的视域相融合。根据伽达默尔哲学解释学，哲学文献的翻译过程就是译者与文本之间通过对话而不断融合的过程。

既然翻译是译者和文本之间的对话，那么译者的地位不再是卑微的，而是和作者平等的。读者是通过译文来了解原作品的，正是译者的努力使原作品获得了重生。因而，翻译不是忠实再现作者原意，而要体现译者的主体性。作为翻译主体的译者，其自身的兴趣、修养、知识及所处的社会环境等因素都会影响他对原文本的解读。译者应充分发挥主体能动性和创造性，积极参与与原文的对话，解读和领悟哲学文献的深刻内涵，使译文既能传达原作之义，又在译者与作者融合后的语境中得到新生。

C. 体现创新性

哲学文献的语言随时代环境的发展而不断演变，进而不断生成新的概念，如后现代哲学文献的语言就具有明显的时代特征和创新性。英语重形合，汉语重意合，为了保证准确达意，译者要造新词。

由于哲学文献中的术语往往具有多重含义，再加上复杂的语境，因而译者在着手翻译哲学术语之前，应仔细研读上下文语境，了解术语的演变过程，同时还要联系时代背景，选准译语，才能准确无误地传达原文献的思想。下面列举两个后现代术语的译法来说明翻译的创新性。

（1）"differance" 延异

德里达是后现代解构主义的代表人物，为了彻底批判并摧毁自柏拉图以来的西方形而上学理性主义的核心思想，即"逻各斯中心主义"或"语音中心主义"，德里达生造了"differance"这个后现代术语。西方传统"逻各斯中心主义"及"语音中心主义"认为"说话"是直接"在场"，因而更接近逻各斯。德里达则认为"书写"比"说话"更优越，因为"书写"能反映语言的差异性。从词源上看，differance 是由 difference 演变而来，两者的区别在于 differance 除了表示"差异"之外，还包含 defer（延迟）之义。德里达认为，语言自身会产生差异并留下痕迹,因而用"differance"来表达"产生差异的差异",译成"延异"。所谓"延异"就是不断产生差异的系统游戏和运动痕迹。

【例12】 Under the rubrics of "language," "power," " Being," "*differance*" and the like, deconstructionist critics have in this way heightened our awareness of the vast and heterogeneous "unconscious" that underlies all conscious practices, including such paradigmatically rational practices as theorizing, reflecting, and criticizing. (David Couzens Hoy and Thomas McCarthy: *Critical Theory*, Blackwell Publishers, 1994, p.74.)

【译文】 在"语言""权力""存在""延异"诸如此类的标题之下,解构主义评论家以这种方式增强我们对巨大的、异质的"无意识"的认识能力,正是"无意识"构成了包括诸如理论化、反省及批判这些范式行为在内的一切意识行为的基础。

(2)"dissemination"撒播

"dissemination"是德里达生造的另一个后现代术语。德里达认为,文本没有内在中心或固定结构,其意义是无限开放的。文本就像无家可归的孤儿,四处"撒播"自己。"撒播"产生出不确定的语义效果,文字符号既无确定指谓,也不含有任何意向,只是不断衍生出差异性、多样性。德里达的解构主义是彻底摧毁性的,不遵循任何逻辑、规律。一种解释总会替代另一种解释,任何解释的意义都没有绝对的确定性。

【例13】 As a result, our meaning always escapes any unitary conscious grasp we may have of it, for language, as "writing," inevitably harbors the possibility of an endless "*dissemination*" of sense, an indefinite multiplicity of recontextualizations and reinterpretations. (David Couzens Hoy and Thomas McCarthy. *Critical Theory*. Blackwell Publishers, 1994, p.34.)

【译文】因此,我们的意义总会逃脱任何我们对它统一的、有意识的掌控。正如"书写",语言蕴含了一种可能性,它包含了意义的无限"撒播"和语境重构及重新解释的无限多样性。

10.3.2　哲学文献英译汉解析

A. 动词名词化

英语中一句话往往只用一个谓语动词，为了使句子结构紧凑、逻辑清晰，经常用名词来表达具有动词意义的词，因而英语中动词的名词化特征明显。此外，哲学思想要体现客观世界的经验、事实、规律，重在说理，使用名词可以忽略主语对文献意义的影响，突出哲学文献的客观性。

【例 14】Despite Heidegger's <u>efforts</u> to avoid any <u>commitment</u> to an ultimate metaphysical reality, Derrida thinks that Heidegger's <u>talk</u> about the <u>presencing</u> of Being and its <u>appropriation</u> involves such a metaphysical metaphor. (David Couzens Hoy. "Forgetting the Text: Derrida's Critique of Heidegger", in *Boundary 2*, 1979(1), pp.224-225.)

【译文】德里达认为，尽管海德格尔<u>努力</u>避免对一个最终的形而上学实在<u>做出任何承诺</u>，但海德格尔关于存在及其<u>占有</u>的<u>在场</u>包含了如此一种形而上学比喻。

B. 被动语态的转化

被动语态在哲学文献中出现频率很高。哲学文献中使用被动语态不仅仅是为了突出动作承受者的重要性，也是为了上下文衔接得更连贯。"去主体化"是当代哲学的一个趋势和特征。为了客观表达思想，避免主观臆断，往往省略行为主体，采用被动句的形式，这样可以突出哲学思想体系的严谨和客观。

【例 15】It <u>was there noticed</u> that, the action of thought <u>is excited by</u> the irritation of doubt, and ceases when belief <u>is attained</u>; so that the production of belief is the sole function of thought. (Charles S. Peirce. "How to Make Our Ideas Clear", in *From Modernism to Postmodernism: An Anthology*. Blackwell Publishers, 1996, p.145.)

【译文】在那里<u>我们注意到</u>，思想的行动会被怀疑的烦躁激活，并且因<u>获得信念</u>而停止；因此信念的产生是思想的唯一功能。

C. 句子冗长、结构复杂、逻辑性强

句子冗长、结构复杂、逻辑性强是哲学文献语言的显著特征。汉语重意合，表现为句中连接词、限定词较少，语义平行展开，多用短句，结构比较松散。英语在思维方式和句法结构上和汉语有着很大区别。英语重形合，表现为完整的长句一般由主干结构后附加多个修饰成分、并列成分、同位成分或者插入成分，多个从句连环相扣，结构复杂严谨，层次感强。哲学文献的语言具有很强的思辨性和逻辑性，因而其句法结构也体现出清晰的逻辑性。

【例 16】It seems to me, however, that we have, by the application of our rule, reached so clear an apprehension of what we mean by reality, and of the fact which the idea rests on, that we should not, perhaps, be making a pretension so presumptuous as it would be singular, if we were to offer a metaphysical theory of existence for universal acceptance among those who employ the scientific method of fixing belief. (Charles S. Peirce. "How to Make Our Ideas Clear", in *From Modernism to Postmodernism: An Anthology*. Blackwell Publishers, 1996, p.154.)

【译文】然而，在我看来，通过规则的运用，我们似乎已经达到关于对事实的意谓以及关于观念所依赖的事实如此清晰的理解，以至于我们也许用不着如此自以为是地假装乃至到了特立独行的地步，如果我们要为那些运用确定信念的科学方法的人们提供一个普遍接受的关于存在的形而上学理论。

【解析】原句包含 70 多个英语词汇，对于这样的冗长句，首先要找准句子主干。句中画线部分是句子的主干，这是一个 if 引导的条件状语从句，主句 It seems to me that we have reached an apprehension...后面用 and 连接两个 of 并列结构，第一个 of 后面接 what 引导的宾语从句，第二个 of the fact 后面接 which 引导的同位语从句，其中还包含一个 so...that...结构。整个句子虽冗长且结构复杂，但逻辑清晰。

D. 用词正式

英文哲学文献用词正式度较高，这是因为哲学家的思想严谨而深邃，单纯依靠日常词汇无法完全表达出哲学家独特的世界观和缜密的逻辑思维。

【例17】A <u>humanistic</u> research that aims at giving a picture of the <u>personality</u> and minds of great men, a literary interpretation that <u>appeals to</u> the <u>biography</u> of the author, and even a traditional literary history that shows <u>antecedents</u> and sources influencing an author's thinking <u>implicitly</u> tend to <u>presuppose</u> such a theory and its explicit <u>advocates</u> are still in evidence. (David Couzens Hoy. *The Critical Circle: Literature, History and Philosophical Hermeneutics*. University of California Press, 1978, p.11.)

【译文】一种旨在提供伟人的人格和心灵的图画，以及旨在提供一种求助于作者传记的文字解释，甚至旨在提供一种表明显著影响作者思想的先前经历和来源的传统文学史，这种人文主义研究往往预设了这种理论，并且这种理论的公开支持者仍然大有人在。

E. 联系语境、准确选词

上文提到，哲学文献语言以抽象著称，因此很难在汉语中为这些词汇、术语找到固定不变的对等词。因此，译者要联系上下文语境，才能准确判断原词的意义，然后确定译语词。

【例18】Unlike Heidegger whose "<u>destruction</u>" of the history of ontology as originally announced in *Being and Time* is to result in a more fundamental ontology that would overcome this tradition, Derrida's method of "<u>deconstruction</u>" aims to dismantle a style of writing and thinking to see how it works (or in the case of traditional philosophy, to see how it does not work) without any intention of replacing it by a more proper one. (David Couzens Hoy. "Forgetting the Text: Derrida's Critique of Heidegger", in *Boundary 2*, 1979 (1), p. 224.)

【译文】海德格尔最初在《存在与时间》中宣称对本体论历史的"<u>拆毁</u>"导致了能克服这一传统的更加基础的本体论，德里达"解构"的方法不同于海德格尔的"摧毁"，前者旨在拆解一种写作和思考风格，这样即便在无意用更为合适的风格替代它的前提下也可以看它如何奏效（或者关于传统哲学方面，看它如何不能奏效）。

【解析】海德格尔为了彻底批判形而上学的本体论基础，创造了"destruction"一词，这时译者要联系语境，不能按照英语惯用意义将这个词译为"毁灭"，而应译为"拆毁"或"分解"。后现代哲学家德里达旨在拆解西方传统哲学的书写和思维模式，彻底摧毁传统形而上学的"语音中心主义"以及二元对立的等级制，因而他生造的"deconstruction"应译为"解构"。

F. 包含大量的专名、术语

从古希腊时代开始，哲学家们就用语言来表达他们对世界的思考。哲学家不同的思想体系形成了众多的流派，各流派衍生出大量的专名、术语等。译者在翻译这些专名、术语时要多查权威资料，避免误译。

【例 19】The proponents of pluralism, represented principally by Empedocles, Anaxagoras, and the Atomists (Leucippus and Democritus), maintained that reality was made up of a multiplicity of entities. Adherence to this doctrine set them in opposition to the monism of the Eleatic School (Parmenides), which taught that reality was an impermeable unity and an unbroken solidarity. It was thus that pluralism came to be defined as a philosophical alternative to monism. (Robert Audi. *The Cambridge Dictionary of Philosophy*. Cambridge University Press, 1995, p.624.)

【译文】以恩培多克勒、阿那克萨戈拉及原子论者（留基伯和德谟克利特）为主要代表的多元论的拥护者们主张，实在是由实体的多样性组成的。对这一原则的坚持使他们反对爱利亚学派（巴门尼德）的一元论主张，这种主张教导人们实在既是一个不可渗透的统一体，又具有连续不断的一致性。因此，多元论被定义为一元论的另类哲学选择。

10.4 英文哲学术语选译

哲学文献中往往包含大量的哲学术语，这些术语高度凝结概括了文献的思想内涵，因此能否正确翻译这些术语体现出译者是否具有深厚的哲学功底。哲学文献翻译的难点之一就是对大量抽象的哲学术语的翻译，对术语的误译会导致对文献的误读。下面列举了10个哲学流派的部分哲学术语英汉对照翻译，供译者翻译哲学文献时参考。

古希腊哲学 ancient Greek philosophy
Academy 学院派哲学(柏拉图哲学)
arche 始基，第一因
first cause 初始因原动力
First philosophy 第一哲学（亚里士多德）
logos 逻各斯（理性、逻辑、概念、定义）
metaphysics 形而上学
ontology 本体论
idea 理念（柏拉图）
substance 实体（亚里士多德）
category 范畴（亚里士多德）
particulars 殊相
universals 共相
realism 唯实论
nominalism 唯名论

经验论 empiricism
theory of tabula rasa 白板说（洛克：心灵是一张白纸，一切知识都来自后天经验）
agnosticism 不可知论（洛克：人类不能透过知识去把握事物本质）
personal identity 人格同一性（洛克）

material empiricism 唯心主义经验论（贝克莱：存在就是被感知）
skepticism 怀疑论（休谟：除了知觉，一切都是不可知的）

唯理论（理性主义）rationalism
Cartisianism 笛卡儿主义
view of endowment 天赋观念论（笛卡儿）
Cogito, ergo sum./ I think, therefore I am. 我思，故我在。（笛卡儿）
dichotomy 二分法
law of causality 因果律
logocentrism 逻各斯中心主义
anthropocentrism 人类中心主义
phonocentrism 语音中心主义
universalism 普遍主义
foundationalism 基础主义
essentialism 本质主义

德国古典哲学 German classical philosophy
thing-in-itself 自在之物/物自体（康德）
critique of pure reason 纯粹理性批判（对形而上学理性的批判）
critique of practical reason 实践理性批判（以善良意志为中心的伦理学批判）
critique of judgement 判断力批判（美学批判）
antinomies 二律背反(两个相互矛盾的命题都成立)
synthetic a priori 先天综合判断
absolute idea 绝对理念（黑格尔）

分析哲学 analytical philosophy
linguistic turn 语言学转向
logical positivism 逻辑实证主义
principle of verification 证实原则
theory of speech act 言语行为理论（奥斯汀）
mind philosophy 心灵哲学（塞尔）

meaning 意义
reference 指称
theory of description 摹状词理论（罗素）
logical atomism 逻辑原子主义（罗素）
knowledge by aquaintance 亲知的知识
knowledge by description 描述的知识
family resemblance 家族相似学说（维特根斯坦）
picture theory of meaning 语言图像论（前期维特根斯坦）
theory of language game 语言游戏学说（后期维特根斯坦）
brain in a vat 缸中之脑（普特南）
mirror philosophy 镜像哲学（罗蒂）

科学哲学 scientific philosophy
positivism 实证主义
falsificationism 证伪主义（波普尔）
scientific community 科学共同体（库恩）
paradigm 范式
incommensurability 不可通约性
scientific anarchism 科学无政府主义（费耶阿本德）
Anything goes! 怎么都行

现象学 phenomenology
intentionality 意向性（胡塞尔）
intersubjectivity 主体间性
noesis 意向活动
noema 意向内容
transcendental ego 先验自我
essence reduction 本质还原
transcendental reduction 先验还原
phenomenological epoche 现象学悬搁（胡塞尔）
phenomenological bracketing 现象学加括号
internal time consciousness 内时间意识

essential intuition 本质直观
categorial intuition 范畴直观

解释学 hermeneutics

hermeneutic circle 解释学循环（伽达默尔）
contextualism 语境论
preunderstanding 前见，前理解
prejudgement 前判断
history of effects 效果历史
fusion of horizons 视域融合
bottomless chessboard 无底的棋盘（德里达）

存在主义 existentialism

dasein 此在，亲在（海德格尔）
being-in-the-world 在世（海德格尔：人存在的基本状态）
concealing 遮蔽（海德格尔）
uncovering 无蔽（海德格尔）
clearing in the forest 林中空地/澄明之境（海德格尔）
Human being's existence is prior to its essence. 人的存在先于本质。（萨特）
being-in-itself 自在的存在（萨特：外部世界）
being-for-itself 自为的存在（萨特：人的意识）
care 烦
gorge 畏
fallen 沉沦

后现代主义 postmodernism

perspectivism 视角主义（尼采）
indeterminacy 不确定性
deconstruction 解构（德里达）
differance 延异（德里达：包含"区别 differ"和"延搁 defer"双重含义）
dissemination 撒播（德里达）

marginalization 边缘化
metanarrative 宏大叙事/元叙事（利奥塔）
disciplinary power 规训权力（福柯）
biopower analysis 微观权力分析（福柯）
desubjectivation 去主体化（福柯）
pluralist genealogy 多元的谱系学（福柯）
critical theory 批判理论
post-critique 后批判
pluralism 多元主义
discontiuity 断裂
poststructualism 后结构主义
nomadic thought 游牧思想（德勒兹：开放、多样、创造性的思想）

10.5 哲学文献翻译实例

在西方的哲学著作中，康德的作品公认为晦涩难懂，主要原因就在于其文献中句子过长，因此在翻译康德著作之前要反复研读作品，对康德思想作整体把握。只有将康德复杂而冗长的句子读透读懂，将康德的作品研究透彻，才能翻译出好的译作。

10.5.1 英译汉实例1：康德《何为启蒙？我之管见》[1]

An Answer to the Question: "What is Enlightenment?"

Immanuel Kant

Konigsberg in Prussia, 30th September

何为启蒙？我之管见

依曼努尔·康德

1784年9月30日，于普鲁士哥尼斯堡

---

[1] 张国敬：《何为启蒙？我之管见》，载《中译外研究》，2014年第1期，第58-70页。

Enlightenment is man's emergence from his self-incurred immaturity. Immaturity is the inability to use one's own understanding without the guidance of another. This immaturity is self-incurred if its cause is not lack of understanding, but lack of resolution and courage to use it without the guidance of another. The motto of enlightenment is therefore: Sapere aude! Have courage to use your own understanding!

启蒙意指人类从自己招致的未成年蒙昧状态中摆脱出来。未成年蒙昧表现为没有他人的指导，就不能运用自己的知性。如果处于未成年状态不是因为缺乏知性，而是因为没有别人的指导就没有运用知性的决心和勇气，那么这种蒙昧状态就是自己招致的。因此，启蒙的口号是：大胆地运用你的知性吧！（Sapere aude!）

Laziness and cowardice are the reasons why such a large proportion of men, even when nature has long emancipated them from alien guidance (naturaliter maiorennes), nevertheless gladly remain immature for life. For the same reasons, it is all too easy for others to set themselves up as their guardians. It is so convenient to be immature! If I have a book to have understanding in place of me, a spiritual adviser to have a conscience for me, a doctor to judge my diet for me, and so on, I need not make any efforts at all. I need not think, so long as I can pay; others will soon enough take the tiresome job over for me. The guardians who have kindly taken upon themselves the work of supervision will soon see to it that by far the largest part of mankind (including the entire fair sex) should consider the step forward to maturity not only as difficult but also as highly dangerous. Having first infatuated their domesticated animals, and carefully prevented the docile creatures from daring to take a single step without the leading-strings to which they are tied, they next show them the danger which threatens them if they try to walk unaided. Now this danger is not in fact so very great, for they would certainly learn to walk eventually after a few falls. But an example of this kind is intimidating, and usually frightens them off from further attempts.

尽管人类早已自然进化到成年阶段（naturaliter maiorennes），然而仍有如此众多的人们乐于终身保持未成年状态，懒惰和怯懦乃其原因。由于同样的原因，别人便可轻而易举地以监护者自居了。处于未成年状态简直是太安逸了！如果有一本书能够让我具备知性，有一位精神劝导者让我保持良知，有一位医生给我安排饮食，诸如此类，我就丝毫用不着劳心费力，只要支付得起，别人会很快地替我做这些令人厌烦的事情。那些欣然地承担起监管工作的监护者们很快就会让绝大多数的人们（包括全部女性）觉得，迈向成年之路不仅艰辛，而且高度危险。他们首先让其驯养的动物沉迷于这种生活，之后为其缚上约束绳索，精心地防范这些驯服的动物，使之在不受约束的情况下不敢越雷池一步。然后再让它们看到，如果试图独立行走，就会面临的危险。而事实上这种危险并非那么大，因为跌倒过几次后它们最终肯定能学会走路。然而一个这样的例子就足以使它们心惊胆战，往往不敢再做进一步的尝试了。

Thus it is difficult for each separate individual to work his way out of the immaturity which has become almost second nature to him. He has even grown fond of it and is really incapable for the time being of using his own understanding, because he was never allowed to make the attempt. Dogmas and formulas, those mechanical instruments for rational use (or rather misuse) of his natural endowments, are the ball and chain of his permanent immaturity. And if anyone did throw them off, he would still be uncertain about jumping over even the narrowest of trenches, for he would be unaccustomed to free movement of this kind. Thus only a few, by cultivating their own minds, have succeeded in freeing themselves from immaturity and in continuing boldly on their way.

因此，对每一个单独的个体而言，摆脱这种未成年蒙昧状态是很困难的，因为这几乎已成为其第二天性。他甚至已经喜欢上这种状态，目前真的不能运用自己的知性了，原因是之前他从未被允许做过这样的尝试。教条和定式化的做法，与其说是天分的合理运用不如说是天分的滥用，这些机械的行为方式乃束缚人们使之永久处于未成年状态的沉重的锁链。即便真有人摆脱了这一锁链，但如果使其跳跃哪怕是最狭窄的沟壑，他仍会战战兢兢，因为他会不习惯这种自由行动。因此，只有极少数人通过磨砺自己的心智，成功地使自己从未成年的状态中挣脱出来，并继续大胆地前进。

There is more chance of an entire public enlightening itself. This is indeed almost inevitable, if only the public concerned is left in freedom. For there will always be a few who think for themselves, even among those appointed as guardians of the common mass. Such guardians, once they have themselves thrown off the yoke of immaturity, will disseminate the spirit of rational respect for personal value and for the duty of all men to think for themselves. The remarkable thing about this is that if the public, which was previously put under this yoke by the guardians, is suitably stirred up by some of the latter who are incapable of enlightenment, it may subsequently compel the guardians themselves to remain under the yoke. For it is very harmful to propagate prejudices, because they finally avenge themselves on the very people who first encouraged them (or whose predecessors did so). Thus a public can only achieve enlightenment slowly. A revolution may well put an end to autocratic despotism and to rapacious or power-seeking oppression, but it will never produce a true reform in ways of thinking. Instead, new prejudices, like the ones they replaced, will serve as a leash to control the great unthinking mass.

对于整个群体而言，实现自身启蒙的机会更多。只要让这个群体处于自由状态，这的确几乎是不可避免的。其原因是，即便在那些被选派作普遍大众的监护者当中，也总会有少数能够独立思考的人。一旦这些人摆脱了那未成年蒙昧的羁绊，他们就会传播合理地尊重个人价值、尊重所有人都有独立思考职责的精神。那些原先被监护者羁勒的群体如果受到监护者中的一些人适时的煽动，而煽动者又不能得到启蒙，其结果可能是，这个群体强迫监护者自己受缚于这种羁勒之中，这一点是必须予以注意的。所以说宣传偏见是非常有害的，因为偏见最终会让那些始传播者本人（或其后辈）遭到报应，自食其果。因此，一个群体只能缓缓地实现启蒙。一场革命可能会终结独裁专制暴政或唯利是图、争取逐势统治的压迫，但它却绝对不会带来一次真正的思想方式上的变革。相反，新的偏见会像那些被取代的旧的偏见一样，成为控制广大无思维能力大众的约束绳索。

　　For enlightenment of this kind, all that is needed is freedom. And the freedom in question is the most innocuous form of all freedom to make public use of one's reason in all matters. But I hear on all sides the cry: Don't argue! The officer says: Don't argue, get on parade! The tax-official: Don't argue, pay! The clergyman: Don't argue, believe! (Only one ruler in the world says: Argue as much as you like and about whatever you like, but obey!) All this means restrictions on freedom everywhere. But which sort of restriction prevents enlightenment, and which, instead of hindering it, can actually promote it? I reply: The public use of man's reason must always be free, and it alone can bring about enlightenment among men; the private use of reason may quite often be very narrowly restricted, however, without undue hindrance to the progress of enlightenment. But by the public use of one's own reason I mean that use which anyone may make of it as a man of learning addressing the entire reading public. What I term the private use of reason is that which a person may make of it in a particular civil post or office with which he is entrusted.

　　实现这种启蒙，自由乃必备条件。并且，这里所谈及的自由是处理各种事务中公开运用自己的理性时所有自由中影响最小的一种。然而我却听到了来自各方面的呵斥声：不许争辩！军官说：住嘴，操练！税吏说：少罗嗦，交钱！神职人员说：不要争辩，信奉吧！（世界上只有一位统治者如是说：尽情地争辩吧，想辩论什么都可以，但要服从！）所有这一切都表明自由处处受到限制。但是，哪些限制会阻碍启蒙的实现，而哪些限制非但无碍于启蒙的实现反而能够推动启蒙的发展呢？我的回答是：人类对其理性的公开运用必须永远是自由的，唯有做到这一点才能使启蒙得以实现；理性的私下运用则往往会受到严格限制，但这并不会严重阻碍启蒙的进程。而我这里所说的公开运用自己的理性指的是，一个有学识的人面对整个有认知能力的群体做公开宣讲时所表现出的理性运用；一个人在其任职的公共岗位或被授权掌管的职位上可以运用的理性。

Now in some affairs which affect the interests of the commonwealth, we require a certain mechanism whereby some members of the commonwealth must behave purely passively, so that they may, by an artificial common agreement, be employed by the government for public ends (or at least deterred from vitiating them). It is, of course, impermissible to argue in such cases; obedience is imperative. But in so far as this or that individual who acts as part of the machine also considers himself as a member of a complete commonwealth or even of cosmopolitan society, and thence as a man of learning who may through his writings address a public in the truest sense of the word, he may indeed argue without harming the affairs in which he is employed for some of the time in a passive capacity. Thus it would be very harmful if an officer receiving an order from his superiors were to quibble openly, while on duty, about the appropriateness or usefulness of the order in question. He must simply obey. But he cannot reasonably be banned from making observations as a man of learning on the errors in the military service, and from submitting these to his public for judgment. The citizen cannot refuse to pay the taxes imposed upon him; presumptuous criticisms of such taxes, where someone is called upon to pay them, may be punished as an outrage which could lead to general insubordination. Nonetheless, the same citizen does not contravene his civil obligations if, as a learned individual, he publicly voices his thoughts on the impropriety or even injustice of such fiscal measures. In the same way, a clergyman is bound to instruct his pupils and his congregation in accordance with the doctrines of the church he serves, for he was employed by it on that condition. But as a scholar, he is completely free as well as obliged to impart to the public all his carefully considered, well-intentioned thoughts on the mistaken aspects of those doctrines, and to offer suggestions for a better arrangement of religious and ecclesiastical affairs. And there is nothing in this which need trouble the conscience. For what he teaches in pursuit of his duties as an active servant of the church is presented by him as something which he is not empowered to teach at his own discretion, but which he is employed to expound in a prescribed manner and in someone else's name. He will say: Our church teaches this or that, and these are the arguments it uses. He then extracts as much practical value as possible for his congregation from precepts to which he would not himself subscribe with full conviction, but which he can nevertheless undertake to expound, since it is not in fact wholly impossible that they may contain truth. At all events, nothing opposed to the essence of religion is present in such doctrines. For if the clergyman thought he could find anything of this sort in them, he would not be able to carry out his official duties in good conscience, and would have to resign. Thus the use which someone employed as a teacher makes of his reason in the presence of his congregation is purely private, since a congregation, however large it is, is never any more than a domestic gathering. In view of this, he is not and cannot be free as a priest, sin? he is acting on a commission imposed from outside. Conversely, as a scholar addressing the real public (i.e. the world at large) through his writings, the clergyman making public use of his reason enjoys unlimited freedom to use his own reason and to speak in his own person. For to maintain that the guardians of the people in spiritual matters should themselves be immature, is an absurdity which amounts to making absurdities permanent.

　　那么，处理影响全体国民利益的事务，我们要建立某一种机制以限制这个国家中的某些成员，使其必须在绝对被动的状态下行事。这样，他们就可以在人为地达成一致承诺的条件下，受雇于政府，为实现公共的目标而工作（至少使其不破坏这些目标的实现）。在这些情况下争辩当然是不能允许的，服从是必须的。但是就这样或那样的个人而言，他既作为这个国家机器的一个组成部分，同时又视自己为全体国民乃至国际社会的一个成员，那么，作为一名有学识的人，在不损害其当时以被动资格所受雇的机构的利益的情况下，完全可以通过自己的作品，用最真诚的语言向大众阐明并坚持自己的观点。鉴于此，假如一位军官接到上司命令时，在执勤期间对该命令的正当性和适用性公开提出质疑，这会是极其有害的，他只能服从命令。但这并不意味着可以理所当然地禁止他以一位有识之士的身份对军事上的错误表达自己的观点，也不能阻止其把自己的观点诉诸公论。公民不能拒绝缴纳对其课征的税费，对其被要求缴纳的赋税提出肆无忌惮的批评可能被视为过激行为从而受到惩罚，因为这可能会引起群体反抗。然而，作为一个学识渊博的个人，对这种财政措施的合理性和公平性公开阐明自己的不同观点，提出这一类的批评，他并未违反其公民义务。同样，一位神职人员必须按照其服务的教堂的教义教导他的弟子和会众，因为这是他当初被雇佣的条件。但是，作为一位学者，对教义中的错误之处，他不仅有义务，而且也有绝对自由，把其所有经深思熟虑的、善意的观点告知公众，并主动对改善宗教和教会事务提出建议。并且他完全可以心安理得地这样做。因为，作为教会的一名忠实仆人，在履行自己职责时所讲授的内容，不能根据自己的见解随意发挥，他没有这样的权力，而只能作为一名受雇者，通过某种规定的方式，以他人的名义向教众传道授意。他可以这样说，我们的教会传授这样或那样的道理，这些内容是教会坚持的观点。然后，对一些他自己都不完全信奉，但又有义务进行宣讲的宗教戒条，他可以竭力为教众取精用弘，萃取出有价值的内容，因为这些戒条中也并非完全没有真理存在。但无论如何，在这些教义中都不会有与宗教本质相违背的内容，因为一旦这位神职人员认为他可以在宗教教义中找到任何与宗教本质相悖的东西，那么他就不可能再心安理得地履行教职，就不得不辞去职务。所以说那些受雇为师的人在教会会众面前所运用的理性纯属私下运用，因为不论其会众的规模有多大，也只能称之为内部聚会。鉴于此，作为一名教士，他不是，也不可能是自由的，因为他是在执行别人赋予他的任务。反之，如果这位神职人员是在以一位学者的身份通过自己的作品向现实中的大众（即整个世界）表达自己的观点，他是在公开运用自己的理性，那么就享有无限的自由，可完全根据自己的见解阐述观点，因为让大众精神上的监护者自己长久处于未成年蒙昧状态是件荒谬绝顶的事，这种做法就等同于让各种荒谬绝顶之事永远地持续下去。

But should not a society of clergymen, for example an ecclesiastical synod or a venerable presbytery (as the Dutch call it), be entitled to commit itself by oath to a certain unalterable set of doctrines, in order to secure for all time a constant guardianship over each of its members, and through them over the people? I reply that this is quite impossible. A contract of this kind, concluded with a view to preventing all further enlightenment of mankind for ever, is absolutely null and void, even if it is ratified by the supreme power, by Imperial Diets and the most solemn peace treaties. One age cannot enter into an alliance on oath to put the next age in a position where it would be impossible for it to extend and correct its knowledge, particularly on such important matters, or to make any progress whatsoever in enlightenment. This would be a crime against human nature, whose original destiny lies precisely in such progress. Later generations are thus perfectly entitled to dismiss these agreements as unauthorised and criminal. To test whether any particular measure can be agreed upon as a law for a people, we need only ask whether a people could well impose such a law upon itself. This might well be possible for a specified short period as a means of introducing a certain order, pending, as it were, a better solution. This would also mean that each citizen, particularly the clergyman, would be given a free hand as a scholar to comment publicly, i.e. in his writings, on the inadequacies of current institutions. Meanwhile, the newly established order would continue to exist, until public insight into the nature of such matters had progressed and proved itself to the point where, by general consent (if not unanimously), a proposal could be submitted to the crown. This would seek to protect the congregations who had, for instance, agreed to alter their religious establishment in accordance with their own notions of what higher insight is, but it would not try to obstruct those who wanted to let things remain as before. But it is absolutely impermissible to agree, even for a single lifetime, to a permanent religious constitution which no-one might publicly question. For this would virtually nullify a phase in man's upward progress, thus making it fruitless and even detrimental to subsequent generations. A man may for his own person, and even then only for a limited period, postpone enlightening himself in matters he ought to know about. But to renounce such enlightenment completely, whether for his own person or even more so for later generations, means violating and trampling underfoot the sacred rights of mankind. But something which a people may not even impose upon itself can still less be imposed upon it by a monarch; for his legislative authority depends precisely upon his uniting the collective will of the people in his own. So long as he sees to it that all true or imagined improvements are compatible with the civil order, he can otherwise leave his subjects to do whatever they find necessary for their salvation, which is none of his business. But it is his business to stop anyone forcibly hindering others from working as best they can to define and promote their salvation. It indeed detracts from his majesty if he interferes in these affairs by subjecting the writings in which his subjects attempt to clarify their religious ideas to governmental supervision. This applies if he does so acting upon his own exalted opinions? In which case he exposes himself to the reproach: Caesar non est supra Grammaticos? But much more so if he demeans his high authority so far as to support the spiritual despotism of a few tyrants within his state against the rest of his subjects.

然而，难道一个神职人员团体，譬如基督教会议或德高望重的长老会会议（如荷兰人所称谓的）就不应该被授予权力使其以誓约的方式为某一不可变更的交易奋斗，以确保永远对其每一个成员提供恒久不变的监护，并通过其成员实现对所有民众的监护吗？我的回答是，这绝对不行。所有这类旨在永久地阻止人类启蒙之进步的契约都是绝对无效的，纵然这类契约获得最高权力机构，获帝国议会或者最神圣的和平条约的批准。一代人不能以盟誓的手段将下一代人的命运依附在自己身上，使下一代人处于知识无法扬弃的境地，特别是在诸如此类的重要事物上，尤其是在有关启蒙方面的任何进步这个问题上。这种行为乃违背人性的犯罪，因为人类基本命运恰恰取决于这些进步过程。因此，子孙后代完全有权把这类协议视作非法甚至是犯罪行为加以摒弃。验证某些特殊措施能否得到国民的赞同而成为法律，我们只需问他们能否将其合理地实施即可。这种情况可能会出现在特定的短暂时期内，为推行某项法令而采取的一种权宜手段，直至更好的解决方案似乎已可呼之欲出为止。这也表明每个公民，尤其是神职人员，可以以一名学者的身份，在其作品中自由地对现行体制的不足之处公开发表评论。与此同时，这项新实施的法令还应继续执行下去，直至公众对这类事务本质的认识得到充分的提高，并证明已达到了绝大多数人（如果不是全体一致通过）都能赞同，并可以向君王呈交方案时方可终止。这样做的目的是，既可以保护那些例如经深思熟虑做出决定，同意按照自己的意愿改变其宗教建制的教会会众，然而又不会阻碍那些坚持一仍旧贯之人的努力。但是，使某一宗教制度永久化，且不容任何人公开质疑是绝对不能允许的，即便是在短短的几十年内也不行，因为这样做就等于实际上宣告了在这段时间里人类不会有任何进步，从而使这一时期毫无建树，这样做甚至会贻害子孙后代。一个人可以在某一有限的时间内，出于自身原因，在其应知晓的事务方面推迟自我启蒙的时间。但是，完全放弃启蒙就等同于严重侵害和践踏人类的神圣权利，于己无益，于子孙后代更是后患无穷。然而民众自己不愿实施的东西君王更不能强制其实施，因为君王立法权威之根基恰恰取决于，他能否把民众的集体的意愿与其自己的意志统一起来。君王只要能够保证所有真实的和想象的改进与国民秩序并行不悖，他大可允许其臣民做他们认为对拯救灵魂所必要的任何事情，因为这与他毫不相干。但是，如果有人要强行阻碍他人为拯救灵魂而尽力阐述自己的观点，做推进工作，那么君王就要出面阻止，这乃是他的职责所在。如果君王通过政府监督的手段来限制其臣民在作品里阐明他们的宗教观点，以干涉这类事务，那的确会使其威严受到伤害。如按其高高在上的主张行事，来干涉此类事物，其威严亦会受到伤害，并且会为自己招致这样的指责：凯撒并不比语法学家高明（Caesar non est supra Grammaticos）。如果君王置自己的无尚权威于不顾，自降身份，竟然支持国内一小撮暴虐统治者对其他臣民进行精神专制统治，那就更为不堪了。

If it is now asked whether we at present live in an enlightened age, the answer is: No, but we do live in an age of enlightenment. As things are at present, we still have a long way to go before men as a whole can be in a position (or can ever be put into a position) of using their own understanding confidently and well in religious matters, without outside guidance. But we do have distinct indications that the way is now being cleared for them to work freely in this direction, and that the obstacles to universal enlightenment, to man's emergence from his self-incurred immaturity, are gradually becoming fewer. In this respect our age is the age of enlightenment, the century of Frederick.

如果现在有人问我们目前是否生活在一个完成启蒙的时代，其答案是：不是。但我们确实是生活在一个正在启蒙的时代。就目前情况而言，人类作为一个整体靠自身的条件（或者即便外界使之具备这种条件），要达到无他人指导，在处理宗教事务方面能够自信并妥善地运用自己知性的程度，我们仍有漫长的路要走。然而种种迹象充分地表明：人们朝这一目标自由奋斗的道路正在被清理；阻挡全人类实现普遍启蒙，摆脱自己招致的未成年蒙昧状态的障碍在逐渐减少。因此可以说，我们所处的时代是启蒙的时代，我们所处的世纪是腓德烈的世纪。

A prince who does not regard it as beneath him to say that he considers it his duty, in religious matters, not to prescribe anything to his people, but to allow them complete freedom, a prince who thus even declines to accept the presumptuous title of tolerant, is himself enlightened. He deserves to be praised by a grateful present and posterity as the man who first liberated mankind from immaturity (as far as government is concerned), and who left all men free to use their own reason in all matters of conscience. Under his rule, ecclesiastical dignitaries, notwithstanding their official duties, may in their capacity as scholars freely and publicly submit to the judgement of the world their verdicts and opinions, even if these deviate here and there from orthodox doctrine. This applies even more to all others who are not restricted by any official duties. This spirit of freedom is also spreading abroad, even where it has to struggle with outward obstacles imposed by governments which misunderstand their own function. For such governments an now witness a shining example of how freedom may exist without in the least jeopardising public concord and the unity of the commonwealth. Men will of their own accord gradually work their way out of barbarism so long as artificial measures are not deliberately adopted to keep them in it.

一位君主如果能够在宗教事务方面非但不对其人民做任何限制，而且准许他们享有绝对的自由，并言明这乃其责任所在，觉得这样做不会使其尊严受损，他甚至不肯接受"宽容"这类自以为是的赞誉，那么这位君主自己就是一位已经启蒙了的君主。第一个将人类从未成年蒙昧状态解放出来（就政府角度而言），并允许所有人在涉及良知的所有问题上自由运用自己理性的人，他是值得受到心存感激的当代人及其后人赞颂的。在他的统治下，教会的显要人物尽管肩负教职，仍可以学者身份根据自己的理解自由地将其观点和意见公之于众，让世人评判，即便这些观点和意见时而会偏离获得普遍赞同的教义精神。对于不受任何职务约束的其他任何人更是如此，他们可以自由公开地阐明观点，发表意见。这种自由的精神也正在国外传播，甚至传播到那些为自由而不得不奋力清除各种外在障碍的国家，这些障碍是由于其政府误解自身职能而强行设置的。这样的政府现在可以见识一个光辉典范，领略一下自由是完全可以在不破坏民众和谐与国家统一的情况下存在的现实。只要不是刻意采取人为的手段使人们处于这种未开化的蒙昧状态，人们就会自觉自愿地逐渐摆脱未成年的状态。

I have portrayed matters of religion as the focal point of enlightenment, i.e. of man's emergence from his self-incurred immaturity. This is firstly because our rulers have no interest in assuming the role of guardians over their subjects so fir as the arts and sciences are concerned, and secondly, because religious immaturity is the most pernicious and dishonourable variety of all. But the attitude of mind of a head of state who favours freedom in the arts and sciences extends even further, for he realises that there is no danger even to his legislation if he allows his subjects to make public use of their own reason and to put before the public their thoughts on better ways of drawing up laws, even if this entails forthright criticism of the current legislation. We have before us a brilliant example of this kind, in which no monarch has yet surpassed the one to whom we now pay tribute.

我之所以把宗教事务阐述成启蒙，即人类从自己招致的未成年蒙昧状态摆脱出来的焦点，首先是因为，就艺术和科学而言，统治者对担任其臣民的监护者这一角色毫无兴趣；其次是因为，宗教方面的未成年蒙昧乃是所有蒙昧中破坏力最强、最臭名昭著者。然而，赞成艺术和科学方面自由的国家首脑的思想态度甚至会进一步延伸，因为他清楚，即使允许其臣民公开运用自己的理性，允许他们把如何更好地制定法律的思想观点公之于众，即便这样做甚至会引起臣民对现行法律的直接批判，但对其法律体系并不会构成任何危险。我们现在就有这样一个活生生的光辉榜样，即我们深怀敬意的君王，在这一点上还没有任何一位君王能够超越他。

But only a ruler who is himself enlightened and has no far of phantoms, yet who likewise has at hand a well-disciplined and numerous army to guarantee public security, may say what no republic would dare to say: Argue as much as you like and about whatever you like, but obey! This reveals to us a strange and unexpected pattern in human affairs (such as we shall always find if we consider them in the widest sense, in which nearly everything is paradoxical). A high degree of civil freedom seems advantageous to a people's intellectual freedom, yet it also sets up insuperable barriers to it. Conversely, a lesser degree of civil freedom gives intellectual freedom enough room to expand to its fullest extent. Thus once the germ on which nature has lavished most care—man's inclination and vocation to think freely—has developed within this hard shell, it gradually reacts upon the mentality of the people, who thus gradually become increasingly able to act freely Eventually, it even influences the principles of governments, which find that they can themselves profit by treating man, who is more than a machine, in a manner appropriate to his dignity.

但是，只有自身已得到启蒙，且不惧鬼神，然而手中又拥有一支人员众多、训练有素的军队以保证公共安全的统治者才可以说出任何一个共和政体都绝不敢说的话：尽情地争辩吧，想辩论什么都可以，但要服从！这为我们揭示了人类事务中一种奇怪而又出人意料的模式（正如我们会经常见到的那样，如果从最广义的角度考虑这些事物，几乎所有事情都是自相矛盾的）。高度的公民自由似乎有利于人民的思想自由，然而高度的公民自由也为人民的思想自由设置了不可逾越的障碍。相反，较低程度公民自由却给思想自由提供足够的空间，使其能够最充分地扩展延伸。所以，一旦这株得到大自然极精心呵护的萌芽，即人类自由思想的意愿与使命，在这个坚硬的外壳中发育成熟，它会逐渐地反作用于人们的精神状态，人们自由行事的能力因此也会逐渐变得越来越强。最终它甚至会影响政府的决策原则，因为政府会发现，以恰当的方式善待人民，让他们有尊严，而不是把他们当成机器，对政府本身也是大有益处的。

10.5.2 英译汉实例2：后现代哲学文献

美国后现代著名学者大卫·卡曾斯·霍伊（David Couzens Hoy）先后出版了"批判三部曲"著作，对"基础主义"（foundationalism）和"普遍主义"（universalism）提出质疑，倡导以多元论为特征的后现代主义批判理论，引起了西方哲学界的关注。国内外学者对霍伊的著作和他所创立的独具特色的"谱系学解释学"（Genealogical Hermeneutics）理论展开了研究和讨论。霍伊的核心术语对研究后现代主义具有重要的理论价值，在西方学界产生了广泛的影响。下面节选了霍伊的论文《谱系学、现象学、批判理论》的原文及译文，供读者研究后现代哲学文献翻译时参考。

Genealogy, Phenomenology, Critical Theory (excerpt)[①]
David Couzens Hoy
谱系学、现象学、批判理论（节选）
大卫·卡曾斯·霍伊

What is genealogy? In Continental philosophy it is a method often ascribed to the poststructuralist philosophers. These philosophers, who are for the most part French, are assumed to have inherited it from Nietzsche and to have wielded it in the 1960s against the two dominant

---

① 参见：*Journal of the Philosophy of History*, 2008(2), pp.276-294. 中文为本章作者译。

trends in French philosophy. One was the phenomenological tradition inspired by Edmund Husserl and carried out by Jean-Paul Sartre and Maurice Merleau-Ponty. The other was the Hegelian or dialectical method inspired by Alexander Kojeve's famous lectures on Hegel in the 1930s in Paris. In this paper I will clarify how genealogy functions as a method of social critique by contrasting it to phenomenology and critical social theory as well as to some other philosophical methods.

什么是谱系学？大陆哲学中经常将这种方法归属于后结构主义哲学家所有。这些哲学家大多数是法国的，他们被认为从尼采那里继承了谱系学方法，并且在20世纪60年代与法国哲学界的两种主导思潮背道而驰来运用谱系学方法。其中一种思潮是受到埃德蒙·胡塞尔启发的现象学传统，被让·保罗·萨特和莫里斯·梅洛·庞蒂发扬光大。另一种是受到亚历山大·科耶夫于20世纪30年代在巴黎发表的关于黑格尔的演说所启发的黑格尔派的或辩证的方法。在这篇论文中，我通过将谱系学与现象学和批判理论以及某些其他的哲学方法进行对比来阐明谱系学作为一种社会批判是如何发挥作用的。

Whereas genealogy can be attributed to several recent French thinkers including Michel Foucault, Gilles Deleuze, and even Jacques Derrida—the attribution becoming more controversial in the order in which I have named them—I note that the term "poststructuralism" could well be questioned. Although these philosophers are often grouped together under the label of poststructuralism, in fact that label says nothing about what they have in common. The most that this label does is to gesture toward whatever comes after structuralism. There was, however, never really any structuralist *philosophy*. The famous structuralists were anthropologists, linguists, or psychoanalysts. Furthermore, the styles of the poststructural-ist philosophers are so different from one another that they can just as easily be pitted against one another as allied under such a vacuous term as poststructuralism.

可以将谱系学归于包括米歇尔·福柯、吉尔·德勒兹甚至雅克·德里达几位法国当代思想家,然而这种归属由于我对他们排名的先后顺序变得颇有争议——我注意到"后结构主义"这一术语备受质疑。尽管这些哲学家经常被贴上后结构主义的标签而归为一类,但实际上那个标签不能表明他们之间任何共同之处。这个标签发挥的最大作用就是表达出结构主义背后的东西。然而,从来都不存在任何真正的结构主义哲学。最著名的结构主义者都是人类学家、语言学家或精神分析学家。此外,后结构主义哲学家的风格如此迥异以至于他们很容易对立起来,正如他们很容易被划归于像后结构主义这样空洞的术语之类。

Unlike the parochial term "poststructuralism," "genealogy" has been adopted as the name for a distinctive method by a variety of philosophers in both the analytic and the Continental traditions. Nietzsche, who is usually credited with the initial use of the genealogical method, in fact attributes it to earlier British philosophers. In a previous paper I argued that one of these must be David Hume.[1] Resemblances and connections should not obscure, of course, the significant differences between Hume's and Nietzsche's employment of genealogy. As Nietzsche understands that difference, Hume and the other British genealogists dig under psychological phenomena to identify the shared features that run through experience. Hume's use of genealogy thereby vindicates standard morality. In *Truth and Truthfulness* Bernard Williams thus calls this usage "vindicatory genealogy."[2] He sees Nietzsche's genealogy, in contrast to Hume's vindicatory genealogy, as an "unmasking" method that explains how

---

[1] 参见: David Couzens Hoy. "Nietzsche, Hume, and the Genealogical Method", in *Nietzsche as Affirmative Thinker*. Yirmiyahu Yovel, ed. Amsterdam: Martinus Nijhoff Publishers, 1986, pp. 20-38.

[2] Bernard Williams. *Truth and Truthfulness*. Princeton: Princeton University Press, 2002, p.36.

morality emerged from non-moral and even anti-moral forces. I will use Williams's distinction between vindicatory and unmasking philosophy in the following discussion of how genealogy functions as critique.

不同于"后结构主义"这个意义狭隘的术语,"谱系学"作为一种独特方法的代名词,已经被分析哲学和大陆哲学领域的众多哲学家采纳。经常被誉为使用谱系学方法第一人的尼采,实际上将谱系学归属于更早的英国哲学家们。在之前的一篇论文中,我认为大卫·休谟必然是这些哲学家中的一员。当然,相似和关联不应混淆休谟和尼采对于谱系学运用的重大差异。就像尼采对那种差异的理解,休谟和其他英国谱系学家挖掘心理现象表面之下,来识别贯穿经验的共同特征。因此,休谟对于谱系学的运用可以为道德标准辩护。于是伯纳德·威廉姆斯在其著作《真理与真实性》中,将这种用法称作"辨明的谱系学"。与休谟的辨明的谱系学相反,他把尼采的谱系学看作一种"揭露的"方法,这种方法解释了道德如何从非道德甚至反道德势力中脱颖而出。我将在下文关于谱系学作为批判力量如何发挥功效的讨论中使用辨明的与揭露的哲学之间的区别。

By calling morality into question, Nietzsche's unmasking genealogy attacks vindicatory genealogy as well. Genealogy that is thoroughly unmasking will challenge everything, including itself. Just as Nietzsche continually questions his own questioning, genealogists have to risk regress by asking whether their own views are not simply perspectives on perspectives. Genealogy thus becomes a methodological challenge to the rationality and coherence of its own interpretations of self and world. I hasten to add, however, that genealogy need not thereby abandon its own interpretations. Doubting is not the same as denying. If the genealogy finds no grounds for suspecting its own rationality, it can assume that its understanding of the phenomena in question is sound, at least for the time being. Vindicatory genealogy can thus survive the attack by the unmasking type of genealogy.

尼采的揭露的谱系学通过质疑道德来抨击辨明的谱系学。完全不加掩饰的谱系学会对包括它自身在内的一切发起挑战。就像尼采不断地质疑他自己的疑问那样，谱系学家们不得不冒着倒退的危险提出问题，他们自己的观点是否不仅仅是关于视角的观点。因此，谱系学成为一种方法论来挑战理性以及它本身关于自我和世界的解释的一致性。然而，我赶紧补充道，谱系学因而不需要抛弃它本身的解释。怀疑不同于否定。如果谱系学不能为怀疑它自身的理性找到理由，那么至少目前可以设想它对于可疑现象的理解是合理的。因此，辨明的谱系学可以在揭露的谱系学的抨击中幸存下来。

Of the principal rivals to genealogy, namely Bergsonism, phenomenology, dialectcs, and critical theory, I suggest that the first two are vindicatory and the second two belong to the unmasking type of philosophy. To explain this distinction, I begin with Bergsonism and then I turn to dialectical critical theory before coming to the relation of genealogy and phenomenology.

在谱系学的主要对手中，也就是，柏格森主义、现象学、辩证法和批判理论，我认为前两个属于辨明的谱系学，而后两个属于揭露的谱系学的类型。为了解释它们的区别，我从柏格森主义开始，然后转向辩证的批判理论，最后才探讨谱系学和现象学之间的关系。

In reflecting on Henri Bergson, the phenomenologist Maurice Merleau-Ponty lists three "Bergsonian" doctrines.[①] The first is that intuition is prior to intellect and logic. The second is that spirit has primacy over matter. The third is that life (or vitality) is more primordial than mechanism. Although Merleau-Ponty insists that these doctrines are merely popularizations of Bergson's real philosophy, the appeal to intuition brings out the unsuspicious character of Bergson's philosophy. Because intuition is in primordial contact with things, intuition is the ultimate arbiter. One could argue that Merleau-Ponty is

---

① Maurice Merleau-Ponty. *In Praise of Philosophy*. John Wild and James M. Edie, trans. Evanston: Northwestern University Press, 1963, pp.9-33.

assimilating Bergson to his own conception of philosophy as phenomenology. For Merleau-Ponty, phenomenology "tries to give a direct description of our experience as it is."[①] If metaphysical reflection distorts immediate experience, phenomenology aims at "re-achieving a direct and primitive contact with the world"[②] and "re-learning to look at the world."[③] This characterization of phenomenology makes it indicatory. The idea is that pre-reflectively we have a basic relation to the world that is distorted by ordinary introspection and reflection. Phenomenology is a more rigorous way of attending to pre-reflective experience. Through phenomenology we can vindicate philosophically what we already understand about experience, even if "understanding" is not equivalent to explicitly knowing. For similar reasons, the recapture of intuition in Berg-sonian philosophy would also be vindicatory. We are finding out the truth that we already understand through intuition, and philosophy is the systematic articulation of this more intuitive knowledge.

仔细研究亨利·柏格森后，现象学家莫里斯·梅洛·庞蒂列出了三点"柏格森主义的"学说。第一点是直觉先于理智与逻辑。第二点是精神优于物质。第三点是生命（或生命力）比机制更加原始。尽管梅洛·庞蒂坚持认为这些学说仅仅是柏格森真正哲学的推广，然而借助直觉可以凸显柏格森哲学不怀疑的特征。因为直觉与事物有着原始的联系，因此直觉是最终裁决者。人们可能认为梅洛·庞蒂将柏格森的学说吸收到他自己的作为现象学的哲学概念中。对梅洛·庞蒂来说，现象学"试图直接描述我们经验的本来面目"。如果形而上学反思歪曲了直接经验，那么现象学则旨在"重新取得一种与世界直接的、原始的联系"以及"重新学会看待世界"。现象学的这种特

---

① Maurice Merleau-Ponty. *Phenomenology of Perception*. Colin Smith, trans. New York: Routledge, 1962, p. vii.

② Ibid., p. vii.

③ Ibid., p. xx.

征使得它成为辨明的。这种观点就是前反思地看,我们与被普通自省和反思所歪曲的世界有一种基本关系。现象学是专注于前反思经验的一种更加严格的方式。我们可以通过现象学在哲学意义上证实我们已经理解的关于经验的东西,即使"理解"不等同于清晰地知道。出于相似的原因,再次体验柏格森哲学中的直觉同样也是辨明的。我们正在发现通过直觉已经理解的真理,并且哲学是这种更加具有直觉性知识的系统表达。

The situation with dialectics and critical theory is markedly different. These methods are more unmasking than vindicatory. From the dialectical perspective the reliance of both Bergsonism and phenomenology on appeals to intuition resembles what is called in the Continental tradition the "myth of presence" and in the analytic tradition the "myth of the given."[①] That is, there is no sensory givenness or immediate presence that is not already permeated by conceptual or linguistic factors. Also, vindication tends to overlook the phenomenon of meaning change. In the Kantian tradition the meaning of concepts stays the same over time. Arranging concepts coherently in a comprehensive system is a Kantian way to vindicate these concepts. In contrast, in the tradition of Hegel's *Phenomenology of Spirit*, there is no immediate given, and the concepts change their meaning as they are combined with other concepts. As Richard Rorty remarks, "it is much easier to formulate specific 'philosophical problems' if, with Kant, you think that there are concepts which stay fixed regardless of historical change rather than, with Hegel, that concepts change as history moves

---

① As Mark Bevir concisely expresses the myth of presence, "no truths are simply given to consciousness." 参见:Mark Bevir. "Meaning, Truth, and Phenomenology", in *Metaphilosophy*, 2000(31), pp.412-426. This paper represents a re-interpretation of phenomenology along Wittgensteinian lines that would exempt it from the myth of presence that Derrida criticizes in Husserl's conception of phenomenology.

along. Hegelian historicism and the idea that the philosopher's job is to draw out the meanings of our statements cannot easily be reconciled."①

辩证法与批判理论的情况就明显不同了。这些方法更加具有揭露性而非辨明性。从辩证的角度看，柏格森主义和现象学依赖于借助直觉，这点与大陆哲学传统中所谓的"在场神话"和分析哲学传统中的"给定神话"很相似。也就是说，没有不被概念或语言因素渗透影响的感官的给定或直接的在场。同样，辩护的行为往往忽视意义变化的现象。在康德的哲学传统中，概念的意义随时间推移却始终保持不变。康德用来辩护这些概念的方式就是将它们有条不紊地安排在一个综合的系统中。相反，在黑格尔的《精神现象学》传统中，没有直接的给定，当这些概念与其他概念结合时，它们的意义也就改变了。就像理查德·罗蒂评论道："如果你认为概念随历史前进而变化，你和黑格尔阐述具体的哲学问题，相比之下，如果你认为不管历史如何变化始终存在着不变的概念，那么和康德阐述具体的哲学问题则容易得多。黑格尔的历史相对主义和哲学的任务就是引出我们陈述的意义这一观点是无法轻易调和的。"

Meaning change is said by its advocates to be holistic. Holism holds that some concepts cannot remain the same while others change. Instead, change in some concepts results in changes in all. Nevertheless, concepts can change at different rates. Foucault notes, for instance, in his study of the history of ethics that the moral rules for sexual conduct have varied relatively little since the ancient Greeks. Where there has been genuine change is at the deeper level of what he calls "ethical substance"— i.e., the underlying self-understanding that explains why one wants to obey the moral rules and what one thereby hopes to become.

---

① Richard Rorty. "A Pragmatist View of Contemporary Analytic Philosophy", in William Eggington and Mike Sandbothe, eds. *The Pragmatic Turn in Philosophy: Contemporary Engagements Between Analytic and Continental Thought*. Albany: The State University of New York Press, 2004, pp.131-144.

据其支持者声称，意义的变化是整体论的。整体论主张在其他概念变化的同时，某些概念不能保持一成不变。相反，某些概念的变化会导致所有概念的变化。然而，概念会在不同的层次发生变化。例如，福柯在其伦理学历史研究中指出，自古希腊开始，性行为的道德准则几乎没有变化。真正的变化发生在他所称作更深层次的"道德实体"——例如，深层的自我理解解释了一个人为何要服从道德准则以及他因此希望成为什么。

This meaning change thus makes it not only possible, but also highly probable that the present understanding of any given particular idea will be decidedly different from earlier understandings of it. Nietzsche's genealogy of morality claims, for instance, that the term "good" changes its meaning from when it was paired with "bad" to when it begins to be contrasted with "evil." We can still hear this meaning change when we use "good" not as an expression of natural aesthetics, as when we say that something tastes good, but as a moral term. The *moral* idea of the good is normative in a different sense for Nietzsche. Moral goodness is not to be vindicated in Hume's fashion, but is instead to be unmasked genealogically. On the Nietzschean analysis, the moral notion of goodness is a double negation and an abstraction. The double negation results first when something that is good in the natural sense is turned into something evil in the moral sense. Nietzsche then concludes that "good" in the moral sense means whatever is not evil. "Good" in the moral sense is thus twice a negation and morality accordingly becomes a string of largely negative commands: "Don't do this, don't do that!"

这种意义变化因此使得下述情况不仅可能，而且很有可能，即关于任何假定的特殊观念的当前理解明显地不同于之前对它的理解。例如，尼采的道德谱系学声称"善"这个术语从与"坏"匹配到开始与"恶"相对，其意义发生了变化。当"善"不再被当作自然美学的一种表述，当它不再被用来表达某物尝起来很好，而是被我们当作一个道德术语来使用时，我们仍能体会到其意义的变化。对于尼采来说，善的道德理念在不同意义上是规范的。道德的善并未按照休谟的方式被证明，而是按照谱系学方式被揭露出来。按照尼采的分析，善的道德理念是一个双重否定以及一种抽象。当自然意义上善的东西被变成道德意义上恶的东西，首先就导致了双重否定。尼采随后得出结论，道德意义上的"善"意指所有不邪恶的东西。因此，道德意义上的"善"是两次否定，并且道德相应地成了一连串总体上否定的命令："不许做这个，不许做那个！"

第十一章　企业规章制度

企业规章制度，指的是企业组织或群体为了维护其生产、工作和生活秩序而制定、颁布执行的书面的企业管理规范、章程、制度、标准、办法、守则等的总称。企业规章制度作为企业及其成员共同的行为规范和准则，其文体具有规范性、强制性、科学性、相对稳定性和群众性等特点。新旧规章制度的更替、新的规章制度的完善，是人们顺应经济发展的客观规律，进行自觉创造的结果，凝结着人的主体性、能动性和对真善美的追求，因而具有重要的文化功能和价值。企业规章制度依法制定后，在本单位范围内对全体职工和单位都具有法律约束力，因此这种文体既具有自身的个性化特点，又带有一定的法律功能和意义。

企业规章制度文本信息量大，句式结构复杂，构成了翻译过程中的主要障碍。而且英文和中文表达习惯截然不同，高质量翻译更是难上加难。韩礼德的功能文体学理论关注文本的文体功能与语言形式之间的密切关系，对企业规章制度的翻译具有实践性的指导意义。本章以这一理论为依据，基于对企业规章制度的文体功能及语言风格的分析，主要探讨功能文体学理论对企业规章制度翻译的指导作用，着重分析该理论在语气、习惯表达、文体风格翻译方面的应用。

11.1　企业规章制度的文体功能

许多国家的劳动法均要求企业规章制度明示用于所有劳动者的、以劳动者的权利和义务为中心的劳动基准，通常又同时要求以劳动合同的方式规定劳动基准。纵观世界各国劳动法，企业等用人单位的规章制度的主要内容和表现形式为：(1) 劳动基准的规定，主要内容为工作时间、劳动报酬的计算和支付方法等、关于辞职或解除劳动合同的相关事项；(2) 劳动安全、卫生制度与工伤制度；(3) 职业培训制度；(4) 劳动者日常劳动纪律；(5) 资产的保管和保全措施；(6) 表彰和惩处制度；(7) 基于企业等用人单位员工身份而应遵守的纪律。由此可见，企业等用人单位的规章制度既发挥着该用人单位范围内强制规范的功能，又体现了以劳动者的权利内容为中心的文化内涵。

作为员工的行为准则，企业规章制度具有以下功能特点：

1. 规范性。它告诉人们应当做什么，应当如何去做。
2. 强制性。它对全体职工都有严格的约束力，任何人不得违反。为此，企业规章制度要有公开性和权威性。
3. 科学性。企业规章制度要成为人们的行为准则，它本身就应当准确、齐全、统一，不能模棱两可，更不能相互矛盾。
4. 相对稳定性。企业规章制度一经批准，在一定的时期内就要保持稳定，不能朝令夕改，使人无所适从。
5. 群众性。企业规章制度要简明扼要，通俗易懂，便于大家掌握和执行。同时，要注意以"鼓励"代替"禁止"，以事前防范代替事后责备，以积极奖赏代替消极处罚。

作为一种行政管理科学化、条理化、规范化、定形化的物化形态，企业规章制度的作用首先就在于传达规范化的管理信息。因此，企业规章制度还具有提供信息的功能，这种功能主要体现在对企业管理规范、章程、制度、标准、办法、守则等的规范描述。从这方面来看，企业规章制度与法律文书在文体特征上具有相似之处，都是具有规范性、强制性的信息文本。

11.2　英文企业规章制度的语言特征

上文在探究企业规章制度的定义时提到，企业规章是企业内部管理规范、章程、制度、标准、办法、守则等的总称。其中，企业章程是企业内部用来约束各股东的内部条例,具有法律法规的功能,是正式书面语,属于法律语言的范畴。鉴于章程内容涉及员工及企业各方的权利和义务问题,因此其语言必须具备精确、严肃、庄重等特点。而关于企业规章制度里的员工守则部分,其功能在于指导和鼓励员工开展或禁止涉及某些活动,因此多选用正式平实、生动灵活、具有亲和力的语言表述。英文企业规章制度重逻辑,多使用简单语汇,下面分别从词汇、语法、语气这三个方面论述英文企业规章制度的语言特征。

11.2.1 词汇特征

A. 用词简单

英文的企业规章制度在叙述企业各条规范、制度、章程、方法、守则等时,往往使用较为简单的词汇,这样可以使材料浅显易懂,照顾到了各个层次的读者,也就照顾到了各个层次的企业员工。在通用型的员工守则部分对员工录用条件、工作时间、休假、请假等事宜作相关规定时,一般不涉及企业业务经营方面的专业词汇及术语,在叙述时用词简单,多为日常生活中常见词汇。

【例1】Company will compensate, according to labor law, the co-worker who is authorized (requested and approved) by the direct leader to work overtime on Weekdays (From Mon. to Fri.). (IKEA Trading China Co-worker Handbook, September, 2008)

【译文】如果员工在工作日加班,而且加班是经其直属上司批准的,公司将根据劳动法的相关规定支付给员工相应的报酬。

例1是宜家贸易(中国)在其员工聘用条款部分对员工如遇工作日(周一至周五)加班,企业该如何补贴报酬这一事项所作的说明。整句话用常见的定语从句规定了享受加班津贴的条件,没有使用复杂或生僻的词汇,浅显易懂。

【例2】Staff shall by himself/herself find a solution to daily commuting between home and the Company. However, the Company may provide assistance from time to time in this respect depending on its resources.

【译文】员工应自行解决其日常上下班交通。但是公司可能根据其资源情况在这一方面提供协助。

同样,例2中企业对如何解决员工上下班交通问题方面的叙述也采用简单句式和常见词汇。

【例 3】All employees will be paid by the 10th day of each month for his/her previous month work. The payment (net) will be wired to the employee's bank account.

【译文】所有员工的前一个月工资应于这个月的第10天或之前发放。工资(税后)将汇入员工的银行账号。

例3是企业对何时以何种方式向员工发放工资的规定作了简短明晰的说明,相信具备相当于中国初级中学英语水平的读者都能明白这句话的意思。

B. 多使用带强制意义的情态动词

系统功能语言学家韩礼德(Halliday)从命题之间的逻辑关系出发,根据命题主张"必要性""可能性"和"不可能性"的特点,以"归一性"为切入点,对英语的情态作了细致、系统的描述,认为情态是表现语言人际功能的手段之一,是体现人际意义的语气系统中的一个子系统。借助情态动词可以表达个人的意愿、应该承担的责任和义务,以及对事物发展趋势的判断等。

企业规章制度的主体通常为权利和义务的约定。情态动词的准确使用旨在明确约定企业法人及员工个人的权利(可以做什么)、企业员工的一般性义务(应当做什么)、强制性义务(必须做什么)和禁止性义务(不得做什么)。企业规章制度中情态动词词义的确定性非常明显。

shall 是企业规章制度中使用频率最高的词汇之一,主要表示企业及员工应当履行的义务。

【例 4】The company shall set up an attendance record system and all staff shall strictly follow the system.

【译文】公司应建立一个考勤系统,所有员工应严格遵守这一制度。

【例5】As a general rule, overtime working applications shall be subject to prior written approval of the General Manager.

【译文】作为一般的规定，加班申请应取得总经理的事先书面批准。

从例4和例5可以看出，shall 主要传达的是义务，经常以代词或第三人称名词为主语。在企业规章制度中，shall 的情态意义体现的人际功能是一种强制性，贯穿于整个企业管理和运营过程中。

与 shall 相比，will 可以表示意愿和决心，但不具备法律约束性，只表示"企业一方的某种建议或对企业或员工某一行为的说明"。

【例6】The Company does not guarantee that one type of disciplinary action will precede another.

【译文】公司不能保证在给予处分时会有先后次序之分。

此外，will 还可用于一般条件句（常省略 if）中，多使用"从句+主句（主语+will+动词原形）"结构。使用这种条件句时，发生条件句中所描述情况的可能性较小。如果该条件句所描述的情况发生了，那么主句所描述的事宜必须完成。

【例7】Any employee who, after investigation, is found to have violated the policies, procedures, rules or regulations outlined in this Regulation, or those established by the Company from time to time, will be subject to appropriate disciplinary action, up to and including early termination of his/her labor contract.

【译文】任何员工在经调查后被发现违反了本员工手册中明确的或公司不时制定的政策、流程、规范，将会受到相应的处分，直至提前解除其劳动合同。

在企业规章制度中，通过 may 提出的要求通常没有强制性，有时还可以添加附加条件；也可以在一定条件下表示"许可"或"允许"。

【例8】From time to time, staff may be asked to work on special projects or to assist with other work necessary or important to the operation of his/her department or the Company on temporary basis and the staff agrees to such arrangement provided that his or her salary does not become lower as a result.

【译文】有时员工可能会被临时安排去完成一个特殊的项目或去协助其他对公司或其部门来说必要的或重要的工作，员工同意上述安排，条件是其薪资不会因此减少。

【例 9】The company may pay employees incentives or bonuses as a form of monetary rewards based on their strong, good and consistent work performance, exemplary work attitudes and behavior, and company profitability.

【译文】公司可能会根据员工突出、良好且一贯的工作表现、榜样式的工作态度和行为以及公司的赢利情况以现金形式给予员工激励或奖金。

may 表示"许可"通常意味着主体可以怎么做，有自由选择的主观性。从这种角度看，may 的意义有些模糊，对规定可以做的事的违反也是合理的。因此，在规章制度的条文中对 may 的使用要慎重，很可能引起对规章制度条文解读的歧义。

should 一般用于条件句中，企业规章制度中多使用 should+S+V"结构。使用这种条件句时，发生条件句中所描述情况的可能性较小。如果该条件句所描述的情况发生了，那么主句所描述的事宜必须完成。这种结构我们也可以理解为从句中采用"主谓部分倒装"的句式。

【例 10】However, should any co-workers be found abusing their discount benefit, the company has the right to withdraw the co-workers' discount benefit or terminate the employment.

【译文】如果员工被发现滥用其折扣福利，公司有权取消员工的折扣福利或者解除与该员工的聘用关系。

此外，企业规章中表示强烈的否定意义时，常使用 should not。

【例 11】Co-workers should not pay airport tax, hotel fees, transportation fares and other costs for visitors and suppliers.

【译文】员工不应该为来访者或供应商支付机场税、住宿费及交通费等费用。

【例12】Employee should not wear suggestive attire, shorts, sandals, ripped clothing, and similar items of casual attire since this clothing does not present a business like appearance and, in certain areas of the operation, could present safety concerns.

【译文】员工不得穿着挑逗性的装束、短裤、拖鞋、有多道裂口的服装以及其他与上述相类似的休闲装,因为这些装束不能展现出商务风格,在某些作业领域,还可能带来安全隐患。

在英文企业规章制度中,表示强制意义的情态意义时,must 的使用不如 shall 普遍,常表示"必须""应当",其人际功能表示一种必要的行为。

【例13】An employee must maintain a personal appearance in a manner that reflects a good image to the public.

【译文】员工必须保持仪表,在公众面前体现出良好的形象。

【例14】Up to 5 days unused annual leave can be carried over to the following years and must be taken within 1 year before expired.

【译文】在未休年假中,最多只能有5天可以延期至下一年度。若在下一年度仍未休完则作废。

C. 不乏专业术语

在遣词造句上,企业规章制度中的企业章程部分常使用具有特定、明确法律含义的专业术语,以便传达其表述企业意图的法律效果,借用法律专业术语的特殊社会功能,体现企业章程的约束性、强制性以及企业章程英语的专业性和行业特性。企业章程的专业术语主要分为两类:一类是表明特定法律概念和意义的专业术语;另一类是由普通词汇转化而来,具有行业特定含义的专业术语。

【例15】Except so far as otherwise provided by or pursuant to these Articles or by the conditions of issue, any new share capital shall be considered as part of the original share capital of the Company, and shall be subject to the same provisions with reference to the payment of calls lien, transfer, transmission, forfeiture and otherwise as the original share capital.

在本例句中,"lien""transfer""transmission"和"forfeiture"属于表明特定法律概念和意义的专业术语,分别表示"扣留""转让""继承"和"没收"。"call"属于由普通词汇转化而来的具有行业特定含义的专业术语,在日常用语中意为"打电话""呼叫",但是在企业章程中是"催缴"的意思。

11.2.2 语法特征

A. 多使用被动语态,表示正式的语气

英语中被动语态的使用十分广泛,尤其常见于报刊文摘、科技文摘和官方文件。企业规章制度可视为企业的"官方文件",在表述企业立场及规定方面尤其会大量使用被动句。

(1)关于企业立场的表述

【例 16】The Human Resource Idea: To give down-to-earth, straightforward people the possibility to grow, both as individuals and in their professional roles, so that, together, we are strongly committed to creating a better everyday life for ourselves and our customers.

【译文】人才理念:我们要为那些脚踏实地、诚实正直的人们提供发展机会,不仅是职业的发展,还有个人能力的发展。由此,我们将矢志不渝地共同创造更美好的日常生活,为我们的顾客,也为我们自己。

【例 17】We were established as a principled ethical enterprise.

【译文】我们是一家坚守原则、道德营商的企业。

【例 18】We are focused on improving every facet of our company and rely on our teams to help us accomplish these goals.

【译文】我们专注于改善公司的方方面面,并依靠团队合作实现这些目标。

（2）关于企业规定的表述

【例19】Probationary period shall be executed according to Labor Contracts. Probationary period may be shortened at the discretion of General Manager.

【译文】所有员工试用期应按其劳动合同中约定执行。总经理有权决定是否缩短试用期。

【例20】If co-workers choose to normally work outside of our standard working hours, an agreement must be reached between the co-worker and his/her direct leader.

【译文】如果员工选择在正常工作时间之外的时间工作，必须征得直属上司的同意。

在英语中，用被动语态来表达企业立场及规定的内容，能够使企业立场及规定相关方面的内容显得客观、自然。与此相反，汉语在表达企业立场及规定的内容时，常使用主动语态。

B. 巧用祈使句，通常以动词祈使开头，表示命令、指示、要求的语气

（1）第二人称祈使句是以听话人为祈使对象的祈使句。在这种祈使句中，祈使对象 you 通常不表示代表，句子以动词祈使式开头，用降调，句尾用句号或感叹号。

【例21】Every employee is expected to understand and follow these basic "Ten Commandments of Safety":

—Learn the safe way to do your job before you start.

—Think safety and work safety at all times, without exception.

—Obey all safety rules and regulations; they are for your protection.

—Wear proper clothing and use required protective equipment on the job

【译文】每个员工都必须理解并遵守下列"安全十诫"：

——在你开始上岗前学习如何安全地工作。

——始终想到劳动安全，不要有例外。

——遵守所有的安全规定。它们是你的保护。

——穿着合适的服装并在工作中使用防护用品。

上面的示例是 SAP 公司关于"基本的安全规定"的部分陈述，可以看到，每项规定条文都是一个第二人称祈使句，语气强烈，引人注目。

（2）第二人称祈使句的否定形式是在句首加 Don't 或 Do not（用于正式语体）或其他否定词。

【例 22】Do not attempt to extinguish only in such cases that it is minor and without potential harm or risk to yourself.

【译文】如果火势很小，可以在不危害自身的情况下将其扑灭的话，您可以尝试将火扑灭。请记住，尝试扑灭您无法控制的火势是十分危险的。

（3）为使祈使句的语气缓和一些，可在句首或句尾加 please。

【例 23】If you have any questions about this handbook or working for China HR, please feel free to speak to the HR department.

【译文】如对此手册或关于中华英才网有任何疑问，请随时和人力资源部门联系。

【例 24】If you are not comfortable with this approach, please speak with your Manager or, if you feel uncomfortable in doing so, please speak to the head of Human Resources.

【译文】若员工觉得不便与该责任人交涉，可与直属经理交涉；若与经理交涉不便，请与人事主管联系。

（4）企业规章制度中偶尔也会使用第三人称祈使句，通常以 let 为引导词，随后接第三人称代词宾格（或名词短语）+不定式。

【例 25】Let the readers and librarians help each other and jointly run the reading room well.

【译文】读者和管理员互相帮助，共同办好阅览室。

C. 条件句

（1）在企业规章制度中，if 引导的真实条件从句用一般现在时表示将来时间，主句常用"主语+shall+动词原形"结构。

【例 26】During his probationary period, the employee will be given training to learn the technical knowledge of the Company's industry and operations, as well as the working policies, procedures, rules and regulations of the Company. He shall have the time and opportunity to determine if it is the type of employment he desires, and the Company has the option of evaluating his capabilities and qualities.

【译文】在试用期内，员工将会获得培训以学习与公司业务和运作相关的技术知识，以及公司的工作政策、流程和规定。他将有时间和机会决定这一份工作是否是他所期望的，公司也有评估他能力的选择。

【例 27】Bills exceeding the limit will only be paid by the Company if a reasonable explanation is submitted and approved by the General Manager.

【译文】电信账单超出该上限的只有在其合理说明提交给总经理并经其批准后方可报销。

（2）企业规章制度中的企业章程英语作为法律英语的一种，要求思维缜密、逻辑严谨，在各项条款的制定上除了规定股东的各项权利和义务，各种潜在的法律后果以及相应的解决方案都应该作一个细致的规定。因此，企业章程英语中普遍使用条件句。

【例 28】If a director is unable to attend the meeting for cause, he may issue a written proxy entrusting another director to attend on his behalf.

【译文】董事因故不能出席，可以书面委托其他董事代为出席董事会。

【例 29】In case of any need to extend the term of the Company, the Company shall submit a written application to the original approving authority six months prior to the expiration thereof.

【译文】如有任何需要延长公司经营期限，公司应当在届满六个月前向原审批机关提出书面申请。

例 28 和例 29 都包含一个条件句，用于阐述事实情景，而主句则表述法律主体应该采取的行为，这是一种典型的"假定与处理"模式。

D. 倒装结构的使用，起强调作用

（1）句首状语为否定词或带有否定意义的词语时，一般采用局部倒装。

【例 30】No other software than those approved by General Manager may be installed and used in the Company's computers.

【译文】未经总经理批准的软件不得在公司计算机内安装和使用。

【例 31】No other person is allowed to stay without registration.

【译文】其他人等未经登记不得逗留。

（2）句首状语由"only+介词词组"或"only+状语分句"构成，也可以采用局部倒装。

【例 32】Only if the co-worker cannot take time off due to BUSINESS REASONs, will OT payment be paid, according to labor law, to the co-worker on the next month salary payment date.

【译文】如果员工因工作关系无法在三十天内补休，则公司将根据劳动法的相关规定于下月的工资发放日支付给员工加班报酬。

【例 33】Only after the handover and termination procedures are completed may the employee receive salary payment.

【译文】离职交接手续完毕后，方可结算工资。

11.3 企业规章制度的翻译

企业规章制度是入职员工必备读本，可以让员工了解企业的相关规章制度，明确自己的职责以及权利与义务，是密切维系员工与企业关系的重要文本，因此其翻译具有一定的特殊性。

11.3.1 功能文体学与企业规章制度翻译

自系统功能语言学家韩礼德于1971年首次提出"功能文体学"

这一概念以来，国内外的学术界就展开了一场热烈讨论。尽管很多语言学家和学者对他的功能文体学理论存在种种不同的看法，但相对于传统的文学文体分析，它提出了一个运用语言学理论进行分析的理论模式和分析框架，并扩大了文体学研究的视野和范围。功能文体学是以系统功能语法为基础的一个现代文体学理论，也是一个在文体分析的现行实践中更具影响力和应用更广泛的理论。该理论在研究企业规章制度翻译的实践中也同样适用，因为功能文体学结合文体和功能，提供了一个研究企业规章制度语言的新方法。

企业规章制度，作为一个有着强制性、规范性的文本，涉及企业和员工双方的义务、权利和经济利益。它有法律文本显著的文体特点，并总以独特的语言形式出现，如选用特殊词汇以及不同句型结构来组织信息等。作为商务活动的一个重要法律文本，企业规章制度有其独特的文体特点和功能。

韩礼德功能文体学主要包括三大元功能理论，即概念功能、人际功能和语篇功能。它提供了一个研究企业规章制度翻译的相对完整、全面和系统的理论模式。语言的文体都与它的功能密切相关。某一语言特征，如某一词汇、语法或修辞格，在某一语篇中出现时若与语篇的情景语境是一致的，那么在这一情景语境中它就是文体特征。各种语言形式和手段都有成为文体特征的潜势，但不是天生就是文体特征，只有在一定情景语境中具有一定功能的形式手段才可称为文体特征。韩礼德指出，语言功能在文体分析中起中介作用。语言形式，包括语法结构、语音结构等，自身不能表明是否与语篇文体相关，而是通过它在语言交流中的"价值"表现出来，也就是说，看它是否在语篇整体中起突出作用，具有"前景化"效应，有利于实现交际者的交际目的。

韩礼德的功能文体学理论对公示语翻译具有重要启示意义。文本的文体功能决定文本的语言形式，反之，语言形式能突显文体功能的文本才是好的译文。由此，译文的文体必须适合表达文本的功能。译者在动笔翻译之前的理解阶段要钻研原文，充分了解原文的文体功能、信息发出者的交际目的以及原文的前景化文体特征；在表达阶段则要洞悉两种语言的文化差异，从汉语中跳出来，摆脱汉语形式束缚，遵循英文企业规章制度的文体特征，创造出简洁准确的译文。

11.3.2 英汉不同层面的翻译难点及应对策略

11.3.2.1 词汇层面

A. 抽象名词及其翻译

抽象名词在英语里使用得相当普遍，尤其常用于社会科学、官方文章、商业材料、法律文件和科技文章。企业规章制度往往也会使用抽象名词，让行文看起来比较正式庄重。而且，英语的文法和后缀也方便了抽象名词的使用。但是，与英语相比，汉语用词倾向于具体，常常以实的形式表达虚构的概念，以具体的形象表达抽象的内容。此外，汉语没有形态变化，形式相同的词，可以是名词，也可以是动词，还可以是形容词或其他词性的词。

因此，企业规章制度中的抽象名词，尤其是由动词或形容词加后缀的抽象名词，一般可以分别转化为汉语的动词或形容词。

【例 34】It's a body for the representation and promotion of the sector's interest specially in the economic, commercial and technological field.

【译文】该机构主要在经济、商业和技术领域代表并促进该部门的利益。

解析：此例中的 representation 和 promotion 两个由动词 represent 和 promote 加后缀转换而来的抽象名词，在翻译成汉语时被转换成汉语的动词"代表"和"促进"。

在企业规章制度的开篇位置通常会呈现总裁或首席执行官寄语，该部分一般包括以下内容：企业当前发展状况、企业文化及核心价值观、企业的未来以及高管的远景。寄语部分通常会出现一些兼有抽象和具体意象且具有一词多义特征的关键性词汇，如 cornerstone，heart，element 等。如何将这些词通顺自然地翻译出来，也是企业规章制度翻译中的难点之一。

【例 35】Quality was an early element found in our company's success.

【译文】质量是我们公司成功的最初基石。

解析:"element"的含义有"要素""成分""元素""材料""部件"等。其中,"成分""部件"倾向于具体释义,而"要素""元素"则偏向于抽象释义。直接选取上文的具体释义或抽象释义均不能恰当地与前文的"early"搭配,我们可将其两种类型的释义进行融合,"成分"和"要素"均体现出了"质量"在企业成功之路上的不可或缺性。我们可以将其理解为"企业的成功必须建立在质量的基础之上"。因此,此处译文中将"element"意译成"基石"再恰当不过了。

B. 专业术语及其翻译

企业规章制度中企业章程英语的专业词汇具有专业性、单一性和不可替代性,用于表示特定的法律概念和意义,汉语里都有与其在语义及形式上对等的专业词汇。因此,在翻译时,应采用这类专业词汇的对等形式,避免不必要的创新翻译。

(1)对于表明特定法律概念和意义的专业术语,可采用紧贴翻译法,即通过查阅相关资料和专业词典找出原文专业术语对应的专业意思。例如,"lien""transfer""transmission""forfeiture"分别译成"扣留""转让""继承"和"没收"。

(2)对于普通词汇转化而来、具有行业特定意义的专业术语,翻译时应避免采用其作为日常英语时的意义,应查找与原文相对应的中文平行文本中对这类词约定俗成的译法。

11.3.2.2 句法层面

A. 被动句及其翻译

企业规章制度主要规定企业及员工双方的权利义务以及相关的法律后果,具有法律上的约束力。因此,企业规章制度英语的叙述必须客观公正,措辞严谨,而被动句的使用能很好地优化法律信息的客观表达。一方面,在被动句中,将企业规章制度英语中具有规定性的信息置于主语的位置,起到了强调的作用。另一方面,被动句的使用可以削弱对动作执行者命令的语气，能够更为客观地传达信息，避免个人偏见的嫌疑。

在处理英文企业规章制度中被动句的翻译时，可灵活运用语态转译法及增词法。本文主要介绍两种翻译策略：（1）保留源语主语，并在其后增加"由""让""依照"等含有被动意义的词语，译成被动句；（2）将源语主语译为译语的宾语，强调动作的执行者，译成主动句。

【例 36】After the Company has paid various taxes and made allocation to various funds, the distribution of the reminder of the profit shall be determined by the board of directors in line with the actual state of the enterprise within 4 months.

【译文1】在每个会计年度结束后4个月内，缴纳各项税费及提取各项基金后的利润分配与否由董事会根据实际情况决定。

【译文2】在每个会计年度结束后4个月内，董事会可以根据实际情况，对缴纳各项税费及提取各项基金后的利润决定是否分配。

解析：对比译文1和译文2，译文1采用了"主语+由……"的汉语被动句模式，但是不免显得有些头重脚轻；而译文2将主语变成动作的执行者"董事会"，而将冗长的受动者"缴纳各项税费及提取各项基金后的利润分配与否"置于句子的后半部分，符合表达习惯，并且语义完整无误。

把英语被动句翻译成汉语时，可以根据英语原文的架构和内容将其译成汉语的主动句，也可以译成被动句，能够顺译的就采用顺译法，不能顺译的，就采用逆译法。英语中有的被动句出现施动者，有的不出现施动者，需要根据汉语的语序和语境译出或者不译出施动者。

（1）顺译法。如果能够译成汉语的被动句，则被动句的表征词可以选用"被""由""受到""加以""予以"。如果译成主动句，英语原文表达被动的意义可以用"经""接受"等词表达出来。

（2）逆译法。在某些语境下，顺译表达不合适，则需要采用逆译法。通常是将源语的主语转译成汉语的宾语。具体而言，英语是按"受动者—be+动词过去分词—by+施动者"的顺序排列。采用逆译法时,其译文的结构则应该是"施动者—动词—受动者"。例如上文例 36 中的译文 2 的处理方式。

关于逆译法,我们再看下面两个示例。

【例 37】The cost of continuing education courses and training and renewal fees for maintaining approved licenses, registrations, and certifications are not reimbursed by the Company.

【译文】公司不为员工报销为维持获批执照、注册和认证的继续教育课程和培训的费用以及续期费用。

【例 38】This Global Employee Handbook in its entirety has been adopted by the Company effective April 15, 2013.

【译文】本公司已全面采用本《全球员工手册》,本手册自 2013 年 4 月 15 日起生效。

B. 平行结构及其翻译

具有相似结构的短语、从句及句子的并列使用为平行结构。平行结构的特点是排列有序、结构对称、层次分明、脉络清晰、前后照应,并确保语句信息的完整性和清晰性,其修辞效果也很好地体现文本的严谨性和严密性。英文企业规章制度主要采用条款形式规定法律事项。而要将大量信息完整清晰地罗列在有限的条款句子中是十分困难的。因此,英文企业规章制度中大量采用了平行结构,不仅能够全面地表述企业规章制度的法律事项,而且清晰的结构更有助于读者的理解。

【例 39】Depending upon severity, a co-worker committing any of the following offenses shall have the following disciplinary action ranging from verbal warning to immediate dismissal without pay in lieu of notice:

—Neglect of duty or refusal to obey lawful instructions

—Conclusion of contracts or agreement beyond the authorization the co-worker has without previous permission

—Abuse of the Company's legal documentation or chops

——Violation of non-disclosure of information regarding the company and its business associates including clients, partners, suppliers, etc.

【译文】根据情况的严重性，有以下行为的员工将受到最轻为口头警告，最严重的为立即解除聘用关系并不予支付经济补偿金：
——玩忽职守或不遵守合法指示的
——未经允许越权签订合同或协议的
——滥用公司法律文件或公章的
——违反规定泄露公司及其相关方（包括客户、合作方、供应商等）机密的。

这一个典型的平行结构，采用四个of名词短语作为"the following offenses"的平行结构。这种平行结构的使用不仅减少了句子的数量，而且还确保在同一语境中信息的完整性，可避免阅读时信息的遗漏。

翻译英文企业规章制度的平行结构时，宜采用结构对等译法，即译文也采用源语的平行结构。英文企业规章制度的平行结构一般为名词词组或动名词词组，一般翻译成对应的汉语名词词组或动宾结构。此外，英文企业规章制度中的平行结构通常用阿拉伯数字标出序号，翻译成汉语时亦如此。

C. 条件句及其翻译

在企业规章制度中，条件句常见的句式架构为"If X, then Y shall do Z"，"X"代表规章制度适用的情况，"Y"代表制度主体，"Z"代表规定行为。在翻译英文企业规章制度中的条件句时，可以采用公式化的译法，即套用"If X, then Y shall do Z"这一句式结构，翻译的关键在于正确理解源语中的"X""Y"和"Z"具体指代的内容。此外，条件从句中连词"if""in case""where"引导的从句部分等可以翻译成"如果……""……时""当……"等，这是长期企业规章制度翻译实践的结果，也可为译者提供借鉴。

【例 40】For staff working under a standard working hour system, deferred rest shall be offered for overtime working which takes place during weekends. Where deferred rest of the current year can not be taken by Mar. 31st of the next year for reasons due to the Company, then compensation equal to 200% of the daily remuneration shall be offered. Where deferred rest of the current year can not be taken by Mar. 31st of the next year for reasons due to the staff, then no compensation shall be offered.

【译文】对于执行标准工时制的员工而言，周末加班给予调休。如当年调休因公司的原因无法在第二年3月31日之前休完的，则按日工资的200%支付补偿。如当年调休因员工的原因无法在第二年3月31日之前休完的，则不给予补偿。

解析：例40采用了"If (Where) X, then Y shall do Z"的公式化译法，译文中先叙述条件事实情况，后阐述制度主体应当采取的规定行为，表述清晰、完整。此外，例句中采用的连词"where"也套用了"如果……""……时""当……"的译法。

11.3.2.3 语篇层面

通过对比可以发现，中外企业的规章制度在语篇内容和风格方面存在着很多差异。中国企业的规章制度多是呈现道德规劝、粗略的规范条例，以及对规章制度条款的摘改。而外企规章制度的内容非常具体，其内容明确规定哪些行为是企业明令禁止的，哪些又是积极提倡的，针对各种行为的奖惩情况，以及该企业的文化和精神具体是什么。此外，中国企业规章制度的语言风格较庄重、严肃，而外企规章制度更偏向于平实、灵活。语篇层面的翻译需要从宏观上把握语篇的整体内容和整体语言风格的转换。这是语篇层面翻译的难点。要使译文在语篇层面与原文的行文风格相契合，就要使译文体现出原文的平实性和灵活性。在翻译过程中，可以灵活地使用汉语祈使句和四字结构，以便体现企业规章制度的正式性，同时彰显企业规章制度的生动灵活性。

在英文企业规章制度中，有关规章制度的表述体现出正式性、平时性，翻译这部分内容时，可以大量地使用汉语的祈使句。朱德熙（1982）在《语法讲义》中指出，"祈使句的作用是要求听话的人做某事",其语体较正式。

【例 41】Receipt of kickbacks in any form is strictly forbidden.

【译文】严禁收取任何形式的回扣。

【例 42】Radical departures from conventional dress or personal grooming and hygiene standards are not permitted.

【译文】不允许穿着与常规装束相去甚远的奇装异服,也不得违反常规的卫生标准。

在企业规章制度中,有关企业文化和精神的表述具有灵活性、通俗性。在翻译这部分内容时,译文可以采用汉语的四字格结构突出汉语的特色,具体可分为两种:四字成语和四字词组。成语的表达形式固定,而四字词组可以自由组合。四字结构言简意赅、形象生动、节奏感强,可增加汉语行文的灵动性。

在翻译企业规章制度时,首先,译者要从宏观上把握文本的语言风格及文本特征;其次,要掌握一定的法律知识及企业内部管理知识;再次,要建立相应的术语表,保持专业术语前后的译文一致,要克服对复杂被动句、条件句的畏惧心理,在翻译之前,要敢于去分析句子的结构并弄懂意思后再开始翻译句子;最后,要对译文反复全面地通读,力求确保译文准确到位。

第十二章 商务信函

商务信函,是指商务往来中的信件,是"人们互相联系,彼此交往、交流思想、沟通信息、洽谈事务所使用的一种应用文"。商务信函属于应用文体,兼具一般公务信函的性质与一般书信的特点。商务信函,"不仅是用来沟通的媒介,还可以有效地取代面对面的登门拜访,建构和维系彼此间的友谊,吸引与争取客户,以及为公司塑造良好的形象",因此商务信函要求特别准确和规范。

12.1 商务信函的文体功能

商务信函具有信息功能和祈使功能。商务信函的信息功能主要体现在,商务信函主要用来向商务伙伴提供有关公司、产品规格、性能、价格、付款、装运、保险等方面的信息。在提供有关信息的同时,商务信函主要促成对方采取行动,如购买产品、装运产品、支付货款等,因此商务信函也具备祈使功能。

商务信函具有实践价值和法律价值。商务信函具有实践价值,因为它是商务往来双方联系业务、交流信息、洽谈磋商、解决问题的重要而有效的手段;商务信函同时还具备法律价值,这些书面记录通常要存档备案,成为商务往来双方"权利、义务的规定和解决争端的法律依据"。

随着科技的发展和社会的进步,联系业务、交流信息、咨询答复的主要途径已逐步转向电话和电子邮件,但商务信函作为书面形式的材料,依然是商务活动中不可或缺的交流工具。商务信函除了可作为法律依据外,作为一种书面材料,可以把问题说得更为透彻,把信息阐述得更为详细,把理由和目的阐述得也更为真切,能够更好地促成双方的业务合作，促进合作顺利而快速地进展。

鉴于此，在翻译商务信函时，不仅要传达原文的信息功能，还要传达原文的祈使功能。

12.2　商务信函的分类

根据功能，商务信函可分为商务应酬函和商务业务函。商务应酬函是用来联络感情、增进友情、促进贸易的信函，可以细分为与商务往来有关的感谢信、祝贺信、慰问信、邀请信等，在商务交往中使用的频率很高；商务业务函是联系业务、洽谈合作、解决经济问题等方面的商务信函，可以细分为建立业务关系函、产品推销函、资信查询函、询盘函、发盘还盘函、订购函、装运通知函、支付结算函、索赔函、保险函等，商务业务函涉及商务活动的全过程。

从正式程度看，应酬函处理的都是一般性或礼节性的事务，篇幅较短，也可以叫做便函；业务函一般篇幅较长，结构完整，内容清晰，处理的都是具有实质内容的商业事务，也可以称作正式函。下面对上述各种业务函做一个简要介绍。

1. 建立商务关系函（cooperation intention）：此类信函主要是介绍己方如何获得对方公司的信息（譬如对方的联系方式、业务描述等），同时表达与对方建立某种业务关系的愿望。在信函中可以介绍己方的业务性质、业务范围，可以主动提出寄送己方产品目录等详细信息。此类信函必须做到言简意赅、情真意切、礼貌得体，从而给对方留下深刻良好的印象，为将来可能的合作打下坚实的基础。

2. 产品推销函（promotion）：产品推销函旨在引起对方的兴趣，激发对方购买产品或服务的欲望，并促使对方订货。该类信函要注意文字简练、通俗易懂。同时，可在信函中有意识地突出自己产品的优势和各种优惠条件。结尾处最好能使用巧妙的文字敦促对方订货，譬如可以告诉对方价格或许会上调、存货有限、大额订购折扣、免费试用等信息。

3. 资信查询函（credit inquiry）：该类信函一般指卖方通过某些途径查询买方的信用情况和业务能力。由于双方初次进行贸易合作，所以互不了解，此时，卖方可以要求买方提供信用资料，以便查询买方的信用状况。此类信函的语气应该非常委婉，不要让对方产生不被信任的感觉。

4. 询盘函（inquiry）：询盘也称询价。该类信函旨在让对方提供产品、服务的相关信息，譬如产品目录、价格单、样品、报价等。该类信函要求语言简单明了，但意图要表达得具体详细，这样，对方才能有针对性地做出答复。

5. 发盘还盘函（offer and counter-offer）：发盘也叫报盘，是商业交易磋商中买卖双方必经的过程。通常是一方先向另一方提出某种交易条件（如商品名称、数量、规格、交货期以及付款条件等），而另一方愿接受此条件，即交易合同成立。卖方的 offer 称为 Selling Offer 或 Offer to sell。买方的 offer 称为 Buying Offer, Offer to buy 或 Bid。报盘有实盘和虚盘两种形式，实盘又称"不可撤销的发盘"，指的是由发盘人向受盘人提出完整、明确、肯定的交易条件，并愿在一定期限内按所提条件与受盘人达成交易的一种肯定表示。虚盘是卖方所作的非承诺性表示，往往附有保留条件，买方接受后卖方仍然可以改变主意。

还盘是指买方针对卖方的报价来进行讨价还价的行为。如果卖方不同意买方的修改意见，再提出新的条件，就叫做反还盘。一笔交易从最初开始询价到最后成功，有时要经历多次还盘和反还盘的过程。发盘和还盘函一定要准确无误，因为一经确定，这些信函就成为双方交易的付款证据，而且在交易发生的过程中具有法律效应。

6. 订购函（purchase）：订购函是购买商品或服务的常用信函。买方收到报盘函后，如果认为卖方的商品及价格合适，确定购买该商品，就写一份正式的订单寄给卖方，这就是订购函。订购函可以是叙述的形式，也可以是表格的形式。但是，不论哪种形式，都要避免出现差错，要写清所订商品的名称、编号、规格、数量、价格、装运方式、交货日期、付款条件以及方式、包装、保险等事宜。因此，订购函最基本的特征就是"准确""清楚"。

7. 装运通知函（shipment）：买卖双方达成交易后，卖方按照合同在规定的期限内将货物交运对方。货物一经装船、车或飞机，卖方应通过信函的方式通知买方，说明该批货物的订单号或合同号，同时随函附上提单、发票、检验证明、重量单、保险单等，以便买方办理提货、付款等事宜。如果更改装运方式或运货途中出现问题，卖方均要通知买方相关事宜，这均属于装运通知函的范畴。

8. 支付结算函（payment）：买方收到货物后要办理付款事宜，付款的方式基本包括汇款、托收和信用证三种。无论采用哪种方式付款，买方应该以信函的形式通知买方付款的方式以及进程。

9. 索赔函（claim）：索赔函指交易双方在买卖过程中遭遇损失的一方向另一方提出赔偿损失要求的信函。譬如，卖方拒绝交货、延期交货、延期装运、数量短缺、产品质量存在问题等情况下使买方蒙受损失，则买方可向卖方提出索赔。索赔函包括：注明原合同条款，然后说明违反合同之处，最后提出损失赔偿办法。

10. 保险函（insurance）：为保证进出口货物在遭受损失后能及时得到补偿，当事人都会按照运输办法、商品性质和合同规定为货物购买保险。货主可根据保险内容和条款申请相应的险种，填写保单，提供可能影响保险条件的因素。保险公司在承诺后履行其职责，在投保人遭受损失后及时根据有关约定给予赔偿。

12.3 商务信函的篇章结构

从基本组成部分来说，英文商务信函与中文商务信函大致相同。区别为，英文的日期放在前面，而中文信函中的日期放在最后。下面分别总结英文商务信函和中文商务信函的结构。

12.3.1 英文商务信函的结构

英文商务信函的结构一般如下：
1) 信头（Heading），包括寄信人的地址和日期

2）信内地址（Inside address），即收信人的地址

3）文档号（Reference），如：Our ref: WFX/SQ, Your ref: JS201/SD707

4）收函方主办人或主要负责人，如 Attention: The Sales Manager 或 To: The Sales Manager

5）称呼（Salutation）

6）事由标题（Caption/Subject/Reference）

7）正文（Body）

8）结束语/函尾套语（Complimentary close）

9）发信人姓名，先签名再打印姓名（Signature & Printed Name）

10) 发信人职务（Position）

11) 发信人以及打信人姓名缩写，如 ST/MS

12) 附件（Enclosure）

13) 副本/抄送（CC., 即 Carbon Copy）

14) 附言/又及事项（P.S., 即 Postscript）

下面以一封完整的英文商务信函为例：

1117 The High Road
Austin, TX 78703
6 June 1996 　　　　　　　　　　　　　　　　　　（信头）
MR. David Patricks
3005 West 29th Suite 130
Waco, TX 77663 　　　　　　　　　　　　　　　　（信内地址）
Our Ref: RI0606 　　　　　　　　　　　　　　　　（文档号）
Attention: International Trade Manager 　　（收函方主办人）
Dear Mr. Patircks, 　　　　　　　　　　　　　　　（称呼）
Subject: Heating Registers' Location 　　　　（事由标题）

I received your June 6th letter requesting consultation and am providing my recommendation in the following.

First, let me review my understanding of your inquiry. The question you raise revolves around whether the heating registers should be located in a low sidewall, or in the ceiling, and if ceiling registers are used, which type—step-down or stamped-faced—will deliver the best results. Additionally, the problem concerns whether there is any benefit to having heating registers near the floor, whether moving heated air "down" in ducts negatively affects blower performance, and whether adequate injection that can be achieved on the low speed of a two-stage furnace.

My recommendations are as follows:

● I can find nothing in either Carder, Trane, or ASHRAE design manuals that indicates drop as being a factor in duct design any different from normal static losses. If you have different information on this, I would like to have references to it.

● I cannot see any advantage to low sidewall application. The problem is injection and pattern. I do see an advantage to low sidewall return; Carrier Design Manual—Air Distribution is a good reference on both items.

● I recommend step-down diffusers with OBD because they have pattern and volume control that is superior to stamped-faced diffusers.

● I am opposed to low sidewall diffusers or floor diffusers in application you describe. The increased static losses that result from trying to get the ducts down through the walls will only increase installation cost and reduce efficiency.

If there is anyone in your organization who is uncomfortable with these recommendations, let me know. I'd be very interested in reviewing any actual documented test results. Let me know if you have any further questions or if I can be of any further assistance.

（以上为正文）

Sincerely　　　　　　　　　　　　　　　　　　（结束语）

Jane A. McMurry　　　　　　　　　　　　　　（手写签名）

Jane A. McMurry　　　　　　　　　　　　（打印签名）
Engineering Manager　　　　　　　　　　（职务）
HVAC Consultants, Inc.　　　　　　　　　（公司名称）
JAM/dmc　　　　　　　（发信人以及打信人姓名缩写）
Encl.: invoice for consulting services　　　（附件）
C.C. Executive Manager of HVAC Consultants, Inc.　（抄送）

英文信函近几年来比较流行的就是齐头式（full blocked style），这样简便明了。英文信函的组成部分中，信头（尤其是日期）、称呼、正文、结束语和签名是必备项，其他部分都是可选的，可以省略。

12.3.2　中文商务信函的结构

中文商务信函的结构一般如下：

1） 标题
2） 发函字号
3） 收函单位或收件人姓名
4） 正文
5） 结束套语
6） 发函单位或发函人姓名
7） 发函时间
8） 附件

下面以一封完整的中文商务信函为例：

　　　　　　　　询价回复　　　　　　　　（标题）
　　　　　（xx）xx 字第 xx 号　　　　　（发函字号）
敬启者：　　　　　　　　　　　　　　　（收函单位）

　　现已收到贵方 5 月 2 日的询价函，内容尽知。兹随函附寄数份附插图的目录和价格表，上面有贵方要了解的情况。同时，我方又为贵方另函寄出部分产品样品，以便贵方更清楚地了解我方产品的质量以及规格。我们相信，当贵方看到产品时，一定会认同我们的产品即使对很多挑剔的顾客来说也是很有吸引力的。

　　按照订货数量的多少，我方可给予适当的折扣。至于支付方式，我方通常要求以即期信用证支付。

  再一次感谢贵方对我方产品的兴趣。如果您还需要了解什么情况，敬请与我们联系。

  我们期待着来自贵方的订货。

（以上为正文）

此致

敬礼 （结束套语）

xxxxx 公司（发函单位）
x 年 x 月 x 日（发函时间）

附件：目录、价格表 （附件）

  在中文信函的组成部分中，称呼、正文、发函单位或发函人姓名、日期是必备项，其他部分都是可选的，可以省略。中文商务信函的格式采用的仍然是传统的中文文章格式，每段开头空两个汉字。

  中英文商务信函的结构一般都分为三个部分，即开头部分（Opening Section）、主题/命题部分（Propositional Section）和结尾部分（Closing Section）。开头部分包括称呼以及称呼之前的部分；主题/命题部分是商务信函的中心内容，是商务信函的核心，这一部分直接决定了商务信函的所属类别；结尾部分就是正文之后的所有内容，包括结束套语、落款等。

12.4　商务信函的词汇特点及翻译

12.4.1　用词准确规范

  商务信函涉及商务合作的各个环节以及各个环节中的各种单据、协议、合同等，因此商务信函的用词在要求准确的同时，也要表现出一定的专业性。有人曾经对部分商贸往来文献的专业术语和行话进行过统计，结果发现相关术语的数量占总字数的 9.1%。① 商务信函的术语使用主要有以下特点，无论在做中翻英还是英翻中的时候，都要注意积累。

A. 使用专业缩略词

随着国际贸易不断发展，业务不断创新，商务信函中一些专业术语常以约定俗成的缩略词的形式出现。这些专业缩略词涉及与国际贸易相关的各个方面，如：

贸易价格术语：CIF（cost, freight and insurance 到岸价）、CFR（cost and freight 成本加运费）、FOB（free on board 船上交货价格，离岸价）

保险：WPA（with particular average 水渍险）、FPA（free from particular average 平安险）

运输：B/L（bill of lading 提单）、LCL（less container load 拼箱货）、FCL（full container load 整箱货）

支付与结算：D/P（documents against payment 付款交单）、L/C（letter of credit 信用证）、M/T（mail transfer 信汇）、D/D（demand draft 票汇）、T/T（telegraphic transfer 电汇）

在英语商务信函中，专业缩略词的恰当使用，有助于增强信函语言的简洁性、专业性，同时能以有限的形式表达出更多的信息，从而节约写作时间。专业缩略词也遵循着一般缩略词的构词特点，一般有以下几种情况：按单个字母发音（initialism），如 D/A、WAP；按整个单词发音的首字母缩拼词（acronym），如 COSCO—China Ocean Shipping Company；截断词（clipping），如 Exp. & Imp. Inc.—export & import incorporated；拼缀词（blending words），如 forex—foreign exchange，EXIMBANK—export-import bank。

在做翻译的时候，要注意这些缩略词的使用，平时多做积累。

B. 普通词汇专业化

在英语商务信函中，很多术语来自普通词汇，这些普通词汇在

---

① 张新红、李明：《商贸英语翻译》，北京：高等教育出版社，2003 年，第 166 页。

商务信函的语境中有特有的含义。在英翻中的时候，切勿望文生义。在中翻英的时候，要注意选词。

【例1】 As this is your trial order, we quote you as follows.

【译文】由于这次贵方写的是试单，特报价如下。

此例中的"order"常用意思为"指令"，"quote"常用意思为"引用""列举"。脱离商务信函的特定语境，此句翻译为"在贵方的指令下，我们向贵方列举如下"，但在商务信函中，"order"意为"订购""订单"，"quote"意为"报价"。

【例2】 Each shipment should be effected at two month intervals.

【译文】每批货物装运须间隔两个月。

此例中的"effect"在商务信函中有特定的含义。如果在商务信函的语境中，将effect翻译为"有效"，此例句翻译为"每批货运间隔限两个月之内有效"就不能准确传达原英文商务信函的表意。

C. 术语多义

术语多义指一个语言形式在不同的语境中有不同的专业含义，在翻译的时候要选择最恰当的含义。

【例3】 We'd like to inform you that your counter sample will be sent to you by DHL by the end of this month. Please confirm it ASAP so that we can start mass production.

【译文】兹通知贵方，我方回样将于本月末用特快专递寄给贵方，请尽快予以确认，以便我方开始批量生产。

【例4】 Payment will be made by a 100% confirmed, irrevocable L/C.

【译文】付款方式为100%保兑不可撤销信用证。

例3中confirm在商务信函中一般意义为"确认"。例4中的confirmed与L/C搭配，翻译为"保兑信用证"，是信用证的一种，由一家银行开具，另一家银行保证兑付。

D. 近义术语

商务信函中存在一些近义术语，在翻译的时候，为了避免造成误译，译者需要把握近义术语之间的区别和确切含义。

【例5】At the time of negotiation, 5% commission to be deducted from invoice value and should be remitted by the negotiating bank in the form of bank draft in favor of ABC Co.

【译文】议付到期时，将按发票金额扣除百分之五的佣金，该扣除金额需由议付行以银行汇票形式开给 ABC 公司。

【例6】The exporters must present shipping documents when they negotiate payment with the bank.

【译文】 出口商向银行议付时必须呈递装船单据。

【例7】This L/C will be duly honored only if the seller submits whole set of documents that all terms and requirements under L/C No. 123456 have been complied with.

【译文】只有出口人提供与信用证 123456 号相符的全套单据，本行才予以承付。

【例8】We trust you will honor our draft on presentation.

【译文】我们相信我方呈递汇票，你方会如期支付。

"negotiate""honor"在信用证中都有"付款"的含义，但 negotiate 在商务信函中是"议付"，指在信用证交易中，银行对卖方的单据进行检查，以判定是否符合信用证的条款要求之意，实际上强调如果单据符合信用证条款，银行可付款给出口商，反之则不能付款。honor 的意思为"兑现""承付"，更为突出的是"如期支付，承付"。

12.4.2 用词庄重规范

尽管随着社会的发展、生活节奏的加快，商务信函的语言有口语化和非正式化的趋势，但通常情况下，无论是英语商务信函，还是中文商务信函，用词都还是非常庄重规范的。"商务信函不是私事和私人活动，而是有关双方组织以及组织与公众利益的事与活动，有明确的公关目的和经济目的"，商务信函多用书面语、谦辞、敬语等，充分体现商务信函规范正式的特点。在翻译的时候，应尽可能使用目的语庄重规范的词汇，从而忠实地表达原文。

在英文商务信函中，日常使用的基本词汇或口语词汇要选择书面词汇和正式词汇。举例来说，"根据"一般英文表达为"according to"，在商务信函中多用"in accordance with/as per"；"……之前"一般英文表达为"before"，在商务信函中多用"in advance of/prior to"；"通知"一般英文表达为"tell"，在商务信函中多用"inform/advice"；"副本"一般英文表达为"copy"，在商务信函中多用"duplicate"；"发货"一般表达为"send"，在商务信函中多用"dispatch"；"否则"一般英文表达为"or"，在商务信函中多用"otherwise"；"因此"一般英文表达为"so"，在商务信函中多用"therefore"；"鉴于"一般英文表达为"about"，在商务信函中多用"in connection with/in view of"等。

另外，英文信函中经常使用一些由 here, there 和 where 加上 after, at, by, from, in, of, to under, upon, with 等介词共同构成的副词，如 hereafter, hereby, thereby, whereas, whereby 等古体词。这些古体词虽然在日常英语中很少使用，但是由于其带有浓厚的法律语体和正式语体色彩，因而常出现在外贸英语信函中，以显示其行文的严肃性和法律意味。此外，这些古体词也可以避免表达上不必要的重复，从而使语言更加简练。

汉语商务信函词汇的庄重规范多表现在使用文言词语，如"兹""获悉""希""承蒙""有关……一事""事宜""均""本函""鉴于"等。

【例9】 Enclosed please find the quotation sheet. All offers and sales are subject to the terms and conditions printed on the reverse side hereof.

【译文】随函附上报价单，所有报盘和销售均应以本报价单背面所印条件为准。

此例中的"hereof"相当于"of the quotation sheet"，使用的是具有正式性和法律性意味的古体词，同时也使得语言更加简练。翻译则为"本报价单"，也是正式的表达。

【例10】鉴于贵方违约造成我方不应有的损失，我方很遗憾地撤销此约，并保留对我方损失的索赔权。

【译文】In view of the fact that your violation of the contract has caused us undeserved losses, we regret to say that we have canceled the contract and we reserve the right to claim damages.

上述例子中使用了庄重词汇"鉴于"，英文翻译选择了"in view of"这个正式词汇。中英文信函都有自己庄重规范的用词，所以翻译时为传达原文的语气，要按照目的语的用词习惯进行处理。

12.4.3 用词礼貌客气

由于商务信函直接关系到商业业务的成败得失，因此礼貌用语和客气措词在商务信函中的使用显得格外重要，因为这不但体现了写信人的素质，同时也可以向对方树立企业的良好形象，有利于建立双方良好的业务合作关系。中英文商务信函都强调用词礼貌客气。在收到对方的询盘（inquiry）、报盘（offer）、还盘（counter-offer）或订货（order）等，不管是否接受，都要用礼貌的语言表达谢意；在传递令人满意的信息时，措词用语也要讲究客气；在提供令对方不满意的信息或向对方表示不满时，更需要注意措词用语的客气、委婉；在向对方提出要求或希望时，同样要使用礼貌客气用语。譬如在中文商务信函中，（1）称呼：使用"贵""尊""高""雅""惠""大"等词称呼对等公司；使用"敝""贱""鄙""小"等称呼自己公司。例如："敝公司"和"贵公司"；"敝方"和"贵方"；"惠函""大函"和"小札""小启"；"高见""尊意""雅教"和"愚见""鄙意"等；（2）请求：使用"恭""拜""垂""请""惠""敬"等敬谦词，如"恭请""拜请""垂询""请教""惠存"等，以示礼貌和文雅；（3）告知：使用"承蒙""承问""惠告"提及对方的告知；使用"谨告""禀告""奉告""敬告""兹"等来引进自己的告知；（4）致谢：用"不胜感谢""谨致谢意""鸣谢肺腑"等来表示谢意；（5）下结语：在信件的结尾，使用"专此奉复""特此谨复""特函奉复""谨祝""此致敬礼""敬启"等套语做结束语。

【例11】贵公司……年……月……日的贸易查询函收悉。

【译文】 We are pleased to have received your trade inquiry of …

此例中使用了"贵公司"来称呼对方公司,英译文无法使用一个礼貌词表示"贵",在英文中添加了英文常用的礼貌用语 pleased。

相比之下,英文商务信函中礼貌用词要比汉语中少,英语商务函电主要通过句型来表达礼貌。英语中表达礼貌主要还通过主情态动词如 can, may, must, will, shall 等和从属情态动词如 could, might, would, ought to, should 等,以及表情感的副词如 faithfully, kindly, respectfully, sincerely, unfortunately 等。从属情态动词比主情态动词更具情态色彩,因而显得更加礼貌。

【例 12】We shall appreciate your providing us with an opinion as to the credit standing, respectability and responsibility of the following firm.

【译文】我们将十分感激你们就如下商行的信用状况、商业地位以及可靠性提出看法。

此例中,英文用"shall appreciate"表示礼貌,中文则翻译为"将十分感激"来传达原文的礼貌语气。

12.4.4　使用模糊措词,留有回旋余地

不同于词义的歧义、模棱两可,商务信函中的模糊措词是指词汇内涵的可塑性、有限性与外延的模糊性、无限性为一体。使用模糊措词或表达弦外之音,或声东击西,或留回旋的余地,或亦此亦彼,推诿搪塞。在翻译的时候,也要注意模糊措词的翻译。

【例 13】As for goods Article No.120, we are not able to make you orders because another supplier is offering us the similar quality at lower price.

【译文】非常抱歉,我方不能向你方购买 120 号订单的货品,因为另一供货商以更低的价格提供了相同品质的货品。

此例中原文并未明确指出对方价格偏高这一表意,而是婉转地使用 another supplier, lower price 来暗示自己的态度。"another supplier"(另一供货商)是谁,"lower price"(更低价格)是多少,

这都是使用了模糊的表达。

12.5 商务信函的句法特点及翻译

12.5.1 句子完整，多用复杂句

商务信函属于正式文体，复杂句式使用频繁，在中英文信函中都有体现，在翻译时，要注意小句之间的逻辑关系，做出准确的翻译。

【例 14】 Goods of a dangerous or damaging nature must not be tendered for shipment unless written notice of their nature and the name and address of the Sender have been previously given to the Carrier, Master or Agent of the vessel and the nature is distinctly marked on the outside of the package or packages as required by statue.

【译文】危险或易损物品严禁送来装运，除非关于其特性、名称、托运人地址的书面通知已事先提交给船主、船长或其代理人，而且货物的性质已按法令要求醒目地打印在包装物表面。

此例中，英文原文是由 and 连接的两个并列分句，前一个分句中有一个 unless 引导的条件状语从句。英文原文句子虽长，但层次分明，并列和互为条件的关系叙述得非常清楚。在翻译的时候，可以将英文原文切分如下，并将每一部分转换为汉语：

1) Goods of a dangerous or damaging nature must not be tendered for shipment
   危险或易损物品严禁送来装运
2) written notice of their nature and the name and address of the Sender have been previously given to the Carrier, Master or Agent of the vessel
   关于其特性、名称、托运人地址的书面通知已事先提交给承运人、船主或其代理人
3) the nature is distinctly marked on the outside of the package or

packages as required by statue

货物的性质已按法令要求醒目地打印在包装物表面

这样切分翻译之后,再根据 unless 和 and 提供的逻辑关系,将上面的汉语进行重新组织,就可以得出符合原文语气和逻辑的汉语译文了。

由于中英文句式长短存在差别,中文信函中的句子不像英文信函中的句子那么复杂,但是一般也会由两三个分句构成。

【例15】从中国驻美国大使馆商务参赞处获悉,贵公司是信誉卓越的轻工产品进口商,我公司系国有单位,以经营轻工产品为主,现寄去商品目录和价目单,用以向贵公司毛遂自荐。

【译文】We have learned from the Commercial Counselor's office of the Embassy of the People's Republic of China to your country that you enjoy the high reputation as a light industrial products importer, which has made us eager to enter into business relations with you. Accordingly, we, as a State-owned corporation dealing exclusively in light industrial products, now introduce ourselves to you by sending you herewith our catalogs and price-lists.

本例中,原文是很长的汉语句子,由几个单句组成,比较复杂。中文中重要的单句可以转换为英文的主谓结构,次要的单句则可以转换为英文中的从句或短语,每个中文小句拆分翻译如下:

1)从中国驻美国大使馆商务参赞处获悉: We have learned from the Commercial Counselor's office of the Embassy of the People's Republic of China to your country

2)贵公司是信誉卓越的轻工产品进口商: you enjoy the high reputation as a light industrial products importer

3)我公司系国有单位,以经营轻工产品为主: we, as a State-owned corporation dealing exclusively in light industrial products

4)现寄去商品目录和价目单,用以向贵公司毛遂自荐: now introduce ourselves to you by sending you herewith our catalogs and price-lists

英文译文在第一句最后加上了定语从句 which has made us eager to enter into business relations with you，为表达原文想建立业务关系的强烈要求。根据前后的逻辑关系，英文译文中还添加了连接副词 accordingly，使译文更加连贯。

12.5.2 多用套语

商务信函属于常用的正式文体，有些固定的表达方式在长期的写作中保留了下来，形成了一些固定的文句，成为套语。在翻译时要特别注意这些程式化的套语的翻译。下面对常用的一些套语做一下总结。

1. 表示感谢的套语

1）Thank you for your order. 谢谢您的订单。

2）It gives us great pleasure to acknowledge receipt of…
非常感谢收到……

3）We should be grateful if you could very shortly let us have your answer to our letter…concerning…
如果贵方能尽快回复我方……月……日关于……的来信，不胜感激。

2. 表示歉意的套语

1）We regret our inability to… 我方因不能……表示歉意

2）We tender you our apologies for… 因……特此道歉

3）We request you to accept our apologies for…
请接受我方对……的道歉

3. 表示自己受到对方的来函时的套语

1）We are in receipt of your letter…

2）We admit receipt of your letter…

3）We acknowledge receipt of…
以上套语均可翻译为：我方已收到贵方来函……

4. 表示自己是在回复某份函电时的套语

1）Regarding your letter of…

2) In reply to your letter of...
3) Referring to your letter of...
以上套语均可翻译为：兹复贵方……函/收到贵方……来函

5. 表示希望得到对方回函时的套语

1) We should be obliged by your early reply. 及时赐复，不胜感激。
2) We hope to receive your favor at an early date. 望早日赐复。
3) We look forward to your early reply. 望早日收到贵公司的答复。

6. 表示报价的套语

1) We have pleasure in offering you the goods listed on the attached offer sheet No…, and hope that they will be of interest to you.
很高兴提供所附的第……号报价单所列货物，希望贵方有兴趣。
3) We have pleasure in recommending to you…and enclose Quotation No...for your reference.
荣幸向贵方推荐……，随函附上第……号报价单，供贵方考虑。

7. 表示付款条件的套语

1) We are prepared to accept payment by confirmed, irrevocable L/C available by draft at sight instead of T/T reimbursement.
我方接受保兑的、不可撤销的信用证，以即期汇票而不是以电汇形式偿付。
2) We regret we cannot accept "cash against documents on arrival of goods at destination".
我方歉难接受"货抵目的港凭单付现"条款。
3) The L/C should be established with its clauses in conformity with the terms and conditions of the contract.
信用证条款应与合同的条款完全相符。

4) Payment should be made by confirmed and irrevocable L/C to be opened in our favor.

货款应用以我方为受益人的、不可撤销的、保兑的信用证支付。

8. 表示价格的套语

1) The above-mentioned article is quoted at...per...CIF.

上述货物的报价为每……CIF……

2) We regret being unable to quote on FOB basis, as it is our general practice to do business with all our clients on CIF terms.

很抱歉，我方不能以 FOB 为基础报价，因为我方与客户做生意按惯例，用 CIF。

3) This is the rock-bottom price and any further reduction is impossible.

这是最低价，无法再降价了。

4) The price quoted herein is based on CIF London with 3% commission.

此报价是 CIF 伦敦价，包括 3%佣金。

9. 表示确认或拒绝订单的套语

1) We thank you very much for your trial order No…and hope that this may be the beginning of a long and friendly connection between us.

非常感谢贵方第……号试订单，希望此订单成为双方长期友好往来的开端。

2) We thank you for this order, and hope we may have the pleasure of supplying you again in the near future.

感谢贵方的订货，希望不久后能再次向供方供货。

3) We want to tell you how pleased we were with your order because it represents our first deal with you. We have always felt that our high quality merchandise should have a ready

sale in your area.

欣告收到贵方订单,因为它代表我们双方第一次交易。我方一直认为我们高质量的商品在贵方地区将非常畅销。

4) We are unable to manufacture the article you ordered. Enclosed, we are returning your order.

我方无法生产贵方定购的产品,现随函退回贵方的订单。

10. 表示索赔、接受或拒绝索赔的套语

1) With mutual cooperation, this case has been settled amicably and we shall remit to you an amount of Stg. 20,000 in compensation for the loss arising therefrom.

由于双方合作,此事现已友好解决,我方将汇两万英镑,赔偿贵方的损失。

2) We are prepared to make you a reasonable compensation but not the amount you claimed, because we cannot see why the loss should be 50% more than the actual value of the goods.

我方准备给予贵方合理的赔偿,但不是贵方提出的赔偿数目,因为我方不能理解为什么损失超过货物实际价值的50%。

3) We have shipping documents to prove that the goods were received by the carrier in perfect condition, therefore, they must have been damaged on route.

我们有装运单据证明货物在送交承运人时完好无损,因此货物一定是在运输途中受损的。

4) As it is a matter concerning the insurance, we hope that you will refer the claim to the insurance company or their agent at your end.

鉴于这是一个涉及保险的问题,希望你方向保险公司或其在贵地的代理人提出索赔。

12.5.3 多用肯定句，少用否定句

商务信函中不宜过多地使用否定，如果直接使用否定句指出对方的问题，就会给人留下冒昧、不礼貌的印象，所以应该尽量使用肯定句，力求使语气委婉、客气。

【例 16】a. Your letter is not clear at all and I cannot understand it.
【译文】贵方的来函不清楚，我方看不明白。
　　　　b. If I understood your letter correctly, I would immediately accept your offer.
【译文】请贵方来函内容更清楚些，这样我便可立即接受贵方报盘。

此例中，对 a 句和 b 句对比发现，b 句的肯定句比 a 句的否定句委婉、客气许多，中文的翻译也是肯定的表达方式更委婉，更符合商务信函的语气。

12.5.4 英语商务信函多用陈述句，少用祈使句；汉语多用祈使句

商务信函的双方彼此的地位应该是平等的，因此，即使一方对另一方有所求，在英文信函中也不会使用祈使句，因为英文中的祈使句有命令的语气，显得盛气凌人。英文信函中往往使用陈述句表示自己的愿望，这样会使信函的语气委婉。汉语商务信函在此种情况下多使用祈使句，主要借助谦词和敬词来显示措辞的礼貌。在翻译时，英文的陈述句翻译成汉语的祈使句，句中加上谦词或者敬词；中文的祈使句在翻译成英文时，翻译为得体的陈述句。

【例 17】It would be appreciated if you could send us your shipping instructions.
【译文】敬请寄来贵方船运要求。

例句中的原文要表达的意思就是 Please send us your shipping instructions，但使用了完整的陈述句，同时主语使用了形式主语 it，主语的转换充分表明写信人的礼貌。为了传达原文的语气，汉语可

加上"敬请"二字。

12.5.5　英语商务信函适当使用被动语态；汉语则很少使用被动语态

在英语商务信函中，被动语态使用频繁。在英文中，被动语态不强调动作的发出者，显得所说出的话不是强加给对方的。在英语信函中，往往会说 It is hoped that the offer is made as soon as possible 而不是 Make the offer as soon as possible。祈使句转换为用含被动语态的陈述句表达，显得更加委婉。汉语被动语态表达对主语而言是不如意或不企望的事，如受祸、受欺骗、受损害，或引起不利的后果。因此，汉语中被动语态使用得很少。

【例 18】By this letter, the undersigned representative hereby declares and agrees that, if and when the tender is awarded and after the formal contract is signed and after the performance bond is established, the Buyer is kindly requested to advance five percent of the contract value as commencement support for the supply of water and electricity and erection of temporary facilities, and the advance thereof shall be deducted from the subsequent monthly progress payments.

【译文】根据该函，下面签名的代表声明并同意，如果标书获得批准，在正式合同、履行保证书签订后，请买方先支付合同规定总价的百分之五作为启动支持，用于供水、供电和临时设施的建设，首付款从随后的分期付款中扣除。

此例中英文原文使用了"is awarded""is signed""is established""is kindly requested"和"shall be deducted"五个被动语态，但是中文翻译中，除了"获得批准"给人感觉被动外，其他被动语态均没有翻译为被动语态的形式，而是用主动语态，以符合中文表达习惯，显示出礼貌与客气。

参考文献

[1] Alcaraz, Enrique & Hughes, Brian. *Legal Translation Explained* [M]. Manchester: St. Jerome Publishing, 2002.

[2] Baigiela-Chiappini & Nickerson, eds. *Writing Business: Genres, Media and Discourse* [M]. Essex: Pearson Education Limited, 1999.

[3] Bell, Allan. *The Language of News Media* [M]. Oxford: Basil Blackwell, 1991.

[4] Casagrande, Joseph B. & Kenneth L. Hale. *The Translator as Communicator* [M]. London: Routledge, 1997.

[5] Halliday, M. A. K. *An Introduction to Functional Grammar* [M]. Beijing: Foreign Language Teaching and Research Press, 2000.

[6] Halliday, M. A. K. *Explorations in the Functions of Language* [C]. London: Edward Arnold, 1973.

[7] Halliday, M. A. K. *Language as Social Semiotic* [M]. London: Edward Arnold, 1978.

[8] Halliday, M. A. K. and Ruqalya Hasan. *Cohesion in English* [M]. Beijing: Foreign Language Teaching and Research Press, 2001.

[9] Joos, Martin. *The Five Clocks* [M]. Bloomington: Indiana University Press, 1962.

[10] Lefevere, André, ed. *Translation, History, Culture: A Sourcebook* [C]. London: Routledge, 1992.

[11] Mark, Shuttleworth and Cowie, Maria. *Dictionary of Translation Studies* [Z]. Shanghai: Shanghai Foreign Language Education Press, 2004.

[12] Mencher, Melven. *News Reporting and Writing* [M]. Boston: Mcgraw-Hill Higher Education, 2003.

[13] Newmark, Peter. *A Textbook of Translation* [M]. Shanghai: Shanghai Foreign Language Education Press, 2001.

[14] Newmark, Peter. *Approaches to Translation* [M]. Shanghai: Shanghai Foreign Language Education Press, 2001.

[15] Nida, Eugene A. *Language, Culture and Translating* [M]. Shanghai: Shanghai Foreign Language Education Press, 2001.

[16] Nida, Eugene A. & Taber R. Charles. *The Theory and Practice of Translation* [M]. Shanghai: Shanghai Foreign Language Education Press, 2004.

[17] Nord, Christina. *Translating as a Purposeful Activity, Functionalist Approaches Explained* [M]. Shanghai: Shanghai Foreign Language Education Press, 2001.

[18] Reiss, Katharina. *Translation Criticism: The Potentials & Limitations* [M]. Shanghai: Shanghai Foreign Language Education Press, 2004.

[19] Sarcevic, Susan. *New Approach to Legal Translation* [M]. The Hague: Kluwer Law International, 1997.

[20] Steiner, George. *After Babel—Aspects of Language and Translation* [M]. Shanghai: Shanghai Foreign Language Education Press, 2001.

[21] Tytler, Alexander. *Essay on the Principles of Translation* [M]. Beijing: Foreign Language Teaching and Research Press, 2007.

[22] Vinay, Jean-Paul. *Comparative Stylistics of French and English* [M]. Amsterdam: John Benjamins Publishing Co., 1995.

[23] Wolfram, Wilss. *The Science of Translation* [M]. Shanghai: Shanghai Foreign Language Education Press, 2001.

[24] 陈小慰. 对德国翻译功能目的论的修辞反思[J]. 外语研究，2012（1）.

[25] 方梦之、毛忠明. 英汉—汉英应用翻译综合教程[M]. 上海：上海外语教育出版社，2008.

[26] 戴宗显、吕和发. 公示语汉英翻译研究[J]. 中国翻译，2005（6）.

[27] 冯庆华. 实用翻译教程[M]. 上海：上海外语教育出版社，2002.

[28] 冯庆华. 报刊语言翻译[M]. 北京：高等教育出版社，2008.

[29] 高莉娟. 伽达默尔解释学的语言维度探究[J]. 语言教育，2015（3）.

[30] 顾维勇. 实用文体翻译（第二版）[M]. 北京：国防工业出版社，2012.

[31] 郭建中. 实用性文章的翻译（上）[J]. 上海科技翻译，2001（3）.

[32] 何庆机. 国内功能派翻译理论研究述评[J]. 上海翻译，2007（4）.

[33] 侯维瑞. 英语的语域及其在文学作品中的运用[J]. 外语教学与研究，1983（2）.

[34] 胡文仲. 现代文体学的沿革、流派和争论[J]. 外国语，1984（5）.

[35] 胡壮麟主编. 语言系统与功能[C]. 北京：北京大学出版社，1990.

[36] 黄龙. 翻译艺术教程[M]. 南京：南京大学出版社，1988.

[37] 黄忠廉、信娜. 应用翻译学创建论[J]. 上海翻译，2011（2）.

[38] 金隄. 等效翻译探索[M]. 北京：中国对外翻译出版公司，1989.

[39] 贾文波. 功能翻译理论对应用翻译的启示[J]. 上海翻译，2007（2）.

[40] 贾文波. 汉英时文翻译高级教程[M]. 北京：中国对外翻译出版公司，2012.

[41] 贾文波. 应用翻译功能论[M]. 北京：中国对外翻译出版公司，2004.

[42] 李长栓. 非文学翻译理论与实践[M]. 中国对外翻译出版公司，2004.

[43] 李道揆. 美国政府和美国政治[M]. 北京：商务印书馆，1999.

[44] 李运兴. 字幕翻译的策略[J]. 中国翻译，2001（4）.

[45] 林本椿. 漫谈汉英实用翻译[J]. 福建外语，1997（1）.

[46] 林煌天. 中国翻译词典[Z]. 武汉：湖北教育出版社，1997.

[47] 刘宓庆. 西方翻译理论概评[J]. 中国翻译，1989（2）.

[48] 刘宓庆. 文体与翻译[M]. 北京：中国对外翻译出版公司，2007.
[49] 刘宓庆、章艳. 翻译美学理论[M]. 北京：外语教学与研究出版社，2011.
[50] 刘世生、宋成方. 功能文体学研究[J]. 外语教学，2010（6）.
[51] 吕和发、蒋璐. 公示语翻译教程[M]. 北京：清华大学出版社，2013.
[52] 吕元. 关联翻译理论视角下文化缺省的英译[J]. 语言教育，2015（1）.
[53] 马祖毅. 中国翻译简史[M]. 北京：中国对外翻译出版公司，2001.
[54] 朴哲浩. 影视翻译研究[M]. 哈尔滨：黑龙江人民出版社，2008.
[55] 申丹. 有关功能文体学的几点思考[J]. 外国语，1997（5）.
[56] 申丹. 功能文体学再思考[J]. 外语教学与研究，2002（3）.
[57] 沈学甫. 伽达默尔解释学视角下的翻译观初探[J]. 作家，2013（10）.
[58] 沈学甫. 英文电影片名汉译：问题与原则[J]. 电影文学，2013（24）.
[59] 孙万彪. 英汉法律翻译教程[M]. 上海：上海外语教育出版社，2003.
[60] 孙正聿. 简明哲学通论[M]. 北京：高等教育出版社，2000.
[61] 天津市政协十三届二次会议大会提案. 关于规范天津市公示语翻译和提升城市国际形象的建议，2014.
[62] 王佐良. 翻译：思考与试笔[M]. 北京：外语教学研究与出版社，1997.
[63] 伍峰等. 应用文体翻译：理论与实践[M]. 杭州：浙江大学出版社，2008.
[64] 夏晓云. 费道罗夫的"等值翻译论"刍议[J]. 作家，2013（7）.
[65] 杨山青. 实用文体英汉翻译[M]. 北京：国防工业出版社，2010.
[66] 张德禄. 功能文体学[M]. 济南：山东教育出版社，1998.
[67] 张德禄. 功能文体学研究方法探索[J]. 四川外语学院学报，2007（6）.
[68] 张德禄. 韩礼德功能文体学理论述评[J]. 外语教学与研究，

1999（1）.

[69] 张德禄. 文体特征分析的框架[J]. 聊城师范学院学报（哲学社会科学版），1988（2）.

[70] 张德禄. 语域理论简介[J]. 现代外语，1987（4）.

[71] 张健. 新闻翻译教程[M]. 上海：上海外语教育出版社，2008.

[72] 郑玉琪、王晓东. 小议电影片名的英汉翻译原则[J]. 中国翻译，2006（3）.

[73] 中华人民共和国国务院法制办公室编. 中华人民共和国涉外法规汇编（2001）[Z]. 北京：中国法制出版社，2006.

[74] 中华人民共和国国务院法制办公室编. 中华人民共和国涉外法规汇编（2007）[Z]. 北京：中国法制出版社，2009.

[75] 朱德熙. 语法讲义[M]. 北京：商务印书馆，1982.

后　记

　　受天津外国语大学出版资助，我们经过几年努力编写的《非文学文体解析与翻译——以功能文体学为理论视角》一书带着我们的期待终于问世了。本书是天津市哲学社会科学规划项目（编号：TJYW10-1-606）的研究成果，该项目经市级评审专家鉴定为 A 级成果。本书旨在以韩礼德（M. A. K. Halliday）的功能文体学为理论视角，对英语非文学文体即实用文体的构成、界定进行分析探讨，对翻译策略和方法的选择进行比较研究，以从客观上澄清形式与内容的关系及相互作用，寻求更合适的翻译手段与措施，规范国内外非文学翻译的活动与效果。要在这样的基础上，给读者提供一点有价值的东西，重要的是提升理论的视野，从学科的高度更多地了解一些文体学和翻译学的宏观面貌。这就犹如提供一幅比例尺很大的地图，让有能力根据地图来辨识地貌和路线的人，可以用它去判断形势和选择目标。

　　本书所涉及的文体涵盖范围广泛，包括法律文书、新闻报道、商贸文本、影视字幕、广告语、旅游宣传、公示语、哲学文献、企业规章制度及商务信函等非文学文体体裁。功能文体学注重对不同的语言结构所产生的不同文体效应的描述，如语言各层面的突出形式与前景化分析、语境与语篇分析等。功能文体学将语言形式、内容和语言功能结合起来考虑，加深了对非文学文本实质的理解，并克服了传统文体分析的缺点和不足。用该理论来指导非文学文体翻译实践，能更好地解决在非文学文体翻译中遇到的诸多问题，超越以往非文学文体翻译过于侧重语言特点以及英汉两种语言之间差异的狭隘。我们编写此书目的是为了规范非文学文体翻译，为翻译教学与实践提供有用的借鉴，从而为培养出更加优秀的翻译人才并进一步促进我国与世界的交流贡献绵薄之力。

本书由天津外国语大学英语学院张国敬教授和天津城建大学外国语学院多名教师合作完成，其构思是由各位作者集体讨论确定的，承担各章写作的情况如下：前言及第一、二章由张国敬执笔；第三、五、六章由吕元执笔；第四、七章由王阳执笔；第八、十章以及参考文献部分由高莉娟执笔；第九、十一章由王文平执笔；第十二章由戴宗琳执笔。吕元和高莉娟耐心细致地进行了后期校对工作，并逐一核对了全部注释。南开大学沈学甫博士在美国卡罗尔大学（Carroll University）访学期间搜集了大量宝贵资料，参加了本书的前期策划工作并协助张国敬教授进行了统稿和技术处理。全书由张国敬教授整体负责，但各章都有一定的独立价值，每位作者也有相应的权利和责任。

我们深信，充实的内容加上突出的特色，必定使本书受到广大读者的青睐。在编写过程中，我们参考借鉴了国内外许多同行专家的相关著述，在此深表谢意。囿于编者的学识和水平，书中肯定还存在很多疏漏乃至舛错之处，恳请读者朋友批评指正，我们将在今后的修订中加以改进。

编　者
2016 年立冬